Charles Raymond Cady

UNIVERSAL CLASSICS LIBRARY

APPLETON PRENTISS CLARK GRIFFIN
LIBRARY OF CONGRESS
EDITORIAL DIRECTOR

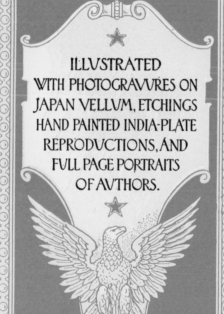

ILLVSTRATED
WITH PHOTOGRAVVRES ON
JAPAN VELLVM, ETCHINGS
HAND PAINTED INDIA-PLATE
REPRODVCTIONS, AND
FVLL PAGE PORTRAITS
OF AVTHORS.

M. WALTER DUNNE, PUBLISHER

WASHINGTON & LONDON

MEMOIRS OF LOUIS XIV
AND THE REGENCY

BY THE

DUKE OF SAINT-SIMON

TRANSLATED BY

BAYLE ST. JOHN

IN THREE VOLUMES

VOL. II

WITH A SPECIAL INTRODUCTION BY

LÉON VALLÉE
Bibliothécaire à la Bibliothèque Nationale

PARIS

M. WALTER DUNNE, PUBLISHER
WASHINGTON & LONDON

ILLUSTRATIONS

CONTENTS OF VOLUME II.

I

CONTENTS

CHAPTER X.

CHAPTER XI.

CHAPTER XII.

CHAPTER XIII.

CHAPTER XIV.

CHAPTER XV.

CHAPTER XVI.

CHAPTER XVII.

CHAPTER XVIII.

CHAPTER XIX.

CHAPTER XX.

CHAPTER XXI.

CONTENTS

CHAPTER XXX.

CHAPTER XXXI.

CHAPTER XXXII.

CHAPTER XXXIII

CHAPTER XXXIV.

CONTENTS

CHAPTER XXXV.

CHAPTER XXXVI.

CHAPTER XXXVII.

MEMOIRS

OF THE

DUKE OF SAINT-SIMON

———

CHAPTER I.

Precedence at the Communion Table — The King Offended with Madame de Torcy — The King's Religion — Atheists and Jansenists —
Project against Scotland — Preparations — Failure — The Chevalier
de St. George — His Return to Court.

I WENT this summer to Forges, to try, by means of the
waters there, to get rid of a tertian fever that *quin-
quina* only suspended. While there I heard of a new
enterprise on the part of the princes of the blood, who,
in the discredit in which the King held them, profited
without measure by his desire for the grandeur of the
illegitimate children, to acquire new advantages which
were suffered because the others shared them. This was
the case in question.

After the elevation of the mass — at the King's communion — a folding chair was pushed to the foot of the
altar, was covered with a piece of stuff, and then with
a large cloth, which hung down before and behind. At
the *Pater* the chaplain rose and whispered in the King's
ear the names of all the dukes who were in the chapel.
The King named two, always the oldest, to each of
whom the chaplain advanced and made a reverence.
During the communion of the priest the King rose, and
went and knelt down on the bare floor behind this folding seat, and took hold of the cloth; at the same time
the two dukes, the elder on the right the other on the

left, each took hold of a corner of the cloth; the two
chaplains took hold of the other two corners of the same
cloth, on the side of the altar, all four kneeling, and the
captain of the guards also kneeling and behind the King.
The communion received and the oblation taken some
moments afterward, the King remained a little while in
the same place, then returned to his own, followed by
the two dukes and the captain of the guards, who took
theirs. If a son of France happened to be there alone,
he alone held the right corner of the cloth, and nobody
the other; and when M. le Duc d'Orléans was there, and
no son of France was present, M. le Duc d'Orléans held
the cloth in like manner. If a prince of the blood were
alone present, however, he held the cloth, but a duke
was called forward to assist him. He was not privileged
to act without the duke.

The princes of the blood wanted to change this; they
were envious of the distinction accorded to M. d'Orléans,
and wished to put themselves on the same footing. Accordingly, at the Assumption of this year, they managed
so well that M. le Duc served alone at the altar at the
King's communion, no duke being called upon to come
and join him. The surprise at this was very great. The
Duc de la Force and the Maréchal de Boufflers, who
ought to have served, were both present. I wrote to
this last to say that such a thing had never happened
before, and that it was contrary to all precedent. I wrote,
too, to M. d'Orléans, who was then in Spain, informing him
of the circumstance. When he returned he complained
to the King. But the King merely said that the dukes
ought to have presented themselves and taken hold of
the cloth. But how could they have done so, without
being requested, as was customary, to come forward?
What would the King have thought of them if they had?
To conclude, nothing could be made of the matter, and
it remained thus. Never then, since that time, did I go
to the communions of the King.

An incident occurred at Marly about the same time,
which made much stir. The ladies who were invited to
Marly, had the privilege of dining with the King. Tables
were placed for them, and they took up positions accord-

ing to their rank. The non-titled ladies had also their special place. It so happened one day, that Madame de Torcy (an untitled lady) placed herself above the Duchess de Duras, who arrived at table a moment after her. Madame de Torcy offered to give up her place, but it was a little late, and the offer passed away in compliments. The King entered, and put himself at table. As soon as he sat down, he saw the place Madame de Torcy had taken, and fixed such a serious and surprised look upon her, that she again offered to give up her place to the Duchess de Duras; but the offer was again declined. All through the dinner the King scarcely ever took his eyes off Madame de Torcy, said hardly a word, and bore a look of anger that rendered everybody very attentive, and even troubled the Duchess de Duras.

Upon rising from the table the King passed, according to custom, into the apartments of Madame de Maintenon, followed by the princesses of the blood, who grouped themselves around him upon stools ; the others who entered kept at a distance. Almost before he had seated himself in his chair he said to Madame de Maintenon, that he had just been witness to an act of «incredible insolence» (that was the term he used) which had thrown him into such a rage that he had been unable to eat: that such an enterprise would have been insupportable in a woman of the highest quality ; but coming as it did, from a mere Bourgeoise, it had so affected him, that ten times he had been upon the point of making her leave the table, and that he was only restrained by consideration for her husband. After this outbreak he made a long discourse upon the genealogy of Madame de Torcy's family, and other matters ; and then, to the astonishment of all present, grew as angry as ever against Madame de Torcy. He went off then into a discourse upon the dignity of the dukes, and in conclusion, he charged the princesses to tell Madame de Torcy to what extent he had found her conduct impertinent. The princesses looked at each other, and not one seemed to like this commission; whereupon the King, growing more angry, said, that it must be undertaken, however, and left the room.

The news of what had taken place, and of the King's choler, soon spread all over the Court. It was believed, however, that all was over, and that nothing more would be heard of the matter. Yet the very same evening the King broke out again with even more bitterness than before. On the morrow, too, surprise was great indeed, when it was found that the King immediately after dinner, could talk of nothing but this subject, and that, too, without any softening of tone. At last he was assured that Madame de Torcy had been spoken to, and this appeased him a little. Torcy was obliged to write him a letter, apologizing for the fault of Madame de Torcy, and the King at this grew content. It may be imagined what a sensation this adventure produced all through the Court.

While upon the subject of the King, let me relate an anecdote of him, which should have found a place ere this. When M. d'Orléans was about to start for Spain, he named the officers who were to be of his suite. Among others was Fontpertius. At that name the King put on a serious look.

"What! my nephew," he said. "Fontpertius! the son of a Jansenist — of that silly woman who ran everywhere after M. Arnould! I do not wish that man to go with you."

"By my faith, Sire," replied the Duc d'Orléans, "I know not what the mother has done; but as for the son, he is far enough from being a Jansenist, I'll answer for it; for he does not believe in God."

"Is it possible, my nephew?" said the King, softening.

"Nothing more certain, Sire, I assure you."

"Well, since it is so," said the King, "there is no harm: you can take him with you."

This scene — for it can be called by no other name — took place in the morning. After dinner M. d'Orléans repeated it to me, bursting with laughter, word for word, just as I have written it. When we had both well laughed at this, we admired the profound instruction of a discreet and religious King, who considered it better not to believe in God than to be a Jansenist, and who thought there was less danger to his nephew from the impiety of

an unbeliever, than from the doctrines of a sectarian.
M. d'Orléans could not contain himself while he told the
story, and never spoke of it without laughing until the
tears came into his eyes. It ran all through the Court
and all over the town, and the marvelous thing was, that
the King was not angry at this. It was a testimony of
his attachment to the good doctrine which withdrew him
further and further from Jansenism. The majority of
people laughed with all their heart. Others, more wise,
felt rather disposed to weep than to laugh, in considering to what excess of blindness the King had reached.

For a long time a most important project had knocked
at every door, without being able to obtain a hearing
anywhere. The project was this: — Hough, an English
gentleman full of talent and knowledge, and who, above
all, knew profoundly the laws of his country, had filled
various posts in England. At first a minister by profession, and furious against King James; afterward a Catholic
and King James's spy, he had been delivered up to King
William who pardoned him. He profited by this only to
continue his services to James. He was taken several
times, and always escaped from the Tower of London and
other prisons. Being no longer able to dwell in England
he came to France, where he occupied himself always with
the same line of business, and was paid for that by the
King (Louis XIV.) and by King James, the latter of whom
he unceasingly sought to re-establish. The union of Scotland with England appeared to him a favorable conjuncture,
by the despair of that ancient kingdom at seeing itself
reduced into a province under the yoke of the English.
The Jacobite party remained there; the vexation caused
by this forced union had increased it, by the desire felt to
break that union with the aid of a king that they would
have re-established. Hough, who was aware of the fer-
mentation going on, made several secret journeys to
Scotland, and planned an invasion of that country; but,
as I have said, for a long time could get no one to listen
to him.

The King, indeed, was so tired of such enterprises, that
nobody dared to speak to him upon this. All drew back.
No one liked to bell the cat. At last, however, Madame

de Maintenon being gained over, the King was induced
to listen to the project. As soon as his consent was
gained to it another scheme was added to the first. This
was to profit by the disorder in which the Spanish Low
Countries were thrown, and to make them revolt against
the Imperials at the very moment when the affairs of
Scotland would bewilder the allies, and deprive them of
all support from England. Bergheyck, a man well acquainted with the state of those countries, was consulted,
and thought the scheme good. He and the Duc de Vendôme conferred upon it in presence of the King.

After talking over various matters, the discussion fell
upon the Meuse, and its position with reference to Maes-
tricht. Vendôme held that the Meuse flowed in a certain direction. Bergheyck opposed him. Vendôme,
indignant that a civilian should dare to dispute military
movements with him, grew warm. The other remained
respectful and cool, but firm. Vendôme laughed at Bergheyck, as at an ignorant fellow who did not know the
position of places. Bergheyck maintained his point.
Vendôme grew more and more hot. If he was right,
what he proposed was easy enough; if wrong, it was impossible. It was in vain that Vendôme pretended to
treat with disdain his opponent, Bergheyck was not to be
put down, and the King, tired out at last with a discussion upon a simple question of fact, examined the maps.
He found at once that Bergheyck was right. Any other
than the King would have felt by this what manner of
man was this general of his taste, of his heart, and of
his confidence; any other than Vendôme would have been
confounded; but it was Bergheyck in reality who was so,
to see the army in such hands and the blindness of the
King for him! He was immediately sent into Flanders
to work up a revolt, and he did it so well, that success
seemed certain, dependent, of course, upon success in
Scotland.

The preparations for the invasion of that country were
at once commenced. Thirty vessels were armed at Dunkerque and in the neighboring ports. The Chevalier de
Forbin was chosen to command the squadron. Four
thousand men were brought from Flanders to Dunkerque;

and it was given out that this movement was a mere change of garrison. The secret of the expedition was well kept; but the misfortune was that things were done too slowly. The fleet, which depended upon Pontchartrain, was not ready in time, and that which depended upon Chamillart, was still more behind hand. The two ministers threw the fault upon each other; but the truth is, both were to blame. Pontchartrain was more than accused of delaying matters from unwillingness; the other from powerlessness.

Great care was taken that no movement should be seen at Saint Germain. The affair, however, began in time to get noised abroad. A prodigious quantity of arms and clothing for the Scotch had been embarked; the movements by sea and land became only too visible upon the coast. At last, on Wednesday, the 6th of March, the King of England set out from Saint Germain. He was attended by the Duke of Perth, who had been his sub-preceptor, by the two Hamiltons, by Middleton, and a very few others. But his departure had been postponed too long. At the moment when all were ready to start, people learned with surprise that the English fleet had appeared in sight, and was blockading Dunkerque. Our troops, who were already on board ship, were at once landed. The King of England cried out so loudly against this, and proposed so eagerly that an attempt should be made to pass the enemy at all risks, that a fleet was sent out to reconnoiter the enemy, and the troops were re-embarked. But then a fresh mischance happened. The Princess of England had had the measles, and was barely growing convalescent at the time of the departure of the King, her brother. She had been prevented from seeing him, lest he should be attacked by the same complaint. In spite of this precaution, however, it declared itself upon him at Dunkerque, just as the troops were re-embarked. He was in despair, and wished to be wrapped up in blankets and carried on board. The doctors said that it would kill him; and he was obliged to remain. The worst of it was, that two of five Scotch deputies who had been hidden at Montrogue, near Paris, had been sent into Scotland a fortnight before, to announce the

immediate arrival of the King with arms and troops.
The movement which it was felt this announcement would
create, increased the impatience for departure. At last,
on Saturday, the 19th of March, the King of England,
half cured and very weak, determined to embark in spite
of his physicians, and did so. The enemy's vessels had
retired; so, at six o'clock in the morning, our ships set
sail with a good breeze, and in the midst of a mist, which
hid them from view in about an hour.

Forty-eight hours after the departure of our squadron,
twenty-seven English ships of war appeared before Dunkerque. But our fleet was away. The very first night
it experienced a furious tempest. The ship in which
was the King of England, took shelter afterward behind
the works of Ostend. During the storm, another ship was
separated from the squadron, and was obliged to take
refuge on the coast of Picardy. This vessel, a frigate,
was commanded by Rambure, a lieutenant. As soon as
he was able he sailed after the squadron that he believed
already in Scotland. He directed his course toward Edinburgh, and found no vessel during all the voyage.
As he approached the mouth of the river, he saw around
him a number of barks and small vessels that he could
not avoid, and that he determined in consequence to approach with as good a grace as possible. The masters
of these ships told him that the King was expected with
impatience, but that they had no news of him, that they
had come out to meet him, and that they would send
pilots to Rambure, to conduct him up the river to Edinburgh, where all was hope and joy. Rambure, equally
surprised that the squadron which bore the King of England, had not appeared, and of the publicity of his forth-
coming arrival, went up toward Edinburgh more and
more surrounded by barks, which addressed to him the
same language. A gentleman of the country passed from
one of these barks upon the frigate. He told Rambure
that the principal noblemen of Scotland had resolved to
act together, that these noblemen could count upon more
than twenty thousand men ready to take up arms, and
that all the towns awaited only the arrival of the King
to proclaim him.

More and more troubled that the squadron did not appear, Rambure, after a time, turned back and went in search of it. As he approached the mouth of the river, which he had so lately entered, he heard a great noise of cannon out at sea, and a short time afterward he saw many vessels of war there. Approaching more and more, and quitting the river, he distinguished our squadron, chased by twenty-six large ships of war and a number of other vessels, all of which he soon lost sight of, so much was our squadron in advance. He continued on his course in order to join them; but he could not do so until all had passed by the mouth of the river. Then steering clear of the rear guard of the English ships, he remarked that the English fleet was hotly chasing the ship of the King of England, which ran along the coast, however, amid the fire of cannon and oftentimes of musketry. Rambure tried, for a long time, to profit by the lightness of his frigate to get ahead; but, always cut off by the enemy's vessels, and continually in danger of being taken, he returned to Dunkerque, where he immediately dispatched to the Court this sad and disturbing news. He was followed, five or six days after, by the King of England, who returned to Dunkerque on the 7th of April, with his vessels badly knocked about.

It seems that the ship in which was the Prince, after experiencing the storm I have already alluded to, set sail again with its squadron, but twice got out of its reckoning within forty-eight hours; a fact not easy to understand in a voyage from Ostend to Edinburgh. This circumstance gave time to the English to join them; thereupon the King held a council, and much time was lost in deliberations. When the squadron drew near the river, the enemy was so close upon us, that to enter, without fighting either inside or out, seemed impossible. In this emergency it was suggested, that our ships should go on to Inverness, about eighteen or twenty leagues further off. But this was objected to by Middleton and the Chevalier Forbin, who declared that the King of England was expected only at Edinburgh, and that it was useless to go elsewhere; and accordingly the project was given up, and the ships returned to France.

2

This return, however, was not accomplished without some difficulty. The enemy's fleet attacked the rear guard of ours, and after an obstinate combat, took two vessels of war and some other vessels. Among the prisoners taken by the English were the Marquis de Lèvi, Lord Griffin, and the two sons of Middleton; who all, after suffering some little bad treatment, were conducted to London.

Lord Griffin was an old Englishman, who deserves a word of special mention. A firm Protestant, but much attached to the King of England, he knew nothing of this expedition until after the King's departure. He went immediately in quest of the Queen. With English freedom he reproached her for the little confidence she had had in him, in spite of his services and his constant fidelity, and finished by assuring her that neither his age nor his religion would hinder him from serving the King to the last drop of his blood. He spoke so feelingly that the Queen was ashamed. After this he went to Versailles, asked M. de Toulouse for a hundred louis and a horse, and without delay rode off to Dunkerque, where he embarked with the others. In London he was condemned to death; but he showed so much firmness and such disdain of death, that his judges were too much ashamed to allow the execution to be carried out. The Queen sent him one respite, then another, although he had never asked for either, and finally he was allowed to remain at liberty in London on parole. He always received fresh respites, and lived in London as if in his own country, well received everywhere. Being informed that these respites would never cease, he lived thus several years, and died very old, a natural death. The other prisoners were equally well treated.

It was in this expedition that the King of England first assumed the title of the Chevalier de St. George, and that his enemies gave him that of the Pretender; both of which have remained to him. He showed much will and firmness, which he spoiled by a docility the result of a bad education, austere and confined, that devotion, ill understood, together with the desire of maintaining him in fear and dependence, caused the Queen (who, with all her sanctity, always wished to dominate) to give him. He asked to serve in the next campaign in Flanders, and wished to go there at once, or remain near Dunkerque. Service was promised him, but he was made to return to St. Germain. Hough, who had been made a peer of Ireland before starting, preceded him with the journals of the voyage, and that of Forbin, to whom the King gave a thousand crowns pension and ten thousand as a recompense.

The King of England arrived at St. Germain on Friday, the 20th of April, and came with the Queen, the following Sunday, to Marly, where our King was. The two Kings embraced each other several times, in the presence of the two Courts. But the visit altogether was a sad one. The Courts, which met in the garden, returned toward the *château*, exchanging indifferent words in an indifferent way.

Middleton was strongly suspected of having acquainted the English with our project. They acted, at all events, as if they had been informed of everything, and wished to appear to know nothing. They made a semblance of sending their fleet to escort a convoy to Portugal; they got in readiness the few troops they had in England and sent them toward Scotland; and the Queen, under various pretexts, detained in London, until the affair had failed, the Duke of Hamilton, the most powerful Scotch lord, and the life and soul of the expedition. When all was over, she made no arrests, and wisely avoided throwing Scotland into despair. This conduct much augmented her authority in England, attached all hearts to her, and took away all desire of stirring again by taking away all hope of success. Thus failed a project so well and so secretly conducted until the end, which was pitiable; and with this project failed that of the Low Countries, which was no longer thought of.

The allies uttered loud cries against this attempt on the part of a power they believed at its last gasp, and which, while pretending to seek peace, thought of nothing less than the invasion of Great Britain. The effect of our failure was to bind closer, and to irritate more and more this formidable alliance.

CHAPTER II.

BRISSAC, Major of the Bodyguards, died of age and *ennui*
about this time, more than eighty years old, at his
country house, to which he had not long retired. The
King had made use of him to put the guards upon that
grand military footing they have reached. He had acquired the confidence of the King by his inexorable exactitude, his honesty, and his aptitude. He was a sort of
wild boar, who had all the appearance of a bad man,
without being so in reality; but his manners were, it
must be admitted, harsh and disagreeable. The King,
speaking one day of the majors of the troops, said that
if they were good, they were sure to be hated.

"If it is necessary to be perfectly hated in order to be
a good major," replied M. de Duras, who was behind the
King with the baton, "behold, Sire, the best major in
France!" and he took Brissac, all confusion, by the arm.
The King laughed, though he would have thought such
a sally very bad in any other; but M. de Duras had put
himself on such a free footing, that he stopped at nothing before the King, and often said the sharpest things.
This major had very robust health, and laughed at the
doctors — very often, even before the King, at Fagon,
whom nobody else would have dared to attack. Fagon
replied by disdain, often by anger, and with all his wit
was embarrassed. These short scenes were sometimes
very amusing.

Brissac, a few years before his retirement, served the
Court ladies a nice turn. All through the winter they

attended evening prayers on Thursdays and Sundays, because the King went there; and, under the pretense of reading their prayer books, had little tapers before them, which cast a light on their faces, and enabled the King to recognize them as he passed. On the evenings when they knew he would not go, scarcely one of them went. One evening, when the king was expected, all the ladies had arrived, and were in their places, and the guards were at their doors. Suddenly, Brissac appeared in the King's place, lifted his baton, and cried aloud, "Guards of the King, withdraw, return to your quarters; the King is not coming this evening." The guards withdrew; but after they had proceeded a short distance, were stopped by brigadiers posted for the purpose, and told to return in a few minutes. What Brissac had said was a joke. The ladies at once began to murmur one to another. In a moment or two all the candles were put out, and the ladies, with but few exceptions, left the chapel. Soon after the King arrived, and, much astonished to see so few ladies present, asked how it was that nobody was there. At the conclusion of the prayers, Brissac related what he had done, not without dwelling on the piety of the Court ladies. The King and all who accompanied him laughed heartily. The story soon spread, and these ladies would have strangled Brissac if they had been able.

The Duchess de Bourgogne being in the family way this spring, was much inconvenienced. The King wished to go to Fontainebleau at the commencement of the fine season, contrary to his usual custom; and had declared this wish. In the meantime he desired to pay visits to Marly. Madame de Bourgogne much amused him; he could not do without her, yet so much movement was not suitable to her state. Madame de Maintenon was uneasy, and Fagon gently intimated his opinion. This annoyed the King, accustomed to restrain himself for nothing, and spoiled by having seen his mistresses travel when big with child, or when just recovering from their confinement, and always in full dress. The hints against going to Marly bothered him, but did not make him give them up. All he would consent to was that the

journey should be put off from the day after Quasimodo
to the Wednesday of the following week; but nothing
could make him delay his amusement beyond that time,
or induce him to allow the Princess to remain at Versailles.

On the following Saturday, as the King was taking a
walk after mass, and amusing himself at the carp basin
between the *château* and the perspective, we saw the
Duchess de Lude coming toward him on foot and all
alone, which as no lady was with the King was a rarity
in the morning. We understood that she had something
important to say to him, and when he was a short distance from her, we stopped so as to allow him to join
her alone. The interview was not long. She went away
again, and the King came back toward us and near the
carps without saying a word. Each saw clearly what was
in the wind, and nobody was eager to speak. At last
the King, when quite close to the basin, looked at the
principal people around, and without addressing anybody,
said, with an air of vexation, these few words: —

« The Duchess de Bourgogne is hurt. »

M. de la Rochefoucauld at once uttered an exclamation. M. de Bouillon, the Duc de Tresmes, and Maréchal
de Boufflers repeated in a low tone the words I have
named; and M. de la Rochefoucauld returning to the
charge, declared emphatically that it was the greatest
misfortune in the world, and that as she had already
wounded herself on other occasions, she might never,
perhaps, have any more children.

« And if so, » interrupted the King all on a sudden,
with anger, « what is that to me? Has she not already
a son; and if he should die, is not the Duc de Berry
old enough to marry and have one? What matters it to
me who succceeds me, — the one or the other? Are they
not all equally my grandchildren? » And immediately,
with impetuosity he added, « Thank God, she is wounded,
since she was to be so; and I shall no longer be annoyed
in my journeys and in everything I wish to do, by the
representations of doctors and the reasonings of matrons.
I shall go and come at my pleasure, and shall be left in
peace. »

A silence so deep that an ant might be heard to walk, succeeded this strange outburst. All eyes were lowered; no one scarcely dared to breathe. All remained stupefied. Even the domestics and the gardeners stood motionless.

This silence lasted more than a quarter of an hour. The King broke it as he leaned upon a balustrade to speak of a carp. Nobody replied. He addressed himself afterward on the subject of these carps to domestics, who did not ordinarily join in the conversation. Nothing but carps was spoken of with them. All was languishing, and the King went away some time after. As soon as we dared look at each other out of his sight, our eyes met and told all. Everybody there was for the moment the confidant of his neighbor. We admired — we marveled — we grieved, we shrugged our shoulders. However distant may be that scene, it is always equally present to me. M. de la Rochefoucauld was in a fury, and this time without being wrong. The chief *écuyer* was ready to faint with affright; I myself examined everybody with my eyes and ears, and was satisfied with myself for having long since thought that the King loved and cared for himself alone, and was himself his only object in life. This strange discourse sounded far and wide — much beyond Marly.

Let me here relate another anecdote of the King — a trifle I was witness of. It was on the 7th of May, of this year, and at Marly. The King walking round the gardens, showing them to Bergheyck, and talking with him upon the approaching campaign in Flanders, stopped before one of the pavilions. It was that occupied by Desmarets, who had recently succeeded Chamillart in the direction of the finances, and who was at work within with Samuel Bernard, the famous banker, the richest man in Europe, and whose money dealings were the largest. The King observed to Desmarets that he was very glad to see him with M. Bernard; then immediately said to this latter:

"You are just the man never to have seen Marly — come and see it now; I will give you up afterward to Desmarets."

Bernard followed, and while the walk lasted the King spoke only to Bergheyck and to Bernard, leading them everywhere, and showing them everything with the grace he so well knew how to employ when he desired to overwhelm. I admired, and I was not the only one, this species of prostitution of the King, so niggard of his words, to a man of Bernard's degree. I was not long in learning the cause of it, and I admired to see how low the greatest kings sometimes find themselves reduced.

Our finances just then were exhausted. Desmarets no longer knew of what wood to make a crutch. He had been to Paris knocking at every door. But the most exact engagements had been so often broken that he found nothing but excuses and closed doors. Bernard, like the rest, would advance nothing. Much was due to him. In vain Desmarets represented to him the pressing necessity for money, and the enormous gains he had made out of the King. Bernard remained unshakable. The King and the minister were cruelly embarrassed. Desmarets said to the King that, after all was said and done, only Samuel Bernard could draw them out of the mess, because it was not doubtful that he had plenty of money everywhere; that the only thing needed was to vanquish his determination and the obstinacy — even insolence — he had shown; that he was a man crazy with vanity, and capable of opening his purse if the King deigned to flatter him.

It was agreed, therefore, that Desmarets should invite Bernard to dinner — should walk with him — and that the King should come and disturb them as I have related. Bernard was the dupe of this scheme; he returned from his walk with the King enchanted to such an extent that he said he would prefer ruining himself rather than leave in embarrassment a Prince who had just treated him so graciously, and whose eulogiums he uttered with enthusiasm! Desmarets profited by this trick immediately, and drew much more from it than he had proposed to himself.

The Prince de Léon had an adventure just about this time, which made much noise. He was a great, ugly, idle, mischievous fellow, son of the Duc de Rohan, who had given him the title I have just named. He had served in one campaign very indolently, and then quitted the army, under pretense of ill health, to serve no more. Glib in speech, and with the manners of the great world, he was full of caprices and fancies; although a great gambler and spendthrift, he was miserly, and cared only for himself. He had been enamored of Florence, an actress, whom M. d'Orléans had for a long time kept, and by whom he had children, one of whom is now Archbishop of Cambrai. M. de Léon also had several children by this creature, and spent large sums upon her. When he went in place of his father to open the States of Brittany, she accompanied him in a coach and six horses, with a ridiculous scandal. His father was in agony lest he should marry her. He offered to insure her five thousand francs a year pension, and to take care of their children, if M. de Léon would quit her. But M. de Léon would not hear of this, and his father accordingly complained to the King. The King summoned M. de Léon into his cabinet; but the young man pleaded his cause so well there, that he gained pity rather than condemnation. Nevertheless, La Florence was carried away from a pretty little house at the Ternes, near Paris, where M. de Léon kept her, and was put in a convent. M. de Léon became furious; for some time he would neither see nor speak of his father or mother, and repulsed all idea of marriage.

At last, however, no longer hoping to see his actress, he not only consented, but wished to marry. His parents were delighted at this, and at once looked about for a wife for him. Their choice fell upon the eldest daughter of the Duc de Roquelaure, who, although humpbacked and extremely ugly, was to be very rich some day, and was, in fact, a very good match. The affair had been arranged and concluded up to a certain point, when all was broken off, in consequence of the haughty obstinacy with which the Duchess de Roquelaure demanded a larger sum with M. de Léon than M. de Rohan chose to give.

The young couple were in despair: M. de Léon, lest his father should always act in this way, as an excuse for giving him nothing; the young lady, because she feared she should rot in a convent, through the avarice of her mother, and never marry. She was more than twenty-four years of age; he was more than eight and twenty. She was in the convent of the Daughters of the Cross in the Faubourg St. Antoine.

As soon as M. de Léon learned that the marriage was broken off, he hastened to the convent; and told all to Mademoiselle de Roquelaure; played the passionate, the despairing; said, that if they waited for their parents' consent they would never marry, and that she would rot in her convent. He proposed, therefore, that in spite of their parents, they should marry and become their own guardians. She agreed to this project, and he went away in order to execute it.

One of the most intimate friends of Madame de Roquelaure was Madame de la Vieuville, and she was the only person (excepting Madame de Roquelaure herself) to whom the Superior of the convent had permission to confide Mademoiselle de Roquelaure. Madame de la Vieuville often came to see Mademoiselle de Roquelaure to take her out, and sometimes sent for her. M. de Léon was made acquainted with this, and took his measures accordingly. He procured a coach of the same size, shape, and fittings as that of Madame de la Vieuville, with her arms upon it, and with three servants in her livery; he counterfeited a letter in her handwriting and with her seal, and sent this coach with a lackey well instructed to carry the letter to the convent, on Tuesday morning, the 29th of May, at the hour Madame de la Vieuville was accustomed to send for her.

Mademoiselle de Roquelaure, who had been let into the scheme, carried the letter to the Superior of the convent, and said Madame de la Vieuville had sent for her. Had the Superior any message to send?

The Superior, accustomed to these invitations, did not even look at the letter, but gave her consent at once. Mademoiselle de Roquelaure, accompanied solely by her governess, left the convent immediately, and entered the coach, which drove off directly. At the first turning it stopped, and the Prince de Léon, who had been in wait-

ing, jumped in. The governess at this began to cry out
with all her might; but at the very first sound M. de
Léon thrust a handkerchief into her mouth and stifled
the noise. The coachman meanwhile lashed his horses,
and the vehicle went off at full speed to Bruyères, near
Ménilmontant, the country house of the Duc de Lorges,
my brother-in-law, and friend of the Prince de Léon,
and who, with the Comte de Rieux, awaited the runaway
pair.

An interdicted and wandering priest was in waiting,
and as soon as they arrived married them. My brother-
in-law then led these nice young people into a fine chamber, where they were undressed, put to bed, and left
alone for two or three hours. A good meal was then
given to them, after which the bride was put into the coach,
with her attendant, who was in despair, and driven back
to the convent.

Mademoiselle de Roquelaure at once went deliberately
to the Superior, told her all that had happened, and then
calmly went into her chamber, and wrote a fine letter to
her mother, giving her an account of her marriage, and
asking for pardon: the Superior of the convent, the attendants, and all the household being, meanwhile, in the
utmost emotion at what had occurred.

The rage of the Duchess de Roquelaure at this incident may be imagined. In her first unreasoning fury,
she went to Madame de la Vieuville, who, all in ignorance of what had happened, was utterly at a loss to
understand her stormy and insulting reproaches. At last
Madame de Roquelaure saw that her friend was innocent
of all connection with the matter, and turned the current
of her wrath upon M. de Léon, against whom she felt
the more indignant, inasmuch as he had treated her with
much respect and attention since the rupture, and had
thus, to some extent, gained her heart. Against her
daughter she was also indignant, not only for what she
had done, but because she had exhibited much gayety
and freedom of spirit at the marriage repast, and had
diverted the company by some songs.

The Duc and Duchess de Rohan were on their side
equally furious, although less to be pitied, and made a

strange uproar. Their son, troubled to know how to extricate himself from this affair, had recourse to his aunt, Soubise, so as to assure himself of the King. She sent him to Pontchartrain to see the chancellor. M. de Léon saw him the day after this fine marriage, at five o'clock in the morning, as he was dressing. The chancellor advised him to do all he could to gain the pardon of his father and of Madame de Roquelaure. But he had scarcely begun to speak, when Madame de Roquelaure sent word to say, that she was close at hand, and wished the chancellor to come and see her. He did so, and she immediately poured out all her griefs to him, saying that she came, not to ask his advice, but to state her complaint as to a friend (they were very intimate), and as to the chief officer of justice to demand justice of him. When he attempted to put in a word on behalf of M. de Léon, her fury burst out anew; she would not listen to his words, but drove off to Marly, where she had an interview with Madame de Maintenon, and by her was presented to the King.

As soon as she was in his presence, she fell down on her knees before him, and demanded justice in its fullest extent against M. de Léon. The King raised her with the gallantry of a prince to whom she had not been indifferent, and sought to console her; but as she still insisted upon justice, he asked her if she knew fully what she asked for, which was nothing less than the head of M. de Léon. She redoubled her entreaties notwithstanding this information, so that the King at last promised her that she should have complete justice. With that, and many compliments, he quitted her, and passed into his own rooms with a very serious air, and without stopping for anybody.

The news of this interview, and of what had taken place soon spread through the chamber. Scarcely had people begun to pity Madame de Roquelaure, than some, by aversion for the grand imperial airs of this poor mother,—the majority, seized by mirth at the idea of a creature, well known to be very ugly and humpbacked, being carried off by such an ugly gallant,—burst out laughing, even to tears, and with an uproar completely scandalous. Madame de Maintenon abandoned herself to mirth, like the rest, and corrected the others at last, by saying it was not very charitable, in a tone that could impose upon no one.

Madame de Saint-Simon and I were at Paris. We knew with all Paris of this affair, but were ignorant of the place of the marriage and the part M. de Lorges had had in it, when the third day after the adventure I was startled out of my sleep at five o'clock in the morning, and saw my curtains and my windows open at the same time, and Madame de Saint-Simon and her brother (M. de Lorges) before me. They related to me all that had occurred, and then went away to consult with a skillful person what course to adopt, leaving me to dress. I never saw a man so crestfallen as M. de Lorges. He had confessed what he had done to a clever lawyer, who had much frightened him. After quitting him, he had hastened to us to make us go and see Pontchartrain. The most serious things are sometimes accompanied with the most ridiculous. M. de Lorges upon arriving knocked at the door of a little room which preceded the chamber of Madame de Saint-Simon. My daughter was rather unwell. Madame de Saint-Simon thought she was worse, and supposing it was I who had knocked, ran and opened the door. At the sight of her brother she ran back to her bed, to which he followed her, in order to relate his disaster. She rang for the windows to be opened, in order that she might see better. It so happened that she had taken the evening before a new servant, a country girl of sixteen, who slept in the little room. M. de Lorges, in a hurry to be off, told this girl to make haste in opening the windows, and then to go away and close the door. At this, the simple girl, all amazed, took her robe and her cotillon, and went up stairs to an old chamber-maid, awoke her, and with much hesitation told her what had just happened, and that she had left by the bedside of Madame de Saint-Simon a fine gentleman, very young, all powdered, curled, and decorated, who had driven her very quickly out of the chamber. She was all of a tremble, and much astonished. She soon learned who he was. The story was told to us, and in spite of our disquietude, much diverted us.

We hurried away to the chancellor, and he advised the priest, the witnesses to the signatures of the marriage, and, in fact, all concerned, to keep out of the way, except M. de Lorges, whom he assured us had nothing to fear. We went afterward to Chamillart, whom we found much displeased, but in little alarm. The King had ordered an account to be drawn up of the whole affair. Nevertheless, in spite of the uproar made on all sides, people began to see that the King would not abandon to public dishonor the daughter of Madame de Roquelaure, nor doom to the scaffold or to civil death in foreign countries the nephew of Madame de Soubise.

Friends of M. and Madame de Roquelaure tried to arrange matters. They represented that it would be better to accept the marriage as it was than to expose a daughter to cruel dishonor. Strange enough, the Duc and Duchess de Rohan were the most stormy. They wished to drive a very hard bargain in the matter, and made proposals so out of the way, that nothing could have been arranged but for the King. He did what he had never done before in all his life; he entered into all the details; he begged, then commanded as master; he had separate interviews with the parties concerned; and finally appointed the Duc d'Aumont and the chancellor to draw up the conditions of the marriage.

As Madame de Rohan, even after this, still refused to give her consent, the King sent for her, and said that if she and her husband did not at once give in, he would make the marriage valid by his own sovereign authority. Finally, after so much noise, anguish, and trouble, the contract was signed by the two families, assembled at the house of the Duchess de Roquelaure. The bans were published, and the marriage took place at the church of the Convent of the Cross, where Mademoiselle de Roquelaure had been confined since her beautiful marriage, guarded night and day by five or six nuns. She entered the church by one door, Prince de Léon by another; not a compliment or a word passed between them; the curate said mass; married them; they mounted a coach, and drove off to the house of a friend some leagues from Paris. They paid for their folly by a cruel indigence which lasted all their lives, neither of them having survived the Duc de Rohan, Monsieur de Roquelaure, or Madame de Roquelaure. They left several children.

CHAPTER III.

THE war this year proceeded much as before. M. d'Orléans went to Spain again. Before taking the field he stopped at Madrid to arrange matters. There he found nothing prepared, and everything in disorder. He was compelled to work day after day, for many hours, in order to obtain the most necessary supplies. This is what accounted for a delay which was maliciously interpreted at Paris into love for the Queen. M. le Duc was angry at the idleness in which he was kept; even Madame la Duchess, who hated him, because she had formerly loved him too well, industriously circulated this report, which was believed at Court, in the city, even in foreign countries, everywhere save in Spain, where the truth was too well known. It was while he was thus engaged that he gave utterance to a pleasantry that made Madame de Maintenon and Madame des Ursins his two most bitter enemies forever afterward.

One evening he was at table with several French and Spanish gentlemen, all occupied with his vexation against Madame des Ursins, who governed everything, and who had not thought of even the smallest thing for the campaign. The supper and the wine somewhat affected M. d'Orléans. Still full of his vexation, he took a glass, and, looking at the company, made an allusion in a toast to the two women, one the captain, the other the lieutenant, who governed France and Spain, and that in so coarse and yet humorous a manner, that it struck at once the imagination of the guests. No comment was made, but everybody burst out laughing, sense of drollery overcoming prudence, for it was well known that the she-captain was

Madame de Maintenon, and the she-lieutenant Madame des Ursins. The health was drunk, although the words were not repeated, and the scandal was strange.

Half an hour at most after this, Madame des Ursins was informed of what had taken place. She knew well who were meant by the toast, and was transported with rage. She at once wrote an account of the circumstances to Madame de Maintenon, who, for her part, was quite as furious. *Inde iræ.* They never pardoned M. d'Orléans, and we shall see how very nearly they succeeded in compassing his death. Until then, Madame de Maintenon had neither liked nor disliked M. de Orléans. Madame des Ursins had omitted nothing in order to please him. From that moment they swore the ruin of this prince. All the rest of the King's life M. d'Orléans did not fail to find that Madame de Maintenon was an implacable and cruel enemy. The sad state to which she succeeded in reducing him influenced him during all the rest of his life. As for Madame des Ursins, he soon found a change in her manner. She endeavored that everything should fail that passed through his hands. There are some wounds that never can be healed; and it must be admitted that the duke's toast inflicted one especially of that sort. He felt this; did not attempt any reconciliation; and followed his usual course. I know not if he ever repented of what he had said, whatever cause he may have had, so droll did it seem to him, but he has many times spoken of it since to me, laughing with all his might. I saw all the sad results which might arise from his speech, and nevertheless, while reproaching M. d'Orléans, I could not help laughing myself, so well, so simply, and so wittily expressed was his ridicule of the government on this and the other side of the Pyrenees.

At last, M. le Duc d'Orléans found means to enter upon his campaign, but was so ill provided, that he never was supplied with more than a fortnight's subsistence in advance. He obtained several small successes; but these were more than swallowed up by a fatal loss in another direction. The island of Sardinia, which was then under the Spanish Crown, was lost through the misconduct of the viceroy, the Duke of Veragua, and taken possession of by the troops of the Archduke. In the month of October, the island of Minorca also fell into the hands of the Archduke. Port Mahon made but little resistance; so that with this conquest and Gibraltar, the English found themselves able to rule in the Mediterranean, to winter entire fleets there, and to blockade all the ports of Spain upon that sea. Leaving Spain in this situation, let us turn to Flanders.

Early in July, we took Ghent and Bruges by surprise, and the news of these successes was received with the most unbridled joy at Fontainebleau. It appeared easy to profit by these two conquests, obtained without difficulty, by passing the Escaut, burning Oudenarde, closing the country to the enemies, and cutting them off from all supplies. Ours were very abundant, and came by water, with a camp that could not be attacked. M. de Vendôme agreed to all this, and alleged nothing against it. There was only one difficulty in the way — his idleness and unwillingness to move from quarters where he was comfortable. He wished to enjoy those quarters as long as possible, and maintained, therefore, that these movements would be just as good if delayed. Monseigneur le Duc de Bourgogne maintained on the contrary, with all the army — even the favorites of M. de Vendôme — that it would be better to execute the operation at once, that there was no reason for delay, and that delay might prove disastrous. He argued in vain. Vendôme disliked fatigue and change of quarters. They interfered with the daily life he was accustomed to lead, and which I have elsewhere described. He would not move.

Marlborough clearly seeing that M. de Vendôme did not at once take advantage of his position, determined to put it out of his power to do so. To reach Oudenarde, Marlborough had a journey to make of twenty-five leagues. Vendôme was so placed that he could have gained it in six leagues at the most. Marlborough put himself in motion with so much diligence that he stole three forced marches before Vendôme had the slightest suspicion or information of them. The news reached him in time, but he treated it with contempt according to his custom, assuring himself that he should outstrip the enemy by setting out the next morning. Monseigneur le Duc de Bourgogne pressed him to start that evening; such as dared represented to him the necessity and the importance of doing so. All was vain — in spite of repeated information of the enemy's march. The neglect was such that bridges had not been thought of for a little brook at the head of the camp, which it was necessary to cross.

On the next day, Wednesday, the 11th of July, a party of our troops, under the command of Biron, which had been sent on in advance to the Escaut, discovered, after passing it as they could, for the bridges were not yet made, all the army of the enemy bending round toward them, the rear of their columns touching at Oudenarde, where they also had crossed. Biron at once dispatched a messenger to the princes and to M. le Vendôme to inform them of this, and to ask for orders. Vendôme, annoyed by information so different to what he expected, maintained that it could not be true. As he was disputing, an officer arrived from Biron to confirm the news; but this only irritated Vendôme anew, and made him more obstinate. A third messenger arrived, and then M. de Vendôme, still affecting disbelief of the news sent him, flew in a passion, but nevertheless mounted his horse, saying that all this was the work of the devil, and that such diligence was impossible. He sent orders to Biron to attack the enemy, promising to support him immediately. He told the princes, at the same time, to gently follow with the whole of the army, while he placed himself at the head of his columns, and pushed on briskly to Biron.

Biron meanwhile placed his troops as well as he could, on ground very unequal and much cut up. He wished to execute the order he had received, less from any hopes of success in a combat so vastly disproportioned than to secure himself from the blame of a general so ready to censure those who did not follow his instructions. But he was advised so strongly not to take so hazardous a step, that he refrained. Maréchal Matignon, who arrived soon after, indeed specially prohibited him from acting.

While this was passing, Biron heard sharp firing on his left, beyond the village. He hastened there, and found an encounter of infantry going on. He sustained it as well as he could, while the enemy were gaining ground on the left, and, the ground being difficult (there was a ravine there), the enemy were kept at bay until M. de Vendôme came up. The troops he brought were all out of breath. As soon as they arrived, they threw themselves amid the hedges, nearly all in columns, and sustained thus the attacks of the enemies, and an engagement which every moment grew hotter, without having the means to arrange themselves in any order. The columns that arrived from time to time to the relief of these were as out of breath as the others, and were at once sharply charged by the enemies, who, being extended in lines and in order, knew well how to profit by our disorder. The confusion was very great; the newcomers had no time to rally; there was a long interval between the platoons engaged and those meant to sustain them; the cavalry and the household troops were mixed up pell-mell with the infantry, which increased the disorder to such a point that our troops no longer recognized each other. This enabled the enemy to fill up the ravine with fascines sufficient to enable them to pass it, and allowed the rear of their army to make a grand tour by our right to gain the head of the ravine, and take us in flank there.

Toward this same right were the princes, who for some time had been looking from a mill at so strange a combat, so disadvantageously commenced. As soon as our troops saw pouring down upon them others much more numerous, they gave way toward their left with so much promptitude that the attendants of the princes became mixed up with their masters, and all were hurried away toward the thick of the fight, with a rapidity and confusion that were indecent. The princes showed themselves everywhere, and in places the most exposed, displaying much valor and coolness, encouraging the men, praising the officers, asking the principal officers what was to be done, and telling M. de Vendôme what they thought.

The inequality of the ground that the enemies found in advancing, after having driven in our right, enabled our men to rally and to resist. But this resistance was of short duration. Everyone had been engaged in hand-to-hand combats; everyone was worn out with lassitude and despair of success, and a confusion so general and so unheard of. The household troops owed their escape to the mistake of one of the enemy's officers, who carried an order to the redcoats, thinking them his own men. He was taken, and seeing that he was about to share the peril with our troops, warned them that they were going to be surrounded. They retired in some disorder, and so avoided this.

The disorder increased, however, every moment. Nobody recognized his troop. All were pell-mell,—cavalry, infantry, dragoons; not a battalion, not a squadron together, and all in confusion, one upon the other.

Night came. We had lost much ground, one-half of the army had not finished arriving. In this sad situation the princes consulted with M. de Vendôme as to what was to be done. He, furious at being so terribly out of his reckoning, affronted everybody. Monseigneur le Duc de Bourgogne wished to speak; but Vendôme, intoxicated with choler and authority, closed his mouth, by saying to him in an imperious voice before everybody, "That he came to the army only on condition of obeying him." These enormous words, pronounced at a moment in which everybody felt so terribly the weight of the obedience rendered to his idleness and obstinacy, made everybody tremble with indignation. The young prince to whom they were addressed, hesitated, mastered himself, and kept silence. Vendôme went on declaring that the battle was not lost — that it could be recommenced the next morning, when the rest of the army had arrived, and so on. No one of consequence cared to reply.

From every side soon came information, however, that the disorder was extreme. Puységur, Matignon, Sousternon, Cheladet, Puyguyon, all brought the same news. Vendôme, seeing that it was useless to resist all this testimony, and beside himself with rage, cried, "Oh, very well, gentlemen! I see clearly what you wish. We

must retire, then;" and looking at Monseigneur le Duc
de Bourgogne, he added, "I know you have long wished
to do so, Monseigneur."

These words, which could not fail to be taken in a
double sense were pronounced exactly as I relate them,
and were emphasized in a manner to leave no doubt as
to their signification. Monseigneur le Duc de Bourgogne
remained silent as before, and for some time the silence
was unbroken. At last Puységur interrupted it, by asking how the retreat was to be executed. Each, then,
spoke confusedly. Vendôme, in his turn, kept silence
from vexation or embarrassment; then he said they
must march to Ghent, without adding how, or anything else.

The day had been very fatiguing; the retreat was long
and perilous. The princes mounted their horses, and took
the road to Ghent. Vendôme set out without giving any
orders, or seeing to anything. The general officers returned to their posts, and of themselves gave the order
for retreat. Yet so great was the confusion, that the
Chevalier Rosel, lieutenant general, at the head of a hundred squadrons, received no orders. In the morning he
found himself with his hundred squadrons, which had been
utterly forgotten. He at once commenced his march; but
to retreat in full daylight was very difficult, as he soon
found. He had to sustain the attacks of the enemy during
several hours of his march.

Elsewhere, also, the difficulty of retreating was great.
Fighting went on at various points all night, and the
enemy were on the alert. Some of the troops on our
right, while debating as to the means of retreat, found
they were about to be surrounded by the enemy. The
Vidame of Amiens saw that not a moment was to be lost.
He cried to the light horse, of which he was captain,
"Follow me," and pierced his way through a line of the
enemy's cavalry. He then found himself in front of a
line of infantry, which fired upon him, but opened to give
him passage. At the same moment, the household troops
and others, profiting by a movement so bold, followed
the Vidame and his men, and all escaped together to
Ghent, led on by the Vidame, to whose sense and courage
the safety of these troops was owing.

M. de Vendôme arrived at Ghent, between seven and eight o'clock in the morning. Even at this moment he did not forget his disgusting habits, and as soon as he set foot to ground . . . in sight of all the troops as they came by,— then at once went to bed, without giving any orders, or seeing to anything, and remained more than thirty hours without rising, in order to repose himself after his fatigues. He learned that Monseigneur de Bourgogne and the army had pushed on to Lawendeghem; but he paid no attention to it, and continued to sup and sleep at Ghent several days running, without attending to anything.

As soon as Monseigneur le Duc de Bourgogne arrived
at Lawendeghem, he wrote a short letter to the
King, and referred him for details to M. de Vendôme. But at the same time he wrote to the Duchess,
very clearly expressing to her where the fault lay. M. de
Vendôme, on his side, wrote to the King, and tried to
persuade him that the battle had not been disadvantageous to us. A short time afterward, he wrote again, telling the King that he could have beaten the enemies had
he been sustained; and that, if, contrary to his advice,
retreat had not been determined on, he would certainly
have beaten them the next day. For the details he referred to Monseigneur le Duc de Bourgogne.

I had always feared that some ill fortune would fall to
the lot of Monseigneur le Duc de Bourgogne if he served
under M. de Vendôme at the army. When I first learned
that he was going to Flanders with M. de Vendôme, I
expressed my apprehensions to M. de Beauvilliers, who
treated them as unreasonable and ridiculous. He soon
had good cause to admit that I had not spoken without justice. Our disasters at Oudenarde were very great. We
had many men and officers killed and wounded, four
thousand men and seven hundred officers taken prisoners,
and a prodigious quantity missing and dispersed. All
these losses were, as I have shown, entirely due to the
laziness and inattention of M. de Vendôme. Yet the
friends of that General — and he had many at the Court
and in the army — actually had the audacity to lay the
blame upon Monseigneur le Duc de Bourgogne. This

was what I had foreseen, viz, M. de Vendôme, in case any misfortune occurred, would be sure to throw the burden of it upon Monseigneur le Duc de Bourgogne.

Albéroni, who, as I have said, was one of M. de Vendôme's creatures, published a deceitful and impudent letter, in which he endeavored to prove that M. de Vendôme had acted throughout like a good general, but that he had been thwarted by Monseigneur le Duc de Bourgogne. This letter was distributed everywhere, and well served the purpose for which it was intended. Another writer, Campistron — a poor, starving poet, ready to do anything to live — went further. He wrote a letter, in which Monseigneur le Duc de Bourgogne was personally attacked in the tenderest points, and in which Maréchal Matignon was said to merit a court-marshal for having counseled retreat. This letter, like the other, although circulated with more precaution, was shown even in the *cafés* and in the theaters; in the public places of gambling and debauchery; on the promenades, and among the newsvenders. Copies of it were even shown in the provinces, and in foreign countries; but always with much circumspection. Another letter soon afterward appeared, apologizing for M. de Vendôme. This was written by Comte d'Evreux, and was of much the same tone as the two others.

A powerful cabal was in fact got up against Monseigneur de Bourgogne. Vaudevilles, verses, atrocious songs against him, ran all over Paris and the provinces with a license and a rapidity that no one checked; while at the Court, the libertines and the fashionables applauded; so that in six days it was thought disgraceful to speak with any measure of this prince, even in his father's house.

Madame de Bourgogne could not witness all this uproar against her husband, without feeling sensibly affected by it. She had been made acquainted by Monseigneur de Bourgogne with the true state of the case. She saw her own happiness and reputation at stake. Though very gentle, and still more timid, the grandeur of the occasion raised her above herself. She was cruelly wounded by the insults of Vendôme to her husband, and by all the atrocities and falsehoods his emissaries published. She gained Madame de Maintenon, and the first result of this step was, that the King censured Chamillart for not speaking of the letters in circulation, and ordered him to write to Albéroni and D'Evreux (Campistron, strangely enough, was forgotten), commanding them to keep silence for the future.

The cabal was amazed to see Madame de Maintenon on the side of Madame de Bourgogne, while M. du Maine (who was generally in accord with Madame de Maintenon) was for M. de Vendôme. They concluded that the King had been led away, but that if they held firm, his partiality for M. de Vendôme, for M. du Maine, and for bastardy in general, would bring him round to them. In point of fact, the King was led now one way, and now another, with a leaning always toward M. de Vendôme.

Soon after this, Chamillart, who was completely of the party of M. de Vendôme, thought fit to write a letter to Monseigneur le Duc de Bourgogne, in which he counseled him to live on good terms with his general. Madame de Bourgogne never forgave Chamillart this letter, and was always annoyed with her husband that he acted upon it. His religious sentiments induced him to do so. Vendôme so profited by the advances made to him by the young prince, that he audaciously brought Albéroni with him when he visited Monseigneur de Bourgogne. This weakness of Monseigneur de Bourgogne lost him many friends, and made his enemies more bold than ever. Madame de Bourgogne, however, did not despair. She wrote to her husband that for M. de Vendôme she had more aversion and contempt than for any one else in the world, and that nothing would make her forget what he had done. We shall see with what courage she knew how to keep her word.

While the discussions upon the battle of Oudenarde were yet proceeding, a league was formed with France against the Emperor by all the states of Italy. The King (Louis XIV.) accepted, however, too late, a project he himself ought to have proposed and executed. He lost perhaps the most precious opportunity he had had during all his reign. The step he at last took was so apparent that it alarmed the allies, and put them on their guard. Except Flanders, they did nothing in any other spot, and turned all their attention to Italy.

Let us return, however, to Flanders.

Prince Eugène, with a large booty gathered in Artois and elsewhere, had fixed himself at Brussels. He wished to bear off his spoil, which required more than five thousand wagons to carry it, and which consisted in great part of provisions, worth three million five hundred thousand francs, and set out with them to join the army of the Duke of Marlborough. Our troops could not, of course, be in ignorance of this. M. de Vendôme wished to attack the convoy with half his troops. The project seemed good, and, in case of success, would have brought results equally honorable and useful. Monseigneur de Bourgogne, however, opposed the attack, I know not why; and M. de Vendôme, so obstinate until then, gave in to him in this case. His object was to ruin the Prince utterly, for allowing such a good chance to escape, the blame resting entirely upon him. Obstinacy and audacity had served M. de Vendôme at Oudenarde: he expected no less a success now from his deference.

Some anxiety was felt just about this time for Lille, which it was feared the enemy would lay siege to. Boufflers went to command there, at his own request, and found the place very ill garrisoned with raw troops, many of whom had never smelt powder. M. de Vendôme, however, laughed at the idea of the siege of Lille, as something mad and ridiculous. Nevertheless, the town was invested on the 12th of August, as the King duly learned on the 14th. Even then, flattery did its work. The friends of Vendôme declared that such an enterprise was the best thing that could happen to France, as the besiegers, inferior in numbers to our army, were sure to be miserably beaten. M. de Vendôme, in the meantime, did not budge from the post he had taken up near Ghent. The King wrote to him to go with his army to the relief of Lille. M. de Vendôme still delayed; another courier was sent with the same result. At this, the King, losing temper, dispatched another courier, with orders to Monseigneur de Bourgogne, to lead the army to Lille, if M. de Vendôme refused to do so. At this, M. de Ven-

dôme awoke from his lethargy. He set out for Lille,
but took the longest road, and dawdled as long as he
could on the way, stopping five days at Mons Puenelle,
among other places.

The agitation, meanwhile, in Paris was extreme. The
King demanded news of the siege from his courtiers,
and could not understand why no couriers arrived. It
was generally expected that some decisive battle had
been fought. Each day increased the uneasiness. The
princes and the principal noblemen of the Court were at
the army. Every one at Versailles feared for the safety
of a relative or friend. Prayers were offered everywhere.
Madame de Bourgogne passed whole nights in the chapel,
when people thought her in bed, and drove her women
to despair. Following her example, ladies who had
husbands at the army stirred not from the churches.
Gaming, conversation ceased. Fear was painted upon
every face, and seen in every speech, without shame.
If a horse passed a little quickly, everybody ran without
knowing where. The apartments of Chamillart were
crowded with lackeys, even into the street, sent by
people desiring to be informed of the moment that a courier
arrived; and this terror and uncertainty lasted nearly a
month. The provinces were even more troubled than
Paris. The King wrote to the Bishop, in order that they
should offer up prayers in terms which suited with the
danger of the time. It may be judged what was the
general impression and alarm.

It is true, that in the midst of this trepidation, the
partisans of M. de Vendôme affected to pity that poor
Prince Eugène, and to declare that he must inevitably
fail in his undertaking; but these discourses did not impose
upon me. I knew what kind of enemies we had to deal
with, and I foresaw the worst results from the idleness
and inattention of M. de Vendôme. One evening, in
the presence of Chamillart and five or six others, annoyed
by the conversation which passed, I offered to bet four
pistoles that there would be no general battle, and that
Lille would be taken without being relieved. This
strange proposition excited much surprise, and caused
many questions to be addressed to me. I would explain

nothing at all; but sustained my proposal in the English manner, and my bet was taken; Cani, who accepted it, thanking me for the present of four pistoles I was making him, as he said. The stakes were placed in the hand of Chamillart.

By the next day, the news of my bet had spread abroad, and made a frightful uproar. The partisans of M. de Vendôme, knowing I was no friend to them, took this opportunity to damage me in the eyes of the King. They so far succeeded that I entirely lost favor with him, without, however, suspecting it, for more than two months. All that I could do then, was to let the storm pass over my head and keep silent, so as not to make matters worse.

Meanwhile, M. de Vendôme continued the inactive policy he had hitherto followed. In despite of reiterated advice from the King, he took no steps to attack the enemy. Monseigneur de Bourgogne was for doing so, but Vendôme would make no movement. As before, too, he contrived to throw all the blame of his inactivity upon Monseigneur de Bourgogne. He succeeded so well in making this believed, that his followers in the army cried out against the followers of Monseigneur de Bourgogne wherever they appeared. Chamillart was sent by the King to report upon the state and position of our troops, and if a battle had taken place and proved unfavorable to us, to prevent such sad results as had taken place after Ramillies.

Chamillart came back on the 18th of September. No battle had been fought, but M de Vendôme felt sure, he said, of cutting off all supplies from the enemy, and thus compelling them to raise the siege.

The King had need of these intervals of consolation and hope. Master as he might be of his words and of his features, he profoundly felt the powerlessness to resist his enemies that he fell into day by day. What I have related about Samuel Bernard, the banker, to whom he almost did the honors of his gardens at Marly, in order to draw from him the assistance he had refused, is a great proof of this. It was much remarked at Fontaine-bleau, just as Lille was invested, that, the city of Paris coming to harangue him on the occasion of the oath taken by Bignon, new *Prévôt des Marchands*, he replied, not only with kindness, but that he made use of the term "gratitude for his good city," and that in doing so he lost countenance,—two things which during all his reign had never escaped him. On the other hand, he sometimes had intervals of firmness which edified less than they surprised. When everybody at the Court was in the anxiety I have already described, he offended them by going out every day hunting or walking, so that they could not know, until after his return, the news which might arrive when he was out.

As for Monseigneur, he seemed altogether exempt from anxiety. After Ramillies, when everybody was waiting for the return of Chamillart, to learn the truth, Monseigneur went away to dine at Meudon, saying he should learn the news soon enough. From this time he showed no more interest in what was passing. When news was brought that Lille was invested, he turned on his heel before the letter announcing it had been read to the end. The King called him back to hear the rest. He returned and heard it. The reading finished, he went away, without offering a word. Entering the apartments of the Princess de Conti, he found there Madame d'Espinoy, who had much property in Flanders, and who had wished to take a trip there.

"Madame," said he, smiling, as he arrived, "how would you do just now to get to Lille?" And at once made them acquainted with the investment. These things really wounded the Princess de Conti. Arriving at Fontainebleau one day, during the movements of the army, Monseigneur set to work reciting, for amusement, a long list of strange names of places in the forest.

"Dear me, Monseigneur," cried she, "what a good memory you have. What a pity it is loaded with such things only!" If he felt the reproach, he did not profit by it.

As for Mgr. le Duc de Bourgogne, Monseigneur (his father) was ill disposed toward him, and readily swallowed all that was said in his dispraise. Monseigneur had no sympathy with the piety of his son; it constrained and bothered him. The cabal well profited by this. They succeeded to such an extent in alienating the father from the son, that it is only strict truth to say that no one dared to speak well of Monseigneur le Duc de Bourgogne in the presence of Monseigneur. From this it may be imagined what was the license and freedom of speech elsewhere against this prince. They reached such a point, indeed, that the King, not daring to complain publicly against the Prince de Conti, who hated Vendôme, for speaking in favor of Monseigneur de Bourgogne, reprimanded him sharply in reality for having done so, but ostensibly because he had talked about the affairs of Flanders at his sister's. Madame de Bourgogne did all she could to turn the current that was setting in against her husband; and in this she was assisted by Madame de Maintenon, who was annoyed to the last degree to see that other people had more influence over the King than she had.

The siege of Lille meanwhile continued, and at last it began to be seen that, instead of attempting to fight a grand battle, the wisest course would be to throw assistance into the place. An attempt was made to do so, but it was now too late.

The besieged, under the guidance of Maréchal Boufflers, who watched over all, and attended to all, in a manner that gained him all hearts, made a gallant and determined resistance. A volume would be necessary in order to relate all the marvels of capacity and valor displayed in this defense. Our troops disputed the ground inch by inch. They repulsed three times running, the enemy from a mill, took it the third time, and burned it. They sustained an attack, in three places at once, of ten thousand men, from nine o'clock in the evening to three o'clock in the morning, without giving way. They recaptured the sole traverse the enemy had been able to take from them. They drove out the besiegers from the projecting angles of the counterscarp, which they had kept possession of for eight days. They twice repulsed seven thousand men who attacked their covered way and an outwork; at the third attack they lost an angle of the outwork, but remained masters of all the rest.

So many attacks and engagements terribly weakened
the garrison. On the 28th of September some assistance
was sent to the besieged by the daring of the Chevalier
de Luxembourg. It enabled them to sustain with vigor
the fresh attacks that were directed against them, to repulse the enemy, and, by a grand sortie, to damage some
of their works, and kill many of their men. But all was
in vain. The enemy returned again and again to the attack. Every attempt to cut off their supplies failed.
Finally, on the 23d of October, a capitulation was signed.
The place had become untenable; three new breaches had
been made on the 20th and 21st; powder and ammunition were failing; the provisions were almost all eaten
up; there was nothing for it but to give in.

Maréchal Boufflers obtained all he asked, and retired
into the citadel with all the prisoners of war, after two
months of resistance. He offered discharge to all the
soldiers who did not wish to enter the citadel. But
not one of the six thousand he had left to him accepted
it. They were all ready for a new resistance, and when
their chief appeared among them their joy burst out in
the most flattering praises of him. It was on Friday,
the 26th of October, that they shut themselves up in the
citadel.

The enemy opened their trenches before the citadel on
the 29th of October. On the 7th of November they made
a grand attack, but were repulsed with considerable loss.
But they did not flinch from their work, and Boufflers
began to see he could not long hold out. By the commencement of December he had only twenty thousand
pounds of powder left; very little of other munitions,
and still less food. In the town and the citadel they had
eaten eight hundred horses. Boufflers, as soon as the
others were reduced to this food, had it served upon his
own table, and ate of it like the rest. The King, learning in what state these soldiers were, personally sent
word to Boufflers to surrender, but the Maréchal, even
after he had received this order, delayed many days to
obey it.

At last, in want of the commonest necessaries, and able
to protract his defense no longer, he beat a parley, signed

a capitulation on the 9th of December, obtaining all he asked, and retired from Lille. Prince Eugène, to whom he surrendered, treated him with much distinction and friendship, invited him to dinner several times,—overwhelmed him, in fact with attention and civilities. The Prince was glad indeed to have brought to a successful issue such a difficult siege.

4

CHAPTER V.

THE position of Monseigneur le Duc de Bourgogne at the army continued to be equivocal. He was constantly in collision with M. de Vendôme. The latter, after the loss of Lille, wished to defend the Escaut without any regard to its extent of forty miles. The Duc de Bourgogne, as far as he dared, took the part of Berwick, who maintained that the defense was impossible. The King, hearing of all these disputes, actually sent Chamillart to the army to compose them; and it was a curious sight to behold this penman, this financier, acting as arbiter between generals on the most delicate operations of war. Chamillart continued to admire Vendôme, and treated the Duc de Bourgogne with little respect, both at the army, and, after his return, in conversation with the King. His report was given in presence of Madame de Maintenon, who listened without daring to say a word, and repeated everything to the Duchess de Bourgogne. We may imagine what passed between them, and the anger of the Princess against the minister. For the present, however, nothing could be done. Berwick was soon afterward almost disgraced. As soon as he was gone M. de Vendôme wrote to the King, saying that he was sure of preventing the enemy from passing the Escaut — that he answered for it on his head. With such a guarantee from a man in such favor at Court, who could doubt? Yet, shortly after, Marlborough crossed the Escaut in four places, and Vendôme actually wrote to the King, begging him to remember that he had always declared the defense of the Escaut to be impossible!

The cabal made a great noise to cover this monstrous audacity, and endeavored to renew the attack against the Duc de Bourgogne. We shall see what success attended their efforts. The army was at Soissons, near Tournai, in a profound tranquillity, the opium of which had gained the Duc de Bourgogne, when news of the approach of the enemy was brought. M. de Vendôme advanced in that direction, and sent word to the Duke, that he thought he ought to advance on the morrow with all his army. The Duke was going to bed when he received the letter; and although it was too late to repulse the enemy, was much blamed for continuing to undress himself, and putting off action till the morrow.

To this fault he added another. He had eaten; it was very early; and it was no longer proper to march. It was necessary to wait fresh orders from M. de Vendôme. Tournai was near. The Duc de Bourgogne went there to have a game at tennis. This sudden party of pleasure strongly scandalized the army, and raised all manner of unpleasant talk. Advantage was taken of the young Prince's imprudence to throw upon him the blame of what was caused by the negligence of M. de Vendôme.

A serious and disastrous action that took place during these operations was actually kept a secret from the King, until the Duc de la Trémoille, whose son was engaged there, let out the truth. Annoyed that the King said nothing to him on the way in which his son had distinguished himself, he took the opportunity, while he was serving the King, to talk of the passage of the Escaut, and said that his son's regiment had much suffered. "How suffered?" cried the King; "nothing has happened." Whereupon the Duke related all to him. The King listened with the greatest attention, and questioned him, and admitted before everybody that he knew nothing of all this. His surprise, and the surprise it occasioned, may be imagined.

It happened that when the King left table, Chamillart unexpectedly came into his cabinet. He was soon asked about the action of the Escaut, and why it had not been reported. The minister, embarrassed, said that it was a thing of no consequence. The King continued to press him, mentioned details, and talked of the regiment of the Prince of Tarento. Chamillart then admitted that what happened at the passage was so disagreeable, and the combat so disagreeable, but so little important, that Madame de Maintenon, to whom he had reported all, had thought it best not to trouble the King upon the matter, and it had accordingly been agreed not to trouble him. Upon this singular answer the King stopped short in his questions, and said not a word more.

The Escaut being forced, the citadel of Lille on the point of being taken, our army exhausted with fatigue was at last dispersed, to the scandal of everybody; for it was known that Ghent was about to be besieged. The princes received orders to return to Court, but they insisted on the propriety of remaining with the army. M. de Vendôme, who began to fear the effect of his rashness and insolence, tried to obtain the permission to pass the winter with the army on the frontier. He was not listened to. The princes received orders most positively to return to Court, and accordingly set out.

The Duchess de Bourgogne was very anxious about the way in which the Duke was to be received, and eager to talk to him and explain how matters stood, before he saw the King or anybody else. I sent a message to him that he ought to contrive to arrive after midnight, in order to pass two or three hours with the Duchess, and perhaps see Madame de Maintenon early in the morning. My message was not received; at any rate not followed. The Duc de Bourgogne arrived on the 11th of December, a little after seven o'clock in the evening, just as Monseigneur had gone to the play, whither the Duchess had not gone, in order to wait for her husband. I know not why he alighted in the Cour des Princes, instead of the Great Court. I was put then in the apartments of the Comtesse de Roncy, from which I could see all that passed. I came down, and saw the Prince ascending the steps between the Ducs de Beauvilliers and De la Rocheguyon, who happened to be there. He looked quite satisfied, was gay, and laughing, and spoke right and left. I bowed to him. He did me the honor to embrace me in a way that showed me he knew better what was going on than how to maintain his dignity. He then talked only to me, and whispered that he knew what I had said. A troop of courtiers met him. In their midst he passed the Great Hall of the Guards, and instead of going to Madame de Maintenon's by the private door, though the nearest way, went to the great public entrance. There was no one there but the King and Madame de Maintenon, with Pontchartrain; for I do not count the Duchess de Bourgogne. Pontchartrain noted well what passed at the interview, and related it all to me that very evening.

As soon as in Madame de Maintenon's apartment was heard the rumor which usually precedes such an arrival, the King became sufficiently embarrassed to change countenance several times. The Duchess de Bourgogne appeared somewhat tremulous, and fluttered about the room to hide her trouble, pretending not to know exactly by which door the Prince would arrive. Madame de Maintenon was thoughtful. Suddenly all the doors flew open: the young Prince advanced toward the King, who, master of himself, more than anyone ever was, lost at once all embarrassment, took two or three steps toward his grandson, embraced him with some demonstration of tenderness, spoke of his voyage, and then pointing to the Princess, said, with a smiling countenance: "Do you say nothing to her?" The Prince turned a moment toward her, and answered respectfully, as if he dared not turn away from the King, and did not move. He then saluted Madame de Maintenon, who received him well. Talk of travel, beds, roads, and so forth, lasted, all standing, some half quarter of an hour; then the King said it would not be fair to deprive him any longer of the pleasure of being alone with Madame la Duchess de Bourgogne, and that they would have time enough to see each other. The Prince made a bow to the King, another to Madame de Maintenon, passed before the few ladies of the palace who had taken courage to put their heads into the room, entered the neighboring cabinet, where he embraced the Duchess, saluted the ladies who

were there, that is, kissed them, remained a few moments,
and then went into his apartment, where he shut himself up with the Duchess de Bourgogne.

Their *tête-à-tête* lasted two hours and more: just toward
the end, Madame d'O was let in; soon after the
Maréchale d'Estrées entered, and soon after that the
Duchess de Bourgogne came out with them, and returned
into the Great Cabinet of Madame de Maintenon. Monseigneur came there as usual, on returning from the
comedy. Madame la Duchess de Bourgogne, troubled
that the Duke did not hurry himself to come and salute
his father, went to fetch him, and came back saying that
he was putting on his powder; but observing that Monseigneur was little satisfied with this want of eagerness,
sent again to hurry him. Just then the Maréchale
d'Estrées, harebrained and light, and free to say just
what came into her head, began to attack Monseigneur
for waiting so tranquilly for his son, instead of going
himself to embrace him. This random expression did not
succeed. Monseigneur replied stiffly that it was not for
him to seek the Duc de Bourgogne; but the duty of the
Duc de Bourgogne to seek him. He came at last. The
reception was pretty good, but did not by any means
equal that of the King. Almost immediately the King
rang, and everybody went to the supper room.

During the supper, M. le Duc de Berry arrived, and
came to salute the King at table. To greet HIM all
hearts opened. The King embraced him very tenderly.
Monseigneur only looked at him tenderly, not daring to
embrace his (youngest) son in presence of the King.
All present courted him. He remained standing near the
King all the rest of the supper, and there was no talk
save of post horses, of roads, and such like trifles. The
King spoke sufficiently at table to Monseigneur le Duc
de Bourgogne; but to the Duc de Berry, he assumed a
very different air. Afterward, there was a supper for the
Duc de Berry in the apartments of the Duchess de
Bourgogne; but the conjugal impatience of the Duc de
Bourgogne cut it rather too short.

I expressed to the Duc de Beauvilliers, with my accustomed freedom, that the Duc de Bourgogne seemed to

me very gay on returning from so sad a campaign. He
could not deny this, and made up his mind to give a
hint on the subject. Everybody indeed blamed so misplaced a gayety. Two or three days after his arrival the
Duc de Bourgogne passed three hours with the King in
the apartments of Madame de Maintenon. I was afraid
that his piety would withhold him from letting out on
the subject of M. de Vendôme, but I heard that he spoke
on that subject without restraint, impelled by the advice
of the Duchess de Bourgogne, and also by the Duc de
Beauvilliers, who set his conscience at ease. His account
of the campaign, of affairs, of things, of advices, of pro-
ceedings, was complete. Another, perhaps, less virtuous,
might have used weightier terms; but at any rate everything was said with a completeness beyond all hope, if
we consider who spoke and who listened. The Duke
concluded with an eager prayer to be given an army in
the next campaign, and with the promise of the King to
that effect. Soon after an explanation took place with
Monseigneur at Meudon, Mademoiselle Choin being present. With the latter he spoke much more in private:
she had taken his part with Monseigneur. The Duchess
de Bourgogne had gained her over. The connection of
this girl with Madame de Maintenon was beginning to
grow very close indeed.

Gamaches had been to the army with the Duc de
Bourgogne, and being a free-tongued man had often
spoken out very sharply on the puerilities in which he
indulged in company with the Duc de Berry, influenced
by his example. One day returning from mass, in company with the Duke on a critical day, when he would
rather have seen him on horseback, he said aloud, "You
will certainly win the kingdom of heaven; but as for the
kingdom of the earth, Prince Eugène and Marlborough
know how to seek it better than you." What he said
quite as publicly to the two princes on their treatment
of the King of England, was admirable. That prince
(known as the Chevalier de St. Georges) served incognito, with a modesty that the princes took advantage of
to treat him with the greatest indifference and contempt.
Toward the end of the campaign, Gamaches, exasperated

with their conduct, exclaimed to them in the presence of everybody: "Is this a wager? speak frankly if so, you have won, there can be no doubt of that; but now, speak a little to the Chevalier de St. George, and treat him more politely." These sallies, however, were too public to produce any good effect. They were suffered, but not attended to.

The citadel of Lille capitulated as we have seen, with the consent of the King, who was obliged to acknowledge that the Maréchal de Boufflers had done all he could, and that further defense was impossible. Prince Eugène treated Boufflers with the greatest possible consideration. The enemy at this time made no secret of their intention to invest Ghent, which made the dispersal of our army the more shameful; but necessity commanded, for no more provisions were to be got.

M. de Vendôme arrived at Versailles on the morning of December 15th, and saluted the King as he left table. The King embraced him with a sort of enthusiasm that made his cabal triumph. He monopolized all conversation during the dinner, but only trifles were talked of. The King said he would talk to him next day at Madame de Maintenon's. This delay, which was new to him, did not seem of good augury. He went to pay his respects to M. de Bourgogne, who received him well in spite of all that had passed. Then Vendôme went to wait on Monseigneur at the Princess de Conti's: here he thought himself in his stronghold. He was received excellently, and the conversation turned on nothings. He wished to take advantage of this, and proposed a visit to Anet. His surprise and that of those present were great at the uncertain reply of Monseigneur, who caused it to be understood, and rather stifly too, that he would not go. Vendôme appeared embarrassed, and abridged his visit. I met him at the end of the gallery of the new wing, as I was coming from M. de Beauvilliers, turning toward the steps in the middle of the gallery. He was alone, without torches or valets, with Albéroni, followed by a man I did not know. I saw him by the light of my torches; we saluted each other politely, though we had not much acquaintance one with the other. He seemed chagrined, and was going to M. du Maine, his counsel and principal support.

Next day he passed an hour with the King at Madame de Maintenon's. He remained eight or ten days at Versailles or at Meudon, and never went to the Duchess de Bourgogne's. This was nothing new for him. The mixture of grandeur and irregularity which he had long affected seemed to him to have freed him from the most indispensable duties. His Abbé Albéroni showed himself at the King's mass in the character of a courtier with unparalleled effrontery. At last they went to Anet. Even before he went he perceived some diminution in his position, since he lowered himself so far as to invite people to come and see him,—he, who in former years made it a favor to receive the most distinguished persons. He soon perceived the falling off in the number of his visitors. Some excused themselves from going; others promised to go and did not. Everyone made a difficulty about a journey of fifteen leagues, which, the year before, was considered as easy and as necessary as that of Marly. Vendôme remained at Anet until the first voyage to Marly, when he came; and he always came to Marly and Meudon, never to Versailles, until the change of which I shall soon have occasion to speak.

The Maréchal de Boufflers returned to Court from his firm but unsuccessful defense of Lille, and was received in a triumphant manner, and overwhelmed with honors and rewards. This contrast with Vendôme was remarkable: the one raised by force of trickery, heaping up mountains like the giants, leaning on vice, lies, audacity, on a cabal inimical to the State and its heirs,* a factitious hero, made such by will in despite of truth;—the other, without cabal, with no support but virtue and modesty, was inundated with favors and the applause of enemies was followed by the acclamations of the public, so that the nature of even courtiers changed, and they were happy in the recompenses showered upon him!

Some days after the return of the Duc de Bourgogne, Cheverny had an interview with him, on leaving which he told me what I cannot refrain from relating here,

* Observe the curious identification of the State and the King.

though it is necessarily with confusion that I write it. He said that, speaking freely with him on what had been circulated during the campaign, the prince observed that he knew how and with what vivacity I had expressed myself, and that he was informed of the manner in which the Prince de Conti had given his opinion, and added that with the approval of two such men, that of others might be dispensed with. Cheverny, a very truthful man, came full of this to tell it to me at once. I was filled with confusion at being placed beside a man as superior to me in knowledge of war as he was in rank and birth; but I felt with gratitude how well M. de Beauvilliers had kept his word and spoken in my favor.

The last evening of this year (1708) was very remarkable, because there had not yet been an example of any such thing. The King having retired after supper to his cabinet with his family, as usual, Chamillart came without being sent for. He whispered in the King's ear that he had a long dispatch from the Maréchal de Boufflers. Immediately the King said good night to Monseigneur and the Princesses, who went out with every one else; and the King actually worked for an hour with his minister before going to bed, so excited was he by the great project for retaking Lille!

Since the fall of Lille, in fact, Chamillart, impressed with the importance of the place being in our possession, had laid out a plan by which we were to lay siege to it and recapture it. One part of his plan was, that the King should conduct the siege in person. Another was, that, as money was so difficult to obtain, the ladies of the Court should not accompany the King, as their presence caused a large increase of expense for carriages, servants, and so on. He confided his project to the King, under a strict promise that it should be kept secret from Madame de Maintenon. He feared, and with reason, that if she heard of it she would object to being separated from the King for such a long time as would be necessary for the siege. Chamillart was warned that if he acted thus, hiding his plan from Madame de Maintenon, to whom he owed everything, she would assuredly ruin him, but he paid no attention to the warning. He felt all the danger he ran, but he was courageous; he loved the State, and, if I may say so, he loved the King as a mistress. He followed his own counsels then, and made the King acquainted with his project.

The King was at once delighted with it. He entered into the details submitted to him by Chamillart with the liveliest interest, and promised to carry out all that was proposed. He sent for Boufflers, who had returned from Lille, and having, as I have said, recompensed him for his brave defense of that place with a peerage and other marks of favor, dispatched him privately into Flanders to make preparations for the siege. The abandonment of Ghent by our troops, after a short and miserable defense, made him more than ever anxious to carry out this scheme.

But the King had been so unused to keep a secret from Madame de Maintenon, that he felt himself constrained in attempting to do so now. He confided to her, therefore, the admirable plan of Chamillart. She had the address to hide her surprise, and the strength to dissimulate perfectly her vexation; she praised the project; she appeared charmed with it; she entered into the details; she spoke of them to Chamillart; admired his zeal, his labor, his diligence, and, above all, his ability, in having conceived and rendered possible so fine and grand a project.

From that moment, however, she forgot nothing in order to insure its failure. The first sight of it had made her tremble. To be separated from the King during a long siege; to abandon him to a minister to whom he would be grateful for all the success of that siege; a minister, too, who, although her creature, had dared to submit this project to the King without informing her; who, moreover, had recently offended her by marrying his son into a family she considered inimical to her, and by supporting M. de Vendôme against Monseigneur de Bourgogne! These were considerations that determined her to bring about the failure of Chamillart's project and the disgrace of Chamillart himself.

She employed her art so well, that after a time the project upon Lille did not appear so easy to the King as at first. Soon after, it seemed difficult; then too hazard-

ous and ruinous; so that at last it was abandoned, and
Boufflers had orders to cease his preparations and return
to France! She succeeded thus in an affair she considered the most important she had undertaken during
all her life. Chamillart was much touched, but little surprised. As soon as he knew his secret had been confided
to Madame de Maintenon he had feeble hope for it. Now
he began to fear for himself.

CHAPTER VI.

ONE of the reasons Madame de Maintenon had brought
forward, which much assisted her in opposing the
siege of Lille, was the excessive cold of this winter. The winter was, in fact, terrible; the memory of
man could find no parallel to it. The frost came suddenly on Twelfth Night, and lasted nearly two months,
beyond all recollection. In four days the Seine and all
the other rivers were frozen, and, what had never been
seen before, the sea froze all along the coasts, so as to
bear carts, even heavily laden, upon it. Curious observ-
ers pretended that this cold surpassed what had ever been
felt in Sweden and Denmark. The tribunals were closed
a considerable time. The worst thing was, that it completely thawed for seven or eight days, and then froze
again as rudely as before. This caused the complete destruction of all kinds of vegetation — even fruit trees,
and others of the most hardy kind, were destroyed. The
violence of the cold was such, that the strongest elixirs
and the most spirituous liquors broke their bottles in cup-
boards of rooms with fires in them, and surrounded by
chimneys, in several parts of the *château* of Versailles.
As I myself was one evening supping with the Duc de
Villeroy in his little bedroom, I saw bottles that had come
from a well-heated kitchen, and that had been put on the
chimney-piece of this bedroom (which was close to the
kitchen), so frozen that pieces of ice fell into our glasses
as we poured out from them. The second frost ruined
everything. There were no walnut trees, no olive trees,
no apple trees, no vines left, — none worth speaking of,

at least. The other trees died in great numbers; the
gardens perished, and all the grain in the earth. It is
impossible to imagine the desolation of this general ruin.
Everybody held tight his old grain. The price of bread
increased in proportion to the despair for the next har-
vest. The most knowing resowed barley where there had
been wheat, and were imitated by the majority. They
were the most successful, and saved all; but the police
bethought themselves of prohibiting this, and repented
too late! Divers edicts were published respecting grain,
researches were made and granaries filled; commissioners
were appointed to scour the provinces, and all these steps
contributed to increase the general dearness and poverty,
and that, too, at a time when, as was afterward proved,
there was enough corn in the country to feed all France
for two years, without a fresh ear being reaped.

Many people believed that the finance gentlemen had
clutched at this occasion to seize upon all the corn in
the kingdom, by emissaries they sent about, in order to
sell it at whatever price they wished for the profit of the
King, not forgetting their own. The fact that a large
quantity of corn that the King had bought, and that
had spoiled upon the Loire, was thrown into the water
in consequence, did not shake this opinion, as the accident could not be hidden. It is certain that the price of
corn was equal in all the markets of the realm; that at
Paris, commissioners fixed the price by force, and often
obliged the vendors to raise it in spite of themselves;
that when people cried out, "How long will this scarcity
last?" some commissioners in a market, close to my
house, near St. Germain des Prés, replied openly, "As
long as you please," moved by compassion and indignation, meaning thereby, as long as the people chose to
submit to the regulation, according to which no corn
entered Paris, except on an order of D'Argenson. D'Argenson was the lieutenant of police. The bakers were
treated with the utmost rigor in order to keep up the
price of bread all over France. In the provinces, officers
called intendants did what D'Argenson did at Paris. On
all the markets, the corn that was not sold at the hour
fixed for closing was forcibly carried off; those who from

pity, sold their corn lower than the fixed rate were punished with cruelty !

Maréchal, the King's surgeon, had the courage and the probity to tell all these things to the King, and to state the sinister opinions it gave rise to among all classes, even the most enlightened. The King appeared touched, was not offended with Maréchal, but did nothing.

In several places large stores of corn were collected by the government authorities, but with the greatest possible secrecy. Private people were expressly forbidden to do this, and informers were encouraged to betray them. A poor fellow, having bethought himself of informing against one of the stores alluded to above, was severely punished for his pains. The Parliament assembled to debate upon these disorders. It came to the resolution of submitting various proposals to the King, which it deemed likely to improve the condition of the country, and offered to send its *conseillers* to examine into the conduct of the monopolists. As soon as the King heard of this, he flew into a strange passion, and his first intention was to send a harsh message to the Parliament to attend to law trials, and not to mix with matters that did not concern it. The chancellor did not dare to represent to the King that what the Parliament wished to do belonged to its province, but calmed him by representing the respect and affection with which the Parliament regarded him, and that he was master either to accept or refuse its offers. No reprimand was given, therefore, to the Parliament, but it was informed that the King prohibited it from meddling with the corn question. However accustomed the Parliament, as well as all the other public bodies, might be to humiliations, it was exceedingly vexed by this treatment, and obeyed with the greatest grief. The public was, nevertheless, much affected by the conduct of the Parliament, and felt that if the finance ministry had been innocent in the matter, the King would have been pleased with what had taken place, which was in no respect an attack on the absolute and unbounded authority, of which he was so vilely jealous.

In the country a somewhat similar incident occurred. The Parliament of Burgundy, seeing the province in the direst necessity, wrote to the Intendant, who did not bestir himself the least in the world. In this pressing danger of a murderous famine, the members assembled to debate upon the course to adopt. Nothing was said or done more than was necessary, and all with infinite discretion, yet the King was no sooner informed of it than he grew extremely irritated. He sent a severe reprimand to this Parliament; prohibited it from meddling again in the matter; and ordered the President, who had conducted the assembly, to come at once to Court to explain his conduct. He came, and but for the intervention of M. le Duc would have been deprived of his post, irreproachable as his conduct had been. He received a sharp scolding from the King, and was then allowed to depart. At the end of a few weeks he returned to Dijon, where it had been resolved to receive him in triumph; but, like a wise and experienced man, he shunned these attentions, arranging so that he arrived at Dijon at four o'clock in the morning. The other Parliaments, with these examples before them, were afraid to act, and allowed the Intendants and their emissaries to have it all their own way. It was at this time that those commissioners were appointed, to whom I have already alluded, who acted under the authority of the Intendants, and without dependence of any kind upon the Parliaments. True, a court of appeal against their decisions was established, but it was a mere mockery. The members who composed it did not set out to fulfill their duties until three months after having been appointed. Then, matters had been so arranged that they received no appeals, and found no cases to judge. All this dark work remained, therefore, in the hands of D'Argenson and the Intendants, and it continued to be done with the same harshness as ever.

Without passing a more definite judgment on those who invented and profited by this scheme, it may be said that there has scarcely been a century which has produced one more mysterious, more daring, better arranged, and resulting in an oppression so enduring, so sure, so cruel. The sums it produced were innumerable; and innumerable were the people who died literally of hunger, and those who perished afterward of the maladies caused by the extremity of misery; innumerable also were the families who were ruined, whose ruin brought down a torrent of other ills.

Despite all this, payments, hitherto most strictly made, began to cease. Those of the customs, those of the divers loans, the dividends upon the Hotel de Ville—in all times so sacred—all were suspended; these last alone continued, but with delays, then with retrenchments, which desolated nearly all the families of Paris and many others. At the same time the taxes—increased, multiplied, and exacted with the most extreme rigor—completed the devastation of France. Everything rose incredibly in price, while nothing was left to buy with, even at the cheapest rate; and although the majority of the cattle had perished for want of food, and by the misery of those who kept them, a new monopoly was established upon horned beasts. A great number of people who, in preceding years, used to relieve the poor, found themselves so reduced as to be able to subsist only with great difficulty, and many of them received alms in secret. It is impossible to say how many others laid siege to the hospitals, until then the shame and punishment of the poor; how many ruined hospitals revomited forth their inmates to the public charge—that is to say, sent them away to die actually of hunger; and how many decent families shut themselves up in garrets to die of want.

It is impossible to say, moreover, how all this misery warmed up zeal and charity, or how immense were the alms distributed. But want increasing each instant, an indiscreet and tyrannical charity imagined new taxes for the benefit of the poor. They were imposed, and, added to so many others, vexed numbers of people, who were annoyed at being compelled to pay, who would have preferred to giving voluntarily. Thus, these new taxes, instead of helping the poor, really took away assistance from them, and left them worse off than before. The strangest thing of all is, that these taxes in favor of the poor were perpetuated and appropriated by the King, and are received by the financiers on his account to this day as a branch of the revenue, the

5

name of them not having even been changed. The same thing has happened with respect to the annual tax for keeping up the highways and thoroughfares of the kingdom. The majority of the bridges were broken, and the high roads had become impracticable. Trade, which suffered by this, awakened attention. The Intendant of Champagne determined to mend the roads by parties of men, whom he compelled to work for nothing, not even giving them bread. He was imitated everywhere, and was made Counselor of State. The people died of hunger and misery at this work, while those who over-looked them made fortunes. In the end the thing was found to be impracticable, and was abandoned, and so were the roads. But the impost for making them and keeping them up did not in the least stop during this experiment or since, nor has it ceased to be appropri-ated as a branch of the King's revenue.

But to return to the year 1709. People never ceased wondering what had become of all the money of the realm. Nobody could any longer pay, because nobody was paid; the country people, overwhelmed with exac-tions and with valueless property, had become insolvent; trade no longer yielded anything — good faith and confi-dence were at an end. Thus the King had no resources, except in terror and in his unlimited power, which, boundless as it was, failed also for want of having some-thing to take and to exercise itself upon. There was no more circulation, no means of re-establishing it. All was perishing step by step; the realm was entirely exhausted; the troops, even, were not paid, although no one could imagine what was done with the millions that came into the King's coffers. The unfed soldiers, disheartened too at being so badly commanded, were always unsuccessful; there was no capacity in generals or ministers; no ap-pointment except by whim or intrigue; nothing was pun-ished, nothing examined, nothing weighed; there was equal impotence to sustain the war and bring about peace; all suffered, yet none dared to put the hand to this arch, tottering as it was and ready to fall.

This was the frightful state to which we were reduced, when envoys were sent into Holland to try and bring about peace. The picture is exact, faithful, and not over-charged. It was necessary to present it as it was, in order to explain the extremity to which we were reduced, the enormity of the concessions which the King made to obtain peace, and the visible miracle of him who sets bounds to the seas, by which France was allowed to escape from the hands of Europe, resolved and ready to destroy her.

Meanwhile the money was recoined; and its increase to a third more than its intrinsic value, brought some profit to the King, but ruin to private people, and a disorder to trade which completed its annihilation.

Samuel Bernard, the banker, overthrew all Lyons by his prodigious bankruptcy, which caused the most terrible results. Desmarets assisted him as much as possible. The discredit into which paper money had fallen, was the cause of his failure. He had issued notes to the amount of twenty millions, and owed almost as much at Lyons. Fourteen millions were given to him in assignations, in order to draw him out of his difficulties. It is pretended that he found means to gain much by his bankruptcy, but this seems doubtful.

The winter at length passed away. In the spring so many disorders took place in the market of Paris, that more guards than usual were kept in the city. At Saint Rock there was a disturbance, on account of a poor fellow who had fallen, and been trampled under foot; and the crowd, which was very large, was very insolent to D'Argenson, Lieutenant of Police, who had hastened there. M. de la Rochefoucauld, who had retired from the Court to Chenil, on account of his loss of sight, received an atrocious letter against the King, in which it was plainly intimated that there were still Ravaillacs left in the world; and to this madness was added an eulogy of Brutus.* M. de la Rochefoucauld at once went in all haste to the King with this letter. His sudden appearance showed that something important had occurred, and the object of his visit, of course, soon became known.

---

* The mind recoils with horror from the wretch to whom such an idea could have presented itself amid the blessings which the absolute authority of Louis XIV. was showering upon the country.

He was very ill received for coming so publicly on such an errand. The Ducs de Beauvilliers and de Bouillon, it seems, had received similar letters, but had given them to the King privately. The King for some days was much troubled, but after due reflection, he came to the conclusion that people who menace and warn have less intention of committing a crime. than of causing alarm.

What annoyed the King more was, the inundation of placards, the most daring and the most unmeasured, against his person, his conduct, and his government — placards, which for a long time were found pasted upon the gates of Paris, the churches, the public places, above all, upon the statues, which during the night were insulted in various fashions, the marks being seen the next morning, and the inscriptions erased. There were · also, multitudes of verses and songs, in which nothing was spared.

We were in this state until the 16th of May. The procession of St. Geneviève took place. This procession never takes place except in times of the direst necessity; and then, only in virtue of orders from the King, the Parliament, or the Archbishop of Paris. On the one hand, it was hoped that it would bring succor to the country; on the other, that it would amuse the people.

It was shortly after this, when the news of the arrogant demands of the allies, and the vain attempts of the King to obtain an honorable peace became known, that the Duchess de Grammont conceived the idea of offering her plate to the King, to replenish his impoverished exchequer, and to afford him means to carry on the war. She hoped that her example would be followed by all the Court, and that she alone would have the merit and the profit of suggesting the idea. Unfortunately for this hope, the Duke, her husband, spoke of the project to Maréchal Boufflers, who thought it so good, that he noised it abroad, and made such a stir, exhorting everybody to adopt it, that he passed for the inventor, and no mention was made of the Duke or the old Duchess de Grammont, the latter of whom was much enraged at this.

The project made a great hubbub at the Court. Nobody dared to refuse to offer his plate, yet each offered it with much regret. Some had been keeping it as a last resource, which they were very sorry to deprive themselves of; others feared the dirtiness of copper and earthenware; others again were annoyed at being obliged to imitate an ungrateful fashion, all the merit of which would go to the inventor. It was in vain that Pontchartrain objected to the project, as one from which only trifling benefit could be derived, and which would do great injury to France by acting as a proclamation of its embarrassed state to all the world, at home and abroad. The King would not listen to his reasonings, but declared himself willing to receive all the plate that was sent to him as a free-will offering. He announced this; and two means were indicated at the same time, which all good citizens might follow. One was, to send their plate to the King's goldsmith; the other, to send it to the mint. Those who made an unconditional gift of their plate, sent it to the former, who kept a register of the names and of the number of marks he received. The King regularly looked over this list, at least at first, and promised in general terms to restore to everybody the weight of metal they gave when his affairs permitted — a promise nobody believed in or hoped to see executed. Those who wished to be paid for their plate sent it to the mint. It was weighed on arrival; the names were written, the marks and the date; payment was made according as money could be found. Many people were not sorry thus to sell their plate without shame. But the loss and the damage were inestimable in admirable ornaments of all kinds, with which much of the plate of the rich was embellished.

When an account came to be drawn up, it was found that not a hundred people were upon the list of Launay, the goldsmith; and the total product of the gift did not amount to three millions. I confess that I was very late in sending my plate. When I found that I was almost the only one of my rank using silver, I sent plate to the value of a thousand pistoles to the mint, and locked up the rest. All the great people turned to earthenware, exhausted the shops where it was sold, and set the trade in it on fire, while common folks continued to use their silver. Even the King thought of using earthenware, having sent his gold vessels to the mint, but afterward decided upon plated metal and silver; the princes and princesses of the blood used crockery.

Ere three months were over his head the King felt all the shame and the weakness of having consented to this surrendering of plate, and avowed that he repented of it. The inundations of the Loire, which happened at the same time, and caused the utmost disorder, did not restore the Court or the public to good humor. The losses they caused, and the damage they did, were very considerable, and ruined many private people, and desolated home trade.

Summer came. The dearness of all things, and of bread in particular, continued to cause frequent commotions all over the realm. Although, as I have said, the guards of Paris were much increased, above all in the markets and the suspected places, they were unable to hinder disturbances from breaking out. In many of these D'Argenson nearly lost his life.

Monseigneur arriving and returning from the opera, was assailed by the populace and by women in great numbers crying, "Bread! Bread!" so that he was afraid, even in the midst of his guards, who did not dare to disperse the crowd for fear of worse happening. He got away by throwing money to the people, and promising wonders; but as the wonders did not follow, he no longer dared to go to Paris.

The King himself from his windows heard the people of Versailles crying aloud in the street. The discourses they held were daring and continual in the streets and public places; they uttered complaints, sharp, and but little measured, against the Government, and even against the King's person; and even exhorted each other no longer to be so enduring, saying that nothing worse could happen to them than what they suffered, dying as they were of starvation.

To amuse the people, the idle and the poor were employed to level a rather large hillock which remained upon the boulevard, between the Portes St. Denis and St. Martin; and for all salary, bad bread in small quantities was distributed to these workers. It happened that on Tuesday morning, the 20th of August, there was no bread for a large number of these people. A woman among others cried out at this, which excited the rest to do likewise. The archers appointed to watch over these laborers, threatened the woman; she only cried the louder; thereupon the archers seized her and indiscreetly put her in an adjoining pillory. In a moment all her companions ran to her aid, pulled down the pillory, and scoured the streets, pillaging the bakers and pastry cooks. One by one the shops closed. The disorder increased and spread through the neighboring streets; no harm was done anybody, but the cry was "Bread! Bread!" and bread was seized everywhere.

It so fell out that Maréchal Boufflers, who little thought what was happening, was in the neighborhood, calling upon his notary. Surprised at the fright he saw everywhere, and learning the cause, he wished of himself to appease it. Accompanied by the Duc de Grammont, he directed himself toward the scene of the disturbance, although advised not to do so. When he arrived at the top of the Rue St. Denis, the crowd and the tumult made him judge that it would be best to alight from his coach. He advanced, therefore, on foot with the Duc de Grammont among the furious and infinite crowd of people, of whom he asked the cause of this uproar, promised them bread, spoke his best with gentleness but firmness, and remonstrated with them. He was listened to. Cries, several times repeated, of "*Vive M. le Maréchal de Boufflers,*" burst from the crowd. M. de Boufflers, walked thus with M. de Grammont all along the Rue aux Ours and the neighboring streets,— into the very center of the sedition, in fact. The people begged him to represent their misery to the King, and to obtain for them some food. He promised this, and upon his word being given all were appeased and all dispersed with thanks and fresh acclamations of "*Vive M. le Maréchal de Boufflers!*" He did a real service that day. D'Argenson had marched to the spot with troops; and had it not been for the Maréchal, blood would have been spilled, and things might have gone very far.

The Maréchal had scarcely reached his own house in the Place Royale than he was informed that the sedition had broken out with even greater force in the Faubourg St. Antoine. He ran there immediately, with the Duc de Grammont, and appeased it as he had appeased the other. He returned to his own home to eat a mouthful or two, and then set out for Versailles. Scarcely had he left the Place Royale than the people in the streets and the shopkeepers cried to him to have pity on them, and to get them some bread, always with "*Vive M. le Maréchal de Boufflers!*" He was conducted thus as far as the quay of the Louvre.

On arriving at Versailles he went straight to the King, told him what had occurred, and was much thanked. He was even offered by the King the command of Paris, —troops, citizens, police, and all; but this he declined, Paris, as he said, having already a governor and proper officers to conduct its affairs. He afterward, however, willingly lent his aid to them in office, and the modesty with which he acted brought him new glory.

Immediately after, the supply of bread was carefully looked to. Paris was filled with patrols, perhaps with too many, but they succeeded so well that no fresh disturbances took place.

CHAPTER VII.

M. de Vendôme Out of Favor — Death and Character of the Prince de Conti — Fall of Vendôme — Puységur's Interview with the King — Madame de Bourgogne against Vendôme — Her Decided Conduct — Vendôme Excluded from Marly — He Clings to Meudon — From Which He is also Expelled — His Final Disgrace and Abandonment — Triumph of Madame de Maintenon.

AFTER his return from the campaign, M. de Vendôme continued to be paid like a general serving in winter, and to enjoy many other advantages. From all this, people inferred that he would serve during the following campaign; nobody dared to doubt as much, and the cabal derived new strength therefrom. But their little triumph was not of long continuance. M. de Vendôme came to Versailles for the ceremony of the Order on Candlemas day. He then learned that he was not to serve, and that he was no longer to receive general's pay. The blow was violent, and he felt it to its fullest extent; but, with a prudence that equaled his former imprudence, he swallowed the pill without making a face, because he feared other more bitter ones, which he felt he had deserved. This it was that, for the first time in his life, made him moderate. He did not affect to conceal what had taken place, but did not. say whether it was in consequence of any request of his, or whether he was glad or sorry, — giving it out as an indifferent piece of news; and changed nothing but his language, the audacity of which he diminished as no longer suited to the times. He sold his equipages.

M. le Prince de Conti died February 22d, aged not quite forty-five. His face had been charming; even the defects of his body and mind had infinite graces. His shoulders were too high; his head was a little on one side; his laugh would have seemed a bray in any one else; his mind was strangely absent. He was gallant with the women, in love with many, well treated by

(73)

several; he was even coquettish with men. He endeavored to please the cobbler, the lacquey, the porter, as well as the minister of state, the Grand Seigneur, the general, — all so naturally that success was certain. He was consequently the constant delight of everyone, of the Court, the armies; the divinity of the people, the idol of the soldiers, the hero of the officers, the hope of whatever was most distinguished, the love of the Parliament, the friend of the learned, and often the admiration of the historian, of jurisconsults, of astronomers, and mathematicians, the most profound. He was especially learned in genealogies, and knew their chimeras and their realities. With him the useful and the polite, the agreeable and the deep, all was distinct and in its place. He had friends, knew how to choose them, cultivate them, visit them, live with them, put himself on their level without haughtiness or baseness. But this man, so amiable, so charming, so delicious, loved nothing. He had and desired friends, as other people have and desire articles of furniture. Although with much self-respect he was a humble courtier, and showed too much how greatly he was in want of support and assistance from all sides; he was avaricious, greedy of fortune, ardent, and unjust. The King could not bear him, and was grieved with the respect he was obliged to show him, and which he was careful never to trespass over by a single jot. Certain intercepted letters had excited a hatred against him in Madame de Maintenon, and an indignation in the King which nothing could efface. The riches, the talents, the agreeable qualities, the great reputation which this prince had acquired, the general love of all, became crimes in him. The contrast with M. du Maine excited daily irritation and jealousy. The very purity of his blood was a reproach to him. Even his friends were odious, and felt that this was so. At last, however, various causes made him to be chosen, in the midst of a very marked disgrace to command the army in Flanders. He was delighted, and gave himself up to the most agreeable hopes. But it was no longer time; he had sought to drown his sorrow at wearing out his life unoccupied in wine and other pleasures, for which

his age and his already enfeebled body were no longer
suited. His health gave way. He felt it soon. The
tardy return to favor which he had enjoyed made him
regret life more. He perished slowly, regretting to have
been brought to death's door by disgrace, and the impossibility of being restored by the unexpected opening
of a brilliant career.

The Prince, against the custom of those of his rank,
had been very well educated. He was full of instruction.
The disorders of his life had clouded his knowledge but
not extinguished it, and he often read to brush up his
learning. He chose M. de la Tour to prepare him, and
help him to die well. He was so attached to life that all
his courage was required. For three months crowds of
visitors filled his palace, and the people even collected in
the place before it. The churches echoed with prayers
for his life. The members of his family often went to
pay for masses for him, and found that others had already
done so. All questions were about his health. People
stopped each other in the street to inquire; passers-by
were called to by shopmen, anxious to know whether the
Prince de Conti was to live or to die. Amid all this, Monseigneur never visited him, and to the indignation of all
Paris, passed along the quay near the Louvre going to
the opera, while the Sacraments were being carried to the
Prince on the other side. He was compelled by public
opinion to make a short visit after this. The Prince died
at last in his armchair, surrounded by a few worthy
people. Regrets were universal; but perhaps he gained
by his disgrace. His heart was firmer than his head.
He might have been timid at the head of an army or in
the Council of the King if he had entered it. The King
was much relieved by his death; Madame de Maintenon
also; M. le Duc much more; for M. du Maine it was a
deliverance, and for M. de Vendôme a consolation. Monseigneur learned it at Meudon as he was going out to
hunt and showed no feeling of any kind.

The death of M. le Prince de Conti seemed to the Duc
de Vendôme a considerable advantage, because he was
thus delivered from a rival most embarrassing by the
superiority of his birth, just when he was about to be

placed in a high military position. I have already mentioned Vendôme's exclusion from command. The fall of this Prince of the Proud had then begun: we have now reached the second step, between which and the third there was a space of between two and three months; but as the third had no connection with any other event, I will relate it at once.

Whatever reasons existed to induce the King to take from M. de Vendôme the command of his armies, I know not, if all the art and credit of Madame de Maintenon would not have been employed in vain, together with the intrigues of M. du Maine, without an adventure, which I must at once explain, to set before the reader's eyes the issue of the terrible struggle, pushed to such extremes, between Vendôme, seconded by his formidable cabal, and the necessary heir of the Crown, supported by his wife, the favorite of the King, and Madame de Maintenon, which last, to speak clearly, as all the Court saw, for thirty years governed him completely.

When M. de Vendôme returned from Flanders, he had a short interview with the King, in which he made many bitter complaints against Puységur, one of his lieutenant generals, whose sole offense was that he was much attached to M. de Bourgogne. Puységur was a great favorite with the King, and often, on account of the business of the infantry regiment, of which the King thought himself the private colonel, had private interviews with him, and was held in high estimation for his capacity and virtue. He, in his turn, came back from Flanders, and had a private audience of the King. The complaints that had been made against him by M. de Vendôme were repeated to him by the King, who, however, did not mention from whom they came. Puységur defended himself so well that the King in his surprise mentioned this latter fact. At the name of Vendôme, Puységur lost all patience. He described to the King all the faults, the impertinences, the obstinacy, the insolence of M. de Vendôme, with a precision and clearness which made his listener very attentive and very fruitful in questions. Puységur, seeing that he might go on, gave himself rein, unmasked M. de Vendôme from top to toe, described his ordinary life at the army, the incapacity of his body, the incapacity of his judgment, the prejudices of his mind, the absurdity and crudity of his maxims, his utter ignorance of the art of war, and showed to demonstration, that it was only by a profusion of miracles France had not been ruined by him — lost a hundred times over.

The conversation lasted more than two hours. The King, long since convinced of the capacity, fidelity, and truthfulness of Puységur, at last opened his eyes to the truth respecting this Vendôme, hidden with so much art until then, and regarded as a hero and the tutelary genius of France. He was vexed and ashamed of his credulity, and from the date of this conversation Vendôme fell at once from his favor.

Puységur, naturally humble, gentle, and modest, but truthful, and on this occasion piqued, went out into the gallery after his conversation, and made a general report of it to all, virtuously braving Vendôme and all his cabal. This cabal trembled with rage; Vendôme still more so. They answered by miserable reasonings, which nobody cared for. This was what led to the suppression of his pay, and his retirement to Anet, where he affected a philosophical indifference.

Crestfallen as he was, he continued to sustain at Meudon and Marly the grand manners he had usurped at the time of his prosperity. After having got over the first embarrassment, he put on again his haughty air, and ruled the roast. To see him at Meudon you would have said he was certainly the master of the salon, and by his free and easy manner to Monseigneur, and, when he dared, to the King, he would have been thought the principal person there. Monseigneur de Bourgogne supported this — his piety made him do so — but Madame de Bourgogne was grievously offended, and watched her opportunity to get rid of M. de Vendôme altogether.

It came, the first journey the King made to Marly after Easter. *Brelan* was then the fashion. Monseigneur, playing at it one day with Madame de Bourgogne and others, and being in want of a fifth player, sent for M. de Vendôme from the other end of the salon, to come and join the party. The instant Madame de Bourgogne said modestly, but very intelligibly, to Monseigneur, that the presence of M. de Vendôme at Marly was sufficiently painful to her, without having him at play with her, and that she begged he might be dispensed with. Monseigneur, who had sent for Vendôme without the slightest reflection, looked round the room, and sent for somebody else. When Vendôme arrived, his place was taken, and he had to suffer this annoyance before all the company. It may be imagined to what an extent this superb gentleman was stung by the affront. He served no longer; he commanded no longer; he was no longer the adored idol; he found himself in the paternal mansion of the prince he had so cruelly offended, and the outraged wife of that prince was more than a match for him. He turned upon his heel, absented himself from the room as soon as he could, and retired to his own chamber, there to storm at his leisure.

Other and more cruel annoyances were yet in store for him however. Madame de Bourgogne reflected on what had just taken place. The facility with which she had succeeded in one respect encouraged her, but she was a little troubled to know how the King would take what she had done, and accordingly, while playing, she resolved to push matters still further, both to ruin her guest utterly and to get out of her embarrassment; for, despite her extreme familiarity, she was easily embarrassed, being gentle and timid. The *brelan* over, she ran to Madame de Maintenon; told her what had just occurred; said that the presence of M. de Vendôme at Marly was a continual insult to her; and begged her to solicit the King to forbid M. de Vendôme to come there. Madame de Maintenon, only too glad to have an opportunity of revenging herself upon an enemy who had set her at defiance, and against whom all her batteries had at one time failed, consented to this request. She spoke out to the King, who, completely weary of M. de Vendôme, and troubled to have under his eyes a man whom he could not doubt was discontented, at once granted what was asked. Before going to bed, he charged one of his valets to tell M. de Vendôme the next morning, that henceforth he was to absent himself from Marly, his presence there being disagreeable to Madame de Bourgogne.

It may be imagined into what an excess of despair M. de Vendôme fell, at a message so unexpected, and which sapped the foundations of all his hopes. He kept silent, however, for fear of making matters worse, did not venture attempting to speak to the King, and hastily retired to Clichy to hide his rage and shame. The news of his banishment from Marly soon spread abroad, and made so much stir, that to show it was not worth attention he returned two days before the end of the visit, and stopped until the end in a continual shame and embarrassment. He set out for Anet at the same time that the King set out for Versailles, and has never since put his foot in Marly.

But another bitter draught was to be mixed for him. Banished from Marly, he had yet the privilege of going to Meudon. He did not fail to avail himself of this every time Monseigneur was there, and stopped as long as he stopped, although in the times of his splendor he had never stayed more than one or two days. It was seldom that Monseigneur visited Meudon without Madame la Duchess de Bourgogne going to see him. And yet M. de Vendôme never failed audaciously to present himself before her, as if to make her feel that at all events in Monseigneur's house he was a match for her. Guided by former experience, the Princess gently suffered this in silence, and watched her opportunity. It soon came.

Two months afterward it happened that, while Monseigneur was at Meudon, the King, Madame de Maintenon, and Madame de Bourgogne, came to dine with him. Madame de Maintenon wished to talk with Mademoiselle Choin without sending for her to Versailles, and the King, as may be believed, was in the secret. I mention this to account for the King's visit. M. de Vendôme, who was at Meudon, as usual, was stupid enough to present himself at the coach door as the King and his companions descended. Madame de Bourgogne was much offended, constrained herself less than usual, and turned away her head with affectation, after a sort of sham salute. He felt the sting, but had the folly to approach her again after dinner, while she was playing. He experienced the same treatment, but this time in a still more marked manner. Stung to the quick and out of countenance, he went up to his chamber, and did not descend until very late. During this time Madame de Bourgogne spoke to Monseigneur of the conduct of M. de Vendôme, and the same evening she addressed herself to Madame de Maintenon, and openly complained to the King. She represented to him how hard it was to her to be treated by Monseigneur with less respect than by the King: for while the latter had banished M. de Vendôme from Marly, the former continued to grant him an asylum at Meudon.

M. de Vendôme, on his side, complained bitterly to Monseigneur of the strange persecution that he suffered everywhere from Madame de Bourgogne; but Monseigneur replied to him so coldly that he withdrew with tears in his eyes, determined, however, not to give up until he had obtained some sort of satisfaction. He set his friends to work to speak to Monseigneur; all they could draw from him was, that M. de Vendôme must avoid Madame de Bourgogne whenever she came to Meudon, and that it was the smallest respect he owed her until she was reconciled to him. A reply so dry and so precise was cruelly felt; but M. de Vendôme was not at the end of the chastisement he had more than merited. The next day put an end to all discussion upon the matter.

He was card playing after dinner in a private cabinet, when D'Antin arrived from Versailles. He approached the players, and asked what was the position of the game, with an eagerness which made M. de Vendôme inquire the reason. D'Antin said he had to render an account to him of the matter he had intrusted him with.

"I!" exclaimed Vendôme, with surprise, "I have intrusted you with nothing."

"Pardon me," replied D'Antin; "you do not recollect, then, that I have an answer to make to you?"

From this perseverance M. de Vendôme comprehended that something was amiss, quitted his game, and went into an obscure wardrobe with D'Antin, who told him that he had been ordered by the King to beg Monseigneur not to invite M. de Vendôme to Meudon any more; that his presence there was as unpleasant to Madame de Bourgogne as it had been at Marly. Upon this, Vendôme, transported with fury, vomited forth all that his rage inspired him with. He spoke to Monseigneur in the evening, but was listened to as coldly as before. Vendôme passed the rest of his visit in a rage and embarrassment easy to conceive, and on the day Monseigneur returned to Versailles he hurried straight to Anet.

But he was unable to remain quiet anywhere; so went off with his dogs, under pretense of going a hunting, to pass a month in his estate of La Ferté Aleps, where he had no proper lodging and no society, and gave there free vent to his rage. Thence he returned again to Anet, where he remained abandoned by everyone. Into this solitude, into this startling and public seclusion, incapable of sustaining a fall so complete, after a long habit of obtaining everything, and doing everything he pleased, of being the idol of the world, of the Court, of the armies, of making his very vices adored, and his greatest faults admired, his defects commended,— so that he dared to conceive the prodigious design of ruining and destroying the necessary heir of the Crown, though he had never received anything but evidences of tenderness from him, and triumphed over him for eight months with the most scandalous success,— it was, I say, thus that this Colossus was overthrown by the breath of a prudent and courageous princess, who earned by this act merited applause. All who were concerned with her, were charmed to see of what she was capable; and all who were opposed to her and her husband trembled. The cabal, so formidable, so lofty, so accredited, so closely united to overthrow them, and reign, after the King, under Monseigneur in their place — these chiefs, male and female, so enterprising and audacious, fell now into mortal discouragement and fear. It was a pleasure to see them work their way back with art and extreme humility, and turn round those of the opposite party who remained influential, and whom they had hitherto despised; and especially to see with what embarrassment, what fear, what terror, they began to crawl before the young Princess, and wretchedly court the Duc de Bourgogne and his friends, and bend to them in the most extraordinary manner.

As for M. de Vendôme, without any resource, save what he found in his vices and his valets, he did not refrain from bragging among them of the friendship of Monseigneur for him, of which he said he was well assured. Violence had been done to Monseigneur's feelings. He was reduced to this misery of hoping that his words would be spread about by these valets, and would procure him some consideration from those who thought of the future. But the present was insupportable to him. To escape from it, he thought of serving in Spain, and wrote to Madame des Ursins asking employment. The King was annoyed at this step, and flatly refused to let him go to Spain. His intrigue, therefore, came to an end at once.

Nobody gained more by the fall of M. de Vendôme than Madame de Maintenon. Besides the joy she felt in overthrowing a man who, through M. du Maine, owed everything to her, and yet dared to resist her so long and successfully, she felt, also, that her credit became still more the terror of the Court; for no one doubted that what had occurred was a great example of her power. We shall presently see how she furnished another, which startled no less.

CHAPTER VIII.

Death of Père La Chaise — His Infirmities in Old Age — Partiality of the King — Character of Père La Chaise — The Jesuits — Choice of a New Confessor — Fagon's Opinion — Destruction of Port Royal — Jansenists and Molinists — Pascal — Violent Oppression of the Inhabitants of Port Royal.

IT IS time now to retrace my steps to the point from which I have been led away in relating all the incidents which arose out of the terrible winter and the scarcity it caused.

The Court at that time beheld the renewal of a ministry, which from the time it had lasted was worn down to its very roots, and which was on that account only the more agreeable to the King. On the 20th of January, the Père La Chaise, the confessor of the King, died at a very advanced age. He was of good family, and his father would have been rich had he not had a dozen children. Père La Chaise succeeded in 1675 to Père Ferrier as confessor of the King, and occupied that post thirty-two years. The festival of Easter often caused him politic absences during the attachment of the King for Madame de Montespan. On one occasion he sent in his place the Père Deschamps, who bravely refused absolution. The Père La Chaise was of mediocre mind but of good character, just, upright, sensible, prudent, gentle, and moderate, an enemy of informers, and of violence of every kind. He kept clear of many scandalous transactions, befriended the Archbishop of Cambrai as much as he could, refused to push the Port Royal des Champs to its destruction, and always had on his table a copy of the New Testament of Père Quesnel, saying that he liked what was good wherever he found it. When near his eightieth year, with his head and his health still good, he wished to retire, but the King would not hear of it. Soon after, his faculties became worn out, and feeling this, he repeated his wish. The Jesuits, who per-

ceived his failing more than he did himself, and felt the
diminution of his credit, exhorted him to make way for
another who should have the grace and zeal of novelty.
For his part he sincerely desired repose, and he pressed
the King to allow him to take it, but all in vain. He
was obliged to bear his burden to the very end. Even
the infirmities and the decrepitude that afflicted could not
deliver him. Decaying legs, memory extinguished, judgment collapsed, all his faculties confused, strange inconveniences for a confessor — nothing could disgust the
King, and he persisted in having this corpse brought to
him and carrying on customary business with it. At
last, two days after a return from Versailles, he grew
much weaker, received the sacrament, wrote with his
own hand a long letter to the King, received a very
rapid and hurried one in reply, and soon after died at
five o'clock in the morning very peaceably. His confessor
asked him two things, whether he had acted according
to his conscience, and whether he had thought of the
interests and honor of the company of Jesuits; and to
both these questions he answered satisfactorily.

The news was brought to the King as he came out of
his cabinet. He received it like a prince accustomed to
losses, praised the Père La Chaise for his goodness, and
then said smilingly, before all the courtiers, and quite
loud, to the two fathers who had come to announce the
death: " He was so good that I sometimes reproached
him for it, and he used to reply to me: 'It is not I who
am good; it is you who are hard.'"

Truly the fathers and all the auditors were so surprised at this that they lowered their eyes. The remark
spread directly; nobody was able to blame the Père La
Chaise. He was generally regretted, for he had done
much good and never harm except in self-defense.
Maréchal, first surgeon of the King, and possessed of his
confidence, related once to me and Madame de Saint-
Simon, a very important anecdote referring to this time.
He said that the King, talking to him privately of the
Père La Chaise, and praising him for his attachment, related one of the great proofs he had given of it. A few
years before his death the Père said that he felt getting

old, and that the King might soon have to choose a new confessor; he begged that that confessor might be chosen from among the Jesuits, that he knew them well, that they were far from deserving all that had been said against them, but — still — he knew them well — and that attachment for the King and desire for his safety induced him to conjure him to act as he requested; because the company contained many sorts of minds and characters which could not be answered for, and must not be reduced to despair, and that the King must not incur a risk — that in fact an unlucky blow is soon given, and had been given before then. Maréchal turned pale at this recital of the King, and concealed as well as he could the disorder it caused in him. We must remember that Henry IV. recalled the Jesuits, and loaded them with gifts merely from fear of them. The King was not superior to Henry IV. He took care not to forget the communication of the Père La Chaise, or expose himself to the vengeance of the company by choosing a confessor out of their limits. He wanted to live, and to live in safety. He requested the Ducs de Chevreuse and de Beauvilliers to make secret inquiries for a proper person. They fell into a trap made, were dupes themselves, and the Church and State the victims.

The Père Tellier, in fact, was chosen as successor of Père La Chaise, and a terrible successor he made. Harsh, exact, laborious, enemy of all dissipation, of all amusement, of all society, incapable of associating even with his colleagues, he demanded no leniency for himself and accorded none to others. His brain and his health were of iron: his conduct was so also; his nature was savage and cruel. He was profoundly false, deceitful, hidden under a thousand folds; and when he could show himself and make himself feared, he yielded nothing, laughed at the most express promises when he no longer cared to keep them, and pursued with fury those who had trusted to them. He was the terror even of the Jesuits, and was so violent to them that they scarcely dared approach him. His exterior kept faith with his interior. He would have been terrible to meet in a dark lane. His physiognomy was cloudy, false, terrible; his eyes were burning, evil, extremely squinting; his aspect struck all with dismay. The whole aim of his life was to advance the interests of his Society; that was his God; his life had been absorbed in that study: surprisingly ignorant, insolent, impudent, impetuous, without measure and without discretion, all means were good that furthered his designs.

The first time Père Tellier saw the King in his cabinet, after having been presented to him, there was nobody but Bloin and Fagon in a corner. Fagon, bent double and leaning on his stick, watched the interview and studied the physiognomy of this new personage — his duckings, and scrapings, and his words. The King asked him if he were a relation of MM. le Tellier. The good father humbled himself in the dust. " I, sire!" answered he, " a relative of MM. le Tellier! I am very different from that. I am a poor peasant of Lower Normandy, where my father was a farmer." Fagon, who watched him in every movement, twisted himself up to look at Bloin, and said, pointing to the Jesuit: " Monsieur, what a cursed ——!" Then shrugging his shoulders, he curved over his stick again. It turned out that he was not mistaken in his strange judgment of a confessor. This Tellier made all the grimaces, not to say the hypocritical monkey tricks of a man who was afraid of his place, and only took it out of deference to his company.

I have dwelt thus upon this new confessor, because from him have come the incredible tempests under which the Church, the State, knowledge, and doctrine, and many good people of all kinds, are still groaning; and because I had a more intimate acquaintance with this terrible personage than had any man at the Court. He introduced himself to me in fact, to my surprise; and although I did all in my power to shun his acquaintance, I could not succeed. He was too dangerous a man to be treated with anything but great prudence.

During the autumn of this year, he gave a sample of his quality in the part he took in the destruction of the celebrated monastery of Port Royal des Champs. I need not dwell at any great length upon the origin and progress of the two religious parties, the Jansenists and the Molinists; enough has been written on both sides to form a whole library. It is enough for me to say that the Molinists were so called because they adopted the views expounded by the Père Molina in a book he wrote against the doctrines of St. Augustin and of the Church of Rome, upon the subject of spiritual grace. The Père Molina was a Jesuit, and it was by the Jesuits his book was brought forward and supported. Finding, however, that the views it expounded met with general opposition, not only throughout France, but at Rome, they had recourse to their usual artifices on feeling themselves embarrassed, turned themselves into accusers instead of defendants, and invented a heresy that had neither author nor follower, which they attributed to Cornelius Jansenius, Bishop of Ypres. Many and long were the discussions at Rome upon this ideal heresy, invented by the Jesuits solely for the purpose of weakening the adversaries of Molina. To oppose his doctrines was to be a Jansenist. That in substance was what was meant by Jansenism.

At the monastery of Port Royal des Champs, a number of holy and learned personages lived in retirement. Some wrote, some gathered youths around them, and instructed them in science and piety. The finest moral works, works which have thrown the most light upon the science and practice of religion, and have been found so by everybody, issued from their hands. These men entered into the quarrel against Molinism. This was enough to excite against them the hatred of the Jesuits, and to determine that body to attempt their destruction.

They were accused of Jansenism, and defended themselves perfectly; but at the same time they carried the war into the enemy's camp, especially by the ingenious « Provincial Letters » of the famous Pascal.

The quarrel grew more hot between the Jesuits and Port Royal, and was telling against the former, when the Père Tellier brought all his influence to bear, to change the current of success. He was, as I have said, an ardent man, whose divinity was his Molinism, and

the company to which he belonged. Confessor to the
King, he saw himself in a good position to exercise
unlimited authority. He saw that the King was very
ignorant, and prejudiced upon all religious matters; that
he was surrounded by people as ignorant and as prejudiced as himself, Madame de Maintenon, M. de Beauvilliers, M. de Chevreuse, and others, and he determined
to take good advantage of this state of things. Step by
step he gained over the King to his views, and convinced
him that the destruction of the monastery of Port Royal
des Champs was a duty which he owed to his conscience,
and the cause of religion. This point gained, the means
to destroy the establishment were soon resolved on.

There was another monastery called Port Royal, at
Paris, in addition to the one in question. It was now
pretended that the latter had only been allowed to exist
by tolerance, and that it was necessary one should cease
to exist. Of the two, it was alleged that it was better
to preserve the one at Paris. A decree in Council was,
therefore, rendered, in virtue of which, on the night from
the 28th to the 29th of October, the abbey of Port Royal
des Champs was secretly invested by troops, and, on the
next morning, the officer in command made all the inmates assemble, showed them a *lettre de cachet*, and,
without giving them more than a quarter of an hour's
warning, carried off everybody and everything. He had
brought with him many coaches, with an elderly woman
in each; he put the nuns in these coaches, and sent them
away to their destinations, which were different monasteries, at ten, twenty, thirty, forty, and even fifty leagues
distant, each coach accompanied by mounted archers,
just as public women are carried away from a house of
ill fame! I pass in silence all the accompaniments to
this scene, so touching and so strangely new. There
have been entire volumes written upon it.

The treatment that these nuns received in their various
prisons, in order to force them to sign a condemnation
of themselves, is the matter of other volumes, which in
spite of the vigilance of the oppressors, were soon in
everybody's hands; public indignation so burst out, that
the Court and the Jesuits even were embarrassed with

it. But the Père Tellier was not a man to stop half way anywhere. He finished this matter directly; decree followed decree, *lettres de cachet* followed *lettres de cachet*. The families who had relatives buried in the cemetery of Port Royal des Champs were ordered to exhume and carry them elsewhere. All the others were thrown into the cemetery of an adjoining parish, with the indecency that may be imagined. Afterward, the house, the church, and all the buildings were razed to the ground, so that not one stone was left upon another. All the materials were sold, the ground was plowed up, and sown — not with salt, it is true, but that was all the favor it received! The scandal at this reached even to Rome. I have restricted myself to this simple and short recital of an expedition so military and so odious.

CHAPTER IX.

Death of D'Avaux—A Quarrel about a Window—Louvois and the King—Anecdote of Boisseuil—Madame de Maintenon and M. de Beauvilliers—Harcourt Proposed for the Council—His Disappointment—Death of M. le Prince—His Character—Treatment of His Wife—His Love Adventures—His Madness—A Confessor Brought —Nobody Regrets Him.

THE death of D'Avaux, who had formerly been our ambassador in Holland, occurred in the early part of this year (1709). D Avaux was one of the first to hear of the project of William of Orange upon England, when that project was still in embryo, and kept profoundly secret. He apprised the King (Louis XIV.) of it, but was laughed at. Barillon, then our ambassador in England, was listened to in preference. He, deceived by Sunderland and the other perfidious ministers of James II., assured our Court that D'Avaux's reports were mere chimeras. It was not until it was impossible any longer to doubt that credit was given to them. The steps that we then took, instead of disconcerting all the measures of the conspirators, as we could have done, did not interfere with the working out of any one of their plans. All liberty was left, in fact, to William to carry out his scheme. The anecdote which explains how this happened is so curious, that it deserves to be mentioned here.

Louvois, who was then minister of war, was also superintendent of the buildings. The King, who liked building, and who had cast off all his mistresses, had pulled down the little porcelain Trianon he had made for Madame de Montespan, and was rebuilding it in the form it still retains. One day he perceived, for his glance was most searching, that one window was a trifle narrower than the others. He showed it to Louvois, in order that it might be altered, which, as it was not then finished, was easy to do. Louvois sustained that the window was all right. The King insisted then, and on the morrow also, but Louvois, pig-headed and inflated with his authority, would not yield.

The next day the King saw Le Notre in the gallery. Although his trade was gardens rather than houses, the King did not fail to consult him upon the latter. He asked him if he had been to Trianon. Le Notre replied that he had not. The King ordered him to go. On the morrow he saw Le Notre again; same question, same answer. The King comprehended the reason of this, and a little annoyed, commanded him to be there that afternoon at a given time. Le Notre did not dare to disobey this time. The King arrived, and Louvois being present, they returned to the subject of the window, which Louvois obstinately said was as broad as the rest. The King wished Le Notre to measure it, for he knew, that, upright and true, he would openly say what he found. Louvois piqued, grew angry. The King, who was not less so, allowed him to say his say. Le Notre, meanwhile did not stir. At last, the King made him go, Louvois still grumbling, and maintaining his assertion with audacity and little measure. Le Notre measured the window and said that the King was right by several inches. Louvois still wished to argue but the King silenced him, and commanded him to see that the window was altered at once, contrary to custom abusing him most harshly.

What annoyed Louvois most was, that this scene passed not only before all the officers of the buildings, but in presence of all who followed the King in his promenades, nobles, courtiers, officers of the guard, and others, even all the rolete. The dressing given to Louvois was smart and long, mixed with reflections upon the fault of this window, which, not noticed so soon, might have spoiled all the façade, and compelled it to be rebuilt.

Louvois, who was not accustomed to be thus treated, returned home in fury, and like a man in despair. His familiars were frightened, and in their disquietude angled to learn what had happened. At last he told them, said he was lost, and that for a few inches the King forgot all his services, which had led to so many conquests; he declared that henceforth he would leave the trowel to the King, bring about a war, and so arrange matters that the King should have good need of him!

He soon kept his word. He caused a war to grow out of the affair of the double election of Cologne, of the Prince of Bavaria, and of the Cardinal of Furstemberg; he confirmed it in carrying the flames into the Palatinate, and in leaving, as I have said, all liberty to the project upon England; he put the finishing touch to his work by forcing the Duke of Savoy into the arms of his enemies, and making him become, by the position of his country, our enemy, the most difficult and the most ruinous. All that I have here related was clearly brought to light in due time.

Boisseuil died shortly after D'Avaux. He was a tall, big man, warm and violent, a great gambler, bad tempered,—who often treated M. le Grand and Madame d Armagnac, great people as they were, so that the company were ashamed,—and who swore in the saloon of Marly as if he had been in a taproom. He was feared; and he said to women whatever came uppermost when the fury of a cutthroat seized him. During a journey the King and Court made to Nancy, Boisseuil one evening sat down to play in the house of one of the courtiers. A player happened to be there who played very high. Boisseuil lost a good deal, and was very angry. He thought he perceived that this gentleman, who was only permitted on account of his play, was cheating, and made such good use of his eyes that he soon found this was the case, and all on a sudden stretched across the table and seized the gambler's hand, which he held upon the table, with the cards he was going to deal. The gentleman, very much astonished, wished to withdraw his hand, and was angry. Boisseuil, stronger than he, said that he was a rogue, and that the company should see it, and immediately shaking his hand with fury put in evidence his deceit. The player, confounded, rose and went away. The game went on and lasted long into the night. When finished, Boisseuil went away. As he was leaving the door he found a man stuck against the wall—it was the player—who called him to account for the insult he had received. Boisseuil replied that he should give him no satisfaction, and that he was a rogue.

"That may be," said the player, "but I don't like to be told so."

They went away directly and fought. Boisseuil received two wounds, from one of which he was like to die. The other escaped without injury.

I have said, that after the affair of M. de Cambrai, Madame de Maintenon had taken a rooted dislike to M. de Beauvilliers. She had become reconciled to him in appearance during the time that Monseigneur de Bourgogne was a victim to the calumnies of M. de Vendôme, because she had need of him. Now that Monseigneur de Bourgogne was brought back to favor, and M. de Vendôme was disgraced, her antipathy for M. de Beauvilliers burst out anew, and she set her wits to work to get rid of him from the Council of State, of which he was a member. The witch wished to introduce her favorite Harcourt there in his place, and worked so well to bring about this result that the King promised he should be received.

His word given, or rather snatched from him, the King was embarrassed as to how to keep it, for he did not wish openly to proclaim Harcourt minister. It was agreed, therefore, that at the next Council Harcourt should be present, as though by accident, in the King's antechamber; that, Spanish matters being brought up, the King should propose to consult Harcourt, and immediately after should direct search to be made for him, to see if, by chance, he was close at hand; that upon finding him, he should be conducted to the Council, made to enter and seat himself, and ever afterward be regarded as a minister of state.

This arrangement was kept extremely secret, according to the express commands of the King. I knew it, however, just before it was to be executed, and I saw at once that the day of Harcourt's entry into the Council would be the day of M. de Beauvilliers's disgrace. I sent, therefore, at once for M. de Beauvilliers, begging him to come to my house immediately, and that I would then tell him why I could not come to him. Without great precaution everything becomes known at Court.

In less than half an hour M. de Beauvilliers arrived, tolerably disturbed at my message. I asked him if he knew anything, and I turned him about, less to pump him than to make him ashamed of his ignorance, and to persuade him the better afterward to do what I wished. When I had well trotted out his ignorance, I apprised him of what I had just learned. He was astounded; he so little expected it! I had not much trouble to persuade him that, although his expulsion might not yet be determined on, the intrusion of Harcourt must pave the way for it. He admitted to me that for some days he had found the King cold and embarrassed with him, but that he had paid little attention to the circumstance, the reason of which was now clear. There was no time to lose. In twenty-four hours all would be over. I therefore took the liberty in the first instance of scolding him for his profound ignorance of what passed at the Court, and was bold enough to say to him that he had only to thank himself for the situation he found himself in. He let me say to the end without growing angry, then smiled, and said, "Well! what do you think I ought to do?"

That was just what I wanted. I replied that there was only one course open to him, and that was to have an interview with the King early the next morning; to say to him, that he had been informed Harcourt was about to enter the Council; that he thought the affairs of State would suffer rather than otherwise if Harcourt did so; and finally, to allude to the change that had taken place in the King's manner toward him lately, and to say, with all respect, affection, and submission, that he was equally ready to continue serving the King or to give up his appointments, as his Majesty might desire.

M. de Beauvilliers took pleasure in listening to me. He embraced me closely, and promised to follow the course I had marked out.

The next morning I went straight to him, and learned that he had perfectly succeeded. He had spoken exactly as I had suggested. The King appeared astonished and piqued that the secret of Harcourt's entry into the Council was discovered. He would not hear a word as to resignation of office on the part of M. de Beauvilliers, and appeared more satisfied with him than ever. Whether, without this interview, he would have been lost, I know not, but by the coldness and embarrassment of the King before that interview, and during the first part of it, I am nearly persuaded that he would. M. de Beauvilliers embraced me again very tenderly — more than once.

As for Harcourt, sure of his good fortune, and scarcely able to contain his joy, he arrived at the meeting place. Time ran on. During the Council there are only the most subaltern people in the antechambers and a few courtiers who pass that way to go from one wing to another. Each of these subalterns eagerly asked M. d'Harcourt what he wanted, if he wished for anything, and importuned him strongly. He was obliged to remain there, although he had no pretext. He went and came, limping with his stick, not knowing what to reply to the passers-by, or the attendants by whom he was remarked. At last, after waiting long, he returned as he came, much disturbed at not having been called. He sent word so to Madame de Maintenon, who, in her turn, was as much disturbed, the King not having said a word to her, and she not having dared to say a word to him. She consoled Harcourt, hoping that at the next Council he would be called. At her wish he waited again, as before, during another Council, but with as little success. He was very much annoyed, comprehending that the affair had fallen through.

Madame de Maintenon did not, however, like to be defeated in this way. After waiting some time she spoke to the King reminding him what he had promised to do. The King replied in confusion that he had thought better of it; that Harcourt was on bad terms with all the ministers, and might, if admitted to the Council, cause them much embarrassment; he preferred, therefore, things to remain as they were. This was said in a manner that admitted of no reply. Madame de Maintenon felt herself beaten; Harcourt was in despair. M. de Beauvilliers was quite re-established in the favor of the King. I pretended to have known nothing of this affair, and inno-

cently asked many questions about it when all was over.
I was happy to the last degree that everything had turned
out so well.

M. le Prince, who for more than two years had not
appeared at the Court, died at Paris a little after midnight on the night between Easter Sunday and Monday,
the last of March and first of April, and in his seventy-
sixth year. No man had ever more ability of all kinds,
—extending even to the arts and mechanics,—more
valor, and, when it pleased him, more discernment, grace,
politeness, and nobility. But then no man had ever before so many useless talents, so much genius of no avail,
or an imagination so calculated to be a bugbear to itself
and a plague to others. Abjectly and vilely servile even
to lackeys, he scrupled not to use the lowest and paltriest
means to gain his ends. Unnatural son, cruel father, terrible husband, detestable master, pernicious neighbor;
without friendship, without friends—incapable of having
any—jealous, suspicious, ever restless, full of slyness and
artifices to discover and to scrutinize all (in which he
was unceasingly occupied, aided by an extreme vivacity
and a surprising penetration), choleric and headstrong to
excess even for trifles, difficult of access, never in accord
with himself, and keeping all around him in a tremble;
to conclude, impetuosity and avarice were his masters,
which monopolized him always. With all this he was a
man difficult to be proof against when he put in play
the pleasing qualities he possessed.

Madame la Princess, his wife, was his continual victim. She was disgustingly ugly, virtuous, and foolish,
a little humpbacked, and stunk like a skunk, even from
a distance. All these things did not hinder M. le Prince
from being jealous of her even to fury up to the very
last. The piety, the indefatigable attention of Madame
la Princess, her sweetness, her novice-like submission,
could not guarantee her from frequent injuries, or from
kicks, and blows with the fist, which were not rare. She
was not mistress even of the most trifling things; she did not
dare to propose or ask anything. He made her set out
from one place to another the moment the fancy took
him. Often when seated in their coach he made her

descend, or return from the end of the street, then recommence the journey after dinner, or the next day. This seesawing lasted once fifteen days running, before a trip to Fontainebleau. At other times he sent for her from church, made her quit high mass, and sometimes sent for her the moment she was going to receive the Sacrament; she was obliged to return at once and put off her communion to another occasion. It was not that he wanted her, but it was merely to gratify his whim that he thus troubled her.

He was always of uncertain habits, and had four dinners ready for him every day; one at Paris, one at Ecouen, one at Chantilly, and one where the Court was. But the expense of this arrangement was not great; he dined on soup, and the half of a fowl roasted upon a crust of bread; the other half serving for the next day. He rarely invited anybody to dinner, but when he did, no man could be more polite or attentive to his guests.

Formerly he had been in love with several ladies of the Court; then, nothing cost too much. He was grace, magnificence, gallantry in person — a Jupiter transformed into a shower of gold. Now he disguised himself as a lackey, another time as a female broker in articles for the toilet; and now in another fashion. He was the most ingenious man in the world. He once gave a grand *fête* solely for the purpose of retarding the journey into Italy of a lady with whom he was enamored, with whom he was on good terms, and whose husband he amused by making verses. He hired all the houses on one side of a street near St. Sulpice, furnished them, and pierced the connecting walls, in order to be able thus to reach the place of rendezvous without being suspected.

Jealous and cruel to his mistresses, he had, among others, the Marquise de Richelieu; whom I name, because she is not worth the trouble of being silent upon. He was hopelessly smitten and spent millions upon her and to learn her movements. He knew that the Comte de Roucy shared her favors (it was for her that sagacious Comte proposed to put straw before the house in order to guarantee her against the sound of the church bells, of which she complained). M. le Prince reproached

7

her for favoring the Count. She defended herself; but he watched her so closely, that he brought home the offense to her without her being able to deny it. The fear of losing a lover so rich as was M. le Prince furnished her on the spot with an excellent suggestion for putting him at ease. She proposed to make an appointment at her own house with the Comte de Roucy, M. le Prince's people to lie in wait, and when the Comte appeared, to make away with him. Instead of the success she expected from a proposition so humane and ingenious, M. le Prince was so horror struck, that he warned the Comte de Roucy, and never saw the Marquise de Richelieu again all his life.

The most surprising thing was, that with so much ability, penetration, activity, and valor, as had M. le Prince, with the desire to be as great a warrior as the Great Condé, his father, he could never succeed in understanding even the first elements of the military art. Instructed as he was by his father, he never acquired the least aptitude in war. It was a profession he was not born for, and for which he could not qualify himself by study.

During the last fifteen or twenty years of his life, he was accused of something more than fierceness and ferocity. Wanderings were noticed in his conduct, which were not exhibited in his own house alone. Entering one morning into the apartment of the Maréchale de Noailles (she herself has related this to me) as her bed was being made, and there being only the counterpane to put on, he stopped short at the door, crying with transport, "Oh, the nice bed, the nice bed!" took a spring, leaped upon the bed, rolled himself upon it seven or eight times, then descended and made his excuses to the Maréchale, saying that her bed was so clean and so well made, that he could not hinder himself from jumping upon it; and this, although there had never been anything between them; and when the Maréchale, who all her life had been above suspicion, was at an age at which she could not give birth to any. Her servants remained stupefied, and she as much as they. She got out of the difficulty by laughing and treating it as a joke. It was whispered that there were times when M. le Prince believed himself a dog, or some other beast, whose manners he imitated; and I have known people very worthy of faith who have assured me they have seen him at the going to bed of the King suddenly throw his head into the air several times running, and open his mouth quite wide, like a dog when barking, yet without making a noise. It is certain, that for a long time nobody saw him except a single valet, who had control over him, and who did not annoy him.

In the latter part of his life he attended in a ridiculously minute manner to his diet and its results, and entered into discussions which drove his doctors to despair. Fever and gout at last attacked him, and he augmented them by the course he pursued. Finot, our physician and his, at times knew not what to do with him. What embarrassed Finot most, as he related to us more than once, was that M. le Prince would eat nothing, for the simple reason, as he alleged, that he was dead, and that dead men did not eat! It was necessary, however, that he should take something, or he would have really died. Finot and another doctor who attended him, determined to agree with him that he was dead, but to maintain that dead men sometimes eat. They offered to produce dead men of this kind; and in point of fact, led to M. le Prince some persons unknown to him, who pretended to be dead, but who ate nevertheless. This trick succeeded, but he would never eat except with these men and Finot. On that condition he ate well, and this jealousy lasted a long time, and drove Finot to despair by its duration; who, nevertheless, sometimes nearly died of laughter in relating to us what passed at these repasts, and the conversation from the other world heard there.

M. le Prince's malady augmenting, Madame la Princess grew bold enough to ask him if he did not wish to think of his conscience, and to see a confessor? He amused himself tolerably long in refusing to do so. Some months before he had seen in secret Père de la Tour. He had sent to the reverend father asking him to come by night and disguised. Père de la Tour, surprised to the last degree at so wild a proposition, replied that the respect he owed to the cloth would prevent him visiting M. le Prince in disguise; but that he would come in his ordinary attire. M. le Prince agreed to this last imposed condition. He made the Père de la Tour enter at night by a little back door, at which an attendant was waiting to receive him. He was led by this attendant, who had a lantern in one hand and a key in the other, through many long and obscure passages, and through many doors, which were opened and closed upon him as he passed. Having arrived at last at the sick chamber, he confessed M. le Prince, and was conducted out of the house in the same manner and by the same way as before. These visits were repeated during several months.

The Prince's malady rapidly increased, and became extreme. The doctors found him so ill on the night of Easter Sunday that they proposed to him the Sacrament for the next day. He disputed with them, and said that if he was so very bad it would be better to take the Sacraments at once, and have done with them. They in their turn opposed this, saying there was no need of so much hurry. At last, for fear of incensing him, they consented, and he received all-hurriedly the last Sacraments. A little while after he called M. le Duc to him, and spoke of the honors he wished at his funeral, mentioning those which had been omitted at the funeral of his father, but which he did not wish to be omitted from his. He talked of nothing but this and of the sums he had spent at Chantilly, until his reason began to wander.

Not a soul regretted him; neither servants nor friends, neither child nor wife. Indeed the Princess was so ashamed of her tears that she made excuses for them. This was scarcely to be wondered at.

CHAPTER X.

IT IS time now that I should speak of our military operations this year and of the progress of the war.
Let me commence by stating the disposition of our
armies at the beginning of the campaign.

Maréchal Boufflers, having become dangerously ill, was
unable to take command in Flanders. Maréchal de Villars was accordingly appointed in his stead under Monseigneur, and with him served the King of England,
under his incognito of the previous year, and M. le Duc
de Berry, as volunteers. The Maréchal d'Harcourt was
appointed to command upon the Rhine under Monseigneur le Duc de Bourgogne. M. d'Orléans commanded
in Spain; Maréchal Berwick in Dauphiny; and the Duc
de Noailles in Roussillon, as usual. The generals went
to their destinations, but the princes remained at the
Court.

Before I relate what we did in war, let me here state
the strange opposition of our ministers in their attempts to bring about peace. Since Villars had introduced Chamillart to Court, he had heard it said that M.
de Louvois did everybody's business as much as he
could; and took it into his head that having succeeded
to M. de Louvois he ought to act exactly like him. For
some time past, accordingly, Chamillart, with the knowledge of the King, had sent people to Holland and elsewhere to negotiate for peace, although he had no right
to do so, Torcy being the minister to whose department
this business belonged. Torcy likewise sent people to
Holland and elsewhere with a similar object, and these

ambassadors of the two ministers, instead of working in
common, did all in their power to thwart each other.
They succeeded so well that it was said they seemed in
foreign countries ministers of different powers, whose interests were quite opposed. This manner of conducting
business gave a most injurious idea of our Government,
and tended very much to bring it into ridicule. Those
who sincerely wished to treat with us, found themselves
so embarrassed between the rival factions, that they did
not know what to do; and others made our disagree-
ments a plausible pretext for not listening to our propositions.

At last Torcy was so annoyed with the interference of
Chamillart, that he called the latter to account for it, and
made him sign an agreement by which he bound himself to enter into no negotiations for peace and to mix
himself in no foreign affairs; and so this absurdity came
to an end.

In Italy, early this year, we received a check of no
small importance. I have mentioned that we were invited to join in an Italian league, having for its object
to oppose the Emperor. We joined this league, but not
before its existence had been noised abroad, and put the
allies on their guard as to the danger they ran of losing
Italy. Therefore the Imperialists entered the Papal
States, laid them under contribution, ravaged them, lived
there in true Tartar style, and snapped their fingers at
the Pope, who cried aloud as he could obtain no redress
and no assistance. Pushed at last to extremity by the
military occupation which desolated his States, he yielded
to all the wishes of the Emperor, and recognized the
Archduke as King of Spain. Philip V. immediately
ceased all intercourse with Rome, and dismissed the
nuncio from Madrid. The Imperialists, even after the
Pope had ceded to their wishes, treated him with the utmost disdain, and continued to ravage his territories.
The Imperialist minister at Rome, actually gave a comedy
and a ball in his palace there, contrary to the express
orders of the Pope, who had forbidden all kinds of
amusement in this period of calamity. When remonstrated with by the Pope, this minister said that he had

promised a *fête* to the ladies, and could not break his
word. The strangest thing is, that after this public instance of contempt the nephews of the Pope went to the
fête, and the Pope had the weakness to suffer it.

In Spain, everything went wrong, and people began
to think it would be best to give up that country to the
House of Austria, under the hope that by this means the
war would be terminated. It was therefore seriously resolved to recall all our troops from Spain, and to give
orders to Madame des Ursins to quit the country. Instructions were accordingly sent to this effect. The King and
Queen of Spain, in the greatest alarm at such a violent
determination, cried aloud against it, and begged that
the execution of it might at least be suspended for
awhile.

At this our King paused and called a Council to discuss the subject. It was ultimately agreed to leave sixty-
six battalions of our troops to the King of Spain, but to
withdraw all the rest. This compromise satisfied nobody.
Those who wished to support Spain said this assistance
was not enough. The other party said it was too much.

This determination being arrived at, it seemed as
though the only thing to be done was to send M. d'Orléans to Spain to take command there. But now will be
seen the effect of that mischievous pleasantry of his upon
Madame de Maintenon and Madame des Ursins, the "she
captain," and the "she lieutenant"—as he called them,
in the gross language to which I have before alluded.
Those two ladies had not forgiven him his witticism,
and had determined to accomplish his disgrace. His own
thoughtless conduct assisted them in bringing about this
result.

The King one day asked him if he had much desire
to return into Spain. He replied in a manner evidenc-
ing his willingness to serve, marking no eagerness. He
did not notice that there might be a secret meaning hidden under this question. When he related to me what
had passed between him and the King, I blamed the
feebleness of his reply, and represented to him the ill
effect it would create if at such a time he evinced any
desire to keep out of the campaign. He appeared con-

vinced by my arguments, and to wish with more eagerness than before to return to Spain.

A few days after, the King asked him, on what terms he
believed himself with the Princess des Ursins; and when M.
d'Orléans replied that he believed himself to be on good
terms with her, as he had done all in his power to be so, the
King said that he feared that it was not thus, since she
had asked that he should not be again sent to Spain, saying that he had leagued himself with all her enemies there,
and that a secretary of his, named Renaut, whom he had
left behind him, kept up such strict and secret intercourse
with those enemies, that she was obliged to demand his
recall lest he might do wrong to the name of his master.

Upon this, M. d'Orléans replied that he was infinitely
surprised at these complaints of Madame des Ursins,
since he had done nothing to deserve them. The King,
after reflecting for a moment, said he thought, all things
considered, that M. d'Orléans had better not return to
Spain. In a few days it was publicly known that he
would not go. The withdrawal of so many of our troops
from Spain was the reason alleged. At the same time
the King gave orders to M. d'Orléans to send for his
equipages from Spain, and added in his ear, that he had
better send some one of sense for them, who might be
the bearer of a protest, if Philip V. quitted his throne.
At least this is what M. d'Orléans told me, although few
people believed him in the end.

M. d'Orléans chose for this errand a man named Flotte,
very skillful in intrigue, in which he had, so to speak,
been always brought up. He went straight to Madrid,
and one of his first employments when he arrived there
was to look for Renaut, the secretary just alluded to.
But Renaut was nowhere to be found, nor could any
news be heard of him. Flotte stayed some time in
Madrid, and then went to the army which was still in
quarters. He remained there three weeks, idling from
quarter to quarter, saluting the maréchal in command,
who was much surprised at his long stay, and who
pressed him to return to France. At last Flotte took
leave of the maréchal, asking him for an escort for himself and a commissary, with whom he meant to go in

company across the Pyrenees. Twenty dragoons were given him as escort, and he and the commissary set out in a chaise.

They had not proceeded far before Flotte perceived that they were followed by other troops besides those guarding them. Flotte fearing that something was meant by this, slipped a pocketbook into the hands of the commissary, requesting him to take care of it. Shortly afterward the chaise was surrounded by troops, and stopped; the two travelers were made to alight. The commissary was ordered to give up the pocketbook, an order that he complied with very rapidly, and Flotte was made prisoner, and escorted back to the spot he had just left.

The news of this occurrence reached the King on the 12th of July, by the ordinary courier from Madrid. The King informed M. d'Orléans of it, who, having learned it by a private courier six days before, affected nevertheless surprise, and said it was strange that one of his people should have been thus arrested, and that as his Majesty was concerned, it was for him to demand the reason. The King replied, that in fact the injury regarded him more than M. d'Orléans, and that he would give orders to Torcy to write as was necessary to Spain.

It is not difficult to believe that such an explosion made a great noise, both in France and Spain; but the noise it made at first was nothing to that which followed. A cabal was formed against Monsieur le Duc d'Orléans. It was said that he had plotted to place himself upon the Spanish throne, by driving out Philip V., under pretext of his incapacity, of the domination of Madame des Ursins, and of the abandonment of the country by France; that he had treated with Stanhope, commander of the English troops in Spain, and with whom he was known to be on friendly terms, in order to be protected by the Archduke. This was the report most widely spread. Others went further. In these M. d'Orléans was accused of nothing less than of intending to divorce himself from Madame la Duchess d'Orléans, as having been married to her by force; of intending to marry the sister of the Empress (widow of Charles II.), and of mounting with her upon the Spanish throne; to marry Madame d'Argenton, as the Queen Dowager was sure to have no children, and finally, to poison Madame d'Orléans.

Meanwhile the reply from Spain came not. The King and Monseigneur treated M. d'Orléans with a coldness which made him sorely ill at ease; the majority of the courtiers, following this example, withdrew from him. He was left almost alone.

I learned at last from M. d'Orléans how far he was deserving of public censure, and what had given coloring to the reports spread against him. He admitted to me, that several of the Spanish grandees had persuaded him that it was not possible the King of Spain could stand, and had proposed to him to hasten his fall, and take his place; that he had rejected this proposition with indignation, but had been induced to promise, that if Philip V. fell of himself, without hope of rising, he would not object to mount the vacant throne, believing that by so doing he would be doing good to our King, by preserving Spain to his house.

As soon as I heard this, I advised him to make a clean breast of it to the King, and to ask his pardon for having acted in this matter without his orders and without his knowledge. He thought my advice good, and acted upon it. But the King was too much under the influence of the enemies of M. d'Orléans, to listen favorably to what was said to him. The facts of the case, too, were much against M. d'Orléans. Both Renaut and Flotte had been intrusted with his secret. The former had openly leagued himself with the enemies of Madame des Ursins, and acted with the utmost imprudence. He had been privately arrested just before the arrival of Flotte. When this latter was arrested, papers were found upon him which brought everything to light. The views of M. d'Orléans and of those who supported him were clearly shown. The King would not listen to anything in favor of his nephew.

The whole Court cried out against M. d'Orléans; never was such an uproar heard. He was accused of plotting to overthrow the King of Spain, he, a prince of the blood, and so closely allied to the two crowns! Monseigneur, usually so plunged in apathy, roused himself to fury against M. d'Orléans, and insisted upon nothing less than a criminal prosecution. He insisted so strongly upon this, that the King at last consented that it should take place, and gave orders to the chancellor to examine the forms requisite in such a case. While the chancellor was about this work, I went to see him one day, and represented to him so strongly, that M. d'Orléans's misdemeanor did not concern France at all, and could only be judged before a Spanish tribunal, that the idea of a criminal trial was altogether abandoned almost immediately after. M. d'Orléans was allowed to remain in peace.

Madame des Ursins and Madame de Maintenon had so far triumphed, however, that M. d'Orléans found himself plunged in the deepest disgrace. He was universally shunned. Whenever he appeared, people flew away, so that they might not be seen in communication with him. His solitude was so great, that for a whole month only one friend entered his house. In the midst of this desertion, he had no resource but debauchery, and the society of his mistress, Madame d'Argenton. The disorder and scandal of his life had for a long time offended the King, the Court, and the public. They now unhappily confirmed everybody in the bad opinion they had formed of him. That the long disgrace he suffered continued to confirm him in his bad habits, and that it explains to some extent his after-conduct, there can be no doubt. But I must leave him now, and return to other matters.

CHAPTER XI.

B<small>UT</small>, meanwhile, a great change had taken place at
Court. Chamillart had committed the mistake of
allowing the advancement of D'Harcourt to the
head of an army. The poor man did not see the
danger; and when warned of it, thought his cleverness would preserve him. Reports of his fall had
already begun to circulate, and D'Antin had been
spoken of in his place. I warned his daughter Dreux,
the only one of the family to whom it was possible
to speak with profit. The mother, with little wit
and knowledge of the Court, full of apparent confidence and sham cunning, received all advice ill. The
brothers were imbecile, the son was a child and a simple-
ton, the two other daughters too light headed. I had
often warned Madame de Dreux of the enmity of the
Duchess de Bourgogne; and she had spoken to her on
the subject. The Princess had answered very coldly that
she was mistaken, that she had no such enmity. At last
I succeeded, in this indirect way, in forcing Chamillart to
speak to the King on the reports that were abroad; but
he did so in a half-and-half way, and committed the capital
mistake of not naming the successor which public rumor
mentioned. The King appeared touched, and gave him
all sorts of assurances of friendship, and made as if he
liked him better than ever. I do not know if Chamillart
was then near his destruction, and whether this conversation set him up again; but from the day it took place
all reports died away, and the Court thought him perfectly re-established.

(108)

But his enemies continued to work against him. Madame de Maintenon and the Duchess de Bourgogne abated not a jot in their enmity. The Maréchal d'Harcourt lost no opportunity of pulling him to pieces. One day, among others, he was declaiming violently against him at Madame de Maintenon's, whom he knew he should thus please. She asked him whom he would put in his place. "M. Fagon, Madame," he replied coldly. She laughed, but said this was not a thing to joke about; but he maintained seriously that the old doctor would make a much better minister than Chamillart, for he had some intelligence, which would make up for his ignorance of many matters; but what could be expected of a man who was ignorant and stupid too? The cunning Norman knew well the effect this strange parallel would have; and it is indeed inconceivable how damaging his sarcasm proved. A short time afterward, D'Antin, wishing also to please, but more imprudent, insulted the son of Chamillart so grossly, and abused the father so publicly, that he was obliged afterward to excuse himself.

The King held, for the first time in his life, a real council of war. He told the Duc de Bourgogne of it, saying rather sharply, "Come, unless you prefer going to vespers." The council lasted nearly three hours, and was stormy. The maréchals were freer in their language than usual, and complained of the ministers. All fell upon Chamillart, who was accused, among other things, of matters that concerned Desmarets, on whom he finished by turning off the King's anger. Chamillart defended himself with so much anger that his voice was heard by people outside.

But he had of late heaped fault on fault. Besides setting Madame de Maintenon and the Duchess de Bourgogne against him, he rather wantonly irritated Monseigneur, at that time more than ever under the government of Mademoiselle Choin. The latter had asked him a favor, and had been refused even with contempt. Various advances at reconciliation she made were also repulsed with contumely. Yet everyone, even the Duchess de Bourgogne, crawled before this creature — the favorite of the heir of the throne. Madame de Maintenon actually caused the King to offer her apartments at Versailles, which she refused, for fear of losing the liberty she enjoyed at Meudon. D'Antin, who saw all that was going on, became the soul of a conspiracy against Chamillart. It was infinitely well managed. Everything moved in order and harmony—always prudently, always knowingly.

The King, quietly attacked on all hands, was shaken; but he had many reasons for sticking to Chamillart. He was his own choice. No minister had stood aside so completely, and allowed the King to receive all the praise of whatever was done. Though the King's reason was, therefore, soon influenced, his heart was not so easily. But Madame de Maintenon was not discouraged. Monseigneur, urged by Mademoiselle Choin, had already spoken out to the King. She labored to make him speak again; for, on the previous occasion, he had been listened to attentively.

So many machines could not be set in motion without some noise being heard abroad. There rose in the Court, I know not what confused murmurs, the origin of which could not be pointed out, publishing that either the State or Chamillart must perish; that already his ignorance had brought the kingdom within an ace of destruction; that it was a miracle this destruction had not yet come to pass; and that it would be madness to tempt Providence any longer. Some did not blush to abuse him; others praised his intentions, and spoke with moderation of faults that many people reproached him bitterly with. All admitted his rectitude, but maintained that a successor of some kind or other was absolutely necessary. Some, believing or trying to persuade others that they carried friendship to as far a point as was possible, protested that they should ever preserve this friendship, and would never forget the pleasure and the services that they had received from Chamillart; but delicately confessed that they preferred the interests of the State to their own personal advantage and the support they would lose; that, even if Chamillart were their brother, they would sorrowfully admit the necessity of removing him! At last, nobody could understand either how such a man could ever have been chosen, or how he could have remained so long in his place! All his faults and all his ridicules formed the staple of Court conversation. If anybody referred to the great things he had done, to the rapid gathering of armies after our disasters, people turned on their heels and walked away. Such were the presages of the fall of Chamillart.

The Maréchal de Boufflers, who had never forgiven the causes that led to the loss of Lille, joined in the attack on Chamillart; and assisted in exciting the King against him. Chamillart has since related to me that up to the last moment he had always been received equally graciously by the King — that is, up to two days before his fall. Then, indeed, he noticed that the King's countenance was embarrassed, and felt inclined to ask if he was displeasing to him, and to offer to retire. Had he done so, he might, if we may judge from what transpired subsequently, have remained in office. But now Madame de Maintenon had come personally into the field, and, believing herself sure of success, openly attacked Chamillart. What passed between her and the King was quite private and never related; but there seems reason to believe that she did not succeed without difficulty.

On Sunday morning, November 9th, the King, on entering the Council of State, called the Duc de Beauvilliers to him, and requested him to go in the afternoon and tell Chamillart that he was obliged, for motives of public interest, to ask him to resign his office; but that, in order to give him a mark of his esteem and satisfaction with his services, he continued his pension of minister — that is to say, twenty thousand francs, and added as much more, with one to his son of twenty thousand francs likewise. He added that he should have liked to see Chamillart, but that at first it would grieve him too much: he was not to come till sent for; he might live in Paris, and go where he liked. The Duc de Beauvilliers did all he could to escape from carrying so harsh a message, but could only obtain permission to let the Duc de Chevreuse accompany him.

They went to Chamillart, and found him alone, working in his cabinet. The air of consternation with which they entered, told the unfortunate Minister that something disagreeable had happened; and without giving them time to speak, he said, with a serene and tranquil countenance, "What is the matter, gentlemen? If what you have to say concerns only me, you may speak: I have long been prepared for everything." This gentle firmness touched them still more. They could scarcely explain what they came about. Chamillart listened without any change of countenance, and said, with the same air and tone as at first: "The King is the master. I have endeavored to serve him to the best of my ability. I hope some one else will please him better, and be more lucky." He then asked if he had been forbidden to write to the King, and being told not, he wrote a letter of respect and thanks, and sent it by the two Dukes, with a Memoir which he had just finished. He also wrote to Madame de Maintenon. He sent a verbal message to his wife; and, without complaint, murmur, or sighs, got into his carriage, and drove to L'Etang. Both then and afterward he showed the greatest magnanimity. Everyone went, from a sort of fashion, to visit him. When I went, the house looked as if a death had taken place; and it was frightful to see, in the midst of cries and tears, the dead man walking, speaking with a quiet, gentle air, and serene brow,—unconstrained, unaffected, attentive to everyone, not at all or scarcely different from what he was accustomed to be.

Chamillart, as I have said, had received permission to live at Paris, if he liked; but soon afterward he innocently gave umbrage to Madame de Maintenon, who was annoyed that his disgrace was not followed by general abandonment. She caused him to be threatened secretly, and he prudently left Paris, and went far away, under pretense of seeking for an estate to buy.

Next day after the fall of Chamillart, it became known that the triumph of Madame de Maintenon was completed, and that Voysin, her creature, was the succeeding secretary of state. This Voysin had the one indispensable quality for admission into the Councils of Louis XIV. —not a drop of noble blood in his veins. He had married, in 1683, the daughter of Trudaine. She had a very agreeable countenance, without any affectation. She appeared simple and modest, and occupied with her household and good works; but in reality had sense, wit, cleverness, above all, a natural insinuation, and the art of bringing things to pass without being perceived. She kept with great tact a magnificent house. It was she who received Madame de Maintenon at Dinan, when the King was besieging Namur; and, as she had been instructed by M. de Luxembourg in the way to please that lady, succeeded most effectually. Among her arts was her modesty, which led her prudently to avoid pressing herself on Madame de Maintenon, or showing herself more than was absolutely necessary. She was sometimes two whole days without seeing her. A trifle, luckily contrived, finished the conquest of Madame de Maintenon. It happened that the weather passed suddenly from excessive heat to a damp cold, which lasted a long time. Immediately, an excellent dressing gown, simple, and well lined, appeared in the corner of the chamber. This present, by so much the more agreeable, as Madame de Maintenon had not brought any warm clothing, touched her also by its suddenness, and by its simple appearance, as if of its own accord.

In this way, the taste of Madame de Maintenon for Madame Voysin was formed and increased. Madame Voysin obtained an appointment for her husband, and coming to Paris, at last grew extremely familiar with Madame de Maintenon. Voysin himself had much need of the wife that Providence had given him. He was perfectly ignorant of everything but the duties of an Intendant. He was, moreover, rough and uncivil, as the courtiers soon found. He was never unjust for the sake of being so, nor was he bad naturally; but he knew nothing but authority, the King, and Madame de Maintenon, whose will was unanswerable — his sovereign law and reason. The choice was settled between the King and Madame de Maintenon after supper, the day of Chamillart's fall. Voysin was conducted to the King by Bloin, after having received the orders and instructions of his benefactress. In the evening of that day, the King found Madame Voysin with Madame de Maintenon, and kissed her several times to please his lady.

8

Voysin's first experience of the duties of his office was unpleasant. He was foolish enough, feeling his ignorance, to tell the King, that at the outset he should be obliged to leave everything to his Majesty, but that when he knew better, he would take more on himself. The King, to whom Chamillart used himself to leave everything, was much offended by this language; and drawing himself up, in the tone of a master, told Voysin to learn, once for all, that his duties were to receive and expedite orders, nothing else. He then took the projects brought to him, examined them, prescribed the measures he thought fit, and very stiffly sent away Voysin, who did not know where he was, and had great want of his wife to set his head to rights, and of Madame de Maintenon to give him completer lessons than she had yet been able to do. Shortly afterward he was forbidden to send any orders without submitting them to the Maréchal de Boufflers. He was supple, and sure of Madame de Maintenon, and through her of the Marèchal, waited for time to release him from this state of tutelage; and showed nothing of his annoyance, especially to Boufflers himself.

Events soon happened to alter the position of the Maréchal de Boufflers.

Flanders, ever since the opening of the campaign, had been the principal object of attention. Prince Eugène and Marlborough, joined together, continued their vast designs, and disdained to hide them. Their prodigious preparations spoke of sieges. Shall I say that we desired them, and that we thought of nothing but how to preserve, not use our army?

Tournai was the first place toward which the enemies directed their arms. After a short resistance it fell into their hands. Villars, as I have said, was commander in Flanders. Boufflers feeling that, in the position of affairs, such a post must weigh very heavily upon one man, and that in case of his death there was no one to take his place, offered to go to assist him. The King, after some little hesitation, accepted this magnanimous offer, and Boufflers set out. I say magnanimous offer, because Boufflers, loaded with honors, and glory, might well have hoped to pass the rest of his life in repose.

It was hardly possible, do what he might, that he could add to his reputation; while, on the other hand, it was not unlikely that he might be made answerable for the faults or shortcomings of others, and return to Paris stripped of some of the laurels that adorned his brow. But he thought only of the welfare of the State, and pressed the King to allow him to depart to Flanders. The King, as I have said, at last consented.

The surprise was great in the army when he arrived there. The general impression was that he was the bearer of news of peace. Villars received him with an air of joy and respect, and at once showed every willingness to act in concert with him. The two generals accordingly worked harmoniously together, taking no steps without consulting each other, and showing great deference for each other's opinions. They were like one man.

After the fall of Tournai, our army took up position at Malplaquet, the right and the left supported by two woods, with hedges and woods before the center, so that the plain was, as it were, cut in two. Marlborough and Prince Eugène marched in their turn, fearing lest Villars should embarrass them as they went toward Mons, which place they had resolved to besiege. They sent on a large detachment of their army, under the command of the Prince of Hesse, to watch ours. He arrived in sight of the camp at Malplaquet at the same time that we entered it, and was quickly warned of our existence by three cannon shots that Villars, out of braggadocio, fired by way of appeal to Marlborough and Prince Eugène. Some little firing took place this day and the next, the 10th of September, but without doing much harm on either side.

Marlborough and Prince Eugène, warned of the perilous state in which the Prince of Hesse was placed — he would have been lost if attacked — hastened at once to join him, and arrived in the middle of the morning of the 10th. Their first care was to examine the position of our army, and to do so, while waiting for their rear guard, they employed a stratagem which succeeded admirably.

They sent several officers, who had the look of subalterns to our lines, and asked to be allowed to speak
to our officers. Their request was granted. Albergotti came down to them, and discoursed with them
a long time. They pretended they came to see whether
peace could not be arranged, but they in reality, spoke
of little but compliments, which signified nothing. They
stayed so long, under various pretexts, that at last we
were obliged to threaten them in order to get rid of them.
All this time a few of their best general officers on horseback, and a large number of engineers and designers on foot,
profited by these ridiculous colloquies to put upon paper
drawings of our position, thus being able to see the best
positions for their cannon, and the best mode, in fact,
in which all their disposition might be made. We learned
this artifice afterward from the prisoners.

It was decided that evening to give us battle on the
morrow, although the deputies of the States-General,
content with the advantages that had been already gained,
and not liking to run the risk of failure, were opposed
to an action taking place. They were, however, persuaded to agree, and on the following morning the battle
began.

The struggle lasted many hours. But our position had
been badly chosen, and, in spite of every effort, we were
unable to maintain it. Villars, in the early part of the
action, received a wound which incapacitated him from
duty. All the burden of command fell upon Boufflers.
He bore it well; but after a time finding his army dispersed, his infantry overwhelmed, the ground slipping
from under his feet, he thought only of beating a good
and honorable retreat. He led away his army in such
good order, that the enemy were unable to interfere
with it in the slightest degree. During all the march,
which lasted until night, we did not lose a hundred
stragglers, and carried off all the cannon with the exception of a few pieces. The enemy passed the night
upon the battlefield, in the midst of twenty-five thousand dead, and marched toward Mons the next evening.
They frankly admitted that in men killed and wounded,
in general officers and privates, in flags and standard,

they had lost more than we. The battle cost them, in fact, seven lieutenant generals, five other generals, about eighteen hundred officers killed or wounded, and more than fifteen thousand men killed or rendered unfit for service. They openly avowed, also, how much they had been surprised by the valor of the majority of our troops, above all of the cavalry, and did not dissimulate that we should have gained the day, had we been better led.

Why the Maréchal Villars waited ten days to be attacked in a position so disadvantageous, instead of at once marching upon the enemies and overcoming, as he might at first easily have done, it is difficult to understand. He threw all the blame upon his wound, although it was well known that the fate of the day was decided long before he was hurt.

Although forced to retire, our men burned with eagerness to engage the enemies again. Mons had been laid siege to. Boufflers tried to make the besiegers give up the undertaking. But his men were without bread and without pay; the subaltern officers were compelled to eat the regulation bread, the general officers were reduced to the most miserable shifts, and were like the privates, without pay, oftentimes for seven or eight days running. There was no meat and no bread for the army. The common soldiers were reduced to herbs and roots for all sustenance. Under these circumstances it was found impossible to persevere in trying to save Mons. Nothing but subsistence could be thought of.

The Court had now become so accustomed to defeats that a battle lost as was Malplaquet seemed half a victory. Boufflers sent a courier to the King with an account of the event, and spoke so favorably of Villars that all the blame of the defeat fell upon himself. Villars was everywhere pitied and applauded, although he had lost an important battle, when it was in his power to beat the enemies in detail, and render them unable to undertake the siege of Mons, or any other siege. If Boufflers was indignant at this, he was still more indignant at what happened afterward. In the first dispatch he sent to the King he promised to send another as soon as possible giving full details, with propositions as to how the vacancies which had occurred in the army might be filled up. On the very evening he sent off his second dispatch, he received intelligence that the King had already taken his dispositions with respect to these vacancies, without having consulted him upon a single point. This was the first reward Boufflers received for the services he had just rendered, and that, too, from a King who had said in public that without Boufflers all was lost, and that assuredly it was God who had inspired him with the idea of going to the army. From that time Boufflers fell into a disgrace from which he never recovered. He had the courage to appear as usual at the Court; but a worm was gnawing him within and destroyed him. Oftentimes he opened his heart to me without rashness, and without passing the strict limits of his virtue; but the poniard was in his heart, and neither time nor reflection could dull its edge. He did nothing but languish afterward, yet without being confined to his bed or to his chamber, but did not live more than two years. Villars, on the contrary, was in greater favor than ever. He arrived at Court triumphant. The King made him occupy an apartment at Versailles, so that his wound might be well attended to.

What a contrast! What a difference between the services, the merit, the condition, the virtue, the situation of these two men! What inexhaustible funds of reflection! *

*It is as well to point out that the silly and ignorant, who are unable to emancipate themselves from the influence of the title of Great, usually given to Louis XIV., and who are yet candid enough to admit that in conduct and tone of thought he never rose above the level of a pious dancing master, or conscientious master of the ceremonies, usually fall back on his mysterious tact in choosing men of genius! Every page of Saint-Simon proves that imbecility, properly combined with dishonesty, was the true passport to his favor. Literature is good enough or servile enough to be grateful to him for not stifling its development. Is France so sure that it might not have done better?

CHAPTER XII.

I HAVE described in its proper place the profound fall
of M. le Duc d'Orléans and the neglect in which he
lived, out of all favor with the King, hated by Madame de Maintenon and Monseigneur, and regarded with
an unfavorable eye by the public, on account of the
scandals of his private life. I had long seen that the
only way in which he could hope to recover his position
would be to give up his mistress, Madame d'Argenton,
with whom he had been on terms of intimacy for many
years past, to the knowledge and the scandal of all the
world. I knew it would be a bold and dangerous game
to play, to try to persuade him to separate himself from
a woman he had known and loved so long; but I determined to engage in it, nevertheless, and I looked about
for some one to assist me in this enterprise. At once I
cast my eyes upon the Maréchal de Besons, who for
many long years had been the bosom friend of M. d'Orléans. He applauded the undertaking, but doubted, he
said, its success; nevertheless he promised to aid me to
the utmost of his power, and, it will be seen, was as
good as his word. For some time I had no opportunity
of accosting M. d'Orléans, and was obliged to keep my
project in abeyance, but I did not lose sight of it; and
when I saw my way clear, I took the matter in hand,
determined to strain every nerve in order to succeed.

It was just at the commencement of the year 1710,
that I first spoke to M. d'Orléans. I began by extract-
ing from him an admission of the neglect into which he
had fallen — the dislike of the King, the hatred of Monseigneur, who accused him of wishing to replace his son

in Spain; that of Madame de Maintenon, whom he had
offended by his *bon mot;* the suspicions of the public,
who talked of his chemical experiments — and then,
throwing off all fear of consequences, I said that before
he could hope to draw back his friends and the world to
him, he must reinstate himself in the favor of the King.
He appeared struck with what I had said, rose after a
profound silence, paced to and fro, and then asked, " But
how ? " Seeing the opportunity so good, I replied in a
firm and significant tone, " How ? I know well enough,
but I will never tell you; and yet it is the only thing to
do." " Ah, I understand you," said he, as though struck
with a thunderbolt; " I understand you perfectly "; and
he threw himself upon the chair at the end of the room.
There he remained some time, without speaking a word,
yet agitated and sighing, and with his eyes lowered. I
broke silence at last, by saying that the state which he
was in had touched me to the quick, and that I had determined in conjunction with the Maréchal de Besons to
speak to him upon the subject, and to propose the only
means by which he could hope to bring about a change
in his position. He considered some time, and then giving me encouragement to proceed, I entered at some
length upon the proposal I had to make to him, and left
him evidently affected by what I had said, when I thought
I had for the time gone far enough.

The next day, Thursday, January 2d, Besons, to whom
I had written, joined me; and after I had communicated
to him what had passed the previous evening, we hastened to M. d'Orléans. He received us well, and we at
once commenced an attack. In order to aid my purpose
as much as possible, I repeated to M. d'Orléans, at this
meeting, the odious reports that were in circulation
against him, viz, that he intended to repudiate his wife
forced upon him by the King, in order to marry the
Queen Dowager of Spain, and by means of her gold to
open up a path for himself to the Spanish throne; that
he intended to wait for his new wife's death, and then
marry Madame d'Argenton, to whom the genii had promised a throne; and I added, that it was very fortunate
that the Duchess d'Orléans had safely passed through

the dangers of her confinement, for already some wretches had begun to spread the saying, that he was not the son of Monsieur for nothing. (An allusion to the death of Henriette d'Angleterre.)

On hearing these words, the Duke was seized with a terror that cannot be described, and at the same time with a grief that is above expression. I took advantage of the effect my discourse had had upon him, to show how necessary it was he should make a great effort in order to win back the favor of the King and of the public. I represented to him that the only way to do this was to give up Madame d'Argenton, at once and forever, and to announce to the King that he had done so. At first he would not hear of such a step, and I was obliged to employ all my eloquence and all my firmness, too, to make him listen to reason. One great obstacle in our way was the repugnance of M. d'Orléans for his wife. He had been married, as I have described in the early part of these " Memoirs," against his will, and with no sort of affection for the woman he was given to. It was natural that he should look upon her with dislike ever since she had become his wife. I did what I could to speak in praise of Madame la Duchess d'Orléans and Besons aided me; but we did little else than waste our breath for some time. Our praises in fact irritated M. de Orléans, and to such a point, that no longer screening things or names, he told us what we should have wished not to hear, but what it was very lucky we did hear. He had suspicions, in fact, of his wife's honor; but fortunately I was able to prove clearly and decisively that those suspicions were unfounded, and I did so. The joy of M. d'Orléans upon finding he had been deceived was great indeed; and when we separated from him after midday, in order to go to dinner, I saw that a point was gained.

A little before three o'clock I returned to M. d'Orléans, whom I found alone in his cabinet with Besons. He received me with pleasure, and made me seat myself between him and the Maréchal, whom he complimented upon his diligence. Our conversation recommenced. I returned to the attack with all the arguments I could

muster, and the Maréchal supported me; but I saw with
affright that M. d'Orléans was less reduced than when we
had quitted him in the morning, and that he had sadly
taken breath during our short absence. I saw that, if we
were to succeed, we must make the best use we could of
our time, and accordingly I brought all my powers into
play in order to gain over M. d'Orléans.

Feeling that everything was now to be lost or gained,
I spoke out with all the force of which I was capable,
surprising and terrifying Maréchal Besons to such a
point, with my hardihood, that he had not a word to say
in order to aid me. When I had finished, M. d'Orléans
thanked me in a piteous tone, by which I knew the profound impression I had made upon his mind. I proposed,
while he was still shaken, that he should at once send
to Madame de Maintenon, to know when she would grant
him an audience; for he had determined to speak to her
first of his intention to give up Madame d'Argenton.
Besons seconded me; and while we were talking together,
not daring to push our point further, M. d'Orléans much
astonished us by rising, running with impetuosity to the
door, and calling aloud for his servants. One ran to him,
whom he ordered in a whisper to go to Madame de
Maintenon, to ask at what hour she would see him on
the morrow. He returned immediately, and threw himself into a chair like a man whose strength fails him and
who is at his last gasp. Uncertain as to what he had
just done, I asked him if he had sent to Madame de
Maintenon. "Yes, Monsieur," said he, in a tone of
despair. Instantly I started toward him, and thanked
him with all the contentment and all the joy imaginable.
This terrible interview, for the struggle we had all gone
through was very great, was soon after brought to a
close, and Besons and myself went our way, congratulat-
ing each other on the success of this day's labor.

On the next day, Friday, the 3d of January, I saw M.
d'Orléans as he preceded the King to mass, and in my
impatience I approached him, and speaking in a low tone,
asked him if he had seen "that woman." I did not dare
to mention names just then. He replied "yes," but in
so lackadaisical a tone that I feared he had seen her to

effect, and I asked him if he had spoken to her. Upon
receiving another "yes," like the other, my emotion redoubled. "But have you told her all?" I said. "Yes,"
he replied, "I have told her all." "And are you content?" said I. "Nobody could be more so," he replied;
"I was nearly an hour with her, she was very much
surprised and ravished."

I saw M. d'Orléans under better circumstances at
another period of the day, and then I learned from him
that since meeting me he had spoken to the King also,
and told him all. "Ah, Monsieur," cried I, with transport, "how I love you!" and advancing warmly toward
him, I added, "How glad I am to see you at last delivered; how did you bring this to pass?" "I mistrusted
myself so much," replied he, "and was so violently
agitated after speaking to Madame de Maintenon, that I
feared to run the risk of pausing all the morning; so,
immediately after mass I spoke to the King, and"—here,
overcome by his grief, his voice faltered, and he burst
into sighs, into tears, and into sobs. I retired into a
corner. A moment after Besons entered: the spectacle
and the profound silence astonished him. He lowered
his eyes, and advanced but little. At last we gently
approached each other. I told him that M. d'Orléans
had conquered himself, and had spoken to the King.
The Maréchal was so bewildered with surprise and joy
that he remained for some moments speechless and
motionless: then running toward M. d'Orléans, he thanked
him, felicitated him, and wept for very joy. M. d'Orléans
was cruelly agitated, now maintaining a ferocious silence,
and now bursting into a torrent of sighs, sobs, and tears.
He said at last that Madame de Maintenon had been
extremely surprised with the resolution he had taken,
and at the same time delighted. She assured him that
it would put him on better terms than ever with the
King, and that Madame d'Argenton should be treated
with every consideration. I pressed M. d'Orléans to let
us know how the King had received him. He replied
that the King had appeared very much surprised, but
had spoken coldly. I comforted him for this disappointment by assuring him that the King's coldness arose

only from his astonishment, and that in the end all would
be well.

It would be impossible to describe the joy felt by Besons and myself at seeing our labors brought to this satisfactory point.   I knew I should make many enemies
when the part I had taken in influencing M. d'Orléans
to give up Madame d'Argenton came to be known, as it
necessarily would; but I felt I had done rightly, and left
the consequences to Providence. · Madame la Duchess
d'Orléans showed me the utmost gratitude for what I had
done.   She exhibited, too, so much intelligence, good
sense, and ability, in the conversation I had with her,
that I determined to spare no pains to unite her husband
to her more closely; being firmly persuaded that he would
nowhere find a better counselor than in her.   The surprise of the whole Court, when it became known that M.
d'Orléans had at last separated himself from Madame
d'Argenton, was great indeed.   It was only equaled by
the vexation of those who were opposed to him.   Of
course in this matter I was not spared.   For several days
nothing was spoken of but this rupture, and everywhere
I was pointed out as the author of it, Besons being
scarcely alluded to.   I parried the thrusts made at me as
well as I could, as much for the purpose of leaving all
the honor to M. d'Orléans, as for the purpose of avoiding the anger of those who were annoyed with me; and
also from a just fear of showing that I had too much influence over the mind of a prince not without faults, and
who could not always be led.

As for Madame d'Argenton, she received the news that
her reign was over with all the consternation, rage, and
despair that might have been expected.   Mademoiselle de
Chausseraye was sent by Madame de Maintenon to announce the ill news to her.   When Mademoiselle de
Chausseraye arrived at Madame d'Argenton's house, Madame d'Argenton was out; she had gone to supper with
the Princess de Rohan.   Mademoiselle de Chausseraye
waited until she returned, and then broke the matter to
her gently, and after much preamble and circumlocution,
as though she were about to announce the death of some
one.   The tears, the cries, the howlings of Madame d'Ar-

genton filled the house, and announced to all the domestics that the reign of felicity was at an end there. After a long silence on the part of Mademoiselle de Chausseraye, she spoke her best in order to appease the poor lady. She represented to her the delicacy and liberality of the arrangements M. d'Orléans had made in her behalf. In the first place she was free to live in any part of the realm except Paris and its appanages. In the next place he assured to her forty-five thousand livres a year, nearly all the capital of which would belong to the son he had had by her, whom he had recognized and made legitimate, and who has since become grandee of Spain, grand prieur of France, and general of the Galleys (for the best of all conditions in France is to have none at all, and to be a bastard). Lastly he undertook to pay all her debts up to the day of the rupture, so that she should not be importuned by any creditor, and allowed her to retain her jewelery, her plate, her furniture — worth altogether about four hundred thousand livres. His liberality amounted to a total of about two million livres, which I thought prodigious.

Madame d'Argenton, in despair at first, became more tractable as she learned the provisions which had been made for her, and the delicacy with which she was treated. She remained four days in Paris, and then returned to her father's house near Port-Sainte-Maxence, the Chevalier d'Orléans, her son, remaining at the Palais Royale. The King, after his first surprise had worn away, was in the greatest joy at the rupture; and testified his gratification to M. d'Orléans, whom he treated better and better every day. Madame de Maintenon did not dare not to contribute a little at first; and in this the Prince felt the friendship of the Jesuits, whom he had contrived to attach to him. The Duchess de Bourgogne did marvels of her own accord; and the Duc de Bourgogne, also, being urged by M. de Beauvilliers. Monseigneur alone remained irritated, on account of the Spanish affair.

I must here mention the death of M. le Duc. He was engaged in a trial which was just about to be pleaded. He had for some time suffered from a strange disease, a mixture of apoplexy and epilepsy, which he concealed so carefully, that he drove away one of his servants for speaking of it to his fellows. For some time he had had a continual headache. This state troubled the gladness he felt at being delivered from his troublesome father and brother-in-law. One evening he was riding in his carriage, returning from a visit to the Hotel de Coislin, without torches, and with only one servant behind, when he felt so ill that he drew the string, and made his lackey get up to tell him whether his mouth was not all on one side. This was not the case, but he soon lost speech and consciousness after having requested to be taken in privately to the Hotel de Condé. They there put him to bed. Priests and doctors came. But he only made horrible faces, and died about four o'clock in the morning.

Madame la Duchess did not lose her presence of mind, and, while her husband was dying, took steps to secure her future fortune. Meanwhile she managed to cry a little, but nobody believed in her grief. As for M. le Duc, I have already mentioned some anecdotes of him that exhibit his cruel character. He was a marvelously little man, short, without being fat. A dwarf of Madame la Princess was said to be the cause. He was of a livid yellow, nearly always looked furious, and was ever so proud, so audacious, that it was difficult to get used to him. His cruelty and ferocity were so extreme that people avoided him, and his pretended friends would not invite him to join in any merriment. They avoided him; he ran after them to escape from solitude, and would sometimes burst upon them during their jovial repasts, reproach them with turning a cold shoulder to him, and change their merriment to desolation.

After the death of M. le Duc, a grand discussion on precedence at the after-suppers, set on foot by the proud Duchess d'Orléans, was, after an elaborate examination by the King, brought to a close. The King ordered his determination to be kept secret until he formally declared it. It is necessary to set forth in a few words the mechanism of the after-suppers every day. The King, on leaving table, stopped less than a half quarter of an hour with his back leaning against the balustrade

of his chamber. He there found in a circle all the
ladies who had been at his supper, and who came there
to wait for him a little before he left table, except the
ladies who sat, who came out after him, and who, in
the suite of the princes and the princesses who had supped
with him, advanced one by one and made him a curtsy,
and filled up the remainder of the standing circle; for a
space was always left for them by the other ladies. The
men stood behind. The King amused himself by observing the dresses, the countenances, and the gracefulness
of the ladies' courtesies, said a word to the princes and
princesses who had supped with him, and who closed the
circle near him on either hand, then bowed to the ladies
on right and left, bowed once or twice more as he went
away, with a grace and majesty unparalleled, spoke sometimes, but very rarely, to some lady in passing, entered
the first cabinet, where he gave the order, and then advanced to the second cabinet, the doors from the first to
the second always remaining open. There he placed
himself in a *fauteuil*, Monsieur, while he was there, in
another; the Duchess de Bourgogne, Madame (but only
after the death of Monsieur), the Duchess de Berry
(after her marriage), the three bastard daughters, and
Madame du Maine (when she was at Versailles), on stools
on each side. Monseigneur, the Duc de Bourgogne, the
Duc de Berry, the Duc d'Orléans, the two bastards, M.
le Duc (as the husband of Madame la Duchess), and
afterward the two sons of M. du Maine, when they had
grown a little, and D'Antin, came afterward, all standing. It was the object of the Duchess d'Orléans to
change this order, and make her daughters take precedence of the wives of the princes of the blood; but the
King declared against her. When he made the public
announcement of his decision, the Duc d'Orléans took
the opportunity of alluding to a marriage which would
console him for everything. " I should think so," replied the King, dryly, and with a bitter and mocking
smile.

CHAPTER XIII.

Proposed Marriage of Mademoiselle — My Intrigues to Bring It About
— The Duchess de Bourgogne and Other Allies — The Attack Begun — Progress of the Intrigue — Economy at Marly — The Marriage
Agreed Upon — Scene at St. Cloud — Horrible Reports — The Marriage — Madame de Saint-Simon — Strange Character of the Duchess de Berry.

IT WAS the desire of the Duc and Duchess d'Orléans to
marry Mademoiselle (their daughter) to the Duke de
Berry (third son of Monseigneur, and consequently
brother of the Duke de Bourgogne and of the King of
Spain). There were many obstacles in the way — partly
the state of public affairs — partly the fact that the
King, though seemingly, was not really quite reconciled —
partly the recollection of that cruel *bon mot* in Spain —
partly the fact that Monseigneur would naturally object
to marry his favorite son with the daughter of a man
toward whom he always testified hatred in the most indecent manner. The recent union between Madame de
Maintenon, Mademoiselle Choin, and Monseigneur was
also a great obstacle. In fact after what M. le Duc
d'Orléans had been accused of in Spain, with his abili-
ties and talents it seemed dangerous to make him the
father-in-law of M. le Duc de Berry.

For my part I passionately desired the marriage of
Mademoiselle, although I saw that all tended to the
marriage of Mademoiselle de Bourbon, daughter of Madame la Duchess, in her place. I had many reasons,
private and public, for acting against the latter marriage;
but it was clear that unless very vigorous steps were
taken it would fall like a millstone upon my head, crush
me, and wound the persons to whom I was attached.
M. le Duc d'Orléans and Madame la Duchess d'Orléans
were immersed in the deepest indolence. They desired
but did not act. I went to them and explained the state

of the case — pointed out the danger of Madame la Duchess — excited their pride, their jealousy, their spite. Will it be believed that it was necessary to put all this machinery in motion ? At last, by working on them by the most powerful motives, I made them attend to their own interests. The natural but extreme laziness of the Duchess d'Orléans gave way this time, but less to ambition than to the desire of defeating a sister who was so inimical to her. We next concerted how we should make use of M. d'Orléans himself.

That Prince, with all his wit and his passion for Mademoiselle — which had never weakened since her birth — was like a motionless beam, which stirred only in obedience to our redoubled efforts, and who remained so to the conclusion of this great business. I often reflected on the causes of this incredible conduct; and was led to suppose that the knowledge of the irremediable nature of what had taken place in Spain was the rein that restrained him. However this may have been, I was throughout obliged to use main force to bring him to activity. I determined to form and direct a powerful cabal in order to bring my views to pass. The first person of whom it was necessary to make sure was the Duchess de Bourgogne. That Princess had many reasons for the preference of Mademoiselle over Mademoiselle de Bourbon (daughter of Madame la Duchess). She knew the King perfectly; and could not be ignorant of the power of novelty over his mind, of which power she had herself made a happy experiment. What she had to fear was another herself — I mean a princess on the same terms with the King as she was, who, being younger than she, would amuse him by new childish playfulness no longer suited to her age, and yet which she (the Duchess) was still obliged to employ. The very contrast of her own untimely childishness, with a childishness so much more natural, would injure her. The new favorite would, moreover, not have a husband to support; for the Duc de Berry was already well liked. The Duc de Bourgogne on the contrary, since the affair of Flanders, had fallen into disgrace with his father, Monseigneur; and his scruples, his preciseness, his retired life, devoted to

literal compliance with the rules of devotion, contrasted
unfavorably with the free life of his younger brother.

The present and the future — whatever was important
in life — were therefore at stake with Madame la Duchess
de Bourgogne; and yet her great duty to herself was
perpetually in danger of being stifled by the fictitious
and petty duties of daily life. It was necessary to stim-
ulate her. She felt these things in general; and that it
was necessary that her sister-in-law should be a princess,
neither able nor willing to give her umbrage, and over
whom she should be mistress. But in spite of her wit
and sense, she was not capable of feeling in a sufficiently
lively manner of herself all the importance of these
things, amid the effervescence of her youth, the occupation of her successive duties, the private and general
favor she seemed to enjoy, the greatness of a rank in
expectation of a throne, the round of amusements which
dissipated her mind and her days: gentle, light, easy —
perhaps too easy. I felt, however, that from the effect
of these considerations upon her I should derive the
greatest assistance, on account of the influence she could
exert upon the King, and still more on Madame de
Maintenon, both of whom loved her exceedingly; and I
felt all that the Duchess d'Orléans would have neither
the grace nor the fire necessary to stick it in deep
enough — on account of her great interest in the matter.

I influenced the Duchess de Villeroy and Madame de
Lévi, who could work on the Duchess, and also Madame
d'O; obtained the indirect assistance of M. du Maine —
and by representing to the Ducs de Chevreuse and de
Beauvilliers, that if M. de Berry married Mademoiselle
de Bourbon, hatred would arise between him and his
brother, and great danger to the state, enlisted them
also on my side. I knew that the Duc de Berry was a
fort that could only be carried by mine and assault.
Working still further, I obtained the concurrence of the
Jesuits; and made the Père de Trevoux our partisan.
Nothing is indifferent to the Jesuits. They became a
powerful instrument. As a last ally I obtained the co-
operation of the Maréchal de Boufflers. Such were the

machines that my friendship for those to whom I was attached, my hatred for Madame la Duchess, my care of my present and future situation, enabled me to discover, to set going, with an exact and compassed movement, a precise agreement, and the strength of a lever — which the space of one Lent commenced and perfected — all whose movements, embarrassments, and progress in their divers lines I knew; and which I regularly wound up in reciprocal cadence every day!

Toward the end of the Lent, the Duchess de Bourgogne, having sounded the King and Madame de Maintenon, had found the latter well disposed, and the former without any particular objection. One day that Mademoiselle had been taken to see the King at the apartments of Madame de Maintenon, where Monseigneur happened to be, the Duchess de Bourgogne praised her, and when she had gone away, ventured, with that freedom and that predetermined impulsiveness and gayety which she sometimes made use of, to say: "What an excellent wife for M. le Duc de Berry!" This expression made Monseigneur redden with anger, and exclaim, "that would be an excellent method of recompensing the Duc d'Orléans for his conduct in Spain!" When he had said these words he hastily left the company, all very much astonished; for no one expected a person seemingly so indifferent and so measured to come out so strongly. The Duchess de Bourgogne, who had only spoken so to feel the way with Monseigneur in presence of the King, was bold and clever to the end. Turning with a bewildered look toward Madame de Maintenon, "My Aunt," quoth she to her, "have I said something foolish?" The King, piqued, answered for Madame de Maintenon, and said, warmly, that if Madame la Duchess was working upon Monseigneur she would have to deal with HIM. Madame de Maintenon adroitly envenomed the matter by wondering at a vivacity so uncommon with Monseigneur, and said that if Madame la Duchess had that much of influence, she would soon make him do other things of more consequence. The conversation, interrupted in various ways and renewed, advanced with emotion, and in the midst of reflections that did more injury to Mademoiselle de Bourbon than the friendship of Monseigneur for Madame la Duchess could serve her.

When I learned this adventure, I saw that it was necessary to attack Monseigneur by piquing the King against Madame la Duchess, and making him fear the influence of that Princess on Monseigneur and through Monseigneur on himself; that no opportunity should be lost to impress on the King the fear of being governed and kept in pupilage by his children; that it was equally important to frighten Madame de Maintenon, and show her the danger she was in from the influence of Monseigneur. I worked on the fears of the Duchess de Bourgogne, by Madame de Villeroy and de Lévi; on the Duc de Bourgogne, by M. de Beauvilliers; on Madame de Maintenon, by the Maréchal de Boufflers; on the King himself, by Père Tellier; and all these batteries succeeded.

In order not to hurry matters too much, I took a turn to La Ferte, and then came back to Marly just as the King arrived. Here I had a little alarm, which did not, however, discourage me. I learned, in fact, that one day the Duchess de Bourgogne, urged perhaps rather too much on the subject of Mademoiselle by Madame d'O, and somewhat annoyed, had shown an inclination for a foreign marriage. Would to God that such a marriage could have been brought about! I should always have preferred it, but there were many reasons to render it impossible.

On my arrival at Marly, I found everything in trouble there: the King so chagrined that he could not hide it—although usually a master of himself and of his face; the Court believing that some new disaster had happened which would unwillingly be declared. Four or five days passed in this way; at last it became known what was in the wind. The King, informed that Paris and all the public were murmuring loudly about the expenses of Marly—at a time when it was impossible to meet the most indispensable claims of a necessary and unfortunate war—was more annoyed this time than on any other occasion, although he had often received the same warnings. Madame de Maintenon had the greatest difficulty to hinder him from returning straight to Versailles.

The upshot was that the King declared with a sort of bitter joy, that he would no longer feed the ladies at Marly; that for the future he would dine alone, simply, as at Versailles; that he would sup every day at a table for sixteen with his family, and that the spare places should be occupied by ladies invited in the morning; that the princesses of his family should each have a table for the ladies they brought with them; and that Madames Voysin and Desmarets should each have one for the ladies who did not choose to eat in their own rooms. He added bitterly, that by making retrenchments at Marly he should not spend more there than at Versailles, so that he could go there when he pleased without being exposed to the blame of any one. He deceived himself from one end of this business to the other, but nobody but himself was deceived, if indeed HE was in any other way but in expecting to deceive the world. The truth is, that no change was made at Marly, except in name. The same expenses went on. The enemies insultingly ridiculed these retrenchments. The King's subjects did not cease to complain.

About this time an invitation to Marly having been obtained by Madame la Duchess for her daughters, Mademoiselles de Bourbon and de Charolois, the King offered one to Mademoiselle. This offer was discussed before the Duc and Duchess d'Orléans and me. We at last resolved to leave Mademoiselle at Versailles; and not to be troubled by seeing Mademoiselle de Bourbon passing her days in the same salon, often at the same play table with the Duc de Berry making herself admired by the Court, fluttering round Monseigneur, and accustoming the eye of the King to her. We knew that these trifles would not bring about a marriage; and it was still more important not to give up Mademoiselle to the malignity of the Court, to exposure, and complaints, from which it might not always be possible to protect her.

But I had felt that it was necessary to act vigorously, and pressed the Duc d'Orléans to speak to the King To my surprise he suddenly heaped up objections, derived from the public disasters, with which a princely marriage would contrast disagreeably. The Duchess d'Orléans was strangely staggered by this admission; it only angered me. I answered by repeating all my arguments. At last he gave way, and agreed to write to the King. Here, again, I had many difficulties to overcome, and was obliged, in fact, to write the letter myself, and dictate it to him. He made one or two changes; and at last signed and sealed it. But I had the greatest difficulty yet in inciting him to give it to the King. I had to follow him, to urge him, to pique him, almost to push him into the presence. The King received the letter very graciously; it had its effect; and the marriage was resolved on.

When the preliminaries were settled, the Duc and Duchess d'Orléans began to show their desire that Madame de Saint-Simon should be lady of honor to their daughter when she had become the Duchess de Berry. I was far from flattered by this distinction, and refused as best I might. Madame de Saint-Simon went to have an audience of the Duchess de Bourgogne, and asked not to be appointed; but her objections were not listened to, or listened to with astonishment. Meanwhile I endeavored to bring about a reconciliation of the Duc d'Orléans with La Choin; but utterly failed. La Choin positively refused to have anything to do with the Duke and Duchess. I was much embarrassed to communicate this news to them, to whom I was attached. It was necessary, however, to do so. I hastened to Saint Cloud and found the Duke and Duchess d'Orléans at table with Mademoiselle and some ladies in a most delightful menagerie, adjoining the railing of the avenue near the village, with a charming pleasure garden attached to it. All this belonged, under the name of Mademoiselle, to Madame de Maré, her governess. I sat down and chatted with them; but the impatience of the Duc d'Orléans to learn the news could not be checked. He asked me if I was very satisfied. " Middling," I replied, not to spoil his dinner; but he rose at once and took me into the garden. He was much affected to hear of the ill success of my negotiation; and returned downcast to table. I took the first opportunity to blame his impatience, and the facility with which he allowed the impressions he received to appear. Always in extreme, he said he cared not; and talked wildly of planting cabbages — talk in which he indulged often without meaning anything.

Soon after, M. le Duc d'Orléans went aside with Mademoiselle, and I found myself placed accidentally near Madame de Fontaine-Martel. She was a great friend of mine, and much attached to M. d'Orléans; and it was by her means that I had become friendly with the Duke. She felt at once that something was going on; and did not doubt that the marriage of Mademoiselle was on the carpet. She said so, but I did not answer, yet without assuming an air of reserve that would have convinced her. Taking her text from the presence of M. le Duc d'Orléans with Mademoiselle, she said to me confidentially, that it would be well to hasten this marriage if it were possible, because all sorts of horrible things were invented to prevent it; and without waiting to be too much pressed, she told me that the most abominable stories were in circulation as to the friendship of father and daughter. The hair of my head stood on end. I now felt more heavily than ever with what demons we had to do; and how necessary it was to hurry on matters. For this reason, after we had walked about a good deal after dark, I again spoke with M. d'Orléans, and told him that if, before the end of this voyage to Marly, he did not carry the declaration of his daughter's marriage, it would never take place.

I persuaded him; and left him more animated and encouraged than I had seen him. He amused himself I know not in what other part of the house. I then talked a little with Madame de Maré, my relation and friend, until I was told that Madame de Fontaine-Martel wished to speak to me in the *château*. When I went there I was taken to the cabinet of the Duchess d'Orléans, when I learned that she had just been made acquainted with the abominable reports spread against her husband and daughter. We deplored together the misfortune of having to do with such furies. The Duchess protested that there was not even any seeming in favor of these calumnies. The Duke had ever tenderly loved his daughter from the age of two years, when he was nearly driven to despair

by a serious illness she had, during which he watched her
night and day; and this tenderness had gone on increasing day by day, so that he loved her more than his son.
We agreed that it would be cruel, wicked, and dangerous
to tell M. d'Orléans what was said.

At length the decisive blow was struck. The King had
an interview with Monseigneur; and told him he had
determined on the marriage, begging him to make up
his mind as soon as possible. The declaration was soon
made. What must have been the state of Madame la
Duchess! I never knew what took place in her house at
this strange moment; and would have dearly paid for a
hiding place behind the tapestry. As for Monseigneur,
as soon as his original repugnance was overcome, and he
saw that it was necessary to comply, he behaved very
well. He received the Duc and Duchess d'Orléans very
well, and kissed her and drank their health and that of
all the family cheerfully. They were extremely delighted
and surprised.

My next visit to Saint Cloud was very different from
that in which I reported the failure of my endeavors with
Mademoiselle Choin. I was received in triumph before
a large company. To my surprise, Mademoiselle, as soon
as I appeared, ran toward me, kissed me on both cheeks,
took me by the hand, and led me into the orangery. Then
she thanked me, and admitted that her father had constantly kept her acquainted with all the negotiations as
they went on. I could not help blaming his easiness and
imprudence. She mingled all with testimonies of the
most lively joy; and I was surprised by her grace, her
eloquence, the dignity and the propriety of the terms she
used. I learned an immense number of things in this
half-hour's conversation. Afterward Mademoiselle took
the opportunity to say and do all manner of graceful
things to Madame de Saint-Simon.

The Duchess d'Orléans now returned once more to the
charge, in order to persuade my wife to be *dame d'honneur* to her daughter. I refused as firmly as I could. But
soon after the King himself named Madame de Saint-
Simon; and when the Duchess de Bourgogne suggested
a doubt of her acceptance, exclaimed, almost piqued:

"Refuse! O no! not when she learns that it is my desire." In fact, I soon received so many menacing warnings that I was obliged to give in; and Madame de Saint-Simon received the appointment. This was made publicly known by the King, who up to that very morning remained doubtful whether he would be met by a refusal or not; and who, as he was about to speak, looked at me with a smile that was meant to please and warn me to be silent. Madame de Saint-Simon learned the news with tears. She was excellently well received by the King, and complimented agreeably by Madame de Maintenon.

The marriage took place with the usual ceremonies. The Duc de Beauvilliers and Madame de Saint-Simon drew the curtains of the couple when they went to bed; and laughed together at being thus employed. The King, who had given a very mediocre present of diamonds to the new Duchess de Berry, gave nothing to the Duc de Berry. The latter had so little money that he could not play during the first days of the voyage to Marly. The Duchess de Bourgogne told this to the King, who feeling the state in which he himself was, said that he had only five hundred pistoles to give him. He gave them with an excuse on the misfortunes of the time, because the Duchess de Bourgogne thought with reason that a little was better than nothing, and that it was insufferable not to be able to play.

Madame de Maré was now set at liberty. The place of Dame d'Atours was offered to her; but she advanced many reasons for not accepting it, and on being pressed, refused with an obstinacy that surprised everyone. We were not long in finding out the cause of her obstinate unwillingness to remain with Madame la Duchess de Berry. The more that Princess allowed people to see what she was — and she never concealed herself — the more we saw that Madame de Maré was in the right; and the more we admired the miracle of care and prudence which had prevented anything from coming to light; and the more we felt how blindly people act in what they desire with the most eagerness, and achieve with much trouble and much joy; and the more we deplored having succeeded in an affair which, so far from having undertaken and carried out as I did, I should have traversed with still greater zeal, even if Mademoiselle de Bourbon had profited thereby without knowing it, if I had known half a quarter — what do I say? the thousandth part — of what we unhappily witnessed! I shall say no more for the present; and as I go on, I shall only say what cannot be concealed; and I say thus much so soon merely because the strange things that soon happened began to develop themselves a little during this first voyage to Marly.

CHAPTER XIV.

Birth of Louis XV.—The Maréchal de la Meilleraye—Saint Ruth's Cudgel—The Cardinal de Bouillon's Desertion from France—Anecdotes of His Audacity.

ON SATURDAY, the 15th of February, the King was waked up at seven o'clock in the morning, an hour earlier than usual, because Madame la Duchess de Bourgogne was in the pains of labor. He dressed himself diligently in order to go to her. She did not keep him waiting long. At three minutes and three seconds after eight o'clock, she brought into the world a Duc d'Anjou, who is the King Louis XV., at present reigning, which caused a great joy. This Prince was soon after sprinkled by Cardinal de Janson in the chamber where he was born, and then carried upon the knees of the Duchess de Ventadour in the sedan chair of the King into the King's apartments, accompanied by the Maréchal de Boufflers and by the bodyguards with officers. A little while after La Vrillière carried to him the *cordon bleu*, and all the Court went to see him, two things which much displeased his brother, who did not scruple to show it. Madame de Saint-Simon, who was in the chamber of Madame la Dauphine, was by chance one of the first who saw this newborn Prince. The *accouchement* passed over very well.

About this time died the Maréchale de la Meilleraye, aged eighty-eight years. She was the paternal aunt of the Maréchal de Villeroy and the Duc de Brissac, his brother-in-law. It was she who unwittingly put that cap on MM. de Brissac, which they have ever since worn in their arms, and which has been imitated. She was walking in a picture gallery of her ancestors one day with her niece, a lively, merry person, whom she obliged to salute and be polite to each portrait, and who in pleasant revenge persuaded her that one of the said portraits wore a cap which proved him to be an Italian prince. She swallowed this, and had the cap introduced into her arms, despite her family, who are now obliged to keep it, but who always call it, "My Aunt's cap." On another occasion, people were speaking in her presence of the death of the Chevalier de Savoie, brother of the Comte de Soissons, and of the famous Prince Eugène, who died very young, very suddenly, very debauched, and full of benefices. The talk became religious. She listened some time, and then, with a profound look of conviction, said: "For my part, I am persuaded that God will think twice about damning a man of such high birth as that!" This caused a burst of laughter, but nothing could make her change her opinion. Her vanity was cruelly punished. She used to affect to apologize for having married the Maréchal de la Meilleraye. After his death, being in love with Saint Ruth, her page, she married him; but took care not to disclose her marriage for fear of losing her distinction at Court. Saint Ruth was a very honorable gentleman, very poor, tall, and well made, whom everybody knew; extremely ugly — I don't know whether he became so after his marriage. He was a worthy man and a good soldier. But he was also a rough customer, and when his distinguished wife annoyed him he twirled his cudgel and belabored her soundly. This went so far that the Maréchale, not being able to stand it any longer, demanded an audience of the King, admitted her weakness and her shame, and implored his protection. The King kindly promised to set matters to rights. He soundly rated Saint Ruth in his cabinet, and forbade him to ill treat the Maréchale. But what is bred in the bone will never get out of the flesh. The Maréchale came to make fresh complaints. The King grew angry in earnest, and threatened Saint Ruth. This kept him quiet for some time. But the habit of the stick was too powerful; and he flourished it again. The Maréchale flew as usual to the King, who, seeing that Saint Ruth was incorrigible, was good enough to send him to Guyenne under pretense of employment. Afterward he was sent to Ireland, where he was killed.

The Maréchale de la Meilleraye had been perfectly beautiful, and was full of wit. She so turned the head

of the Cardinal de Retz, that he wanted to turn everything topsy-turvy in France, in order to make himself a
necessary man and force the King to use his influence
at Rome in order to obtain a dispensation by which he
(the Cardinal) should be allowed, though a priest and a
consecrated Bishop, to marry the Maréchale de la Meilleraye while her husband was alive and she on very good
terms with him! This madness is inconceivable and yet
existed.

I have described in its place the disgrace of Cardinal
de Bouillon, and the banishment to which he was sen-
tenced. Exile did not improve him. He languished in
weariness and rage, and saw no hope that his position
would ever change. Incapable of repose, he had passed
all his long enforced leisure in a monastic war. The
monks of Cluni were his antagonists. He was constantly
bringing actions against them, which they as constantly
defended. He accused them of revolt — they accused
him of scheming. They profited by his disgrace, and
omitted nothing to shake off the yoke, which when in
favor, he had imposed upon them. These broils went
on, until at last a suit, which Cardinal de Bouillon had
commenced against the refractory monks, and which had
been carried into the Grand Council of Paris, was decided
against him, notwithstanding all the efforts he made to
obtain a contrary verdict. This was the last drop which
made the too full cup overflow, and which consummated
the resolution that Cardinal had long since had in his
head, and which he now executed.

By the terms of his exile, he was allowed to visit without restraint, his various abbeys, situated in different
parts of the realm. He took advantage of this privilege,
gave out that he was going to Normandy, but instead of
doing so, posted away to Picardy, stopped briefly at Ab-
beville, gained Arras, where he had the Abbey of Saint
Waast, thence feigning to go and see his Abbey of Vi-
gogne, he passed over into the camp of the enemy, and
threw himself into the arms of the Duke of Marlborough
and Prince Eugène. The Prince d'Auvergne, his nephew,
had deserted from France in a similar manner some time
before, as I have related in its place, and was in wait-

ing to receive the Cardinal, who was also very graciously welcomed by Prince Eugène and the Duke of Marlborough, who introduced him to the heads of the army, and lavished upon him the greatest honors.

Such a change of condition appeared very sweet to this spirit so haughty and so ulcerated, and marvelously inflated the Cardinal's courage. He recompensed his dear hosts by discourses, which were the most agreeable to them, upon the misery of France (which his frequent journeys through the provinces had placed before his eyes), upon its powerlessness to sustain the war; upon the discontent which reigned among the people; upon the exhaustion of the finances; in fine, he spared nothing that perfidy or ingratitude could suggest to flatter them and gain their favor.

No sooner had the Cardinal had time to turn round among his new friends than he wrote a letter to the King announcing his flight — a letter which was such a monstrous production of insolence, of madness, of felony, and which was written in a style so extravagant and confused that it deserves to be thus specially alluded to. In this letter, as full of absurdities, impudence, and of madness, as of words, the Cardinal, while pretending much devotion for the King, and much submission to the Church, plainly intimated that he cared for neither. Although this was as the sting of a gnat upon an elephant, the King was horribly piqued at it. He received the letter on the 24th of May, gave it the next day to D'Aguesseau, attorney-general, and ordered him to commence a suit against Cardinal de Bouillon, as guilty of felony. At the same time the King wrote to Rome, inclosing a copy of Bouillon's letter, so that it might be laid before the Pope. This letter received little approbation. People considered that the King had forgotten his dignity in writing it, it seemed so much like a justification and so little worthy of a great monarch. As for the Cardinal de Bouillon, he grew more haughty than ever. He wrote a letter upon the subject of this trial with which he was threatened, even more violent than his previous letter, and proclaimed that cardinals were not in any way amenable to secular justice, and could not be judged except by the Pope and all the sacred college.

So in fact it seemed to be; for although the Parliament commenced the trial, and issued an order of arrest against the Cardinal, they soon found themselves stopped by difficulties which arose, and by this immunity of the cardinals, which was supported by many examples. After all the fuss made, therefore, this cause fell by its own weakness, and exhaled itself, so to speak, in insensible perspiration. A fine lesson this for the most powerful princes, and calculated to teach them that if they want to be served by Rome they should favor those that are there, instead of raising their own subjects, who, out of Rome, can be of no service to the State, and who are good only to seize three or four hundred thousand livres a year in benefices, with the quarter of which an Italian would be more than recompensed. A French cardinal in France is the friend of the Pope, but the enemy of the King, the Church and the State; a tyrant very often to the clergy and the ministers, at liberty to do what he likes without ever being punished for anything.

As nothing could be done in this way against the Cardinal, other steps were taken. The fraudulent "Genealogical History of the House of Auvergne," which I have previously alluded to, was suppressed by royal edict, and orders given that all the copies of it should be seized. Baluze, who had written it, was deprived of his chair of Professor of the Royal College, and driven out of the realm. A large quantity of copies of this edict were printed and publicly distributed. The little patrimony that Cardinal de Bouillon had not been able to carry away, was immediately confiscated: the temporality of his benefices had been already seized, and on the 7th of July appeared a declaration from the King, which, depriving the Cardinal of all his advowsons, distributed them to the bishops of the dioceses in which those advowsons were situated.

These blows were very sensibly felt by the other Bouillons, but it was no time for complaint. The Cardinal himself became more enraged than ever. Even up to this time he had kept so little within bounds that he had pontifically officiated in the church of Tournai at the *Te Deum* for the taking of Douai (by the enemies); and from that town (Tournai), where he had fixed his residence, he wrote a long letter to M. de Beauvais, bishop of the place, when it yielded, and who would not sing the *Te Deum*, exhorting him to return to Tournai and submit to the new rule. Some time after this, that is to say, toward the end of the year, he was guilty of even greater presumption. The Abbey of Saint Arnaud in Flanders, had just been given by the King to Cardinal La Trémoille, who had been confirmed in his possession by bulls from the Pope. Since then the abbey had fallen into the power of the enemy. Upon this, Cardinal de Bouillon caused himself to be elected abbot by a minority of the monks and in spite of the opposition of the others. It was curious to see this dutiful son of Rome, who had declared in his letter to the King, that he thought of nothing except the dignity of the King, and how he could best serve God and the church, thus elect himself in spite of the bulls of the Pope, in spite of the orders of the King, and enjoy by force the revenues of the abbey, protected solely by heretics!

But I have in the above recital alluded to the taking of Douai: this reminds me that I have got to speak of our military movements, our losses, and our victories, of this year. In Flanders and in Spain they were of some importance, and had better, perhaps, have a chapter or more to themselves.

CHAPTER XV.

THE King, who had made numberless promotions, appointed this year the same generals to the same armies. Villars was chosen for Flanders, as before. Having arrived at the very summit of favor, he thought he might venture, for the first time in his life, to bring a few truths before the King. He did nothing then but represent to the ministers, nay, even to the King and Madame de Maintenon themselves, the wretched state of our magazines and our garrisons; the utter absence of all provision for the campaign, and the piteous condition of the troops and their officers, without money and without pay. This was new language in the mouth of Villars, who hitherto had owed all his success to the smiling, rose-tinted account he had given of everything. It was the frequency and the hardihood of his falsehoods in this respect that made the King and Madame de Maintenon look upon him as their sole resource; for he never said anything disagreeable, and never found difficulties anywhere. Now that he had raised this fatal curtain, the aspect appeared so hideous to them, that they found it easier to fly into a rage than to reply. From that moment they began to regard Villars with other eyes. Finding that he spoke now the language which everybody spoke, they began to look upon him as the world had always looked upon him, — to find him ridiculous, silly, impudent, lying, insupportable; to reproach themselves with having elevated him from nothing, so rapidly and so enormously; they began to shun him, to put him aside, to make him perceive what they thought, and to let others perceive it also.

10

Villars in his turn was frightened. He saw the prospect of losing what he had gained, and of sinking into hopeless disgrace. With the effrontery that was natural to him, he returned therefore to his usual flatteries, artifices and deceits; laughed at all dangers and inconveniences, as having resources in himself against everything! The coarseness of this variation was as plain as possible; but the difficulty of choosing another general was equally plain, and Villars thus got out of the quagmire. He set forth for the frontier, therefore, in his coach, and traveling easy stages, on account of his wound, arrived in due time at the army.

Neither Prince Eugène nor the Duke of Marlborough wished for peace; their object was, the first, from personal vengeance against the King, and a desire to obtain a still greater reputation; the second, to get rich, for ambition was the prominent passion of one, and avarice of the other — their object was, I say, to enter France, and profiting by the extreme weakness and straitened state of our troops and of our places, to push their conquests as far as possible.

As for the King, stung by his continual losses, he wished passionately for nothing so much as a victory, which should disturb the plans of the enemies, and deliver him from the necessity of continuing the sad and shameful negotiations for peace he had set on foot at Gertruydemberg. But the enemies were well posted, and Villars had imprudently lost a good opportunity of engaging them. All the army had noticed this fault; he had been warned in time by several general officers, and by the Maréchal de Montesquieu, but he would not believe them. He did not dare to attack the enemies now, after having left them leisure to make all their dispositions. The army cried aloud against so capital a fault. Villars answered with his usual effrontery. He had quarreled with his second in command, the Maréchal de Montesquieu, and now knew not what to do.

In this crisis, no engagement taking place, the King thought it fitting to send Berwick into Flanders to act as mediator, even, to some extent, as dictator to the army. He was ordered to bring back an account of all things, so that it might be seen whether a battle could or could not be fought.

I think I have already stated who Berwick was; but I will here add a few more words about him to signalize his prodigious and rapid advancement.

We were in the golden age of bastards, and Berwick was a man who had reason to think so. Bastard of James II., of England, he had arrived in France, at the age of eighteen, with that monarch, after the Revolution of 1688. At twenty-two he was made lieutenant general, and served as such in Flanders, without having passed through any other rank. At thirty-three he commanded in chief in Spain with a patent of general. At thirty-four he was made, on account of his victory at Almanza, grandee of Spain, and chevalier of the Golden Fleece. He continued to command in chief until February, 1706, when he was made maréchal of France, being then not more than thirty-six years old. He was an English duke, and although as such he had no rank in France, the King had awarded it to him, as to all who came over with James. This was making a rapid fortune with a vengeance, under a King who regarded people of thirty odd as children, but who thought no more of the ages of bastards than of those of the gods.

For more than a year past Berwick had coveted to be made duke and peer. But he could not obtain his wish. Now, however, that he was to be sent into Flanders for the purpose I have just described, it seemed a good opportunity to try again. He did try, and was successful. He was made duke and peer. He had been twice married. By his first wife he had had a son. By his second several sons and daughters. Will it be believed that he was hardy enough to propose, and that we were weak enough to accord to him, that his son of the first bed should be formally excluded from the letters patent of duke and peer, and that those of the second bed should alone be entered there? Yet so it was. Berwick was, in respect to England, like the Jews who await for the Messiah. He coaxed himself always with the hope of a revolution in England, which should put the Stuarts on the throne again, and reinstate him in his wealth and honors. He was son of the sister of the Duke of Marlborough, by which general he was much loved, and with whom, by permission of the King, and of King James, he kept up a secret intercourse, of which all three were the dupes, but which enabled Berwick to maintain other intercourses in England, and to establish his batteries there, hoping thus for his reinstatement even under the government established. This explains his motive for the arrangement he made in the letters patent. He wished his eldest son to succeed to his English dukedom and his English estates; to make the second duke and peer of France, and the third grandee of Spain. Three sons hereditarily elevated to the three chief dignities of the three chief realms in Europe, it must be agreed was not bad work for a man to have achieved at fifty years of age! But Berwick failed in his English projects. Do what he could all his life to court the various ministers who came from England, he never could succeed in re-establishing himself.

The scandal was great at the complaisance of the King in consenting to a family arrangement, by which a cadet was put over the head of his elder brother; but the time of the monsters had arrived. Berwick bought an estate that he created under the name of FITZ-JAMES. The King, who allowed him to do so, was shocked by the name; and, in my presence, asked Berwick the meaning of it; he, without any embarrassment, thus explained it:

The Kings of England, in legitimatizing their children, give them a name and arms, which pass to their posterity. The name varies. Thus the Duke of Richmond, bastard of Charles II., had the name of "Lennox;" the Dukes of Cleveland and of Grafton, by the same King, that of "Fitz-Roi," which means "son of the king;" in fine, the Duke of Berwick had the name of "Fitz-James;" so that his family name for his posterity is thus "Son of James;" as a name, it is so ridiculous in French, that nobody could help laughing at it, or being astonished at the scandal of imposing it in English upon France.

Berwick, having thus obtained his recompense beforehand, started off for Flanders, but not until he had seen everything signed and sealed and delivered in due form.

He found the enemy so advantageously placed, and so well prepared, that he had no difficulty in subscribing to the common opinion of the general officers, that an attack could no longer be thought of. He gathered up all the opinions he could, and then returned to Court, having been only about three weeks absent. His report dismayed the King, and those who penetrated it. Letters from the army soon showed the fault of which Villars had been guilty, and everybody revolted against this wordy bully.

He soon after was the subject of common talk at the Court, and in the army, in consequence of a ridiculous adventure, in which he was the hero. His wound, or the airs that he gave himself in consequence of it, often forced him to hold his leg upon the neck of his horse, almost in the same manner as ladies do. One day, he let slip the remark that he was sick to death of mounting on horseback like those "harlots" in the suite of Madame de Bourgogne. These "harlots," I will observe parenthetically, were all the young ladies of the Court, and the daughters of Madame la Duchess! Such a remark uttered by a general not much loved, speedily flew from one end of the camp to the other, and was not long in making its way to the Court and to Paris. The young horsewomen alluded to were offended; their friends took up arms for them, and Madame la Duchess de Bourgogne could not help showing irritation, or avoid complaining.

Villars was apprised of all, and was much troubled by this increase of enemies so redoubtable, of whom just then he assuredly had no need. He took it into his head to try and discover who had blabbed; and found it was Heudicourt, whom Villars, to advance his own interests, by means of Heudicourt's mother (who was the evil genius of Madame de Maintenon), had protected; and to whom even, much against his custom, he had actually not lent, but given money.

This Heudicourt (whom I have previously alluded to, *apropos* of a song he wrote), was a merry wag, who excelled in making fun of people, in highly-seasoned pleasantry, and in comic songs. Spoiled by the favor which had always sustained him, he gave full license to his

tongue, and by this audacity had rendered himself redoubtable. He was a scurrilous wretch, a great drunkard,
and a debauchee; not at all cowardly, and with a face
hideous as that of an ugly satyr. He was not insensible
to this; and so, unfitted for intrigues himself, he assisted
others in them, and, by this honest trade, had acquired
many friends among the flower of the courtiers of both
sexes — above all with the ladies. By way of contrast
to his wickedness, he was called "the good little fellow";
and "the good little fellow" was mixed up in all intrigues; the ladies of the Court positively struggled for
him; and not one of them, even of the highest ranks,
would have dared to fall out with him. Thus protected,
he was rather an embarrassing customer for Maréchal de
Villars, who, nevertheless, falling back as usual upon his
effrontery, hit upon a bright project to bring home to
Heudicourt the expedient he had against him.

He collected together about fifteen general officers,
and Heudicourt with them. When they had all arrived,
he left his chamber, and went to them. A number of
loiterers had gathered round. This was just what Villars
wanted. He asked all the officers in turn, if they remembered hearing him utter the expression attributed to
him. Albergotti said he remembered to have heard
Villars apply the term "harlots" to the sutlers and the
camp creatures, but never to any other woman. All the
rest followed in the same track. Then Villars, after
letting out against this frightful calumny, and against
the impostor who had written and sent it to the Court,
addressed himself to Heudicourt, whom he treated in the
most cruel fashion. "The good little fellow" was
strangely taken aback and wished to defend himself;
but Villars produced proofs that could not be contradicted.
Thereupon the ill-favored dog avowed his turpitude, and
had the audacity to approach Villars in order to speak
low to him; but the Maréchal, drawing back, and repel-
ling him with an air of indignation, said to him aloud,
that with scoundrels like him he wished for no privacy.
Gathering up his pluck at this, Heudicourt gave rein to
all his impudence, and declared that they who had been
questioned had not dared to own the truth for fear of

offending the Maréchal; that as for himself he might have been wrong in speaking and writing about it, but he had not imagined that words said before such a numerous company, and in such a public place, could remain secret, or that he had done more harm in writing about them than so many others who had acted likewise.

The Maréchal, outraged upon hearing so bold and so truthful a reply, let out with greater violence than ever against Heudicourt, accused him of ingratitude and villainy, drove him away, and a few minutes after had him arrested and conducted as a prisoner to the *château* at Calais. This violent scene made as much stir at the Court and in the army as that which had caused it. The consistent and public conduct of Villars was much approved. The King declared that he left Heudicourt in his hands; Madame de Maintenon and Madame de Bourgogne, that they abandoned him; and his friends avowed that his fault was inexcusable. But the tide soon turned. After the first hubbub, the excuse of "the good little fellow" appeared excellent to the ladies who had their reasons for liking him and for fearing to irritate him; and also to the army, where the Maréchal was not liked. Several of the officers who had been publicly interrogated by Villars, now admitted that they had been taken by surprise, and had not wished to compromise themselves. It was even, going into base details, argued that the Maréchal's expression could not apply to the *vivandières* and the other camp women, as they always rode astride, one leg on this side, one leg on the other, like men, a manner very different from that of the ladies of Madame de Bourgogne. People contested the power of a general to deal out justice upon his inferiors for personal matters in which the service was in no wise concerned; in a word, Heudicourt was soon let out of Calais, and remained "the good little fellow" in fashion in spite of the Maréchal, who, tormented by so many things in this campaign, sought for and obtained permission to go and take the waters; and did so. He was succeeded by Harcourt, who was himself in weak health. Thus one cripple replaced another. One began, the other ended, at Bourbonne.

Douai, Saint Venant, and Aire fell into the hands of the enemy during this campaign, who thus gained upon us more and more, while we did little or nothing. This was the last campaign in Flanders of the Duke of Marlborough. On the Rhine our troops observed and subsisted: nothing more; but in Spain there was more movement, and I will therefore turn my glances toward that country, and relate what took place there.

CHAPTER XVI.

BEFORE I commence speaking of the affairs of Spain, let me pass lightly over an event which, engrafted upon some others, made much noise, notwithstanding the care taken to stifle it.

Madame la Duchess de Bourgogne supped at Saint Cloud one evening with Madame la Duchess de Berry and others — Madame de Saint-Simon absenting herself from the party. Madame la Duchess de Berry and M. d'Orléans — but she more than he — got so drunk, that Madame la Duchess d'Orléans, Madame la Duchess de Bourgogne, and the rest of the numerous company there assembled, knew not what to do. M. le Duc de Berry was there, and him they talked over as well as they could; and the numerous company was amused by the Grand Duchess as well as she was able. The effect of the wine, in more ways than one, was such, that people were troubled. In spite of all, the Duchess de Berry could not be sobered, so that it became necessary to carry her, drunk as she was, to Versailles. All the servants saw her state, and did not keep it to themselves; nevertheless, it was hidden from the King, from Monseigneur, and from Madame de Maintenon.

And now, having related this incident, let me turn to Spain.

The events which took place in that country were so important, that I have thought it best to relate them in a continuous narrative without interruption. We must go back to the commencement of the year, and remember the dangerous state which Spain was thrown into, delivered up to her own weakness, France being too feeble to defend her; finding it difficult enough, in fact, to defend herself, and willing to abandon her ally entirely in the hope by this means to obtain peace.

Toward the end of March the King of Spain set out from Madrid to put himself at the head of his army in Aragon. Villadarias, one of his best and oldest general officers, was chosen to command under him. The King of Spain went from Saragossa to Lerida, where he was received with acclamations by the people and his army. He crossed the Sègre on the 14th of May, and advanced toward Balaguier, designing to lay siege to it. But heavy rains falling and causing the waters to rise, he was obliged to abandon his project. Joined a month afterward by troops arrived from Flanders, he sought to attack the enemy, but was obliged to content himself for the moment by scouring the country, and taking some little towns where the Archduke had established stores. All this time the Count of Staremberg, who commanded the forces of the Archduke, was ill; this circumstance the King of Spain was profiting by. But the Count grew well again quicker than was expected; promptly assembled his forces; marched against the army of the King of Spain; engaged it, and obliged it, all astonished, to retire under Saragossa. This ill success fell entirely on Villadarias, who was accused of imprudence and negligence. The King of Spain was desperately in want of generals, and M. de Vendôme knowing this, and sick to death of banishment, had asked some little time before to be allowed to offer his services. At first he was snubbed. But the King of Spain, who eagerly wished for M. de Vendôme, dispatched a courier, after this defeat, begging the King to allow him to come and take command. The King held out no longer.

The Duc de Vendôme had prepared everything in advance; and having got over a slight attack of gout, hastened to Versailles. M. du Maine had negotiated with Madame de Maintenon to obtain permission to take Vendôme to the Duchess de Bourgogne. The opportunity seemed favorable to them. Vendôme was going to Spain to serve the brother and sister of the Duchess; and his departure without seeing her would have had a very disagreeable effect. The Duc du Maine, followed by Vendôme, came then that day to the toilet of the Duchess de Bourgogne. There happened that there was a very large company of men and ladies. The Duchess rose for them, as she always did for the princes of the blood and others, and for all the dukes and duchesses, and sat down again as usual; but after this first glance, which could not be refused, she, though usually very talkative and accustomed to look round, became for once attentive to her adornment, fixed her eyes on her mirror, and spoke no more to any one. M. du Maine, with M. de Vendôme stuck by his side, remained very disconcerted; and M. du Maine, usually so free and easy, dared not utter a single word. Nobody went near them or spoke to them. They remained thus about half a quarter of an hour, with an universal silence throughout the chamber — all eyes being fixed on them; and not being able to stand this any longer, slunk away. This reception was not sufficiently agreeable to induce Vendôme to pay his respects at parting; for it would have been more embarrassing still if, when according to custom he advanced to kiss the Duchess de Bourgogne, she had given him the unheard-of affront of a refusal. As for the Duc de Bourgogne, he received Vendôme tolerably politely, that is to say, much too well.

Staremberg meanwhile profited by the advantage he had gained; he attacked the Spanish army under Saragossa and totally defeated it. Artillery, baggage, all was lost; and the rout was complete. This misfortune happened on the 20th of August. The King, who had witnessed it from Saragossa, immediately afterward took the road for Madrid. Bay, one of his generals, gathered together eighteen thousand men, with whom he retired to Tudela, without any impediment on the part of the enemy.

M. de Vendôme learned the news of this defeat while on his way to Spain. Like a prudent man as he was, for his own interests, he stopped at once so as to see what turn affairs were taking, and to know how to act. He waited at Bayonne, gaining time there by sending a courier to the King for instructions how to act, and remaining until the reply came. After its arrival he set out to continue his journey, and joined the King of Spain at Valladolid.

Staremberg, after his victory, was joined by the Archduke, and a debate soon took place as to the steps next to be taken. Staremberg was for giving battle to the army of eighteen thousand men under Bay, which I have just alluded to, beating it, and then advancing little by little into Spain, to make head against the vanquished army of the King. Had this advice been acted on, it could scarcely have failed to ruin the King of Spain, and the whole country must have fallen into the hands of the enemy. But it was not acted on. Stanhope, who commanded the English and Dutch troops, said that his Queen had ordered him to march upon Madrid when possible, in preference to every other place. He therefore proposed that they should go straight to Madrid with the Archduke, proclaim him King there, and thus terrify all Spain by seizing the capital. Staremberg, who admitted that the project was dazzling, sustained, however, that it was of little use, and of great danger. He tried all in his power to shake the inflexibility of Stanhope, but in vain, and at last was obliged to yield as being the feebler of the two. The time lost in this dispute saved the wreck of the army which had just been defeated. What was afterward done saved the King of Spain.

When the plan of the allies became known, however, the consternation at Madrid, which was already great, was extreme. The King resolved to withdraw from a place which could not defend itself, and to carry away with him the Queen, the Prince, and the Councils. The grandees declared that they would follow the King and his fortune everywhere, and very few failed to do so; the departure succeeded the declaration in twenty-four hours. The Queen, holding the Prince in her arms, at a balcony of the palace, spoke to the people assembled beneath, with so much grace, force, and courage, that the success she had is incredible. The impression that the people received was communicated everywhere, and soon gained all the provinces. The Court thus left Madrid for the second time in the midst of the most lamentable cries, uttered from the bottom of their heart, by people who came from town and country, and who so wished to follow the King and Queen that considerable effort was required in order to induce them to return, each one to his home.

Valladolid was the retreat of this wretched Court, which in the most terrible trouble it had yet experienced, lost neither judgment nor courage. Meanwhile the grandest and rarest example of attachment and of courage that had ever been heard of or seen was seen in Spain. Prelates and the humblest of the clergy, noblemen and the poorest people, lawyers and artisans, all bled themselves of the last drop of their substance, in order to form new troops and magazines, and to provide all kinds of provisions for the Court, and those who had followed it. Never nation made efforts so surprising with a unanimity and a concert which acted everywhere at once. The Queen sold off all she possessed, received with her own hands sometimes even as little as ten pistoles, in order to content the zeal of those who brought, and thanked them with as much affection as they themselves displayed. She would continually say that she should like to put herself at the head of her troops, with her son in her arms. With this language and her conduct she gained all hearts, and was very useful in such a strange extremity.

The Archduke meanwhile arrived in Madrid with his army. He entered there in triumph, and caused himself to be proclaimed King of Spain, by the violence of his troops, who dragged the trembling Corregidor through the streets, which for the most part were deserted, while the majority of the houses were without inhabitants, the few who remained having barricaded their doors and windows, and shut themselves up in the most remote places, where the troops did not dare to break in upon them, for fear of increasing the visible and general despair, and in the hope of gaining by gentleness. The entry of the Archduke was not less sad than his proclamation. A few scarcely audible and feeble acclamations were heard, but were so forced that the Archduke, sensibly astonished, made them cease of himself. He did not dare to lodge in the palace, or in the center of Madrid, but slept at the extremity of the city, and even there only for two or three nights. Scarcely any damage was inflicted upon the town. Staremberg was careful to gain over the inhabitants by conciliation and clemency; yet his army perished of all kinds of misery. Not a single person could be found to supply it with subsistence for man or beast — not even when offered money. Prayers, menaces, executions, all were perfectly useless. There was not a Castilian who would not have believed himself dishonored in selling the least thing to the enemies, or in allowing them to take it. It is thus that this magnanimous people, without any other help than their courage and their fidelity, sustained themselves in the midst of their enemies, whose army they caused to perish, while at the same time, by inconceivable prodigies, they formed a new army for themselves, perfectly equipped and furnished, and put thus, by themselves, alone, and for the second time, the crown upon the head of their King, with a glory forever an example to all the people of Europe; so true it is that nothing approaches the strength which is found in the heart of a nation for the succor and re-establishment of Kings!*

Stanhope, who had not failed to see the excellence of Staremberg's advice from the first moment of their dispute, now said insolently, that having executed the orders of his Queen, it was for Staremberg to draw the army out of its embarrassment. As for himself, he had nothing more to do in the matter! When ten or twelve days had elapsed, it was resolved to remove from Madrid toward Toledo. From the former place nothing was taken away, except some of the King's tapestry, which Stanhope was not ashamed to carry off, but which he did not long keep. This act of meanness was blamed even by his own countrymen. Staremberg did not make a long stay at Toledo, but in quitting the town, burned the superb palace in the Moorish style that Charles Quint had built there, and that was called the Alcazar. This

---

* This is a wiser observation, perhaps, than Saint-Simon thought. Human nature is too apt to attribute its degradation to external violence, and to forget that the strongest allies of those that enslave it are found within its own breast.

was an irreparable damage, which he made believe happened accidentally.

As nothing now hindered the King of Spain from going to see his faithful subjects at Madrid, he entered that city on the 2d of December, in the midst of an infinite crowd and incredible acclamations. He descended at the church of Notre Dame d'Atocha, and was three hours in arriving at the palace, so prodigious was the crowd. The city made a present to him of twenty thousand pistoles. On the fourth day after his arrival at Madrid, the King left, in order to join M. de Vendôme and his army.

But a little while before, this monarch was a fugitive wanderer, almost entirely destroyed, without troops, without money, and without subsistence. Now he found himself at the head of ten or fifteen thousand men well armed, well clad, well paid, with provisions, money, and ammunition in abundance; and this magical change was brought about by the sudden universal conspiracy of the unshakable fidelity and attachment without example, of all the orders of his subjects; by their efforts and their industry, as prodigious the one as the other.

Vendôme, in the utmost surprise at a change so little to be hoped for, wished to profit by it by joining the army under Bay, which was too weak itself to appear before Staremberg. Vendôme accordingly set about making this junction, which Staremberg thought only how to hinder. He knew well the Duc de Vendôme. In Savoy he had gained many a march upon him; had passed five rivers in front of him; and in spite of him had led his troops to M. de Savoie. Staremberg thought only therefore in what manner he could lay a trap for M. de Vendôme, in which he, with his army, might fall and break his neck without hope of escape. With this view he put his army into quarters, access to which was easy everywhere, which were near each other, and which could assist each other in case of need. He then placed all his English and Dutch, Stanhope at their head, in Brighuega, a little fortified town in good condition for defense. It was at the head of all the quarters of Staremberg's army, and at the entrance of a plain over which M. de Vendôme had to pass to join Bay.

Staremberg was on the point of being joined by his army of Estremadura, so that in the event of M. de Vendôme attacking Brighuega, as he hoped, he had a large number of troops to depend upon.

Vendôme, meanwhile, set out on his march. He was informed of Staremberg's position, but in a manner just as Staremberg wished; that is to say, he was led to believe that Stanhope had made a wrong move in occupying Brighuega, that he was too far removed from Staremberg to receive any assistance from him, and that he could be easily overpowered. That is how matters appeared to Vendôme. He hastened his march, therefore, made his dispositions, and on the 8th of December, after midday, approached Brighuega, called upon it to surrender, and upon its refusal, prepared to attack it.

Immediately afterward his surprise was great, upon discovering that there were so many troops in the town, and that instead of having to do with a mere outpost, he was engaged against a place of some consequence. He did not wish to retire, and perhaps he could not have done so with impunity. He set to, therefore, storming in his usual manner, and did what he could to excite his troops to make short work of a conquest so different from what he had imagined, and so dangerous to delay.

Nevertheless, the weight of his mistake pressed upon him as the hours passed and he saw fresh enemies arrive. Two of his assaults had failed: he determined to play at double or quits, and ordered a third assault. While the dispositions were being made, on the 9th of December he learned that Staremberg was marching against him with four or five thousand men, that is to say, with just about half what he really led. In this anguish, Vendôme did not hesitate to stake even the Crown of Spain upon the hazard of the die. His third attack was made with all the force of which he was capable. Every one of the assailants knew the extremity of the danger, and behaved with so much valor and impetuosity, that the town was carried in spite of an obstinate resistance. The besieged were obliged to yield, and to the number of eight battalions and eight squadrons, surrendered themselves prisoners of war, and with them, Stanhope, their general, who so triumphant in Madrid, was here obliged to disgorge the King's tapestries that he had taken from the palace.

While the capitulation was being made, various information came to Vendôme of Staremberg's march, which it was necessary, above all, to hide from the prisoners, who had they known their liberator was only a league and a half distant from them, as he was then, would have broken the capitulation, and defended themselves. M. de Vendôme's embarrassment was great. He had, and at the same time, to march out and meet Staremberg and to get rid of his numerous prisoners. All was done, however, very successfully. Sufficient troops were left in Brighuega to attend to the evacuation, and when it was at an end, those troops, left the place themselves and joined their comrades, who, with M. de Vendôme, were waiting for Staremberg outside the town, at Villaviciosa, a little place that afterward give its name to the battle. Only four hundred men were left in Brighuega.

M. de Vendôme arranged his army in order of battle in a tolerably open plain, but embarrassed by little knolls in several places, very disadvantageous for the cavalry. Immediately afterward the cannon began to fire on both sides, and almost immediately the two lines of the King of Spain prepared to charge. After the battle had proceeded some time, M. de Vendôme perceived that his center began to give way, and that the left of his cavalry could not break the right of the enemies'. He thought all was lost, and gave orders accordingly to his men to retire toward Torija. Straightway, too, he directed himself in that direction, with the King of Spain and a good part of his troops. While thus retreating, he learned that two of his officers had charged the enemy's infantry with the cavalry they had at their orders, had much knocked it about, and had rendered themselves masters, on the field of battle, of a large number of prisoners, and of the artillery that the enemy had abandoned. News so agreeable and so little expected determined the Duc de Vendôme and the King of Spain to return to the battle with the troops that had followed them. The day was, in fact, won just as night came on. The enemies abandoned twenty pieces of cannon, two mortars, their wounded, and their equipages; and numbers of them were taken prisoners. But Staremberg, having all the night to himself, succeeded in retiring in good order with seven or eight thousand men. His baggage and a majority of his wagons fell a prey to the vanquisher. Counting the garrison of Brighuega, the loss to the enemy was eleven thousand men killed or taken, their ammunition, artillery, baggage, and a great number of flags and standards.

When we consider the extreme peril the crown of Spain ran in these engagements, and that this time, if things had gone ill there was no resource, we tremble still. Had a catastrophe happened, there was nothing to hope from France. Its exhaustion and its losses would not have enabled it to lend aid. In its desire for peace, in fact, it would have hailed the loss of the Spanish crown as a relief. The imprudence, therefore, of M. de Vendôme in so readily falling into the snare laid for him, is all the more to be blamed. He takes no trouble to inform himself of the dispositions of the enemy; he comes upon a place which he believes a mere post, but soon sees it contains a numerous garrison, and finds that the principal part of the enemy's army is ready to fall upon him as he makes the attack. Then he begins to see in what ship he has embarked; he sees the double peril of a double action to sustain against Stanhope, whom he must overwhelm by furious assault, and against Staremberg, whom he must meet and defeat; or leave to the enemies the crown of Spain, and perhaps the person of Philip V. as price of his folly. Brighuega is gained, but it is without him. Villaviciosa is gained, but it is also without him. This hero is not sharp-sighted enough to see success when it comes. He thinks it defeat, aud gives orders for retreat. When informed that the battle is gained, he returns to the field, and as daylight comes, perceives the fact to be so. He is quite without shame for his stupid mistake, and cries out that he has vanquished, with an impudence to which the Spaniards were not accustomed; and, to conclude, he allows Staremberg's army to get clean off, instead of destroying it at once, as he might have done, and so finished the war. Such were the exploits of this great warrior, so desired in Spain to resuscitate it, and such were the first proofs of his capacity upon arriving in that country!*

At the moment that the King of Spain was led back to the battlefield by Vendôme, and that they could no longer doubt their good fortune, he sent a courier to the Queen. Her mortal anguish was on the instant changed into so great a joy, that she went out immediately on foot into the streets of Vittoria, where all was delight; as it soon was over all Spain. The news of the victory was brought to the King (of France) by Don Gaspard de Zuniga, who gave an exact account of all that had occurred, hiding nothing respecting M. de Vendôme, who was thus unmasked and disgraced, in spite of every effort on the part of his cabal to defend him.

Among the allies, all the blame of this defeat fell upon Stanhope. Seven or eight hours more of resistance on his part at Brighuega would have enabled Staremberg to come up to his assistance, and all the resources of Spain would then have been annihilated. Staremberg, outraged at the ill success of his undertaking, cried out loudly against Stanhope. Some of the principal officers who had been at Brighuega seconded these complaints. Stanhope even did not dare to deny his fault. He was allowed to demand leave of absence to go home and defend himself. He was badly received, stripped of all military rank in England and Holland, and (as well as the officers under him) was not without fear of his degradation, and was even in danger of his life.

This recital of the events that took place in Spain, has led me away from other matters of earlier date. It is time now that I should return to them.

* Despite Vendôme's abominable character, it cannot but be evident that Saint-Simon here gives way to his hatred, and carps unjustifiably. If we were to deprive a general of the benefit of the chances of war, and duly separate from surrounding circumstances what is due to his own unaided genius, how many modern heroes would dwindle to no better than scare-crows! As to the effect of Vendôme's conduct at Court and on the mind of the King, it is perfectly indifferent. Defeats formerly made him a hero; victories now prove him a fool. This is perhaps the most striking instance in the whole of Saint-Simon's « Memoirs » of the absolute nullity of this Great Louis XIV.

CHAPTER XVII.

ALTHOUGH, as we have just seen, matters were beginning to brighten a little in Spain, they remained as dull and overcast as ever in France. The impossibility of obtaining peace, and the exhaustion of the realm, threw the King into the most cruel anguish, and Desmarets into the saddest embarrassment. The paper of all kinds with which trade was inundated, and which had all more or less lost credit, made a chaos for which no remedy could be perceived. State bills, bank bills, receiver general's bills, title bills, utensil bills, were the ruin of private people, who were forced by the King to take them in payment, and who lost half, two-thirds, and sometimes more by the transaction. This depreciation enriched the money people, at the expense of the public; and the circulation of money ceased, because there was no longer any money; because the King no longer paid anybody, but drew his revenues still; and because all the specie out of his control was locked up in the coffers of the possessors.

The capitation tax was doubled and trebled, at the will of the Intendants of the Provinces, merchandise and all kinds of provision were taxed to the amount of four times their value; new taxes of all kinds and upon all sorts of things were exacted; all this crushed nobles and *roturiers*, lords and clergy, and yet did not bring enough to the King, who drew the blood of all his subjects, squeezed out their very marrow, without distinction, and who enriched an army of tax gatherers and officials of all kinds, in whose hands the best part of what was collected remained.

Desmarets, in whom the King had been forced to put all his confidence in finance matters, conceived the idea of establishing, in addition to so many taxes, that Royal Tithe upon all the property of each community and of each private person of the realm, that the Maréchal de Vauban, on the one hand, and Boisguilbert on the other, had formerly proposed; but, as I have already described, as a simple and sole tax which would suffice for all, which would all enter the coffers of the King, and by means of which every other impost would be abolished.

We have seen what success this proposition met with; how the financiers trembled at it; how the ministers blushed at it, with what anathemas it was rejected, and to what extent these two excellent and skillful citizens were disgraced. All this must be recollected here, since Desmarets, who had not lost sight of this system (not as relief and remedy — unpardonable crimes in the financial doctrine), now had recourse to it.

He imparted his project to three friends, councilors of state, who examined it well, and worked hard to see how to overcome the obstacles which arose in the way of its execution. In the first place, it was necessary, in order to collect this tax, to draw from each person a clear statement of his wealth, of his debts, and so on. It was necessary to demand sure proofs on these points so as not to be deceived. Here was all the difficulty. Nothing was thought of the desolation this extra impost must cause to a prodigious number of men, or of their despair upon finding themselves obliged to disclose their family secrets; to have a lamp thrown, as it were, upon their most delicate parts; all these things, I say, went for nothing. Less than a month sufficed these humane commissioners to render an account of this gentle project to the Cyclop who had charged them with it. Desmarets thereupon proposed it to the King, who, accustomed as he was to the most ruinous imposts, could not avoid being terrified at this. For a long while he had heard nothing talked of but the most extreme misery; this increase saddened him in a manner so evident, that his valets perceived it several days running, and were so disturbed at it, that Maréchal (who related all this curious anecdote to me) made bold to speak to the King upon this sadness, fearing for his health. The King avowed to him that he felt infinite trouble, and threw himself vaguely upon the state of affairs. Eight or ten days after (during which he continued to feel the same melancholy), the King regained his usual calmness, and called Maréchal to explain the cause of his trouble.

The King related to Maréchal that the extremity of his affairs had forced him to put on furious imposts; that setting aside compassion, scruples had much tormented him for taking thus the wealth of his subjects; that at last he had unbosomed himself to the Père Tellier, who had asked for a few days to think upon the matter, and that he had returned after having had a consultation with some of the most skillful doctors of the Sorbonne, who had decided that ALL THE WEALTH OF HIS SUBJECTS WAS HIS, AND THAT WHEN HE TOOK IT HE ONLY TOOK WHAT BELONGED TO HIM! The King added, that this decision had taken away all his scruples, and had restored to him the calm and tranquillity he had lost. Maréchal was so astonished, so bewildered to hear this recital, that he could not offer one word. Happily for him, the King quitted him almost immediately, and Maréchal remained some time in the same place, scarcely knowing where he was.

After the King had been thus satisfied by his confessor, no time was lost in establishing the tax. On Tuesday, the 30th of September, Desmarets entered the Finance Council with the necessary edict in his bag.

For some days everybody had known of this bombshell in the air, and had trembled with that remnant of hope which is founded only upon desire; all the Court as well as all Paris waited in a dejected sadness to see what would happen. People whispered to each other, and even when the project was rendered public, no one dared to talk of it aloud.

On the day above named, the King brought forward this measure in the Council, by saying, that the impossibility of obtaining peace, and the extreme difficulty of sustaining the war, had caused Desmarets to look about in order to discover some means, which should appear good, of raising money; that he had pitched upon this

tax; that he (the King), although sorry to adopt such a
resource, approved it, and had no doubt the Council
would do so likewise, when it was explained to them.
Desmarets, in a pathetic discourse, then dwelt upon the
reasons which had induced him to propose this tax, and
afterward read the edict through from beginning to end
without interruption.

No one spoke, moreover, when it was over, until the
King asked D'Aguesseau his opinion. D'Aguesseau replied, that it would be necessary for him to take home
the edict and read it through very carefully before expressing an opinion. The King said that D'Aguesseau
was right — it WOULD take a long time to examine the
edict — but after all, examination was unnecessary, and
would only be loss of time. All remained silent again,
except the Duc de Beauvilliers, who, seduced by the
nephew of Colbert, whom he thought an oracle in finances,
said a few words in favor of the project.

Thus was settled this bloody business, and immediately
after signed, sealed, and registered, among stifled sobs,
and published amid the most gentle but most piteous
complaints. The product of this tax was nothing like so
much as had been imagined in this bureau of Cannibals;
and the King did not pay a single farthing more to anyone than he had previously done. Thus all the fine relief
expected by this tax ended in smoke.

The Maréchal de Vauban had died of grief at the ill
success of his task and his zeal, as I have related in its
place. Poor Boisguilbert, in the exile his zeal had
brought him, was terribly afflicted, to find he had innocently given advice which he intended for the relief of
the State, but which had been made use of in this
frightful manner. Every man, without exception, saw
himself a prey to the taxgatherers: reduced to calculate
and discuss with them his own patrimony, to receive
their signature and their protection under the most
terrible pains; to show in public all the secrets of his
family; to bring into the broad open daylight domestic
turpitudes enveloped until then in the folds of precaution
the wisest and the most multiplied. Many had to convince the taxagents, but vainly, that although proprie-

tors, they did not enjoy the tenth part of their property. All Languedoc offered to give up its entire wealth, if allowed to enjoy, free from every impost, the tenth part of it. The proposition not only was not listened to, but was reputed an insult and severely blamed.

Monseigneur le Duc de Bourgogne spoke openly against this tax, and against the finance people, who lived upon the very marrow of the people; spoke with a just and holy anger that recalled the memory of Saint Louis, of Louis XII., father of the people, and of Louis the Just. Monseigneur, too, moved by this indignation, so unusual, of his son, sided with him, and showed anger at so many exactions as injurious as barbarous, and at so many insignificant men so monstrously enriched with the nation's blood. Both father and son infinitely surprised those who heard them, and made themselves looked upon in some sort, as resources from which something might hereafter be hoped for. But the edict was issued, and though there might be some hope in the future, there was none in the present. And no one knew who was to be the real successor of Louis XIV., and how under the next government we were to be still more overwhelmed than under this one.

One result of this tax was, that it enabled the King to augment all his infantry with five men per company.

A tax was also levied upon the usurers, who had much gained by trafficking in the paper of the King, that is to say, had taken advantage of the need of those to whom the King gave this paper in payment. These usurers are called *agioteurs*. Their mode was, ordinarily, to give, for example, according as the holder of paper was more or less pressed, three or four hundred francs (the greater part often in provisions), for a bill of a thousand francs! This game was called *agio*. It was said that thirty millions were obtained from this tax. Many people gained much by it; I know not if the King was the better treated.

Soon after this the coin was recoined, by which great profit was made for the King, and much wrong done to private people and to trade. In all times it has been regarded as a very great misfortune to meddle with corn and money. Desmarets has accustomed us to tricks with the money; M. le Duc and Cardinal Fleury to interfere with corn and to fictitious famine.

At the commencement of December, the King declared that he wished there should be, contrary to custom, plays and "apartments" at Versailles even when Monseigneur should be at Meudon. He thought apparently he must keep his Court full of amusements, to hide, if it was possible, abroad and at home, the disorder and the extremity of affairs. For the same reason, the carnival was opened early this season, and all through the winter there were many balls of all kinds at the Court, where the wives of the ministers gave very magnificent displays, like *fêtes*, to Madame la Duchess de Bourgogne and to all the Court.

But Paris did not remain less wretched or the provinces less desolated.

And thus I have arrived at the end of 1710.*

At the commencement of the following year, 1711,— that is to say, a few days after the middle of March,— a cruel misfortune happened to the Maréchal de Boufflers. His eldest son was fourteen years of age, handsome, well made, of much promise, and who succeeded marvelously at the Court, when his father presented him there to the King to thank his Majesty for the reversion of the govern-

---

* I cannot refrain, at the end of this short narrative, containing so terrible an exposure of the principles and conduct of the Great King of the Great Age, from referring to the trite observation — trite from its extreme truth — that we have here sufficient explanation, not only of the occurrence, but of the horrors of the French Revolution. We must remember that with rare exceptions, for a thousand years France was subject to tyrants of the same nature; and that almost always when the country was not desolated by oppression and taxation, it was desolated by bigotry or licentiousness. All kings as such — unless they have been taught to be mere magistrates, instances of which are few — look, as Louis XIV. did, upon the nation as their property. This is why they not only seize money wherever they can find it, but interfere with everything, from the religious belief, to the wives and daughters of their subjects. A calculation has been made that six thousand persons perished by executions of various kinds during the French Revolution. If we compare this number with the multitudes who suffered each famine brought on by the arrangements of the King and his ministers and the connivance of the nobility, we shall be astonished at the clemency shown by the people in the hour of vengeance and triumph.— TRANSLATOR.

ment of Flow and of Lille. He returned afterward to the College of the Jesuits, where he was being educated. I know not what youthful folly he was guilty of with the two sons of D'Argenson; but the Jesuits, wishing to show that they made no distinction of persons, whipped the little lad, because, to say the truth, they had nothing to fear from the Maréchal de Boufflers; but they took good care to let the others off, although equally guilty, because they had to reckon with D'Argenson, lieutenant of the police, of much credit in book matters, Jansenism, and all sorts of things and affairs in which they were interested.

Little Boufflers, who was full of courage, and who had done no more than the two Argensons, and with them, was seized with such despair that he fell ill that same day. He was carried to the Maréchal's house, but it was impossible to save him. The heart was seized, the blood diseased, the purples appeared; in four days all was over. The state of the father and mother may be imagined! The King, who was much touched by it, did not let them ask or wait for him. He sent one of his gentlemen to testify to them the share he had in their loss, and announced that he would give to their remaining son what he had already given to the other. As for the Jesuits, the universal cry against them was prodigious; but that was all. This would be the place, now that I am speaking of the Jesuits, to speak of another affair in which they were concerned. But I pass over, for the present, the dissensions that broke out at about this time, and that ultimately led to the famous Papal Bull Unigenitus, so fatal to the Church and to the State, so shameful for Rome, and so injurious to religion; and I proceed to speak of the great event this year which led to others so memorable and so unexpected.

CHAPTER XVIII.

My Interview with Du Mont — A Mysterious Communication — Anger of Monseigneur against Me — Household of the Duchess de Berry — Monseigneur Taken Ill of the Smallpox — Effect of the News — The King Goes to Meudon — The Danger Diminishes — Madame de Maintenon at Meudon — The Court at Versailles — Hopes and Fears — The Danger Returns — Death of Monseigneur — Conduct of the King.

BUT in order to understand the part I played in the event I have alluded to and the interest I took in it, it is necessary for me to relate some personal matters that occurred in the previous year. Du Mont was one of the confidants of Monseigneur; but also had never forgotten what his father owed to mine. Some days after the commencement of the second voyage to Marly, subsequently to the marriage of the Duchess de Berry, as I was coming back from the King's mass, the said Du Mont, in the crush at the door of the little salon of the chapel, took an opportunity when he was not perceived, to pull me by the coat, and when I turned round put a finger to his lips, and pointed toward the gardens which are at the bottom of the river, that is to say, of that superb cascade which the Cardinal Fleury has destroyed, and which faced the rear of the *château*. At the same time Du Mont whispered in my ear; "To the arbors!" That part of the garden was surrounded with arbors palisaded so as to conceal what was inside. It was the least frequented place at Marly, leading to nothing; and in the afternoon even, and the evening, few people within them.

Uneasy to know what Du Mont wished to communicate with so much mystery, I gently went toward the arbors where, without being seen, I looked through one of the openings until I saw him appear. He slipped in by the corner of the chapel, and I went toward him. As he joined me he begged me to return toward the river, so as to be still more out of the way; and then we set

ourselves against the thickest palisades, as far as possible
from all openings, so as to be still more concealed.* All
this surprised and frightened me: I was still more so when
I learned what was the matter.

Du Mont then told me, on condition that I promised
not to show that I knew it, and not to make use of my
knowledge in any way without his consent, that two days
after the marriage of the Duc de Berry, having entered
toward the end of the morning the cabinet of Monseigneur, he found him alone, looking very serious. He
followed Monseigneur, through the gardens alone, until
he entered by the window the apartments of the Princess
de Conti, who was also alone. As he entered Monseigneur said with an air not natural to him, and very inflamed — as if by way of interrogation — that she "sat
very quietly there." This frightened her so, that she
asked if there was any news from Flanders, and what
had happened? Monseigneur answered, in a tone of great
annoyance, that there was no news except that the Duc
de Saint-Simon had said, that now that the marriage of
the Duc de Berry was brought about, it would be proper
to drive away Madame la Duchess and the Princess
de Conti, after which it would be easy to govern "the
great imbecile," meaning himself. This was why he
thought she ought not to be so much at her ease. Then,
suddenly, as if lashing his sides to get into a greater
rage, he spoke in a way such a speech would have deserved, added menaces, said that he would have the Duc
de Bourgogne to fear me, to put me aside, and separate
himself entirely from me. This sort of soliloquy lasted
a long time, and I was not told what the Princess
de Conti said to it; but from the silence of Du Mont,
her annoyance at the marriage I had brought about, and
other reasons, it seems to me unlikely that she tried to
soften Monseigneur.

Du Mont begged me not, for a long time at least, to
show that I knew what had taken place, and to behave

* To understand all this precaution, it is necessary to remember
what has previously been told of the company of Swiss spies set on
foot by the King for the gardens of Marly. What real man would
be a courtier here on such conditions?

with the utmost prudence. Then he fled away by the path he had come by, fearing to be seen. I remained walking up and down in the arbor all the time, reflecting on the wickedness of my enemies, and the gross credulity of Monseigneur. Then I ran away, and escaped to Madame de Saint-Simon, who, as astonished and frightened as I, said not a word of the communication I had received.

I never knew who had served me this ill turn with Monseigneur, but I always suspected Mademoiselle de Lillebonne. After a long time, having obtained with difficulty the consent of the timid Du Mont, I made Madame de Saint-Simon speak to the Duchess de Bourgogne, who undertook to arrange the affair as well as it could be arranged. The Duchess spoke indeed to Monseigneur, and showed him how ridiculously he had been deceived, when he was persuaded that I could ever have entertained the ideas attributed to me. Monseigneur admitted that he had been carried away by anger; and that there was no likelihood that I should have thought of anything so wicked and incredible.

About this time the house of the Duc and Duchess de Berry was constituted. Racilly obtained the splendid appointment of first surgeon, and was worthy of it; but the Duchess de Berry wept bitterly, because she did not consider him of high family enough. She was not so delicate about La Haye, whose appointment she rapidly secured. The fellow looked in the glass more complaisantly than ever. He was well made, but stiff, and with a face not at all handsome, and looking as if it had been skinned. He was happy in more ways than one, and was far more attached to his new mistress than to his master. The King was very angry when he learned that the Duc de Berry had supplied himself with such an assistant.

Meantime, I continued on very uneasy terms with Monseigneur, since I had learned his strange credulity with respect to me. I began to feel my position very irksome, not to say painful, on this account. Meudon I would not go to—for me it was a place infested with demons —yet by stopping away I ran great risks of losing the

favor and consideration I enjoyed at Court. Monseigneur
was a man so easily imposed upon, as I had already experienced, and his intimate friends were so unscrupulous that there was no saying what might be invented on
the one side and swallowed by the other, to my discredit.
Those friends, too, were, I knew, enraged against me
for divers weighty reasons, and would stop at nothing, I
was satisfied, to procure my downfall. For want of
better support I sustained myself with courage. I said
to myself, "We never experience all the evil or all the
good that we have apparently the most reason to expect."
I hoped, therefore, against hope, terribly troubled it
must be confessed on the score of Meudon. At Easter,
this year, I went away to La Ferté, far from the Court
and the world, to solace myself as I could; but this
thorn in my side was cruelly sharp! At the moment the
most unlooked-for it pleased God to deliver me from it.

At La Ferté I had but few guests: M. de Saint Louis,
an old brigadier of cavalry, and a Normandy gentleman,
who had been in my regiment, and who was much attached to me. On Saturday, the 11th of the month, and
the day before Quasimodo, I had been walking with them
all the morning, and I had entered all alone into my
cabinet a little before dinner, when a courier sent by
Madame de Saint-Simon, gave me a letter from her, in
which I was informed that Monseigneur was ill.

I learned afterward that this Prince, while on his way
to Meudon for the Easter *fêtes*, met at Chaville a priest,
who was carrying Our Lord to a sick person. Monseigneur, and Madame de Bourgogne, who was with him,
knelt down to adore the host, and then Monseigneur inquired what was the malady of the patient. "The smallpox," he was told. That disease was very prevalent just
then. Monseigneur had had it, but very lightly, and
when young. He feared it very much, and was struck
with the answer he now received. In the evening he
said to Boudin, his chief doctor, "I should not be surprised if I were to have the smallpox." The day, however, passed over as usual.

On the morrow, Thursday, the 9th, Monseigneur rose,
and meant to go out wolf hunting; but as he was dress-

ing, such a fit of weakness seized him, that he fell into his chair. Boudin made him get into bed again; but all the day his pulse was in an alarming state. The King, only half informed by Fagon of what had taken place, believed there was nothing the matter, and went out walking at Marly after dinner, receiving news from time to time. Monseigneur le Duc de Bourgogne and Madame de Bourgogne dined at Meudon, and they would not quit Monseigneur for one moment. The Princess added to the strict duties of a daughter-in-law all that her gracefulness could suggest, and gave everything to Monseigneur with her own hand. Her heart could not have been troubled by what her reason foresaw; but, nevertheless, her care and attention were extreme, without any airs of affectation or acting. The Duc de Bourgogne, simple and holy as he was, and full of the idea of his duty, exaggerated his attention; and although there was a strong suspicion of the smallpox, neither quitted Monseigneur, except for the King's supper.

The next day, Friday, the 10th, in reply to his express demands, the King was informed of the extremely dangerous state of Monseigneur. He had said on the previous evening that he would go on the following morning to Meudon, and remain there during all the illness of Monseigneur whatever its nature might be. He was now as good as his word. Immediately after mass he set out for Meudon. Before doing so, he forbade his children, and all who had not had the smallpox, to go there, which was suggested by a motive of kindness. With Madame de Maintenon and a small suite, he had just taken up his abode in Meudon, when Madame de Saint-Simon sent me the letter of which I have just made mention.

I will continue to speak of myself with the same truthfulness I speak of others, and with as much exactness as possible. According to the terms on which I was with Monseigneur and his intimates, may be imagined the impression made upon me by this news. I felt that one way or other, well or ill, the malady of Monseigneur would soon terminate. I was quite at my ease at La Ferté. I resolved therefore to wait there until I received fresh particulars. I dispatched a courier to Madame de Saint-Simon, requesting her to send me another the next day, and I passed the rest of this day, in an ebb and flow of feelings; the man and the Christian struggling against the man and the courtier, and in the midst of a crowd of vague fancies catching glimpses of the future, painted in the most agreeable colors.

The courier I expected so impatiently arrived the next day, Sunday, after dinner. The smallpox had declared itself, I learned, and was going on as well as could be wished. I believed Monseigneur saved, and wished to remain at my own house; nevertheless I took advice, as I have done all my life, and with great regret set out the next morning. At La Queue, about six leagues from Versailles, I met a financier of the name of La Fontaine, whom I knew well. He was coming from Paris and Versailles, and came up to me as I changed horses. Monseigneur, he said, was going on admirably; and he added details which convinced me he was out of all danger. I arrived at Versailles, full of this opinion, which was confirmed by Madame de Saint-Simon and everybody I met, so that nobody any longer feared, except on account of the treacherous nature of this disease in a very fat man of fifty.

The King held his Council, and worked in the evening with his ministers as usual. He saw Monseigneur morning and evening, oftentimes in the afternoon, and always remained long by the bedside. On the Monday I arrived he had dined early, and had driven to Marly, where the Duchess de Bourgogne joined him. He saw in passing on the outskirts of the garden of Versailles his grandchildren, who had come out to meet him, but he would not let them come near, and said "good day" from a distance. The Duchess de Bourgogne had had the smallpox, but no trace was left.

The King only liked his own houses, and could not bear to be anywhere else. This was why his visits to Meudon were few and short, and only made from complaisance. Madame de Maintenon was still more out of her element there. Although her chamber was everywhere a sanctuary, where only ladies entitled to the most extreme familiarity entered, she always wanted another retreat near at hand entirely inaccessible except to the Duchess de Bourgogne alone, and that only for a few instants at a time. Thus she had Saint Cyr for Versailles and for Marly; and at Marly also a particular retiring place; at Fontainebleau she had her town house. Seeing therefore that Monseigneur was getting on well, and that a long sojourn at Meudon would be necessary, the upholsterers of the King were ordered to furnish a house in the park which once belonged to the Chancellor le Tellier, but which Monseigneur had bought.

When I arrived at Versailles, I wrote to M. de Beauvilliers at Meudon praying him to apprise the King that I had returned on account of the illness of Monseigneur, and that I would have gone to see him, but that, never having had the smallpox, I was included in the prohibition. M. de Beauvilliers did as I asked, and sent word back to me that my return had been very well timed, and that the King still forbade me as well as Madame de Saint-Simon to go to Meudon. This fresh prohibition did not distress me in the least. I was informed of all that was passing there, and that satisfied me.

There were yet contrasts at Meudon worth noticing. Mademoiselle Choin never appeared while the King was with Monseigneur, but kept close in her loft. When the coast was clear she came out, and took up her position at the sick man's bedside. All sorts of compliments passed between her and Madame de Maintenon, yet the two ladies never met. The King asked Madame de Maintenon if she had seen Mademoiselle Choin, and upon learning that she had not, was but ill pleased. Therefore Madame de Maintenon sent excuses and apologies to Mademoiselle Choin, and hoped, she said, to see her soon, — strange compliments from one chamber to another under the same roof. They never saw each other afterward.

It should be observed, that Père Tellier was also incognito at Meudon, and dwelt in a retired room from which he issued to see the King, but never approached the apartments of Monseigneur.

Versailles presented another scene. Monseigneur le Duc and Madame la Duchess de Bourgogne held their

12

Court openly there; and this Court resembled the first gleamings of the dawn. All the Court assembled there; all Paris also; and as discretion and precaution were never French virtues, all Meudon came as well. People were believed on their word when they declared that they had not entered the apartments of Monseigneur that day, and consequently could not bring the infection. When the Prince and Princess rose, when they went to bed, when they dined and supped with the ladies,—all public conversations—all meals—all assemblies—were opportunities of paying court to them. The apartments could not contain the crowd. The characteristic features of the room were many. Couriers arrived every quarter of an hour, and reminded people of the illness of Monseigneur—he was going on as well as could be expected; confidence and hope were easily felt; but there was an extreme desire to please at the new Court. The young Prince and Princess exhibited majesty and gravity, mixed with gayety; obligingly received all, continually spoke to every one; the crowd wore an air of complaisance; reciprocal satisfaction showed in every face, the Duc and Duchess de Berry were treated almost as nobody. Thus five days fled away in increasing thought of future events —in preparation to be ready for whatever might happen.

On Tuesday, the 14th of April I went to see the Chancellor, and asked for information upon the state of Monseigneur. He assured me it was good, and repeated to me the words Fagon had spoken to him, "that things were going on according to their wishes, and beyond their hopes." The Chancellor appeared to me very confident, and I had faith in him, so much the more, because he was on an extremely good footing with Monseigneur. The Prince, indeed, had so much recovered, that the fish women came in a body the self-same day to congratulate him, as they did after his attack of indigestion. They threw themselves at the foot of his bed, which they kissed several times, and in their joy said they would go back to Paris and have a *Te Deum* sung. But Monseigneur, who was not insensible to these marks of popular affection, told them it was not yet time, thanked them, and gave them a dinner, and some money.

As I was going home, I saw the Duchess d'Orléans walking on a terrace. She called to me; but I pretended not to notice her, because La Montauban was with her, and hastened home, my mind filled with this news, and withdrew to my cabinet. Almost immediately afterward Madame la Duchess d'Orléans joined me there. We were bursting to speak to each other alone, upon a point on which our thoughts were alike. She had left Meudon not an hour before, and she had the same tale to tell as the Chancellor. Everybody was at ease there she said; and then she extolled the care and capacities of the doctors, exaggerating their success; and, to speak frankly and to our shame, she and I lamented together to see Monseigneur, in spite of his age and his fat, escape from so dangerous an illness. She reflected seriously but wittily, that after an illness of this sort, apoplexy was not to be looked for; that an attack of indigestion was equally unlikely to arise, considering the care Monseigneur had taken not to over-gorge himself since his recent danger; and we concluded more than dolefully, that henceforth we must make up our minds that the Prince would live and reign for a long time. In a word, we let ourselves loose in this rare conversation, although not without an occasional scruple of conscience which disturbed it. Madame de Saint-Simon all-devoutly tried what she could to put a drag upon our tongues, but the drag broke, so to speak, and we continued our free discourse, humanly speaking very reasonable on our parts, but which we felt, nevertheless, was not according to religion. Thus two hours passed, seemingly very short. Madame d'Orléans went away, and I repaired with Madame de Saint-Simon to receive a numerous company.

While thus all was tranquillity at Versailles, and even at Meudon, everything had changed its aspect at the *château*. The King had seen Monseigneur several times during the day; but in his after-dinner visit he was so much struck with the extraordinary swelling of the face and of the head, that he shortened his stay, and on leaving the *château* shed tears. He was reassured as much as possible, and after the council he took a walk in the garden.

Nevertheless Monseigneur had already mistaken Madame la Princess de Conti for some one else; and Boudin, the doctor, was alarmed. Monseigneur himself had been so from the first, and he admitted that, for a long time before being attacked, he had been very unwell, and so much on Good Friday, that he had been unable to read his prayer book at chapel.

Toward four o'clock he grew worse, so much so that Boudin proposed to Fagon to call in other doctors, more familiar with the disease than they were. But Fagon flew into a rage at this, and would call in nobody. He declared that it would be better to act for themselves, and to keep Monseigneur's state secret, although it was hourly growing worse, and toward seven o'clock was perceived by several valets and courtiers. But nobody dared to open his mouth before Fagon, and the King was actually allowed to go to supper and to finish it without interruption, believing on the faith of Fagon that Monseigneur was going on well.

While the King supped thus tranquilly, all those who were in the sick chamber began to lose their wits. Fagon and the others poured down physic on physic, without leaving time for any to work. The *curé*, who was accustomed to go and learn the news every evening, found, against all custom, the doors thrown wide open, and the valets in confusion. He entered the chamber, and perceiving what was the matter, ran to the bedside, took the hand of Monseigneur, spoke to him of God, and seeing him full of consciousness, but scarcely able to speak, drew from him a sort of confession, of which nobody had hitherto thought, and suggested some acts of contrition. The poor Prince repeated distinctly several words suggested to him, and confusedly answered others, struck his breast, squeezed the *curé's* hand, appeared penetrated with the best sentiments, and received with a contrite and willing air the absolution of the *curé*.

As the King rose from the supper table, he well nigh fell backward when Fagon, coming forward, cried in great trouble that all was lost. It may be imagined what terror seized all the company at this abrupt passage from perfect security to hopeless despair. The King, scarcely master of himself, at once began to go toward the apartment of Monseigneur, and repelled very stiffly the indiscreet eagerness of some courtiers who wished to prevent him, saying that he would see his son again, and be quite certain that nothing could be done. As he was about to enter the chamber, Madame la Princess de Conti presented herself before him, and prevented him from going in. She pushed him back with her hands, and said that henceforth he had only to think of himself. Then the King, nearly fainting from a shock so complete and so sudden, fell upon a sofa that stood near. He asked unceasingly for news of all who passed, but scarce anybody dared to reply to him. He had sent for Père Tellier who went into Monseigneur's room; but it was no longer time. It is true the Jesuit, perhaps to console the King, said that he gave him a well-founded absolution. Madame de Maintenon hastened after the King, and sitting down beside him on the same sofa, tried to cry. She endeavored to lead away the King into the carriage already waiting for him in the courtyard, but he would not go, and sat thus outside the door until Monseigneur had expired.

The agony, without consciousness, of Monseigneur lasted more than an hour after the King had come into the cabinet. Madame la Duchess and Madame la Princess de Conti divided their cares between the dying man and the King, to whom they constantly came back; while the faculty confounded, the valets bewildered, the courtiers hurrying and murmuring, hustled against each other, and moved unceasingly to and fro, backward and forward, in the same narrow space. At last the fatal moment arrived. Fagon came out, and allowed so much to be understood.

The King, much afflicted, and very grieved that Monseigneur's confession had been so tardily made, abused Fagon a little; and went away led by Madame de Maintenon and the two Princesses. He was somewhat struck by finding the vehicle of Monseigneur outside; and made a sign that he would have another coach, for that one made him suffer, and left the *château*. He was not, however, so much occupied with his grief that he could not call Pontchartrain to arrange the hour of the council

of the next day. I will not comment on this coolness,
and shall merely say it surprised extremely all present;
and that if Pontchartrain had not said the council could
be put off, no interruption to business would have taken
place. The King got into his coach with difficulty, supported on both sides. Madame de Maintenon seated
herself beside him. A crowd of officers of Monseigneur
lined both sides of the court on their knees, as he passed
out, crying to him with strange howlings to have compassion on them, for they had lost all, and must die of
hunger.

CHAPTER XIX.

WHILE Meudon was filled with horror, all was tranquil at Versailles, without the least suspicion. We had supped. The company some time after had retired, and I was talking with Madame de Saint-Simon, who had nearly finished undressing herself to go to bed, when a servant of Madame la Duchess de Berry, who had formerly belonged to us, entered, all terrified. He said that there must be some bad news from Meudon, since Monseigneur le Duc de Bourgogne had just whispered in the ear of M. le Duc de Berry, whose eyes had at once become red, that he left the table, and that all the company shortly after him rose with precipitation. So sudden a change rendered my surprise extreme. I ran in hot haste to Madame la Duchess de Berry's. Nobody was there. Everybody had gone to Madame la Duchess de Bourgogne. I followed on with all speed.

I found all Versailles assembled on arriving, all the ladies hastily dressed — the majority having been on the point of going to bed — all the doors open, and all in trouble. I learned that Monseigneur had received the extreme unction, that he was without consciousness and beyond hope, and that the King had sent word to Madame de Bourgogne that he was going to Marly, and that she was to meet him as he passed through the avenue between the two stables.

The spectacle before me attracted all the attention I could bestow. The two Princes and the two Princesses were in the little cabinet behind the bed. The bed toilet was as usual in the chamber of the Duchess de Bourgogne, which was filled with all the Court in confusion. She came and went from the cabinet to the chamber, waiting for the moment when she was to meet the King; and her demeanor, always distinguished by the same graces, was one of trouble and compassion, which the trouble and compassion of others induced them to take for grief. Now and then, in passing, she said a few rare words. All present were in truth expressive personages. Whoever had eyes, without any knowledge of the Court, could see the interests of all interested painted on their faces, and the indifference of the indifferent; these tranquil, the former penetrated with grief, or gravely attentive to themselves to hide their emancipation and their joy.

For my part, my first care was to inform myself thoroughly of the state of affairs, fearing lest there might be too much alarm for too trifling a cause; then, recovering myself, I reflected upon the misery common to all men, and that I myself should find myself some day at the gates of death. Joy nevertheless found its way through the momentary reflections of religion and of humanity, by which I tried to master myself. My own private deliverance seemed so great and so unhoped for, that it appeared to me that the State must gain everything by such a loss. And with these thoughts I felt, in spite, of myself, a lingering fear lest the sick man should recover, and was extremely ashamed of it.

Wrapped up thus in myself, I did not fail, nevertheless, to cast clandestine looks upon each face, to see what was passing there. I saw Madame la Duchess d'Orléans arrive, but her countenance, majestic and constrained, said nothing. She went into the little cabinet, whence she presently issued with the Duc d'Orléans, whose activity and turbulent air marked his emotion at the spectacle more than any other sentiment. They went away, and I noticed this expressly, on account of what happened afterward in my presence.

Soon afterward I caught a distinct glimpse of the Duc de Bourgogne, who seemed much moved and troubled; but the glance with which I probed him rapidly, revealed nothing tender, and told merely of a mind profoundly occupied with the bearings of what had taken place.

Valets and chamber-women were already indiscreetly crying out; and THEIR grief showed well that they were about to lose something.

Toward half past twelve we had news of the King, and immediately after Madame de Bourgogne came out of the little cabinet with the Duke, who seemed more touched than when I first saw him. The Princess took her carf and her coifs from the toilet, standing with a deliberate air, her eyes scarcely wet — a fact betrayed by inquisitive glances cast rapidly to the right and left — and, followed only by her ladies, went to her coach by the great stair-case.

I took the opportunity to go to the Duchess d'Orléans, where I found many people. Their presence made me very impatient; the Duchess, who was equally impatient, took a light and went in. I whispered in the ear of the Duchess de Villeroy, who thought as I thought of this event. She nudged me, and said in a very low voice that I must contain myself. I was smothered with silence, amid the complaints and the narrative surprises of these ladies; but at last M. le Duc d'Orléans appeared at the door of his cabinet, and beckoned me to come to him.

I followed him into the cabinet where we were alone. What was my surprise, remembering the terms on which he was with Monseigneur, to see the tears streaming from his eyes.

"Sir!" exclaimed I, rising. He understood me at once; and answered in a broken voice, really crying: "You are right to be surprised — I am surprised myself; but such a spectacle touches. He was a man with whom I passed much of my life, and who treated me well when he was uninfluenced. I feel very well that my grief wont last long; in a few days I shall discover motives of joy; at present, blood, relationship, humanity, — all work; and my entrails are moved." I praised his sentiments, but repeated my surprise. He rose, thrust his head into a corner, and with his nose there, wept bitterly and sobbed, which if I had not seen I could not have believed.

After a little silence, however, I exhorted him to calm himself. I represented to him that, everybody knowing on what terms he had been with Monseigneur, he would be laughed at, as playing a part, if his eyes showed that he had been weeping. He did what he could to remove the marks of his tears, and we then went back into the other room.

The interview of the Duchess de Bourgogne with the King had not been long. She met him in the avenue between the two stables, got down, and went to the door of the carriage. Madame de Maintenon cried out, « Where are you going? We bear the plague about with us. » I do not know what the King said or did. The Princess returned to her carriage, and came back to Versailles, bringing in reality the first news of the actual death of Monseigneur.

Acting upon the advice of M. de Beauvilliers, all the company had gone into the *salon*. The two Princes, Monseigneur de Bourgogne and M. de Berry, were there, seated on one sofa, their Princesses at their side; all the rest of the company were scattered about in confusion, seated or standing, some of the ladies being on the floor, near the sofa. There could be no doubt of what had happened. It was plainly written on every face in the chamber and throughout the apartment. Monseigneur was no more: it was known: it was spoken of: constraint with respect to him no longer existed. Amid the surprise, the confusion, and the movements that prevailed, the sentiments of all were painted to the life in looks and gestures.

In the outside rooms were heard the constrained groans and sighs of the valets — grieving for the master they had lost as well as for the master that had succeeded. Farther on began the crowd of courtiers of all kinds. The greater number — that is to say the fools — pumped up sighs as well as they could, and with wandering but dry eyes, sung the praises of Monseigneur — insisting especially on his goodness. They pitied the King for the loss of so good a son. The keener began already to be uneasy about the health of the King; and admired themselves for preserving so much judgment amid so much trouble, which could be perceived by the frequency of their repetitions. Others, really afflicted — the discomfited Cabal — wept bitterly, and kept themselves under with an effort as easy to notice as sobs. The most strongminded or the wisest, with eyes fixed on the ground, in corners, meditated on the consequences of such an event — and especially on their own interests. Few words passed in conversation — here and there an exclamation wrung from grief was answered by some neighboring grief — a word every quarter of an hour — somber and haggard eyes — movements quite involuntary of the hands — immobility of all other parts of the body. Those who already looked upon the event as favorable in vain exaggerated their gravity so as to make it resemble chagrin and severity; the veil over their faces was transparent and hid not a single feature. They remained as motionless as those who grieved most, fearing opinion, curiosity, their own satisfaction, their every movement; but their eyes made up for their immobility. Indeed they could not refrain from repeatedly changing their attitude like people ill at ease, sitting or standing, from avoiding each other too carefully, even from allowing their eyes to meet — nor repress a manifest air of liberty — nor conceal their increased liveliness — nor put out a sort of brilliancy which distinguished them in spite of themselves.

The two princes, and the two princesses who sat by their sides, were more exposed to view than any other. The Duc de Bourgogne wept with tenderness, sincerity, and gentleness, the tears of nature, of religion, and patience. M. le Duc de Berry also sincerely shed abundance of tears, but bloody tears, so to speak, so great appeared their bitterness; and he uttered not only sobs, but cries, nay, even yells. He was silent sometimes, but from suffocation, and then would burst out again with such a noise, such a trumpet sound of despair, that the majority present burst out also at these dolorous repetitions, either impelled by affliction or decorum. He became so bad, in fact, that his people were forced to undress him then and there, put him to bed, and call in the doctor. Madame la Duchess de Berry was beside herself, and we shall soon see why. The most bitter

despair was painted with horror on her face. There was
seen written, as it were, a sort of furious grief, based
on interest, not affection; now and then came dry lulls
deep and sullen, then a torrent of tears and involuntary
gestures, yet restrained, which showed extreme bitterness
of mind, fruit of the profound meditation that had preceded. Often aroused by the cries of her husband,
prompt to assist him, to support him, to embrace him,
to give her smelling bottle, her care for him was evident;
but soon came another profound reverie—then a gush of
tears assisted to suppress her cries. As for Madame la
Duchess de Bourgogne she consoled her husband with
less trouble than she had to appear herself in want of
consolation. Without attempting to play a part, it was
evident that she did her best to acquit herself of a pressing duty of decorum. But she found extreme difficulty
in keeping up appearances. When the Prince her brother-
in-law howled, she blew her nose. She had brought
some tears along with her and kept them up with care;
and these combined with the art of the handkerchief,
enabled her to redden her eyes, and make them swell,
and smudge her face; but her glances often wandered
on the sly to the countenances of all present.

Madame arrived, in full dress she knew not why, and
howling she knew not why, inundated everybody with
her tears in embracing them, making the *château* echo
with renewed cries, and furnished the odd spectacle of
a princess putting on her robes of ceremony in the dead
of night to come and cry among a crowd of women with
but little on except their nightdresses,—almost as mas-
queraders.

In the gallery several ladies, Madame la Duchess d'Orléans, Madame de Castries, and Madame de Saint-Simon
among the rest, finding no one close by, drew near
each other by the side of a tent bedstead, and began to
open their hearts to each other, which they did with the
more freedom, inasmuch as they had but one sentiment
in common upon what had occurred. In this gallery, and
in the *salon*, there were always during the night several
beds in which, for security's sake, certain Swiss guards
and servants slept. These beds had been put in their usual

place this evening before the bad news came from Meudon. In the midst of the conversation of the ladies, Madame de Castries touched the bed, felt something move, and was much terrified. A moment after they saw a sturdy arm, nearly naked, raise on a sudden the curtains, and thus show them a great brawny Swiss under the sheets, half awake, and wholly amazed. The fellow was a long time in making out his position, fixing his eyes upon every face one after the other; but at last, not judging it advisable to get up in the midst of such a grand company, he reburied himself in his bed, and closed the curtains. Apparently the good man had gone to bed before anything had transpired, and had slept so soundly ever since that he had not been aroused until then. The saddest sights have often the most ridiculous contrasts. This caused some of the ladies to laugh, and made Madame d'Orléans fear lest the conversation should have been overheard. But after reflection, the sleep and the stupidity of the sleeper reassured her.

I had some doubts yet as to the event that had taken place; for I did not like to abandon myself to belief, until the word was pronounced by some one in whom I could have faith. By chance I met D'O, and I asked him. He answered me clearly that Monseigneur was no more. Thus answered, I tried not to be glad. I know not if I succeeded well, but at least it is certain, that neither joy nor sorrow blunted my curiosity, and that while taking due care to preserve all decorum, I did not consider myself in any way forced to play the doleful. I no longer feared any fresh attack from the citadel of Meudon, nor any cruel charges from its implacable garrison. I felt, therefore, under no constraint, and followed every face with my glances, and tried to scrutinize them unobserved. It must be admitted, that for him who is well acquainted with the privacies of a Court, the first sight of rare events of this nature, so interesting in so many different respects, is extremely satisfactory. Every countenance recalls the cares, the intrigues, the labors employed in the advancement of fortunes — in the overthrow of rivals; the relations, the coldness, the hatreds, the evil offices done, the baseness of all; hope, despair, rage, satisfaction, express themselves in the features. See how all eyes wander to and fro examining what passes around — how some are astonished to find others more mean, or less mean than was expected! Thus this spectacle produced a pleasure, which, hollow as it may be, is one of the greatest a Court can bestow.

The turmoil in this vast apartment lasted about an hour, at the end of which M. de Beauvilliers thought it was high time to deliver the Princes of their company. The rooms were cleared. M. le Duc de Berry went away to his rooms, partly supported by his wife. All through the night he asked, amid tears and cries, for news from Meudon; he would not understand the cause of the King's departure to Marly. When at length the mournful curtain was drawn from before his eyes, the state he fell into cannot be described. The night of Monseigneur and Madame de Bourgogne was more tranquil. Some one having said to the Princess, that having no real cause to be affected, it would be terrible to play a part, she replied, quite naturally, that without feigning, pity touched her and decorum controlled her; and indeed she kept herself within these bounds with truth and decency. Their chamber, in which they invited several ladies to pass the night in armchairs, became immediately a palace of Morpheus. All quietly fell asleep. The curtains were left open, so that the Prince and Princess could be seen sleeping profoundly. They woke up once or twice for a moment. In the morning the Duke and Duchess rose early, their tears quite dried up. They shed no more for this cause, except on special and rare occasions. The ladies who had watched and slept in their chamber, told their friends how tranquil the night had been. But nobody was surprised, and as there was no longer a Monseigneur, nobody was scandalized. Madame de Saint-Simon and I remained up two hours before going to bed, and then went there without feeling any want of rest. In fact, I slept so little that at seven in the morning I was up; but it must be admitted that such restlessness is sweet, and such reawakenings are savory.

Horror reigned at Meudon. As soon as the King left, all the courtiers left also, crowding into the first carriages that came. In an instant Meudon was empty. Mademoiselle Choin remained alone in her garret, and unaware of what had taken place. She learned it only by the cry raised. Nobody thought of telling her. At last some friends went up to her, hurried her into a hired coach, and took her to Paris. The dispersion was general. One or two valets, at the most, remained near the body. La Vrillière, to his praise be it said, was the only courtier who, not having abandoned Monseigneur during life, did not abandon him after his death. He had some difficulty to find somebody to go in search of Capuchins to pray over the corpse. The decomposition became so rapid and so great, that the opening of windows was not enough; the Capuchins, La Vrillière, and the valets, were compelled to pass the night outside.

At Marly everybody had felt so confident that the King's return there was not dreamed of. Nothing was ready, no keys of the rooms, no fires, scarcely an end of candle. The King was more than an hour thus with Madame de Maintenon and other ladies in one of the antechambers. The King retired into a corner, seated between Madame de Maintenon and two other ladies, and wept at long intervals. At last the chamber of Madame de Maintenon was ready. The King entered, remained there an hour, and then went to bed at nearly four o'clock in the morning.

Monseigneur was rather tall than short; very fat, but without being bloated; with a very lofty and noble aspect without any harshness; and he would have had a very agreeable face if M. le Prince de Conti had not unfortunately broken his nose in playing while they were both young. He was of a very beautiful fair complexion; he had a face everywhere covered with a healthy red, but without expression; the most beautiful legs in the world; his feet singularly small and delicate. He wavered always in walking, and felt his way with his feet; he was always afraid of falling, and if the path was not perfectly even and straight, he called for assistance. He was a good horseman, and looked well when mounted; but he was not a bold rider. When hunting—they had persuaded him that he liked this amusement—a servant rode before him; if he lost sight of this servant he gave himself up for lost, slacked his pace to a gentle trot, and oftentimes waited under a tree for the hunting party, and returned to it slowly. He was very fond of the table, but always without indecency. Ever since that great attack of indigestion, which was taken at first for apoplexy, he made but one real meal a day, and was content,— although a great eater, like the rest of the royal family. Nearly all his portraits well resemble him.

As for his character he had none; he was without enlightenment or knowledge of any kind, radically incapable of acquiring any; very idle, without imagination or productiveness; without taste, without choice, without discernment; neither seeing the weariness he caused others, nor that he was as a ball moving at haphazard by the impulsion of others; obstinate and little to excess in everything; amazingly credulous and accessible to prejudice, keeping himself, always, in the most pernicious hands, yet incapable of seeing his position or of changing it; absorbed in his fat and his ignorance; so that without any desire to do ill he would have made a pernicious King.

His avariciousness, except in certain things, passed all belief. He kept an account of his personal expenditure, and knew to a penny what his smallest and his largest expenses amounted to. He spent large sums in building, in furniture, in jewels, and in hunting, which he made himself believe he was fond of.

It is inconceivable the little he gave to La Choin, whom he so much loved. It never exceeded four hundred louis a quarter in gold, or sixteen hundred louis a year, whatever the louis might be worth. He gave them to her with his own hand, without adding or subtracting a pistole, and, at the most, made her but one present a year, and that he looked at twice before giving. It was said that they were married, and certain circumstances seemed to justify this rumor. As, for instance, during the illness of Monseigneur, the King, as I have said, asked Madame de Maintenon if she had seen Mademoiselle Choin, and upon receiving a negative reply, was displeased. Instead of driving her away from the *château* he inquired particularly after her! This, to say the least, looked as though Mademoiselle Choin was Monseigneur's Maintenon; but the matter remained incomprehensible to the last. Mademoiselle Choin threw no light upon it, although she spoke on many other things concerning Monseigneur in the modest home at Paris, to which she had retired for the rest of her days. The King gave her a pension of twelve thousand livres.

Monseigneur was, I have said, ignorant to the last degree, and had a thorough aversion for learning; so that, according to his own admission, ever since he had been released from the hands of teachers he had never read anything except the articles in the «Gazette de France,» in which deaths and marriages are recorded. His timidity, especially before the King, was equal to his ignorance, which indeed contributed not a little to cause it. The King took advantage of it and never treated him as a son, but as a subject. He was the monarch always, never the father. Monseigneur had not the slightest influence with the King. If he showed any preference for a person it was enough! That person was sure to be kept back by the King. The King was so anxious to show that Monseigneur could do nothing, that Monseigneur after a time did not even try. He contented himself by complaining occasionally in monosyllables, and by hoping for better times.

The body of Monseigneur so soon grew decomposed, that immediate burial was necessary. At midnight on Wednesday he was carried, with but little ceremony, to St. Denis, and deposited in the royal vaults. His funeral services were said at St. Denis on the 18th of the following June, and at Notre Dame on the 3d of July. As the procession passed through Paris nothing but cries, acclamations, and eulogiums of the defunct were heard. Monseigneur had, I know not how, much endeared himself to the common people of Paris, and this sentiment soon gained the provinces, so true it is, that in France it costs little to its princes to make themselves almost adored!

The King soon got over his affliction for the loss of

13

this son of fifty. Never was a man so ready with tears, so backward with grief, or so promptly restored to his ordinary state. The morning after the death of Monseigneur he rose late, called M. de Beauvilliers into his cabinet, shed some more tears, and then said that from that time Monseigneur le Duc de Bourgogne and Madame la Duchess de Bourgogne were to enjoy the honors, the rank, and the name of Dauphin and of Dauphine. Henceforth I shall call them by no other names.

My joy at this change may be imagined. In a few days all my causes of disquietude had been removed, and I saw a future opening before me full of light and promise. Monseigneur le Duc de Bourgogne became Dauphin, heir to the throne of France; what favor might I not hope for? I could not conceal or control my satisfaction.

But alas! it was soon followed by sad disappointment and grievous sorrow.*

* The death of Monseigneur leaving Louis XIV. almost in his dotage, on the throne, surrounded by young princes and princesses impatient for a new reign, worked a wonderful change in the Court of France. The subsequent part of these «Memoirs» will show the steps that led to the Regency of the Duc d'Orléans, and describe the state of France under that prince.

CHAPTER XX.

State of the Court at Death of Monseigneur — Conduct of the Dauphin and the Dauphine — The Duchess de Berry — My Interview with the Dauphin — He is Reconciled with M. d'Orléans.

THE death of Monseigneur, as we have seen, made a great change in the aspect of the Court and in the relative positions of its members. But the two persons to whom I must chiefly direct attention are the Duchess de Bourgogne and the Duchess de Berry. The former, on account of her husband's fall in the opinion of his father, had long been out of favor likewise. Although Monseigneur had begun to treat her less well for a long time, and most harshly during the campaign of Lille, and above all after the expulsion of the Duc de Vendôme from Mailly and Meudon; yet after the marriage of the Duc de Berry his coldness had still further increased. The adroit Princess, it is true, had rowed against the current with a steadiness and grace capable of disarming even a well-founded resentment; but the persons who surrounded him looked upon the melting of the ice as dangerous for their projects. The Duc and Duchess de Bourgogne were every day still further removed in comparative disgrace.

Things even went so far, that *apropos* of an engagement broken off, the Duchess resolved to exert her power instead of her persuasion, and threatened the two Lillebonnes. A sort of reconciliation was then patched up, but it was neither sincere nor apparently so.

The cabal which labored to destroy the Duc and Duchess de Bourgogne was equally assiduous in augmenting the influence of the Duc de Berry, whose wife had at once been admitted without having asked into the sanctuary of the Parvulo. The object was to disunite the two brothers and excite jealousy between them. In this they did not succeed even in the slightest degree. But they found a formidable ally in the Duchess de Berry, who proved as full of wickedness and ambition as any among them. The Duc d'Orléans often called his Duchess Madame Lucifer, at which she used to smile with complacency. He was right, for she would have been a prodigy of pride had she not had a daughter who far surpassed her. This is not yet the time to paint their portraits; but I must give a word or two of explanation on the Duchess de Berry.

That princess was a marvel of wit, of pride, of ingratitude and folly — nay, of debauchery and obstinacy. Scarcely had she been married a week when she began to exhibit herself in all these lights, — not too manifestly it is true, for one of the qualities of which she was most vain was her falsity and power of concealment, but sufficient to make an impression on those around her. People soon perceived how annoyed she was to be the daughter of an illegitimate mother, and to have lived under her restraint however mild; how she despised the weakness of her father, the Duc d'Orléans, and how confident she was of her influence over him; and how she had hated all who had interfered in her marriage — merely because she could not bear to be under obligations to anyone — a reason she was absurd enough publicly to avow and boast of. Her conduct was now based on those motives. This is an example of how in this world people work with their heads in a sack, and how human prudence and wisdom are sometimes confounded by successes which have been reasonably desired and which turn out to be detestable. We had brought about this marriage to avoid a marriage with Mademoiselle de Bourbon and to cement the union of the two brothers. We now discovered that there was little danger of Mademoiselle de Bourbon, and then instead of her we had a Fury who had no thought but how to ruin those who had established her, to injure her benefactors, to make her husband and her brother quarrel, and to put herself in the power of her enemies because they were the enemies of her natural friends. It never occurred to her that the cabal would not be

likely to abandon to her the fruit of so much labor
and so many crimes.

It may easily be imagined that she was neither gentle
nor docile when Madame la Duchess began to give her
advice. Certain that her father would support her, she
played the stranger and daughter of France with her
mother. Estrangement, however, soon came on. She
behaved differently in form, but in effect the same with
the Duchess de Bourgogne, who wished to guide her as
a daughter, but who soon gave up the attempt. The
Duchess de Perry's object could only be gained by bringing about disunion between the two brothers, and for
this purpose she employed as a spring the passion of her
husband for herself.

The first night at Versailles after the death of Monseigneur was sleepless. The Dauphin and Dauphine heard
mass early next morning. I went to see them. Few
persons were present on account of the hour. The
Princess wished to be at Marly at the King's waking.
Their eyes were wonderfully dry, but carefully managed,
and it was easy to see they were more occupied with
their new position than with the death of Monseigneur.
A smile which they exchanged as they spoke in whispers
convinced me of this. One of their first cares was to endeavor to increase their good relations with the Duc and
Duchess de Berry. They were to see them before they
were up. The Duc de Berry showed himself very sensible to this act, and the Duchess was eloquent, clever,
and full of tears. But her heart was wrung by these
advances of pure generosity. The separation she
had planned soon followed; and the two princesses
felt relieved at no longer being obliged to dine together.

Thus never was change greater or more marked than
that brought about by the death of Monseigneur. That
prince had become the center of all hope and of all fear,
a formidable cabal had seized upon him, yet without
awakening the jealousy of the King, before whom all
trembled, but whose anxieties did not extend beyond his
own lifetime, during which and very reasonably, he feared
nothing.

Before I go any further, let me note a circumstance
characteristic of the King. Madame la Dauphine went
every day to Marly to see him. On the day after the
death of Monseigneur she received, not without surprise,
easily understood, a hint from Madame de Maintenon.
It was to the effect that she should dress herself with
some little care, inasmuch as the negligence of her attire displeased the King! The Princess did not think
that dress ought to occupy her then; and even if she
had thought so, she would have believed, and with good
reason, that she was committing a grave fault against
decorum, a fault which would have been less readily
pardoned, since in every way she had gained too much
by what had just occurred not be very guarded in her
behavior. On the next day she took more pains with
her toilet: but what she did, not being found sufficient
the day following she carried with her some things and
dressed herself secretly in Madame de Maintenon's rooms;
and resumed there her ordinary apparel before returning
to Versailles. Thus she avoided offense both to the King
and to society. The latter certainly would with difficulty have been persuaded that in this ill-timed adornment of her person, her own tastes went for nothing.
The Comtesse de Mailly, who invented the scheme, and
Madame de Nogaret, who both liked Monseigneur, related this to me and were piqued by it. From this fact
and from the circumstance that all the ordinary pleasures
and occupations were resumed immediately after the
death of Monseigneur, the King passing his days without any constraint,—it may be assumed that if the royal
grief was bitter its evidences were of a kind to promise
that it would not be of long duration.

M. le Dauphin, for, as I have said, it is by that title
I shall now name Monseigneur le Duc de Bourgogne —
M. le Dauphin, I say, soon gained all hearts. In the
first days of solitude following upon the death of Monseigneur, the King intimated to M. de Beauvilliers that
he should not care to see the new Dauphin go very often
to Meudon. This was enough. M. le Dauphin at once
declared that he would never set his foot in that palace,
and that he would never quit the King. He was as good

as his word, and not one single visit did he ever afterward pay to Meudon. The King wished to give him fifty thousand livres a month, Monseigneur having had that sum. M. le Dauphin would not accept them. He had only six thousand livres per month. He was satisfied with double that amount and would not receive more. This disinterestedness much pleased the public. M. le Dauphin wished for nothing special on his account, and persisted in remaining in nearly everything as he was during the life of Monseigneur. These auguries of a prudent and measured reign, suggested the brightest of hopes.

Aided by his adroit spouse, who already had full possession of the King's heart and of that of Madame de Maintenon, M. le Dauphin redoubled his attentions in order to possess them also. These attentions, addressed to Madame de Maintenon, produced their fruit. She was transported with pleasure at finding a Dauphin upon whom she could rely, instead of one whom she did not like, gave herself up to him accordingly, and by that means secured to him the King's favor. The first fortnight made evident to everybody at Marly the extraordinary change that had come over the King with respect to the Dauphin. His Majesty, generally severe beyond measure with his legitimate children, showed the most marked graciousness for this prince. The effect of this, and of the change that had taken place in his state, were soon most clearly visible in the Dauphin. Instead of being timid and retiring, diffident in speech, and more fond of his study than of the *salon*, he became on a sudden easy and frank, showing himself in public on all occasions, conversing right and left in a gay, agreeable, and dignified manner; presiding, in fact, over the Salon of Marly, and over the groups gathered round him, like the divinity of a temple, who receives with goodness the homage to which he is accustomed, and recompenses the mortals who offer it with gentle regard.

In a short time hunting became a less usual topic of conversation. History, and even science, were touched upon lightly, pleasantly, and discreetly, in a manner that charmed while it instructed. The Dauphin spoke with

an eloquent freedom that opened all eyes, ears, and
hearts. People sometimes, in gathering near him, were
less anxious to make their court than to listen to his
natural eloquence, and to draw from it delicious instruction.   It is astonishing with what rapidity he gained
universal esteem and admiration. The public joy could
not keep silent. People asked each other if this was
really the same man they had known as the Duc de
Bourgogne, whether he was a vision or a reality? One
of M. le Dauphin's friends, to whom this question was
addressed, gave a keen reply. He answered, that the
cause of all this surprise was, that previously the people
did not, and would not, know this prince, who, nevertheless, to those who had known him, was the same now
as he had ever been; and that this justice would be
rendered to him when time had shown how much it was
deserved.

From the Court to Paris, and from Paris to the provinces, the reputation of the Dauphin flew on rapid wings.
However founded might be this prodigious success, we
need not believe it was entirely due to the marvelous
qualities of the young prince. It was in a great measure a reaction against the hostile feeling toward him
which had been excited by the cabal, whose efforts I
have previously spoken of. Now that people saw how
unjust was this feeling, their astonishment added to
their admiration. Everybody was filled with a sentiment of joy at seeing the first dawn of a new state of
things, which promised so much order and happiness
after such a long confusion and so much obscurity.

Gracious as the King showed himself to M. le Dauphin, and accustomed as the people grew to his graciousness, all the Court was strangely surprised at a fresh
mark of favor that was bestowed one morning by his
Majesty on this virtuous prince. The King, after having
been closeted alone with him for some time, ordered his
ministers to work with the Dauphin whenever sent for,
and, whether sent for or not, to make him acquainted with
all public affairs; this command being given once for all.

It is not easy to describe the prodigious movement
caused at the Court by this order, so directly opposed to

the tastes, to the disposition, to the maxims, to the usage of the King, who thus showed a confidence in the Dauphin which was nothing less than tacitly transferring to him a large part of the disposition of public affairs. This was a thunderbolt for the ministers,—who, accustomed to have almost everything their own way, to rule over everybody and browbeat everybody at will, to govern the State abroad and at home, in fact,—fixing all punishments, all recompenses, and always sheltering themselves behind the royal authority—"the King wills it so" being the phrase ever on their lips,—to these officers, I say, it was a thunderbolt which so bewildered them that they could not hide their astonishment or their confusion. The public joy at an order which reduced these ministers, or rather these kings, to the condition of subjects, which put a curb upon their power, and provided against the abuses they committed, was great indeed! The ministers were compelled to bend their necks, though stiff as iron, to the yoke. They all went, with a hangdog look, to show the Dauphin a feigned joy and a forced obedience to the order they had received.

Here, perhaps, I may as well speak of the situation in which I soon afterward found myself with the Dauphin, the confidence as to the present and the future that I enjoyed with him, and the many deliberations we had upon public affairs. The matter is curious and interesting, and need no longer be deferred.

The Court being changed by the death of Monseigneur, I soon began indeed to think of changing my conduct with regard to the new Dauphin. M. de Beauvilliers spoke to me about this matter first, but he judged, and I shared his opinion, that slandered as I had been on previous occasions, and remaining still, as it were, half in disgrace, I must approach the Dauphin only by slow degrees, and not endeavor to shelter myself under him until his authority with the King had become strong enough to afford me a safe asylum. I believed, nevertheless, that it would be well to sound him immediately; and one evening, when he was but thinly accompanied, I joined him in the gardens at Marly, and profited by his gracious welcome to say to him, on the sly, that many

reasons, of which he was not ignorant, had necessarily
kept me until then removed from him, but that now I
hoped to be able to follow with less constraint my attachment and my inclination, and that I flattered myself this
would be agreeable to him. He replied in a low tone,
that there were sometimes reasons which fettered people,
but in our case such no longer existed; that he knew of
my regard for him, and reckoned with pleasure that we
should soon see each other more frequently than before.
I am writing the exact words of his reply, on account of
the singular politeness of the concluding ones. I regarded that reply as the successful result of a bait that
had been taken as I wished. Little by little I became
more assiduous at his promenades, but without following
them when the crowd or any dangerous people do so; and I
spoke more freely. I remained content with seeing the
Dauphin in public, and I approached him in the *salon*
only when I saw a good opportunity.

Some days after, being in the *salon*, I saw the Dauphin
and the Dauphine enter together and converse. I approached and heard their last words; they stimulated me
to ask the Prince what was in debate, not in a straightforward manner, but in a sort of respectful, insinuating
way which I already adopted. He explained to me that
he was going to St. Germain to pay an ordinary visit;
that on this occasion there would be some change in the
ceremonial; explained the matter and enlarged with
eagerness on the necessity of not abandoning legitimate
rights.

"How glad I am to see you think thus," I replied,
"and how well you act in advocating these forms, the
neglect of which tarnishes everything."

He responded with warmth; and I seized the moment
to say, that if he, whose rank was so great and so decided, was right to pay attention to these things, how
much we dukes had reason to complain of our losses,
and to try to sustain ourselves! Thereupon he entered
into the question so far as to become the advocate of our
cause, and finished by saying that he regarded our res-
toration as an act of justice important to the State; that
he knew I was well instructed in these things, and that I

should give him pleasure by talking of them some day.* He rejoined at that moment the Dauphine, and they set off for St. Germain.

A few days after this the Dauphin sent for me. I entered by the wardrobe, where a sure and trusty valet was in waiting; he conducted me to a cabinet in which the Dauphin was sitting alone. Our conversation at once commenced. For a full hour we talked upon the state of affairs, the Dauphin listening with much attention to all I said, and expressing himself with infinite modesty, sense, and judgment. His views, I found, were almost entirely in harmony with mine. He was sorry, and touchingly said so, for the ignorance of all things in which the King was kept by his minister; he was anxious to see the power of those ministers restricted; he looked with dislike upon the incredible elevation of the illegitimate children; he wished to see the order to which I belonged restored to the position it deserved to occupy.

It is difficult to express what I felt in quitting the Dauphin. A magnificent and near future opened out before me. I saw a prince, pious, just, debonair, enlightened, and seeking to become more so; with principles completely in accord with my own, and capacity to carry out those principles when the time for doing so arrived. I relished deliciously a confidence so precious and so full, upon the most momentous matters, and at a first interview. I felt all the sweetness of this perspective, and of my deliverance from a servitude which, in spite of myself, I sometimes could not help showing myself impatient of. I felt, too, that I now had an opportunity of elevating myself, and of contributing to those grand works, for the happiness and advantage of the state I so much wished to see accomplished.

A few days after this I had another interview with the Dauphin. I was introduced secretly as before, so that no one perceived either my coming or my departure. The same subjects we had previously touched upon we now entered into again, and more amply than on the former occasion. The Dauphin, in taking leave of me, gave me

---

* This incredibly serious tone adopted in reference to mere questions of etiquette and precedence is worthy of remark.

full permission to see him in private as often as I desired, though in public I was still to be circumspect.

Indeed there was need of great circumspection in carrying on even private intercourse with the Dauphin. From
this time I continually saw him in his cabinet, talking with
him in all liberty upon the various persons of the Court,
and upon the various subjects relating to the State; but
always with the same secrecy as at first. This was absolutely necessary; as I have just said, I was still in a sort
of half disgrace: the King did not regard me with the
eyes of favor; Madame de Maintenon was resolutely averse
to me. If these two had suspected my strict intimacy
with the heir to the throne, I should have been assuredly
lost.

To show what need there was of precaution in my
private interviews with the Dauphin, let me here relate
an incident which one day occurred when we were
closeted together, and which might have led to the
gravest results.

The Prince lodged then in one of the four grand suites
of apartments, on the same level as the *salon*,—the suite
that was broken up during an illness of Madame la
Princess de Conti, to make way for a grand staircase,
the narrow and crooked one in use annoying the King
when he ascended it. The chamber of the Dauphin was
there; the bed had its foot toward the windows; by the
chimney was the door of the obscure wardrobe by which
I entered; between the chimney and one of the two
windows was a little portable bureau; in front of the
ordinary entrance door of the chamber and behind the
bureau was the door of one of the Dauphin's rooms;
between the two windows was a chest of drawers which
was used for papers only.

There were only some moments of conversation before
the Dauphin set himself down at his bureau, and ordered
me to place myself opposite him. Having become more
free with him, I took the liberty to say one day in these
first moments of our discourse, that he would do well to
bolt the door behind him, the door I mean of the Dauphine's chamber. He said that the Dauphine would not
come, it not being her hour. I replied that I did not

fear that princess herself, but the crowd that always accompanied her. He was obstinate, and would not bolt the door. I did not dare to press him more. He sat down before his bureau, and ordered me to sit also. Our deliberation was long; afterward we sorted our papers. Here let me say this — Every time I went to see the Dauphin I garnished all my pockets with papers, and I often smiled within myself passing through the *salon*, at seeing there many people who at that moment were in my pockets, and who were far indeed from suspecting the important discussion that was going to take place. To return: the Dauphin gave me his papers to put in my pocket, and kept mine. He locked up some in his cupboard, and instead of locking up the others in his bureau, kept them out, and began talking to me, his back to the chimney, his papers in one hand, his keys in the other. I was standing at the bureau looking for some other papers, when on a sudden the door in front of me opened, and the Dauphine entered!

The first appearance of all three — for, thank God! she was alone — the astonishment, the countenance of all have never left my memory. Our fixed eyes, our statue-like immobility, and our embarrassment were all alike, and lasted longer than a slow Paternoster. The Princess spoke first. She said to the Prince in a very ill-assured voice, that she had not imagined him in such good company; smiling upon him and upon me. I had scarce time to smile also and to lower my eyes, before the Dauphin replied.

"Since you find me so," said he, smiling in turn, "leave me so."

For an instant she looked on him, he and she both smiling at each other more; then she looked on me, still smiling with greater liberty than at first, made a pirouette, went away and closed the door, beyond the threshold of which she had not come.

Never have I seen woman so astonished; never man so taken aback, as the Prince after the Dauphine's departure; and never man, to say truth, was so afraid as I was at first, though I quickly reassured myself when I found that our intruder was alone. As soon as she had

closed the door, "Well, Monsieur," said I to the Dauphin,
"if you had drawn the bolt?"

"You were right," he replied, "and I was wrong. But
no harm is done. She was alone fortunately, and I guarantee to you her secrecy."

"I am not troubled," said I to him (yet I was so
mightily), "but it is a miracle she was alone. With her
suite you would have escaped with a scolding perhaps,
but for me, I should have been utterly lost."

He admitted again he had been wrong, and assured
me more and more that our secret was safe. The
Dauphine had caught us, not only *tête-à-tête* — of which
no one had the least suspicion — she had caught us in
the fact, so to say, our crimes in our hands. I felt that
she would not expose the Dauphin, but I feared an
after-revelation through some over-easy confidant. Nevertheless our secret was so well kept if confided that it
never transpired. We finished, I to pocket, the Prince
to lock up, the papers. The rest of the conversation
was short, and I withdrew by the wardrobe as usual.
M. de Beauvilliers, to whom I related this adventure
shortly afterward, grew pale at first, but recovered when
I said the Dauphine was alone. He blamed the imprudence of the Dauphin, but assured me my secret was
safe. Ever since that adventure the Dauphine often
smiled upon me when we met, as if to remind me of it,
and showed marked attention to me.

No sooner did I feel myself pretty firmly established
on this footing of delicious intimacy with the Dauphin
than I conceived the desire to unite him with M. le Duc
d'Orléans through the means of M. de Beauvilliers. At
the very outset, however, an obstacle rose in my path.

I have already said that the friendship of M. d'Orléans for his daughter, Madame la Duchess de Berry,
had given employment to the tongues of Satan, set in
motion by hatred and jealousy. Evil reports even
reached M. le Duc de Berry, who on his part, wishing
to enjoy the society of his wife in full liberty, was importuned by the continual presence near her of her
father. To ward off a quarrel between son-in-law and
father-in-law, based upon so false and so odious a founda-

tion, appeared to Madame de Saint-Simon and myself a pressing duty.

I had already tried to divert M. le Duc d'Orléans from an assiduity which wearied M. le Duc de Berry; but I had not succeeded. I believed it my duty then to return to the charge more hotly; and remembering my previous ill success, I prefaced properly, and then said what I had to say. M. d'Orléans was astonished; he cried out against the horror of such a vile imputation and the villainy that had carried it to M. le Duc de Berry. He thanked me for having warned him of it, a service few besides myself would have rendered him. I left him to draw the proper and natural conclusion on the conduct he should pursue. This conversation passed one day at Versailles about four o'clock in the afternoon.

On the morrow Madame de Saint-Simon related to me, that returning home the previous evening, from the supper and the cabinet of the King with Madame la Duchess de Berry, the Duchess had passed straight into the wardrobe and called her there; and then with a cold and angry air, said she was very much astonished that I wished to get up a quarrel between her and M. le Duc d'Orléans. Madame Saint-Simon exhibited surprise, but Madame la Duchess de Berry declared that nothing was so true; that I wished to estrange M. d'Orléans from her, but that I should not succeed; and immediately related all that I had just said to her father. He had had the goodness to repeat it to her an hour afterward! Madame de Saint-Simon still more surprised, listened attentively to the end, and replied that this horrible report was public, that she herself could see what consequences it would have, false and abominable as it might be, and feel whether it was not important that M. le Duc d'Orléans should be informed of it. She added, that I had shown such proofs of my attachment for them and of my desire for their happiness, that I was above all suspicion. Then she courtesied and leaving the Princess went to bed. This scene appeared to me enormous.

For some time after this I ceased entirely to see M. le Duc d'Orléans and Madame la Duchess de Berry. They cajoled me with all sorts of excuses, apologies, and so forth, but I remained frozen. They redoubled their excuses and their prayers. Friendship, I dare not say compassion, seduced me, and I allowed myself to be led away. In a word, we were reconciled. I kept aloof, however, from Madame la Duchess de Berry as much as possible, visiting her only for form's sake; and as long as she lived never changed in this respect.

Being reconciled with M. d'Orléans, I again thought of my project of uniting him to the Dauphin through M. de Beauvilliers. He had need of some support, for on all sides he was sadly out of favor. His debauchery and his impiety, which he had quitted for a time after separating himself from Madame d'Argenton, his mistress, had now seized on him again as firmly as ever. It seemed as though there were a wager between him and his daughter, Madame la Duchess de Berry, which should cast most contempt on religion and good manners.

The King was nothing ignorant of the conduct of his nephew. He had been much shocked with the return to debauchery and low company. The enemies of M. d'Orléans, foremost among which was M. Du Maine, had therefore everything in their favor. As I have said, without some support M. d'Orléans seemed in danger of being utterly lost.

It was no easy matter to persuade M. de Beauvilliers to fall in with the plan I had concocted, and lend his aid to it. But, I worked him hard. I dwelt upon the taste of the Dauphin for history, science, and the arts, and showed what a ripe knowledge of those subjects M. d'Orléans had, and what agreeable conversation thereon they both might enjoy together. In brief I won over M. de Beauvilliers to my scheme. M. d'Orléans, on his side, saw without difficulty the advantage to him of union with the Dauphin. To bring it about I laid before him two conditions. One, that when in the presence of the Prince he should suppress that detestable heroism of impiety he affected more than he felt, and allow no licentious expressions to escape him. The second was to go less often into evil company at Paris, and if he must continue his debauchery, to do so at the least within closed doors, and avoid all public scandal. He promised obedience, and was faithful to his promise. The Dauphin perceived and approved the change; little by little the object of my desire was gained.

As I have already said, it would be impossible for me to express all the joy I felt at my deliverance from the dangers I was threatened with during the lifetime of Monseigneur. My respect, esteem, and admiration for the Dauphin grew more and more day by day, as I saw his noble qualities blossom out in richer luxuriance. My hopes, too, took a brighter color from the rising dawn of prosperity that was breaking around me. Alas! that I should be compelled to relate the cruel manner in which envious fortune took from me the cup of gladness just as I was raising it to my lips.

14

CHAPTER XXI.

Warnings to the Dauphin and Dauphine — The Dauphine Sickens and Dies — Illness of the Dauphin — His Death — Character and Manners of the Dauphine — And of the Dauphin.

ON MONDAY, the 18th of January, 1712, after a visit to Versailles, the King went to Marly. I mark expressly this journey. No sooner were we settled there than Boudin, chief doctor of the Dauphine, warned her to take care of herself, as he had received sure information that there was a plot to poison her and the Dauphin, to whom he made a similar communication. Not content with this he repeated it with a terrified manner to everybody in the *salon*, and frightened all who listened to him. The King spoke to him about it in private. Boudin declared that this information was good, and yet that he did not know whence it came; and he stuck to this contradiction. For, if he did not know where the information came from, how could he be assured it was trustworthy?

The most singular thing is, that twenty-four hours after Boudin had uttered this warning, the Dauphin received a similar one from the King of Spain, vague, and without mentioning whence obtained, and yet also declared to be of good source. In this only the Dauphin was named distinctly — the Dauphine obscurely and by implication — at least, so the Dauphin explained the matter, and I never heard that he said otherwise. People pretended to despise these stories of origin unknown, but they were struck by them nevertheless, and in the midst of the amusements and occupations of the Court, seriousness, silence, and consternation were spread.*

* These stories, and the subsequent events that seemed to confirm them, have never been explained. It is unfortunate, however, that Saint-Simon should just previously have brought about an intimacy between the Duc d'Orléans and the Dauphin, the Duke having so repeatedly been accused of poisoning practices.

The King, as I have said, went to Marly on Monday, the 18th of January, 1712. The Dauphine came there early with a face very much swelled, and went to bed at once; yet she rose at seven o'clock in the evening, because the King wished her to preside in the *salon*. She played there, in morning dress, with her head wrapped up, visited the King in the apartment of Madame de Maintenon just before his supper, and then again went to bed, where she supped. On the morrow, the 19th, she rose only to play in the *salon*, and see the King, returning to her bed and supping there. On the 20th, her swelling diminished, and she was better. She was subject to this complaint, which was caused by her teeth. She passed the following days as usual. On Monday, the 1st of February, the Court returned to Versailles.

On Friday, the 5th of February, the Duc de Noailles gave a very fine box full of excellent Spanish snuff to the Dauphine, who took some, and liked it. This was toward the end of the morning. Upon entering her cabinet (closed to everybody else), she put this box upon the table, and left it there. Toward the evening she was seized with trembling fits of fever. She went to bed, and could not rise again even to go to the King's cabinet after the supper. On Saturday, the 6th of February, the Dauphine, who had had fever all night, did not fail to rise at her ordinary hour, and to pass the day as usual; but in the evening the fever returned. She was but middling all that night, a little worse the next day; but toward ten o'clock at night she was suddenly seized by a sharp pain under the temple. It did not extend to the dimensions of a ten sous piece, but was so violent that she begged the King who was coming to see her, not to enter. This kind of madness of suffering lasted without intermission until Monday, the 8th, and was proof against tobacco chewed and smoked, a quantity of opium, and two bleedings in the arms. Fever showed itself more when this pain was a little calmed; the Dauphin said she had suffered more than in childbirth.

Such a violent illness filled the chamber with rumors concerning the snuffbox given to the Dauphine by the Duc de Noailles. In going to bed the day she had received it and was seized by fever, she spoke of the snuff to her ladies, highly praising it and the box, which she told one of them to go and look for upon the table in the cabinet, where, as I have said, it had been left. The box could not be found, although looked for high and low. This disappearance had seemed very extraordinary from the first moment it became known. Now, joined to the grave illness with which the Dauphine was so cruelly assailed, it aroused the most somber suspicions. Nothing, however, was breathed of these suspicions, beyond a very restricted circle; for the Princess took snuff with the knowledge of Madame de Maintenon, but without that of the King, who would have made a fine scene if he had discovered it. This was what was feared, if the singular loss of the box became divulged.

Let me here say, that although one of my friends, the Archbishop of Rheims, believed to his dying day that the Duc de Noailles had poisoned the Dauphine by means of this box of Spanish snuff, I never could induce myself to believe so too. The Archbishop declared that in the manner of the Duc de Noailles, after quitting the chamber of the Princess, there was something which suggested both confusion and contentment. He brought forward other proofs of guilt, but they made no impression upon me. I endeavored, on the contrary, to shake his belief, but my labor was in vain. I entreated him, however, at least to maintain the most profound silence upon this horrible thought, and he did so.

Those who afterward knew the history of the box — and they were in good number — were as inaccessible to suspicion as I; and nobody thought of charging the Duc de Noailles with the offense it was said he had committed. As for me, I believed in his guilt so little that our intimacy remained the same; and although that intimacy grew even up to the death of the King, we never spoke of this fatal snuffbox.

During the night, from Monday to Tuesday, the 9th of February, the lethargy was great. During the day the King approached the bed many times: the fever was strong, the awakenings were short; the head was confused, and some marks upon the skin gave tokens of measles, because they extended quickly, and because many people at Versailles and at Paris were known to be, at this time, attacked with that disease. The night from Tuesday to Wednesday passed so much the more badly, because the hope of measles had already vanished. The King came in the morning to see Madame la Dauphine, to whom an emetic had been given. It operated well, but produced no relief. The Dauphin, who scarcely ever left the bed-side of his wife, was forced into the garden to take the air, of which he had much need; but his disquiet led him back immediately into the chamber. The malady increased toward the evening, and at eleven o'clock there was a considerable augmentation of fever. The night was very bad. On Thursday, the 11th of February, at nine o'clock in the morning, the King entered the Dauphine's chamber, which Madame de Maintenon scarcely ever left, except when he was in her apartments. The Princess was so ill that it was resolved to speak to her of receiving the Sacrament. Prostrated though she was she was surprised at this. She put some questions as to her state; replies as little terrifying as possible were given to her, and little by little she was warned against delay. Grateful for this advice, she said she would prepare herself.

After some time, accidents being feared, Father la Rue, her (Jesuit) confessor, whom she had always appeared to like, approached her to exhort her not to delay confession. She looked at him, replied that she understood him, and then remained silent. Like a sensible man he saw what was the matter, and at once said that if she had any objection to confess to him to have no hesitation in admitting it. Thereupon she indicated that she should like to have M. Bailly, priest of the mission of the parish of Versailles. He was a man much esteemed, but not altogether free from the suspicion of Jansenism. Bailly, as it happened, had gone to Paris. This being told her, the Dauphine asked for Father Noël, who was instantly sent for.

The excitement that this change of confessor made at a moment so critical may be imagined. All the cruelty of the tyranny that the King never ceased to exercise over every member of his family was now apparent.

They could not have a confessor not of his choosing! What was his surprise and the surprise of all the Court, to find that in these last terrible moments of life the Dauphine wished to change her confessor, whose Order even she repudiated!

Meanwhile the Dauphin had given way. He had hidden his own illness as long as he could, so as not to leave the pillow of his Dauphine. Now the fever he had was too strong to be dissimulated; and the doctors who wished to spare him the sight of the horrors they foresaw, forgot nothing to induce him to stay in his chamber, where, to sustain him, false news was, from time to time, brought him of the state of his spouse.

The confession of the Dauphine was long. Extreme unction was administered immediately afterward; and the holy viaticum directly. An hour afterward the Dauphine desired the prayers for the dying to be said. They told her she was not yet in that state, and with words of consolation exhorted her to try and get to sleep. Seven doctors of the Court and of Paris were sent for. They consulted together in the presence of the King and Madame de Maintenon. All with one voice were in favor of bleeding at the foot; and in case it did not have the effect desired, to give an emetic at the end of the night. The bleeding was executed at seven o'clock in the evening. The return of the fever came and was found less violent than the preceding. The night was cruel. The King came early next morning to see the Dauphine. The emetic she took at about nine o'clock had little effect. The day passed in symptoms each more sad than the other; consciousness only at rare intervals. All at once toward evening, the whole chamber fell into dismay. A number of people were allowed to enter although the King was there. Just before she expired he left, mounted into his coach at the foot of the grand staircase, and with Madame de Maintenon and Madame de Caylus went away to Marly. They were both in the most bitter grief, and had not the courage to go to the Dauphin. Upon arriving at Marly the King supped in his own room; and passed a short time with M. d'Orléans and his natural children. M. le Duc de Berry, entirely occupied with his affliction which was great and real, had remained at Versailles with Madame la Duchess de Berry, who, transported with joy upon seeing herself delivered from a powerful rival, to whom, however, she owed all, made her face do duty for her heart.

Monseigneur le Dauphin, ill and agitated by the most bitter grief, kept his chamber; but on Saturday morning the 13th, being pressed to go to Marly to avoid the horror of the noise overhead where the Dauphine was lying dead, he set out for that place at seven o'clock in the morning. Shortly after arriving he heard mass in the chapel, and thence was carried in a chair to the window of one of his rooms. Madame de Maintenon came to see him there afterward; the anguish of the interview was speedily too much for her, and she went away. Early in the morning I went uninvited to see M. le Dauphin. He showed me that he perceived this with an air of gentleness and of affection which penetrated me. But I was terrified with his looks, constrained, fixed, and with something wild about them, with the change in his face and with the marks there, livid rather than red, that I observed in good number and large; marks observed by the others also. The Dauphin was standing. In a few minutes he was apprised that the King had awaked. The tears that he had restrained, now rolled from his eyes; he turned round at the news but said nothing, remaining stock-still. His three attendants proposed to him, once or twice, that he should go to the King. He neither spoke nor stirred. I approached and made signs to him to go, then softly spoke to the same effect. Seeing that he still remained speechless and motionless, I made bold to take his arm, representing to him that sooner or later he must see the King, who expected him, and assuredly with the desire to see and embrace him; and pressing him in this manner, I took the liberty to gently push him. He cast upon me a look that pierced my soul and went away. I followed him some few steps and then withdrew to recover breath; I never saw him again. May I, by the mercy of God, see him eternally where God's goodness doubtless has placed him!

The Dauphin reached the chamber of the King, full just then of company. As soon as he appeared the King called him and embraced him tenderly again and again. These first moments, so touching, passed in words broken by sobs and tears.

Shortly afterward the King looking at the Dauphin was terrified by the same things that had previously struck me with affright. Everybody around was so, also the doctors more than the others. The King ordered them to feel his pulse; that they found bad, so they said afterward; for the time they contented themselves with saying it was not regular, and that the Dauphin would do wisely to go to bed. The King embraced him again, recommended him very tenderly to take care of himself, and ordered him to go to bed. He obeyed and rose no more!

It was now late in the morning. The King had passed a cruel night and had a bad headache; he saw at his dinner the few courtiers who presented themselves, and after dinner went to the Dauphin. The fever had augmented; the pulse was worse than before. The King passed into the apartments of Madame de Maintenon, and the Dauphin was left with his attendants and his doctors. He spent the day in prayers and holy reading.

On the morrow, Sunday, the uneasiness felt on account of the Dauphin augmented. He himself did not conceal his belief that he should never rise again, and that the plot Boudin had warned him of, had been executed. He explained himself to this effect more than once, and always with a disdain of earthly grandeur and an incomparable submission and love of God. It is impossible to describe the general consternation. On Monday, the 15th, the King was bled. The Dauphin was no better than before. The King and Madame de Maintenon saw him separately several times during the day, which was passed in prayers and reading.

On Tuesday, the 16th, the Dauphin was worse. He felt himself devoured by a consuming fire, which the external fever did not seem to justify; but the pulse was very extraordinary and exceedingly menacing. This was a deceptive day. The marks on the Dauphin's face extended over all the body. They were regarded as the marks of measles. Hope arose thereon, but the doctors and the most clear sighted of the Court could not forget that these same marks had shown themselves on the body of the Dauphine; a fact unknown out of her chamber until after death.

On Wednesday, the 17th, the malady considerably increased. I had news at all moments of the Dauphin's state from Cheverny, an excellent apothecary of the King and of my family. He hid nothing from us. He had told us what he thought of the Dauphine's illness; he told us now what he thought of the Dauphin's. I no longer hoped, therefore, or rather I hoped to the end, against all hope.

On Wednesday the pains increased. They were like a devouring fire, but more violent than ever. Very late into the evening the Dauphin sent to the King for permission to receive the communion early the next morning, without ceremony and without display, at the mass performed in his chamber. Nobody heard of this that evening; it was not known until the following morning. I was in extreme desolation; I scarcely saw the King once a day. I did nothing but go in quest of news several times a day, and to the house of M. de Chevreuse, where I was completely free. M. de Chevreuse — always calm, always sanguine — endeavored to prove to us by his medical reasonings that there was more reason to hope than to fear, but he did so with a tranquillity that roused my impatience. I returned home to pass a very cruel night.

On Thursday morning, the 18th of February, I learned that the Dauphin, who had waited for midnight with impatience, had heard mass immediately after the communion, had passed two hours in devout communication with God, and that his reason then became embarrassed. Madame de Saint-Simon told me afterward that he had received extreme unction: in fine, that he had died at half past eight. These "Memoirs" are not written to describe my private sentiments. But in reading them,—if, long after me, they shall ever appear,— my state and that of Madame de Saint-Simon will only too keenly be felt. I will content myself with saying, that the first days after the Dauphin's death scarcely appeared to us more than moments; that I wished to quit all, to withdraw from the Court and the world, and that I was only hindered by the wisdom, conduct and power over me of Madame de Saint-Simon, who yet had much trouble to subdue my sorrowful desires.

Let me say something now of the young prince and his spouse, whom we thus lost in quick succession.

Never did princess arrive among us so young with so much instruction, or with such capacity to profit by instruction. Her skillful father, who thoroughly knew our Court, had painted it to her, and had made her acquainted with the only manner of making herself happy there. From the first moment of her arrival she had acted upon his lessons. Gentle, timid, but adroit, fearing to give the slightest pain to anybody, and though all lightness and vivacity, very capable of far-stretching views; constraint, even to annoyance, cost her nothing, though she felt all its weight. Complacency was natural to her, flowed from her, and was exhibited toward every member of the Court.

Regularly plain, with cheeks hanging, a forehead too prominent, a nose without meaning, thick biting lips, hair and eyebrows of dark chestnut, and well planted; the most speaking and most beautiful eyes in the world; few teeth, and those all rotten, about which she was the first to talk and jest; the most beautiful complexion and skin; not much bosom, but what there was admirable; the throat long, with the suspicion of a goitre, which did not ill become her; her head carried gallantly, majestically, gracefully; her mein noble; her smile most expressive; her figure long, round, slender, easy, perfectly shaped; her walk that of a goddess upon the clouds: with such qualifications she pleased supremely. Grace accompanied her every step, and shone through her manners and her most ordinary conversation. An air always simple and natural, often naïve, but seasoned with wit —this with the ease peculiar to her, charmed all who approached her, and communicated itself to them. She wished to please even the most useless and the most ordinary persons, and yet without making an effort to do so. You were tempted to believe her wholly and solely devoted to those with whom she found herself. Her gayety—young, quick, and active—animated all; and her nymph-like lightness carried her everywhere, like a whirlwind which fills several places at once, and gives them movement and life. She was the ornament of all diversions, the life and soul of all pleasure, and at balls ravished everybody by the justness and perfection of her dancing. She could be amused by playing for small sums but liked high gambling better, and was an excellent, good-tempered, and bold gamester.

She spared nothing, not even her health, to gain Madame de Maintenon, and through her the King. Her suppleness toward them was without example, and never for a moment was at fault. She accompanied it with all the discretion that her knowledge of them, acquired by study and experience, had given her, and could measure their dispositions to an inch. In this way she had acquired a familiarity with them such as none of the King's children, not even the bastards, had approached.

In public, serious, measured, with the King, and in timid decorum with Madame de Maintenon, whom she never addressed except as MY AUNT, thus prettily confounding friendship and rank. In private, prattling, skipping, flying around them, now perched upon the sides of their armchairs, now playing upon their knees, she clasped them round the neck, embraced them, kissed them, caressed them, rumpled them, tickled them under the chin, tormented them, rummaged their tables, their papers, their letters, broke open the seals, and read the contents in spite of opposition, if she saw that her waggeries were likely to be received in good part. When the King was with his ministers, when he received couriers, when the most important affairs were under discussion, she was present, and with such liberty, that, hearing the King and Madame de Maintenon speak one evening with affection of the Court of England, at the time when peace was hoped for from Queen Anne, "My aunt," she said, "you must admit that in England the queens govern better than the kings; and do you know why, my aunt?" asked she, running about and gamboling all the time, "because under kings it is women who govern, and men under queens." The joke is that they both laughed, and said she was right.

The King really could not do without her. Everything went wrong with him if she was not by; even at his public supper, if she were away an additional cloud of seriousness and silence settled around him. She took great care to see him every day upon arriving and departing; and if some ball in winter, or some pleasure party in summer, made her lose half the night, she nevertheless adjusted things so well that she went and embraced the King the moment he was up, and amused him with a description of the *fête*.

She was so far removed from the thoughts of death, that on Candlemas day she talked with Madame de Saint-Simon of people who had died since she had been at Court, and of what she would herself do in old age, of the life she would lead, and of such like matters. Alas! it pleased God, for our misfortune, to dispose of her differently.

With all her coquetry—and she was not wanting in it—never woman seemed to take less heed of her appearance; her toilet was finished in a moment, she cared nothing for finery except at balls and *fêtes;* if she displayed a little at other times it was simply in order to please the King. If the Court subsisted after her it was only to languish. Never was princess so regretted, never one so worthy of it: regrets have not yet passed away, the involuntary and secret bitterness they caused still remain, with a frightful blank not yet filled up.

Let me now turn to the Dauphin.

The youth of this prince made everyone tremble. Stern and choleric to the last degree, and even against inanimate objects; impetuous with frenzy, incapable of suffering the slightest resistance even from the hours and the elements, without flying into a passion that threatened to destroy his body; obstinate to excess; passionately fond of all kind of voluptuousness, of women, with even a worse passion strongly developed at the same time; fond not less of wine, good living, hunting, music, and gaming, in which last he could not endure to be beaten; in fine, abandoned to every passion, and transported by every pleasure; oftentimes wild, naturally disposed toward cruelty; barbarous in raillery, and with an all-powerful capacity for ridicule. He looked down upon all men as from the sky, as atoms with whom he had nothing in common; even his brothers scarcely appeared connecting links between himself and human nature, although all had been educated together in perfect equality. His sense and penetration shone through everything. His replies, even in anger, astonished everybody. He amused himself with the most abstract knowledge. The extent and vivacity of his intellect were prodigious, and rendered him incapable of applying himself to one study at a time.

So much intelligence and of such a kind, joined to such vivacity, sensibility, and passion, rendered his education difficult. But God, who is the master of all hearts, and whose divine spirit breathes where he wishes, worked a miracle on this prince between his eighteenth and twentieth years. From this abyss he came out affable, gentle, humane, moderate, patient, modest, penitent, and humble; and austere, even more than harmonized with his position. Devoted to his duties, feeling them to be immense, he thought only how to unite the duties of son and subject with those he saw to be destined for himself. The shortness of each day was his only sorrow. All his force, all his consolation, was in prayer and pious reading. He clung with joy to the cross of his Savior, repenting sincerely of his past pride. The King, with his outside devotion, soon saw with secret displeasure his own life censured by that of a prince so young, who refused himself a new desk in order to give the money it would cost to the poor, and who did not care to accept some new gilding with which it was proposed to furnish his little room.

Madame la Duchess de Bourgogne, alarmed at so austere a spouse, left nothing undone in order to soften him. Her charms, with which he was smitten, the cunning and the unbridled importunities of the young ladies of her suite, disguised in a hundred different forms — the attraction of parties and pleasures to which he was far from insensible,—all were displayed every day. But for a long time he behaved not like a prince but like a novice. On one occasion he refused to be present at a ball on Twelfth Night, and in various ways made himself ridiculous at Court.

In due time, however, he comprehended that the faithful performance of the duties proper to the state in which he had been placed, would be the conduct most agreeable to God. The bark of the tree, little by little, grew softer without affecting the solidity of the trunk. He applied himself to the studies which were necessary, in order to instruct himself in public affairs, and at the same time he lent himself more to the world, doing so with so much grace, with such a natural air, that everybody soon began to grow reconciled to him.

The discernment of this prince was such, that, like the bee, he gathered the most perfect substance from the best and most beautiful flowers. He tried to fathom men, to draw from them the instruction and the light that he could hope for. He conferred sometimes, but rarely, with others besides his chosen few. I was the only one, not of that number, who had complete access to him; with me he opened his heart upon the present and the future with confidence, with sageness, with discretion. A volume would not describe sufficiently my private interviews with this prince,— what love of good! what forgetfulness of self! what researches! what fruit! what purity of purpose!—May I say it? what reflection of the divinity in that mind, candid, simple, strong, which as much as is possible here below had preserved the image of its maker!

If you had business, and thought of opening it to him, say for a quarter of an hour or half an hour, he gave you oftentimes two hours and more, according as he found himself at liberty. Yet he was without verbiage, compliments, prefaces, pleasantries, or other hindrances; went straight to the point, and allowed you to go also.

His undue scruples of devotion diminished every day, as he found himself face to face with the world; above all, he was well cured of the inclination for piety in preference to talent, that is to say, for making a man ambassador, minister, or general, rather on account of his devotedness than of his capacity or experience. He saw the danger of inducing hypocrisy by placing devotion too high as a qualification for employ.

It was he who was not afraid to say publicly, in the *salon* of Marly, "that a king is made for his subjects, and not the subjects for him;" a remark that, except under his own reign, which God did not permit, would have been the most frightful blasphemy.

Great God! what a spectacle you gave to us in him. What tender but tranquil views he had! What submission and love of God! What a consciousness of his own nothingness, and of his sins! What a magnificent idea of the infinite mercy! What religious and humble fear! What tempered confidence! What patience! What constant goodness for all who approached him! France fell, in fine, under this last chastisement. God showed to her a prince she merited not. The earth was not worthy of him; he was ripe already for the blessed eternity!*

* Whatever deduction we may make from this panegyric, it is evident that we are in presence of the results of the teaching of Fenelon, on which the prejudiced Saint-Simon lays far too little stress.

CHAPTER XXII.

THE consternation at the event that had taken place was real and general; it penetrated to foreign lands and courts. While the people wept for him who thought only of their relief, and all France lamented a prince who only wished to reign in order to render it flourishing and happy, the sovereigns of Europe publicly lamented him whom they regarded as their example, and whose virtues were preparing him to be their arbitrator, and the peaceful and revered moderator of nations. The Pope was so touched that he resolved of himself to set aside all rule and hold expressly a consistory; deplored there the infinite loss the Church and all Christianity had sustained, and pronounced a complete eulogium of the Prince who caused the just regrets of all Europe.

On Saturday, the 13th, the corpse of the Dauphine was left in its bed with uncovered face, and opened the same evening at eleven in presence of all the faculty. On the 15th it was placed in the grand cabinet, were masses were continually said.

On Friday, the 19th, the corpse of Monseigneur le Dauphin was opened, a little more than twenty-four hours after his death, also in presence of all the faculty. His heart was immediately carried to Versailles, placed by the side of that of Madame la Dauphine. Both were afterward taken to the Val de Grâce. They arrived at midnight with a numerous cortège. All was finished in two hours. The corpse of Monseigneur le Dauphin was afterward carried from Marly to Versailles, and placed by the side of Madame la Dauphine on the same estrade.

On Tuesday, the 23d of February, the two bodies were taken from Versailles to St. Denis in the same chariot. The procession began to enter Paris by the Porte St.

Honoré at two o'clock in the morning, and arrived between seven and eight o'clock in the morning at St. Denis. There was great order in Paris, and no confusion.

On Tuesday, the 8th of March, Monseigneur le Duc de Bretagne, eldest son of Monseigneur le Dauphin, who had succeeded to the name and rank of his father, being then only five years and some months old, and who had been seized with measles within a few days, expired, in spite of all the remedies given him. His brother, M. le Duc d'Anjou, who still sucked, was taken ill at the same time, but thanks to the care of the Duchess de Ventadour, whom in after life he never forgot, and who administered an antidote, escaped, and is now King.

Thus three Dauphins died in less than a year, and father, mother, and eldest son in twenty-four days! On Wednesday, the 9th of March, the corpse of the little Dauphin was opened at night, and without any ceremony his heart was taken to the Val de Grâce, his body to St. Denis, and placed by the side of those of his father and mother. M. le Duc d'Anjou, now sole remaining child, succeeded to the title and to the rank of Dauphin.

I have said that the bodies of the Dauphin and the Dauphine were opened in presence of all the faculty. The report made upon the opening of the latter was not consolatory. Only one of the doctors declared there were no signs of poison; the rest were of the opposite opinion. When the body of the Dauphin was opened, everybody was terrified. His *viscera* were all dissolved; his heart had no consistency; its substance flowed through the hands of those who tried to hold it; an intolerable odor, too, filled the apartment. The majority of the doctors declared they saw in all this the effect of a very subtle and very violent poison, which had consumed all the interior of the body, like a burning fire. As before, there was one of their number who held different views, but this was Maréchal, who declared that to persuade the King of the existence of secret enemies of his family would be to kill him by degrees.

This medical opinion that the cause of the Dauphin's and the Dauphine's death was poison, soon spread like

15

wildfire over the Court and the city. Public indignation fell upon M. d'Orléans, who was at once pointed out as the poisoner. The rapidity with which this rumor filled the Court, Paris, the provinces, the least frequented places, the most isolated monasteries, the most deserted solitudes, all foreign countries and all the peoples of Europe, recalled to me the efforts of the cabal, which had previously spread such black reports against the honor of him for whom all the world now wept, and showed that that cabal, though dispersed, was not dissolved.

In effect M. du Maine, now the head of the cabal, who had all to gain and nothing to lose by the death of the Dauphin and Dauphine, from both of whom he had studiously held aloof, and who thoroughly disliked M. d'Orléans, did all in his power to circulate this odious report. He communicated it to Madame de Maintenon, by whom it reached the King. In a short time all the Court, down to the meanest valets, publicly cried vengeance upon M. d'Orléans, with an air of the most unbridled indignation and of perfect security.

M. d'Orléans, with respect to the two losses that afflicted the public, had an interest the most directly opposite to that of M. du Maine; he had everything to gain by the life of the Dauphin and Dauphine, and unless he had been a monster vomited forth from hell he could not have been guilty of the crime with which he was charged. Nevertheless, the odious accusation flew from mouth to mouth, and took refuge in every breast.

Let us compare the interest M. d'Orléans had in the life of the Dauphin with the interest M. du Maine had in his death, and then look about for the poisoner.*

* The whole course of Saint-Simon's narrative would seem to point rather to the Duchess de Berry as the guilty person than to any other. An attempt was made to poison the whole family of the heir to the throne—and only one child at the breast escaped by accident. If this child, afterward Louis XV. had died, the Duc de Berry would have succeeded to the crown. What, therefore, can Saint-Simon mean by averring that the Duc d'Orléans had no interest in the death of the victims? If the whole plot had been successful, his favorite and too-beloved daughter would have been Queen. A better argument for his innocence is, that he afterward suffered Louis XV. to live.

But this is not all. Let us remember how M. le Duc d'Orléans was treated by Monseigneur, and yet what genuine grief he displayed at the death of that prince. What a contrast was this conduct with that of M. du Maine at another time, who, after leaving the King (Louis XIV.) at the point of death, delivered over to an ignorant peasant, imitated that peasant so naturally and so pleasantly, that bursts of laughter extended to the gallery, and scandalized the passers-by. This is a celebrated and very characteristic fact, which will find its proper place if I live long enough to carry these « Memoirs » up to the death of the King.

M. d'Orléans was, however, already in such bad odor, that people were ready to believe anything to his discredit. They drank in this new report so rapidly, that on the 17th of February, as he went with Madame to give the holy water to the corpse of the Dauphine, the crowd of the people threw out all sorts of accusations against him, which both he and Madame very distinctly heard, without daring to show it, and were in trouble, embarrassment, and indignation as may be imagined. There was even ground for fearing worse from an excited and credulous populace when M. d'Orléans went alone to give the holy water to the corpse of the Dauphin. For he had to endure on his passage atrocious insults from a populace which uttered aloud the most frightful observations, which pointed the finger at him with the coarsest epithets, and which believed it was doing him a favor in not falling upon him and tearing him to pieces!

Similar circumstances took place at the funeral procession. The streets resounded more with cries of indignation against M. d'Orléans and abuse of him than with grief. Silent precautions were not forgotten in Paris in order to check the public fury, the boiling over of which was feared at different moments. The people recompensed themselves by gestures, cries, and other atrocities, vomited against M. d'Orléans. Near the Palais Royal, before which the procession passed, the increase of shouts, of cries, of abuse, was so great, that for some minutes everything was to be feared.

It may be imagined what use M. du Maine contrived to
make of the public folly, the rumors of the Paris *cafés*,
the feeling of the *salon* of Marly, that of the Parliament,
the reports that arrived from the provinces and foreign
countries. In a short time so overpowered was M.
d'Orléans by the feeling against him everywhere exhibited, that acting upon very ill-judged advice he spoke to
the King upon the subject, and begged to be allowed to
surrender himself as a prisoner at the Bastille, until his
character was cleared from stain.

I was terribly annoyed when I heard that M. d'Orléans had taken this step, which could not possibly lead
to good. I had quite another sort of scheme in my head
which I should have proposed to him had I known of his
resolve. Fortunately, however, the King was persuaded
not to grant M. d'Orléans's request, out of which therefore nothing came. The Duke meanwhile lived more
abandoned by everybody than ever; if in the *salon* he
approached a group of courtiers, each, without the least
hesitation, turned to the right or to the left and went
elsewhere, so that it was impossible for him to accost
anybody except by surprise, and if he did so he was left
alone directly after with the most marked indecency. In
a word, I was the only person, I say distinctly, the only
person, who spoke to M. d'Orléans as before. Whether
in his own house or in the palace I conversed with him,
seated myself by his side in a corner of the *salon*, where
assuredly we had no third person to fear, and walked
with him in the gardens under the very windows of the
King and of Madame de Maintenon.

Nevertheless, all my friends warned me that if I pursued this conduct so opposite to that in vogue, I should
assuredly fall into disgrace. I held firm. I thought
that when we did not believe our friends guilty we
ought not to desert them, but, on the contrary, to draw
closer to them, as by honor bound, give them the consolation due from us, and show thus to the world our
hatred for calumny. My friends insisted; gave me to
understand that the King disapproved my conduct, that
Madame de Maintenon was annoyed at it; they forgot
nothing to awaken my fears. But I was insensible to

all they said to me, and did not omit seeing M. d'Orléans a single day; often stopping with him two and three hours at a time.

A few weeks had passed over thus, when one morning M. de Beauvilliers called upon me, and urged me to plead business, and at once withdraw to La Ferté; intimating that if I did not do so of my own accord, I should be compelled by an order from the King. He never explained himself more fully, but I have always remained persuaded that the King or Madame de Maintenon had sent him to me, and had told him that I should be banished if I did not banish myself. Neither my absence nor my departure made any stir; nobody suspected anything. I was carefully informed, without knowing by whom, when my exile was likely to end: and I returned, after a month or five weeks, straight to the Court, where I kept up the same intimacy with M. d'Orléans as before.

But he was not yet at the end of his misfortunes. The Princess des Ursins had not forgiven him his pleasantry at her expense. Chalais, one of her most useful agents, was dispatched by her on a journey so mysterious that its obscurity has never been illuminated. He was eighteen days on the road, unknown, concealing his name, and passing within two leagues of Chalais, where his father and mother lived without giving them any signs of life, although all were on very good terms. He loitered secretly in Poitou, and at last arrested there a Cordelier monk, of middle age, in the convent of Bressuire, who cried, "Ah! I am lost!" upon being caught. Chalais conducted him to the prison of Poitiers, whence he dispatched to Madrid an officer of dragoons he had brought with him, and who knew this Cordelier, whose name has never transpired, although it is certain he was really a Cordelier, and that he was returning from a journey in Italy and Germany that had extended as far as Vienna. Chalais pushed on to Paris, and came to Marly on the 27th of April, a day on which the King had taken medicine. After dinner he was taken by Torcy to the King, with whom he remained half an hour, delaying thus the council of state for the same time, and then returned immediately to

Paris. So much trouble had not been taken for no purpose: and Chalais had not prostituted himself to play the
part of prevôt to a miserable monk without expecting
good winnings from the game. Immediately afterward
the most dreadful rumors were everywhere in circulation
against M. d'Orléans, who, it was said, had poisoned the
the Dauphin and Dauphine by means of this monk, who,
nevertheless, was far enough away from our Prince and
Princess at the time of their death. In an instant Paris
resounded with these horrors; the provinces were inundated with them, and immediately afterward foreign countries — this too with an incredible rapidity, which plainly
showed how well the plot had been prepared — and a
publicity that reached the very caverns of the earth.
Madame des Ursins was not less served in Spain than
M. du Maine and Madame de Maintenon in France. The
anger of the public was doubled. The Cordelier was
brought, bound hand and foot, to the Bastille, and delivered up to D'Argenson, lieutenant of Police.*

This D'Argenson rendered an account to the King of
many things which Pontchartrain, as Secretary of State,
considered to belong to his department. Pontchartrain
was vexed beyond measure at this, and could not see
without despair his subaltern become a kind of minister
more feared, more valued, more in consideration than he,
and conduct himself always in such manner that he
gained many powerful friends, and made but few enemies, and those of but little moment. M. d'Orléans
bowed before the storm that he could not avert; it could
not increase the general desertion; he had accustomed
himself to his solitude, and, as he had never heard this
monk spoken of, had not the slightest fear on his account.
D'Argenson, who questioned the Cordelier several times,
and carried his replies daily to the King, was sufficiently
adroit to pay his court to M. d'Orléans, by telling him
that the prisoner had uttered nothing which concerned
him, and by representing the services he did M. d'Orléans

---

* It is to be observed that whenever Saint-Simon comes to talk of
things in which he was himself engaged or particularly interested, he
becomes declamatory and magniloquent, losing much of his picturesque-
ness and almost all his wit.

with the King. Like a sagacious man, D'Argenson saw the madness of popular anger devoid of all foundation, and which could not hinder M. d'Orléans from being a very considerable person in France, during a minority that the age of the King showed to be pretty near. He took care, therefore, to avail himself of the mystery which surrounded his office, to ingratiate himself more and more with M. d'Orléans, whom he had always carefully though secretly served; and this conduct, as will be seen in due time, procured him a large fortune.

But I have gone too far. I must retrace my steps, to speak of things I have omitted to notice in their proper place.

The two Dauphins and the Dauphine were interred at St. Denis, on Monday, the 18th of April. The funeral oration was pronounced by Maboul, bishop of Aleth, and pleased; M. de Metz, chief chaplain, officiated; the service commenced at about eleven o'clock. As it was very long, it was thought well to have at hand a large vase of vinegar, in case anybody should be ill. M. de Metz having taken the first oblation, and observing that very little wine was left for the second, asked for more. This large vase of vinegar was supposed to be wine, and M. de Metz, who wished to strengthen himself, said, washing his fingers over the chalice, "fill right up." He swallowed all at a draught, and did not perceive until the end that he had drunk vinegar; his grimace and his complaint caused some little laughter round him; and he often related this adventure, which much soured him.

On Monday, the 10th of May, the funeral service for the Dauphin and Dauphine was performed at Notre Dame.

Let me here say, that before the Prince and his spouse were buried, that is to say, the 6th of April, the King gave orders for the recommencement of the usual play at Marly; and that M. le Duc de Berry and Madame la Duchess de Berry presided in the *salon* at the public lansquenet and *brelan*, and the different gaming tables for all the Court. In a short time the King dined in Madame de Maintenon's apartments once or twice a

week, and had music there. And all this, as I have remarked, with the corpse of the Dauphin and that of the
Dauphine still above ground!

The gap left by the death of the Dauphine could not,
however, be easily filled up. Some months after her loss,
the King began to feel great *ennui* steal upon him in
the hours when he had no work with his ministers. The
few ladies admitted into the apartments of Madame de
Maintenon when he was there, were unable to entertain
him. Music, frequently introduced, languished from that
cause. Detached scenes from the comedies of Molière
were thought of, and were played by the King's musicians, comedians for the nonce. Madame de Maintenon
introduced, too, the Maréchal de Villeroy, to amuse the
King by relating their youthful adventures.

Evening amusements became more and more frequent
in Madame de Maintenon's apartments, where, however,
nothing could fill up the void left by the poor Dauphine.

I have said little of the grief I felt at the loss of the
prince whom everybody so deeply regretted. As will be
believed, it was bitter and profound. The day of his
death, I barricaded myself in my own house, and only
left it for one instant in order to join the King at his
promenade in the gardens. The vexation I felt upon
seeing him followed almost as usual, did not permit me
to stop more than an instant. All the rest of the stay
at Versailles I scarcely left my room, except to visit M.
de Beauvilliers. I will admit that, to reach M. de Beauvilliers's house, I made a circuit between the canal and the
gardens of Versailles, so as to spare myself the sight of
the chamber of death, which I had not force enough to
approach. I admit that I was weak. I was sustained
neither by the piety, superior to all things, of M. de Beauvilliers, nor by that of Madame de Saint-Simon, who nevertheless not the less suffered. The truth is, I was in
despair. To those who know my position, this will appear
less strange than my being able to support at all, so complete a misfortune. I experienced this sadness precisely
at the same age as that of my father when he lost Louis
XIII.; but he at least had enjoyed the results of favor,

while I, *Gustavi paululum mellis, et ecce morior.* Yet this was not all.

In the casket of the Dauphin there were several papers he had asked me for. I had drawn them up in all confidence; he had preserved them in the same manner. There was one, very large, in my hand, which if seen by the King, would have robbed me of his favor forever; ruined me without hope of return. We do not think in time of such catastrophes. The King knew my handwriting; he did not know my mode of thought, but might pretty well have guessed it. I had sometimes supplied him with means to do so; my good friends of the Court had done the rest. The King when he discovered my paper would also discover on what close terms of intimacy I had been with the Dauphin, of which he had no suspicion. My anguish was then cruel, and there seemed every reason to believe that if my secret was found out, I should be disgraced and exiled during all the rest of the King's reign.

What a contrast between the bright heaven I had so recently gazed upon and the abyss now yawning at my feet! But so it is in the Court and the world! I felt then the nothingness of even the most desirable future, by an inward sentiment, which, nevertheless, indicates how we cling to it. Fear on acccount of the contents of the casket had scarcely any power over me. I was obliged to reflect in order to return to it from time to time. Regret for this incomparable Dauphin pierced my heart, and suspended all the faculties of my soul. For a long time I wished to fly from the Court, so that I might never again see the deceitful face of the world; and it was some time before prudence and honor got the upper hand.

It so happened that the Duc de Beauvilliers himself was able to carry this casket to the King, who had the key of it. M. de Beauvilliers in fact resolved not to trust it out of his own hands, but to wait until he was well enough to take it to the King, so that he might then try to hide my papers from view. This task was difficult for he did not know the position in the casket of these dangerous documents, and yet it was our only resource. This terrible uncertainty lasted more than a fortnight.

On Tuesday, the 1st of March, M. de Beauvilliers carried the casket to the King. He came to me shortly after and before sitting down, indicated by signs that there was no further occasion for fear. He then related to me that he had found the casket full of a mass of documents, finance projects, reports from the provinces, papers of all kinds; that he had read some of them to the King on purpose to weary him, and had succeeded so well that the King soon was satisfied by hearing only the titles; and, at last, tired out by not finding anything important, said it was not worth while to read more, and that there was nothing to do but to throw everything into the fire. The Duke assured me that he did not wait to be told twice, being all the more anxious to comply, because at the bottom of the casket he had seen some of my handwriting, which he had promptly covered up in taking other papers to read their titles to the King; and that immediately the word " fire " was uttered, he confusedly threw all the papers into the casket, and then emptied it near the fire, between the King and Madame de Maintenon, taking good care, as he did so that my documents should not be seen,— even cautiously using the tongs in order to prevent any piece flying away, and not quitting the fireplace until he had seen every page consumed. We embraced each other, in the relief we reciprocally felt, relief proportioned to the danger we had run.

CHAPTER XXIII.

LET me here relate an incident which should have found a place earlier, but which has been omitted in order that what has gone before, might be uninterrupted. On the 16th of the previous July the King made a journey to Fontainebleau, where he remained until the 14th of September. I should suppress the *bagatelle* which happened on the occasion of this journey, if it did not serve more and more to characterize the King.

Madame la Duchess de Berry was in the familyway for the first time, and had been so for nearly three months, was very much inconvenienced, and had a pretty strong fever. M. Fagon, the doctor, thought it would be imprudent for her not to put off traveling for a day or two. Neither she nor M. d'Orléans dared to speak about it. M. le Duc de Berry timidly hazarded a word, and was ill received. Madame la Duchess d'Orléans more timid still, addressed herself to Madame, and to Madame de Maintenon, who indifferent as they might be respecting Madame la Duchess de Berry, thought her departure so hazardous that, supported by Fagon, they spoke of it to the King. It was useless. They were not daunted, however, and this dispute lasted three or four days. The end of it was, that the King grew thoroughly angry and agreed, by way of capitulation, that the journey should be performed in a boat instead of a coach.

It was arranged that Madame la Duchess de Berry should leave Marly, where the King then was, on the 13th, sleep at the Palais Royal that night and repose herself there all the next day and night, that on the 15th she should set out for Petit-Bourg, where the King was to halt for the night, and arrive like him, on the 16th, at Fontainebleau, the whole journey to be by the river.

M. le Duc de Berry had permission to accompany his wife; but during the two nights they were to rest in Paris the King angrily forbade them to go anywhere, even to the opera, although that building joined the Palais Royal, and M. d'Orléans's box could be reached without going out of the palace.

On the 14th the King, under pretense of inquiry after them, repeated this prohibition to M. le Duc de Berry and Madame his wife, and also to M. d'Orléans and Madame d'Orléans, who had been included in it. He carried his caution so far as to enjoin Madame de Saint-Simon to see that Madame la Duchess de Berry obeyed the instructions she had received. As may be believed, his orders were punctually obeyed. Madame de Saint-Simon could not refuse to remain and sleep in the Palais Royal, where the apartment of the queen mother was given to her. All the while the party were shut up there was a good deal of gaming in order to console M. le Duc de Berry for his confinement.

The provost of the merchants had orders to prepare boats for the trip to Fontainebleau. He had so little time that they were ill chosen. Madame la Duchess de Berry embarked, however, on the 15th, and arrived, with fever, at ten o'clock at night at Petit-Bourg, where the King appeared rejoiced by an obedience so exact.

On the morrow the journey recommenced. In passing Melun, the boat of Madame la Duchess de Berry struck against the bridge, was nearly capsized, and almost swamped, so that they were all in great danger. They got off, however, with fear and a delay. Disembarking in great disorder at Valvin, where their equipages were waiting for them, they arrived at Fontainebleau two hours after midnight. The King, pleased beyond measure, went the next morning to see Madame la Duchess de Berry in the beautiful apartment of the queen mother that had been given to her. From the moment of her arrival she had been forced to keep her bed, and at six o'clock in the morning of the 21st of July she miscarried and was delivered of a daughter, stillborn. Madame de Saint-Simon ran to tell the King; he did not appear much moved; he had been obeyed! The Duchess de

Beauvilliers and the Marquise de Chatillon were named by the King to carry the embryo to St. Denis. As it was only a girl, and as the miscarriage had no ill effect, consolation soon came.

It was some little time after this occurrence, that we heard of the defeat of the Czar by the Grand Vizier upon the Pruth. The Czar annoyed by the protection the Porte had accorded to the King of Sweden (in retirement at Bender), made an appeal to arms, and fell into the same error as that which had occasioned the defeat of the King of Sweden by him. The Turks drew him to the Pruth across deserts supplied with nothing; if he did not risk all, by a very unequal battle, he must perish. The Czar was at the head of sixty thousand men; he lost more than thirty thousand on the Pruth, the rest were dying of hunger and misery; and he without any resources, could scarcely avoid surrendering himself and his forces to the Turks. In this pressing extremity, a common woman whom he had taken away from her husband, a drummer in the army, and whom he had publicly espoused after having repudiated and confined his own wife in a convent,—proposed that he should try by bribery to induce the Grand Vizier to allow him and the wreck of his forces to retreat. The Czar approved of the proposition, without hoping for success from it. He sent to the Grand Vizier and ordered him to be spoken to in secret. The Vizier was dazzled by the gold, the precious stones, and several valuable things that were offered to him. He accepted and received them; and signed a treaty by which the Czar was permitted to retire, with all who accompanied him, into his own states by the shortest road, the Turks to furnish him with provisions, with which he was entirely unprovided. The Czar, on his side, agreed to give up Azof as soon as he returned; destroy all the forts and burn all the vessels that he had upon the Black Sea; allow the King of Sweden to return by Pomerania; and to pay the Turks and their prince all the expenses of the war.

The Grand Vizier found such an opposition in the Divan to this treaty, and such boldness in the minister of the King of Sweden, who accompanied him, in exciting against him all the chiefs of the army, that it was within an ace of being broken; and the Czar, with every one left to him, of being made prisoner. The latter was in no condition to make even the least resistance. The Grand Vizier had only to will it, in order to execute it on the spot. In addition to the glory of leading captive to Constantinople the Czar, his Court, and his troops, there would have been his ransom, which must have cost not a little. But if he had been thus stripped of his riches, they would have been for the Sultan, and the Grand Vizier preferred having them for himself. He braved it then with authority and menaces, and hastened the Czar's departure and his own. The Swedish minister, charged with protests from the principal Turkish chiefs, hurried to Constantinople, where the Grand Vizier was strangled upon arriving.

The Czar never forgot this service of his wife, by whose courage and presence of mind he had been saved. The esteem he conceived for her, joined to his friendship, induced him to crown her Czarina, and to consult her upon all his affairs and all his schemes. Escaped from danger, he was a long time without giving up Azof, or demolishing his forts on the Black Sea. As for his vessels, he kept them nearly all, and would not allow the King of Sweden to return into Germany, as he had agreed, thus almost lighting up a fresh war with the Turk.

On the 6th of November, 1711, at about eight o'clock in the evening, the shock of an earthquake was felt at Paris and at Versailles; but it was so slight that few people perceived it. In several places toward Touraine and Poitou, in Saxony, and in some of the German towns near, it was very perceptible at the same day and hour. At this date a new tontine was established in Paris.

I have so often spoken of Marshal Catinat, of his virtue, wisdom, modesty, and disinterestedness; of the rare superiority of his sentiments, and of his great qualities as captain, that nothing remains for me to say except that he died at this time very advanced in years, at his little house of Saint Gratien, near Saint Denis, where he had retired, and which he seldom quitted although receiving there but few friends. By his simplicity and frugality, his contempt for worldly distinction, and his

uniformity of conduct, he recalled the memory of those
great men, who after the best merited triumphs, peacefully returned to their plow, still loving their country
and but little offended by the ingratitude of the Rome
they had so well served. Catinat placed his philosophy
at the service of his piety. He had intelligence, good
sense, ripe reflection; and he never forgot his origin; his
dress, his equipages, his furniture, all were of the greatest
simplicity. His air and his deportment were so also.
He was tall, dark, and thin; had an aspect pensive, slow,
and somewhat mean; with very fine and expressive eyes.
He deplored the signal faults that he saw succeed each
other unceasingly; the gradual extinction of all emulation; the luxury, the emptiness, the ignorance, the confusion of ranks; the inquisition in the place of the police:
he saw all the signs of destruction, and he used to say
it was only a climax of dangerous disorder that could
restore order to the realm.

Vendôme was one of the few to whom the death of the
Dauphin and the Dauphine brought hope and joy. He
had deemed himself expatriated for the rest of his life.
He saw, now, good chances before him of returning to
our Court, and of playing a part there again. He had
obtained some honor in Spain; he aimed at others even
higher, and hoped to return to France with all the honors of a prince of the blood. His idleness, his free living, his debauchery had prolonged his stay upon the
frontier, where he had more facilities for gratifying his
tastes than at Madrid. In that city, it is true, he did
not much constrain himself, but he was forced to do so
to some extent by courtly usages. He was, then, quite
at home on the frontier; there was nothing to do; for
the Austrians weakened by the departure of the English,
were quite unable to attack; and Vendôme, floating upon
the delights of his new dignities, thought only of enjoying himself in the midst of profound idleness, under
pretext that operations could not at once be commenced.

In order to be more at liberty he separated from the
general officers, and established himself with his valets
and two or three of his most familiar friends, cherished
companions everywhere, at Vignarez, a little isolated

hamlet, almost deserted, on the seashore and in the kingdom of Valencia. His object was to eat fish there to
his heart's content. He carried out that object, and
filled himself to repletion for nearly a month. He became unwell — his diet, as may be believed, was enough
to cause this — but his illness increased so rapidly, and
in so strange a manner, after having for a long time
seemed nothing, — that the few around him suspected
poison, and sent on all sides for assistance. But the
malady would not wait; it augmented rapidly with strange
symptoms. Vendôme could not sign a will that was
presented to him; nor a letter to the King, in which he
asked that his brother might be permitted to return to
Court. Everybody near flew from him and abandoned
him, so that he remained in the hands of three or four
of the meanest valets, while the rest robbed him of
everything and decamped. He passed thus, the last two
or three days of his life, without a priest, — no mention
even had been made of one, — without other help than
that of a single surgeon. The three or four valets who
remained near him, seeing him at his last extremity,
seized hold of the few things he still possessed, and for
want of better plunder, dragged off his bedclothes and
the mattress from under him. He piteously cried to
them at least not to leave him to die naked upon the
bare bed. I know not whether they listened to him.

Thus died on Friday, the 10th of June, 1712, the
haughtiest of men; and the happiest, except in the latter
years of his life. After having been obliged to speak of
him so often, I get rid of him now, once, and forever.
He was fifty-eight years old; but in spite of the blind
and prodigious favor he had enjoyed, that favor had
never been able to make aught but a cabal hero out of
a captain who was a very bad general, and a man whose
vices were the shame of humanity. His death restored
life and joy to all Spain.

Aguilar, a friend of the Duc de Noailles, was accused
of having poisoned him, but took little pains to defend
himself, inasmuch as little pains were taken to substan-
tiate the accusation. The Princess des Ursins, who had
so well profited by his life in order to increase her own

greatness, did not profit less by his death. She felt her
deliverance from a new Don Juan of Spain who had
ceased to be supple in her hands, and who might have
revived, in the course of time, all the power and authority he had formerly enjoyed in France. She was not
shocked then by the joy which burst out without constraint;
nor by the free talk of the Court, the city, the army, of
all Spain. But in order to sustain what she had done,
and cheaply pay her court to M. du Maine, Madame de
Maintenon, and even to the King, she ordered that the
corpse of this hideous monster of greatness and of fortune should be carried to the Escurial. This was crown-
ing the glory of M. de Vendôme in good earnest; for no
private persons are buried in the Escurial, although
several are to be found in St. Denis. But meanwhile,
until I speak of the visit I made to the Escurial — I shall
do so if I live long enough to carry these "Memoirs" up
to the death of M. d'Orléans,—let me say something of
that illustrious sepulcher.

The Pantheon is the place where only the bodies of
Kings and Queens who have had posterity are admitted.
In a separate place, near, though not on the same floor,
and resembling a library, the bodies of children, and of
Queens who have had no posterity, are ranged. A third
place, a sort of antechamber to the last named, is rightly
called "the rotting room"; while the other improperly
bears the same name. In this third room, there is nothing to be seen but four bare walls and a table in the
middle. The walls being very thick, openings are made
in them in which the bodies are placed. Each body has
an opening to itself, which is afterward walled up, so
that nothing is seen. When it is thought that the corpse
has been closed up sufficiently long to be free from odor
the wall is opened, the body taken out, and put in a
coffin which allows a portion of it to be seen toward the
feet. This coffin is covered with a rich stuff and carried
into an adjoining room.

The body of the Duc de Vendôme had been walled up
nine years when I entered the Escurial. I was shown
the place it occupied, smooth like every part of the four
walls and without mark. I gently asked the monks who did

16

me the honors of the place, when the body would be removed to the other chamber. They would not satisfy
my curiosity, showed some indignation, and plainly intimated that this removal was not dreamed of, and that as
M. de Vendôme had been so carefully walled up he might
remain so.

Harlay, formerly chief president, of whom I have so
often had occasion to speak, died a short time after M.
de Vendôme. I have already made him known. I will
simply add an account of the humiliation to which this
haughty cynic was reduced. He hired a house in the
Rue de l'Université with a partition wall between his garden
and that of the Jacobins of the Faubourg St. Germain.
The house did not belong to the Jacobins, like the houses
of the Rue St. Dominique, and the Rue du Bac, which,
in order that they might command higher rents, were put
in connection with the convent garden. These mendicant
Jacobins thus derive fifty thousand livres a year. Harlay, accustomed to exercise authority, asked them for a
door into their garden. He was refused. He insisted,
had them spoken to, and succeeded no better. Nevertheless, the Jacobins comprehended that although this mag-
istrate, recently so powerful, was now nothing by himself,
he had a son and a cousin, councilors of state, whom
they might some day have to do with, and who for
pride's sake might make themselves very disagreeable.
The argument of interest is the best of all with monks.
The Jacobins changed their mind. The Prior, accompanied by some of the notabilities of the convent, went
to Harlay with excuses, and said he was at liberty, if he
liked, to make the door. Harlay, true to his character,
looked at them askance, and replied, that he had changed
his mind and would do without it. The monks, much
troubled by his refusal, insisted; he interrupted them and
said, "Look you, my Fathers, I am grandson of Achille
du Harlay, chief president of the Parliament, who so well
served the State and the Kingdom, and who for his support of the public cause, was dragged to the Bastille,
where he expected to be hanged by those rascally
Leaguers; it would ill become me, therefore, to enter the
house, or pray to God there, of folks of the same stamp

as that Jacques Clement.» And he immediately turned his back upon them, leaving them confounded. This was his last act of vigor. He took it into his head afterward to go out visiting a good deal, and as he preserved all his old unpleasant manners, he afflicted all he visited; he went even to persons who had often cooled their heels in his antechambers. By degrees, slight but frequent attacks of apoplexy troubled his speech, so that people had great difficulty in understanding him, and he in speaking. In this state he did not cease his visits and could not perceive that many doors were closed to him. He died in this misery, and this neglect, to the great relief of the few who by relationship were obliged to see him, above all of his son and his domestic.

On the 17th of July, a truce between France and England, was published in Flanders, at the head of the troops of the two crowns. The Emperor, however, was not yet inclined for peace and his forces under Prince Eugène continued to oppose us in Flanders, where, however, the tide at last turned in our favor. The King was so flattered by the overflow of joy that took place at Fontainebleau on account of our successes, that he thanked the country for it, for the first time in his life. Prince Eugène in want of bread and of everything, raised the siege of Landrecies, which he had been conducting, and terrible desertion took place among his troops.

About this time, there was an irruption of wolves, which caused great disorders in the Orleannais; the King's wolf hunters were sent there, and the people were authorized to take arms and make a number of grand *battues*.

CHAPTER XXIV.

PEACE was now all but concluded between France and England. There was, however, one great obstacle still in its way. Queen Anne and her Council were stopped by the consideration, that the King of Spain would claim to succeed to the Crown of France, if the little Dauphin should die. Neither England nor any of the other powers at war, would consent to see the two principal crowns of Europe upon the same head. It was necessary then above all things to get rid of this difficulty, and so arrange the order of succession to our throne, that the case to be provided against, could never happen. Treaties, renunciation, and oaths, all of which the King had already broken, appeared feeble guarantees in the eyes of Europe. Something stronger was sought for. It could not be found; because there is nothing more sacred among men than engagements, which they consider binding on each other. What was wanting then in mere forms it was now thought could be supplied by giving to those forms the greatest possible solemnity.

It was a long time before we could get over the difficulty. The King would accord nothing except promises in order to guarantee to Europe that the two crowns should never be united upon the same head. His authority was wounded at the idea of being called upon to admit, as it were, a rival near it. Absolute without reply, as he had become, he had extinguished and absorbed even the minutest trace, idea, and recollection, of all other authority, all other power in France except that which emanated from himself alone. The English, little accustomed to such maxims, proposed that the States-General should assemble in order to give weight to the renunciations to be made. They said, and with reason, that it was not enough that the King of Spain should renounce France unless France renounced Spain; and that this formality was necessary in order to break the double bonds which attached Spain to France, as France was attached to Spain. Accustomed to their Parliaments, which are in effect their States-General, they believed ours preserved the same authority, and they thought such authority the greatest to be obtained and the best capable of solidly supporting that of the King.

The effect of this upon the mind of a prince almost deified in his own eyes, and habituated to the most unlimited despotism cannot be expressed. To show him that the authority of his subjects was thought necessary in order to confirm his own, wounded him in his most delicate part. The English were made to understand the weakness and the uselessness of what they asked; for the powerlessness of our States-General was explained to them, and they saw at once how vain their help would be, even if accorded.

For a long time nothing was done; France saying that a treaty of renunciation and an express confirmatory declaration of the King, registered in the Parliament, were sufficient; the English replying by reference to the fate of past treaties. Peace meanwhile was arranged with the English, and much beyond our hopes remained undisturbed.

In due time matters were so far advanced in spite of obstacles thrown in the way by the allies, that the Duc d'Aumont was sent as ambassador into England; and the Duke of Hamilton was named as ambassador for France. This last, however, losing his life in a duel with Lord Mohun, the Duke of Shrewsbury was appointed in his stead.

At the commencement of the new year [1713] the Duke and Duchess of Shrewsbury arrived in Paris. The Duchess was a great fat masculine creature, more than past the meridian, who had been beautiful and who affected to be so still; bare bosomed; her hair behind her ears; covered with rouge and patches, and full of

finicking ways. All her manners were that of a mad
thing, but her play, her taste, her magnificence, even her
general familiarity made her the fashion. She soon
declared the women's headdresses ridiculous, as indeed
they were. They were edifices of brass wire, ribbons,
hair, and all sorts of tawdry rubbish more than two feet
high, making women's faces seem in the middle of their
bodies. The old ladies wore the same, but made of black
gauze. If they moved ever so lightly the edifice trembled and the inconvenience was extreme. The King
could not endure them, but master as he was of everything was unable to banish them. They lasted for ten
years and more, despite all he could say and do. What
this monarch had been unable to perform, the taste
and example of a silly foreigner accomplished with the
most surprising rapidity. From extreme height, the ladies
descended to extreme lowness, and these headdresses,
more simple, more convenient, and more becoming, last
even now. Reasonable people wait with impatience for
some other mad stranger who would strip our dames of
these immense baskets, thoroughly insupportable to themselves and to others.

Shortly after the Duke of Shrewsbury arrived in Paris
the Hotel de Powis in London, occupied by our ambassador the Duc d'Aumont, was burned to the ground. A
neighboring house was pulled down to prevent others
catching fire. The plate of M. d'Aumont was saved. He
pretended to have lost everything else. He pretended
also to have received several warnings that his house was
to be burned and himself assassinated, and that the Queen
to whom he had mentioned these warnings, offered to give
him a guard. People judged otherwise in London and
Paris, and felt persuaded he himself had been the in-
cendiary in order to draw money from the King and also
to conceal some monstrous smuggling operations, by which
he gained enormously, and which the English had complained of ever since his arrival. This is at least what
was publicly said in the two courts and cities, and nearly
everybody believed it.

But to return to the peace. The renunciations were
ready toward the middle of March and were agreed upon.

The King was invited to sign them by his own most pressing interest; and the Court of England, to which we owed all, was not less interested in consummating this grand work so as to enjoy with the glory of having imposed it upon all the powers, that domestic repose which was unceasingly disturbed by the party opposed to the government, which party, excited by the enemies of peace abroad, could not cease to cause disquiet to the Queen's minister, while, by delay in signing, vain hopes of disturbing the peace or hindering its ratification existed in people's minds. The King of Spain had made his renunciations with all the solidity and solemnity which could be desired from the laws, customs, and usages of Spain. It only remained for France to imitate him.

For the ceremony that was to take place, all that could be obtained in order to render it more solemn was the presence of the peers. But the King was so jealous of his authority, and so little inclined to pay attention to that of others, that he wished to content himself with merely saying in a general way that he hoped to find all the peers at the Parliament when the renunciations were made. I told M. d'Orléans that if the King thought such an announcement as this was enough he might rely upon finding not a single peer at the Parliament. I added, that if the King did not himself invite each peer, the master of the ceremonies ought to do so for him, according to the custom always followed. This warning had its effect. We all received written invitations, immediately. Wednesday, the 18th of May, was fixed for the ceremony.

At six o'clock on the morning of that day I went to the apartments of M. le Duc de Berry, in parliamentary dress, and shortly afterward M. d'Orléans came there also, with a grand suite. It had been arranged that the ceremony was to commence by a compliment from the Chief President de Mesmes to M. le Duc de Berry, who was to reply to it. He was much troubled at this. Madame de Saint-Simon, to whom he unbosomed himself, found means, through a subaltern, to obtain the discourse of the Chief President, and gave it to M. le Duc de Berry, to regulate his reply by. This, however, seemed too much for him; he admitted so to Madame de Saint-Simon, and that he knew not what to do. She proposed that I should take the work off his hands; and he was delighted with the expedient. I wrote, therefore, a page and a half full of common sized paper in an ordinary handwriting. M. le Duc de Berry liked it, but thought it too long to be learned. I abridged it; he wished it to be still shorter, so that at last there was not more than three quarters of a page. He had learned it by heart, and repeated it in his cabinet the night before the ceremony to Madame de Saint-Simon, who encouraged him as much as she could.

At about half past six o'clock we set out — M. le Duc d'Orléans, M. le Duc de Berry, myself, and M. le Duc de Saint Aignan, in one coach, several other coaches following. M. le Duc de Berry was very silent all the journey, appearing to be much occupied with the speech he had learned by heart. M. d'Orléans, on the contrary, was full of gayety, and related some of his youthful adventures, and his wild doings by night in the streets of Paris. We arrived gently at the Porte de la Conference, that is to say — for it is now pulled down — at the end of the terrace, and of the Quai of the Tuileries.

We found there the trumpeters and drummers of M. le Duc de Berry's guard, who made a great noise all the rest of our journey, which ended at the Palais de Justice. Thence we went to the Sainte Chapelle to hear mass. The Chapelle was filled with company, among which were many people of quality. The crowd of people from this building to the grand chamber was so great that a pin could not have fallen to the ground. On all sides, too, folks had climbed up to see what passed.

All the princes of the blood, the bastards, the peers, and the Parliament, were assembled in the palace. When M. le Duc de Berry entered, everything was ready. Silence having with difficulty been obtained, the Chief President paid his compliment to the Prince. When he had finished, it was for M. le Duc de Berry to reply. He half took off his hat, immediately put it back again, looked at the Chief President, and said, " Monsieur "; after a moment's pause he repeated — " Monsieur." Then he looked at the assembly, and again said, "Monsieur." Afterward he turned toward M. d'Orléans, who, like himself, was as red as fire, next to the Chief President, and finally stopped short, nothing else than "Monsieur" having been able to issue from his mouth.

I saw distinctly the confusion of M. le Duc de Berry, and sweated at it; but what could be done? The Duke turned again toward M. d'Orléans, who lowered his head. Both were dismayed. At last the Chief President, seeing there was no other resource, finished this cruel scene, by taking off his cap to M. le Duc de Berry, and inclining himself very low, as if the response was finished. Immediately after he told the King's people to begin. The embarrassment of all the courtiers and the surprise of the magistracy may be imagined!

The renunciations were then read; and by these the King of Spain and his posterity gave up all claim to the throne of France, and M. le Duc d'Orléans, and M. le Duc de Berry to succeed to that of Spain. These and other forms occupied a long time. The chamber was all the while crowded to excess. There was not room for a single other person to enter. It was very late when all was over.

When everything was at an end M. de Saint Aignan and I accompanied M. le Duc de Berry and M. le Duc d'Orléans in a coach to the Palais Royal. On the way the conversation was very quiet. M. le Duc de Berry appeared dispirited, embarrassed, and vexed. Even after we had partaken of a splendid and delicate dinner, to which an immense number of other guests sat down, he did not improve. We were conducted to the Porte St. Honoré with the same pomp as that in the midst of which we had entered Paris. During the rest of the journey to Versailles M. le Duc de Berry was as silent as ever.

To add to his vexation, as soon as he arrived at Versailles the Princess de Montauban, without knowing a word of what had passed, set herself to exclaim, with her usual flattery, that she was charmed with the grace and the appropriate eloquence with which he had spoken at the Parliament, and paraphrased this theme with all the praises of which it was susceptible. M. le Duc de Berry blushed with vexation without saying a word; she recommenced extolling his modesty, he blushing the more, and saying nothing. When at last he had got rid of her, he went to his own apartments, said not a word to the persons he found there, scarcely one to Madame his wife, but taking Madame de Saint-Simon with him, went into his library, and shut himself up alone there with her.

Throwing himself into an armchair he cried out that he was dishonored, and wept scalding tears. Then he related to Madame de Saint-Simon, in the midst of sobs, how he had stuck fast at the Parliament, without being able to utter a word, said that he should everywhere be regarded as an ass and a blockhead, and repeated the compliments he had received from Madame de Montauban, who, he said, had laughed at and insulted him, knowing well what had happened; then infuriated against her to the last degree, he called her by all sorts of names. Madame de Saint-Simon spared no exertion in order to calm M. de Berry, assuring him that it was impossible Madame de Montauban could know what had taken place at the Parliament, the news not having then reached Versailles, and that she had had no other object than flattery in addressing him. Nothing availed. Complaints and silence succeeded each other in the midst of tears. Then, suddenly falling upon the Duc de Beauvilliers and the King, and accusing the defects of his education: "They thought only," he exclaimed, "of making me stupid, and of stifling all my powers. I was a younger son. I coped with my brother. They feared the consequences; they annihilated me. I was taught only to play and to hunt, and they have succeeded in making me a fool and an ass, incapable of anything, the laughingstock and disdain of everybody." Madame de Saint-Simon was overpowered with compassion, and did everything to calm M. de Berry. Their strange *tête-à-tête* lasted nearly two hours, and resumed the next day but with less violence. By degrees M. le Duc de Berry became consoled, but never afterward did anyone dare to speak to him of his misadventure at the peace ceremony.

Let me here say that, the ceremony over, peace was signed at Utrecht on the 10th of April, 1713, at a late hour of the night. It was published in Paris with great solemnity on the 22d. Monsieur and Madame du Maine, who wished to render themselves popular, came from Sceaux to see the ceremony in the Place Royale, showed themselves on a balcony to the people to whom they threw some money — a liberality that the King would not have permitted in anybody else. At night fires were lighted before the houses, several of which were illuminated. On the 25th a *Te Deum* was sung at Notre Dame, and in the evening there was a grand display of fireworks at the Grève, which was followed by a superb banquet given at the Hotel de Ville by the Duc de Tresmes, the Governor of Paris, to a large number of distinguished persons of both sexes of the Court and the city, twenty-four violins playing during the repast.

I have omitted to mention the death of M. de Chevreuse, which took place between seven and eight o'clock in the morning on Saturday, the 5th of November, of the previous year (1712). I have so often alluded to M. de Chevreuse in the course of these pages, that I will content myself with relating here two anecdotes of him, which serve to paint a part of his character.

He was very forgetful, and adventures often happened to him in consequence, which diverted us amazingly. Sometimes his horses were put to and kept waiting for him twelve or fifteen hours at a time. Upon one occasion in summer this happened at Vaucresson, whence he was going to dine at Dampierre. The coachman, first, then the postilion, grew tired of looking after the horses, and left them. Toward six o'clock at night the horses themselves were in their turn worn out, bolted, and a din was heard which shook the house. Everybody ran out, the coach was found smashed, the large door shivered in pieces; the garden railings, which inclosed both sides of the court, broken down; the gates in pieces; in short, damage was done that took a long time to repair. M. de Chevreuse, who had not been disturbed by this uproar even for an instant, was quite astonished when he heard of it. M. de Beauvilliers amused himself for a long time by reproaching him with it, and by asking the expense.

Another adventure happened to him also at Vaucresson, and covered him with real confusion, comical to see, every time it was mentioned. About ten o'clock one morning a M. Sconin, who had formerly been his steward, was announced. "Let him take a turn in the garden," said M. de Chevreuse, "and come back in half an hour." He continued what he was doing, and completely forgot his man. Toward seven o'clock in the evening Sconin was again announced. "In a moment," replied M. de Chevreuse, without disturbing himself. A quarter of an hour afterward he called Sconin, and admitted him. "Ah, my poor Sconin!" said he, "I must offer you a thousand excuses for having caused you to lose your day."

"Not at all, Monseigneur," replied Sconin. "As I have had the honor of knowing you for many years, I comprehended this morning that the half hour might be long, so I went to Paris, did some business there, before and after dinner, and here I am again."

M. de Chevreuse was confounded. Sconin did not keep silence, nor did the servants of the house. M. de Beauvilliers made merry with the adventure when he heard of it, and accustomed as M. de Chevreuse might be to his raillery, he could not bear to have this subject alluded to. I have selected two anecdotes out of a hundred others of the same kind, because they characterize the man.

The liberality of M. du Maine which we have related on the occasion of the proclamation of peace at Paris, and which was so popular, and so surprising when viewed in connection with the disposition of the King, soon took new development. The Jesuits, so skillful in detecting the foibles of monarchs, and so clever in seizing hold of everything which can protect themselves and answer their ends, showed to what extent they were masters of these arts. A new and assuredly a very original "History of France," in three large folio volumes, appeared under the name of Father Daniel, who lived at Paris in the establishment of the Jesuits. The paper and the printing of the work were excellent; the style was admirable. Never was French so clear, so pure, so flow-

ing, with such happy transitions; in a word, everything
to charm and entice the reader; admirable preface, magnificent promises, short, learned dissertations, a pomp,
an authority of the most seductive kind. As for the
history, there was much romance in the first race, much
in the second, and much mistiness in the early times of
the third. In a word, all the work evidently appeared
composed in order to persuade people — under the simple
air of a man who set aside prejudices with discernment,
and who only seeks the truth — that the majority of
the Kings of the first race, several of the second,
some, even of the third, were bastards, whom this defect did not exclude from the throne, or affect in any
way.

I say bluntly here what was very delicately veiled in
the work, and yet plainly seen. The effect of the book
was great; its vogue such that everybody, even women,
asked for it. The King spoke of it to several of his
Court, asked if they had read it; the most sagacious
early saw how much it was protected; it was the sole
historical book the King and Madame de Maintenon had
ever spoken of. Thus the work appeared at Versailles
upon every table, nothing else was talked about, marvelous eulogies were lavished upon it, which were sometimes comical in the mouths of persons either very
ignorant, or who, incapable of reading, pretended to read
and relish this book.

But this surprising success did not last. People perceived that this history, which so cleverly unraveled the
remote past, gave but a meagre account of modern days,
except in so far as their military operations were concerned, of which even the minutest details were recorded.
Of negotiations, cabals, Court intrigues, portraits, ele-
vations, falls, and the mainsprings of events, there was
not a word in all the work, except briefly, dryly, and
with precision as in the gazettes, often more superficially.
Upon legal matters, public ceremonies, *fêtes* of different
times, there was also silence at the best, the same la-
conism; and when we came to the affairs of Rome and
of the League, it is a pleasure to see the author glide
over that dangerous ice on his Jesuit skates!

In due time critics condemned the work which, after so much applause, was recognized as a very wretched history, which had very industriously and very fraudulently answered the purpose for which it was written. It fell to the ground then; learned men wrote against it; but the principal and delicate point of the work was scarcely touched in France with the pen, so great was the danger.

Father Daniel obtained two thousand francs' pension for his history — a prodigious recompense, — with a title of Historiographer of France. He enjoyed the fruits of his falsehood, and laughed at those who attacked him. Foreign countries did not swallow quite so readily these stories that declared such a number of our early kings bastards; but great care was taken not to let France be infected by the disagreeable truths therein published.

CHAPTER XXV.

The Bull *Unigenitus* — My Interview with Father Tellier — Curious Inadvertence of Mine — Peace — Duc de la Rochefoucauld — A Suicide in Public — Charmel — Two Gay Sisters.

I<small>T</small> is now time that I should say something of the infamous bull *Unigenitus*, which by the unsurpassed audacity and scheming of Father Le Tellier and his friends was forced upon the Pope and the world.

I need not enter into a very lengthy account of the celebrated Papal decree which has made so many martyrs, depopulated our schools, introduced ignorance, fanaticism, and misrule, rewarded vice, thrown the whole community into the greatest confusion, caused disorder everywhere, and established the most arbitrary and the most barbarous inquisition; evils which have doubled within the last thirty years. I will content myself with a word or two, and will not blacken further the pages of my "Memoirs." Many pens have been occupied, and will be occupied, with this subject. It is not the apostleship of Jesus Christ that is in question, but that of the reverend fathers and their ambitious clients.

It is enough to say that the new bull condemned in set terms the doctrines of St. Paul (respected like oracles of the Holy Spirit ever since the time of our Savior), and also those of St. Augustin, and of other fathers; doctrines which have always been adopted by the Popes, by the Councils, and by the Church itself. The bull, as soon as published, met with a violent opposition in Rome from the cardinals there, who went by sixes, by eights, and by tens, to complain of it to the Pope. They might well do so, for they had not been consulted in any way upon this new constitution. Father Tellier and his friends had had the art and the audacity to obtain the publication of it without submitting it to them. The Pope, as I have said, had been forced into acquiescence,

and now, all confused, knew not what to say. He protested, however, that the publication had been made
without his knowledge, and put off the cardinals with
compliments, excuses, and tears, which last he could
always command.

The constitution had the same fate in France as in
Rome. The cry against it was universal. The cardinals
protested that it would never be received. They were
shocked by its condemnation of the doctrines of St.
Augustin and of the other fathers; terrified at its condemnation of St. Paul. There were not two opinions
upon this terrible constitution. The Court, the city, and
the provinces, as soon as they knew the nature of it, rose
against it like one man.

In addition to the articles of this constitution which I
have already named, there was one which excited infinite
alarm and indignation, for it rendered the Pope master
of every crown! As is well known, there is a doctrine
of the church, which says:

AN UNJUST EXCOMMUNICATION OUGHT NOT TO HINDER [US]
FROM DOING OUR DUTY.

The new constitution condemned this doctrine, and
consequently proclaimed that—

AN UNJUST EXCOMMUNICATION OUGHT TO HINDER [US]
FROM DOING OUR DUTY.

The enormity of this last is more striking than the
simple truth of the proposition condemned. The second
is a shadow which better throws up the light of the first.
The results and the frightful consequences of the condemnation are as clear as day.

I think I have before said that Father Tellier, without
any advances on my part, without, in fact, encouragement of any kind, insisted upon keeping up an intimacy
with me, which I could not well repel, for it came from
a man whom it would have been very dangerous indeed
to have for an enemy. As soon as this matter of the
constitution was in the wind, he came to me to talk about
it. I did not disguise my opinion from him, nor did he
disguise in any way from me the unscrupulous means he
meant to employ in order to get this bull accepted by
the clergy. Indeed, he was so free with me, showed me

so plainly his knavery and cunning, that I was, as it were, transformed with astonishment and fright. I never could comprehend this openness in a man so false, so artificial, so profound, or see in what manner it could be useful to him.

One day he came to me by appointment, with a copy of the constitution in his hand in order that we might thoroughly discuss it. I was at Versailles. In order to understand what I am going to relate, I must give some account of my apartments there. Let me say, then, that I had a little back cabinet, leading out of another cabinet, but so arranged that you would not have thought it was there. It received no light except from the outer cabinet, its own windows being boarded up. In this back cabinet I had a bureau, some chairs, books, and all I needed; my friends called it "my shop," and in truth it did not ill resemble one.

Father Tellier came at the hour he had fixed. As chance would have it, M. le Duc and Madame la Duchess de Berry had invited themselves to a collation with Madame de Saint-Simon that morning. I knew that when they arrived I should no longer be master of my chamber or of my cabinet. I told Father Tellier this, and he was much vexed. He begged me so hard to find some place where we might be inaccessible to the company, that at last, pressed by him to excess, I said I knew of only one expedient by which we might become free: and I told him that he must dismiss his *vatblé* (as the brother who always accompanies a monk is called), and that then, furnished with candles, we would go and shut ourselves up in my back cabinet, where we could neither be seen nor heard, if we took care not to speak loud when anybody approached. He thought the expedient admirable, dismissed his companion, and we sat down opposite each other, the bureau between us, with two candles alight upon it.

He immediately began to sing the praises of the "*Constitution Unigenitus,*" a copy of which he placed on the table. I interrupted him so as to come at once to the EXCOMMUNICATION proposition. We discussed it with much politeness, but with little accord. I shall not pretend to

17

report our dispute. It was warm and long. I pointed out to Father Tellier, that supposing the King and the little Dauphin were both to die, and this was a misfortune which might happen, the crown of France would by right of birth belong to the King of Spain; but according to the renunciation just made, it would belong to M. le Duc de Berry and his branch, or in default to M. le Duc d'Orléans. "Now," said I, "if the two brothers dispute the crown, and the Pope favoring the one should excommunicate the other, it follows, according to our new constitution, that the excommunicated must abandon all his claims, all his partisans, all his forces, and go over to the other side. For you say, AN UNJUST EXCOMMUNICATION OUGHT TO HINDER US FROM DOING OUR DUTY. So that in one fashion or another the Pope is master of all the crowns in his communion, is at liberty to take them away or to give them as he pleases, a liberty so many Popes have claimed and so many have tried to put in action."

My argument was simple, applicable, natural, and pressing; it offered itself, of itself. Therefore the confessor was amazed by it; he blushed, he beat about the bush, he could not collect himself. By degrees he did so, and replied to me in a manner that he doubtless thought would convince me at once. "If the case you suggest were to happen," he said, "and the Pope declaring for one disputant were to excommunicate the other and all his followers, such excommunication would not merely be UNJUST, it would be FALSE; and it has never been decided that a FALSE excommunication should hinder us from doing our duty."

"Ah! my father," I said, "your distinction is subtle and clever I admit. I admit, too, I did not expect it, but permit me some few more objections, I beseech you. Will the Ultramontanes admit the nullity of the excommunication? Is it not null as soon as it is unjust? If the Pope has the power to excommunicate unjustly, and to enforce obedience to his excommunication, who can limit power so unlimited, and why should not his FALSE (or nullified) excommunication be as much obeyed and respected as his UNJUST excommunication? Suppose the case I have imagined were to happen. Suppose the Pope were to excommunicate one of the two brothers. Do you think it would be easy to make your subtle distinction between a false and an unjust excommunication understood by the people, the soldiers, the bourgeois, the officers, the lords, the women, at the very moment when they would be preparing to act and to take up arms? You see I point out great inconveniences that may arise if the new doctrine be accepted, and if the Pope should claim the power of deposing kings, disposing of their crowns, and releasing their subjects from the oath of fidelity in opposition to the formal words of Jesus Christ and of all the Scripture.»

My words transported the Jesuit, for I had touched the right spring in spite of his effort to hide it. He said nothing personal to me, but he fumed. The more he restrained himself for me the less he did so for the matter in hand. As though to indemnify himself for his moderation on my account, he launched out the more, upon the subject we were discussing. In his heat, no longer master of himself, many things escaped him, silence upon which I am sure he would afterward have bought very dearly. He told me so many things of the violence that would be used to make his constitution accepted, things so monstrous, so atrocious, so terrible, and with such extreme passion that I fell into a veritable syncope. I saw him right in front of me between two candles, only the width of the table between us (I have described elsewhere his horrible physiognomy). My hearing and my sight became bewildered. I was seized, while he was speaking, with a full idea of what a Jesuit was. He was a man who by his state and his vows, could hope for nothing for his family or for himself, who could not expect an apple or a glass of wine more than his brethren; who was approaching an age when he would have to render an account of all things to God, and who, with studied deliberation and mighty artifice, was going to throw the State and religion into the most terrible flames, and commence a most frightful persecution for questions which affected him in nothing, nor touched in any way the honor of the School of Molina.

His profundities, the violence he spoke of—all this
together, threw me into such an ecstasy, that suddenly
I interrupted him by saying:

"My father, how old are you?"

The extreme surprise which painted itself upon his face
as I looked at him with all my eyes, fetched back my
senses, and his reply brought me completely to myself.
"Why do you ask?" he replied, smiling. The effort that
I made over myself to escape such a unique *proposito*, the
terrible value of which I fully appreciated, furnished me
an issue. "Because," said I, "never have I looked at you
so long as I have now, you in front of me, these two
candles between us, and your face is so fresh and so
healthy, with all your labors, that I am surprised at it."

He swallowed the answer, or so well pretended to do
so, that he said nothing of it then nor since, never ceasing
when he met me to speak to me openly, and as frequently
as before, I seeking him as little as ever. He replied at
that time that he was seventy-four years old, that in truth
he was very well; that he had accustomed himself, from
his earliest years, to a hard life and to labor; and then
went back to the point at which I had interrupted him. We
were compelled, however, to be silent for a time, because
people came into my cabinet, and Madame de Saint-Simon,
who knew of our interview, had some difficulty to keep
the coast clear.

For more than two hours we continued our discussion,
he trying to put me off with his subtleties and authorita-
tiveness, I offering but little opposition to him, feeling
that opposition was of no use, all his plans being already
decided. We separated without having persuaded each
other, he with many flatteries upon my intelligence, praying me to reflect well upon the matter; I replying that
my reflections were all made, and that my capacity could
not go farther. I let him out by the little back door of
my cabinet, so that nobody perceived him, and as soon
as I had closed it, I threw myself into a chair like a man
out of breath, and I remained there a long time alone,
reflecting upon the strange kind of ecstasy I had been in,
and the horror it had caused me.

The results of this CONSTITUTION were, as I have said,

terrible to the last degree; every artifice, every cruelty, was used in order to force it down the throats of the clergy, and hence the confusion and sore trouble which arose all over the realm. But it is time now for me to touch upon other matters.

Toward the close of this year, 1713, peace with the Emperor seemed so certain, that the King disbanded sixty battalions and eighteen men per company of the regiment of the guards, and one hundred and six squadrons; of which squadrons twenty-seven were dragoons. At peace now with the rest of Europe he had no need of so many troops, even although the war against the Empire had continued; fortunately, however, it did not. Negotiations were set on foot, and on the 6th of March of the following year, 1714, after much debate, they ended successfully. On that day, in fact, peace was signed at Rastadt. It was shortly afterward published at Paris, a *Te Deum* sung, and bonfires lighted at night; a grand collation was given at the Hotel de Ville by the Duc de Tresmes, who at midnight also gave, in his own house, a splendid banquet, at which were present many ladies, foreigners, and courtiers.

This winter was fertile in balls at the Court; there were several, fancy dress and masked, given by M. le Duc de Berry, by Madame la Duchess de Berry, M. le Duc, and others. There were some also at Paris, and at Sceaux, where Madame du Maine gave many *fêtes* and played many comedies, everybody going there from Paris and the Court — M. du Maine doing the honors. Madame la Duchess de Berry was in the family way, and went to no dances out of her own house. The King permitted her, on account of her condition, to sup with him in a *robe de chambre*, as under similar circumstances he had permitted the two Dauphines to do.

At the opera, one night this winter, the Abbé Servien, not liking certain praises of the King contained in a Prologue, let slip a bitter joke in ridicule of them. The pit took it up, repeated it, and applauded it. Two days afterward the Abbé Servien was arrested and taken to Vincennes, forbidden to speak to anybody and allowed no servant to wait upon him. For form's sake seals

were put upon his papers, but he was not a man likely
to have any fit for aught else than to light the fire.
Though more than sixty-five years old, he was strangely
debauched.

The Duc de la Rochefoucauld died on Thursday, the
11th of January, at Versailles, seventy-nine years of age,
and blind. I have spoken of him so frequently in the
course of these "Memoirs," that I will do nothing more
now than relate a few particulars respecting him, which
will serve in some sort to form his portrait.

He had much honor, worth, and probity. He was
noble, good, magnificent, ever willing to serve his
friends; a little too much so, for he oftentimes wearied
the King with importunities on their behalf. Without
any intellect or discernment he was proud to excess,
coarse and rough in his manners—disagreeable even,
and embarrassed with all except his flatterers; like a
man who does not know how to receive a visit, enter or
leave a room. He scarcely went anywhere except to pay
the indispensable compliments demanded by marriage,
death, etc., and even then as little as he could. He lived
in his own house so shut up that no one went to see
him except on these same occasions. He gave himself
up almost entirely to his valets, who mixed themselves in
the conversation; and you were obliged to treat them with
all sorts of attentions if you wished to become a fre-
quenter of the house.

I shall never forget what happened to us at the death
of the Prince of Vaudemont's son, by which M. de la
Rochefoucauld's family came in for a good inheritance.
We were at Marly. The King had been stag hunting.
M. de Chevreuse, whom I found when the King was being unbooted, proposed that we should go and pay our
compliments to M. de la Rochefoucauld. We went. Upon
entering, what was our surprise, nay, our shame to find
M. de la Rochefoucauld playing at chess with one of his
servants in livery, seated opposite to him! Speech failed
us. M. de la Rochefoucauld perceived it, and remained
confounded himself. He stammered, he grew confused,
he tried to excuse what we had seen, saying that this
lackey played very well, and that chess players played

with everybody. M. de Chevreuse had not come to contradict him, neither had I; we turned the conversation, therefore, and left as soon as possible. As soon as we were outside we opened our minds to each other, and said what we thought of this rare meeting, which, however, we did not make public.

M. de la Rochefoucauld, toward the end of his career at Court, became so importunate, as I have said, for his friends, that the King was much relieved by his death. Such have been his sentiments at the death of nearly all those whom he had liked and favored.

Of the courage of M. de la Rochefoucauld, courtier as he was in speaking to the King, I will relate an instance. It was during one of the visits at Marly, in the gardens of which the King was amusing himself with a fountain that he set at work. I know not what led to it, but the King, usually so reserved, spoke with him of the bishop of Saint-Pons, then in disgrace on account of the affairs of Port Royal. M. de la Rochefoucauld let him speak on to the end, and then began to praise the bishop. The discouraging silence of the King warned him; he persisted, however, and related how the bishop, mounted upon a mule, and visiting one day his diocese, found himself in a path, which grew narrower at every step, and which ended in a precipice. There were no means of getting out of it except by going back, but this was impossible, there not being enough space to turn round or to alight. The holy bishop (for such was his term as I well remarked) lifted his eyes to Heaven, let go the bridle, and abandoned himself to Providence. Immediately his mule rose up upon its hind legs, and thus upright, the bishop still astride, turned round until its head was where its tail had been. The beast thereupon returned along the path until it found an opening into a good road. Everybody around the King imitated his silence, which excited the Duke to comment upon what he had just related. This generosity charmed me, and surprised all who were witness of it.

The day after the death of M. de la Rochefoucauld, the Chancellor took part in a very tragic scene. A vice *bailli* of Alençon had just lost a trial, in which, apparently,

his honor, or his property, was much interested. He
came to Ponchartrain's where the Chancellor was at the
moment, and waited until he came out into the court to
get into his carriage. The vice *bailli* then asked him
for a revision of the verdict. The Chancellor, with much
gentleness and goodness, represented to the man that
the law courts were open to him if he insisted to appeal,
but that as to a revision of the verdict, it was contrary to usage; and turned to get into his coach. While
he was getting in, the unhappy *bailli* said there was a
shorter way of escaping from trouble, and stabbed himself
twice with a poniard. At the cries of the domestics the
Chancellor descended from the coach, had the man carried
into a room, and sent for a doctor, and a confessor. The
bailli made confession very peacefully, and died an hour
afterward.

I have spoken in its time of the exile of Charmel and
its causes, of which the chief was his obstinate refusal
to present himself before the King. The vexation of the
King against people who withdrew from him was always
very great. In this case, it never passed away, but hard-
ened into a strange cruelty, to speak within limits.
Charmel attacked with the stone, asked permission to
come to Paris to undergo an operation. The permission
was positively refused. Time pressed. The operation
was obliged to be done in the country. It was so severe,
and perhaps so badly done, that Charmel died three days
afterward full of penitence and piety. He had led a life
remarkable for its goodness, was without education, but
had religious fervor that supplied the want of it. He
was sixty-eight years of age.

The Maréchale de la Ferté died at Paris, at the same
time, more than eighty years old. She was sister of the
Comtesse d'Olonne, very rich and a widow. The beauty
of the two sisters, and the excesses of their lives, made
a great stir. No women, not even those most stigma-
tized for their gallantry, dared to see them, or to be
seen anywhere with them. That was the way then; the
fashion has changed since. When they were old and
nobody cared for them, they tried to become devout.
They lodged together, and one Ash Wednesday went and

heard a sermon. This sermon, which was upon fasting and penitence, terrified them.

"My sister," they said to each other on their return, "it was all true; there was no joke about it; we must do penance, or we are lost. But, my sister, what shall we do?" After having well turned it over: "My sister," said Madame d'Olonne, "this is what we must do; we must make our servants fast." Madame d'Olonne thought she had very well met the difficulty. However, at last, she set herself to work in earnest, at piety and penitence, and died three months after her sister, the Maréchale de la Ferté. It will not be forgotten, that it was under cover of the Maréchale that a natural child was first legitimated without naming the mother, in order that by this example, the King's natural children might be similarly honored, without naming Madame de Montespan, as I have related in its place.

CHAPTER XXVI.

The King of Spain a Widower—Intrigues of Madame des Ursins—
Choice of the Princess of Parma—The King of France Kept in
the Dark—Celebration of the Marriage—Sudden Fall of the Princess des Ursins—Her Expulsion from Spain.

THE Queen of Spain, for a long time violently attacked
with the king's evil around the face and neck, was
just now at the point of death. Obtaining no relief from the Spanish doctors, she wished to have Helvetius, and begged the King by an express command to
send him to her. Helvetius much inconvenienced, and
knowing besides the condition of the princess, did not
wish to go, but the King expressly commanded him. He
set out then in a post chaise, followed by another in case
his own should break down, and arrived thus at Madrid
on the 11th of February, 1714. As soon as he had seen
the Queen, he said there was nothing but a miracle could
save her. The King of Spain did not discontinue sleeping with her until the 9th. On the 14th she died, with
much courage, consciousness, and piety.

Despair was general in Spain, where this Queen was
universally adored. There was not a family which did
not lament her, not a person who has since been consoled. The King of Spain was extremely touched, but
somewhat in a royal manner. Thus, when out shooting one
day, he came close to the convoy by which the body of
his queen was being conveyed to the Escurial; he looked
at it, followed it with his eyes, and continued his sport!
Are these princes made like other human beings?

The death of the Queen led to amazing changes, such
as the most prophetic could not have foreseen. Let me
here, then, relate the events that followed this misfortune.

I must commence by saying, that the principal cause
which had so long and scandalously hindered us from
making peace with the Emperor, was a condition, which
Madame des Ursins wished to insert in the treaty, (and

which the King of Spain supported through thick and thin) to the effect that she should be invested with a *bona fide* sovereignty. She had set her heart upon this, and the King of Spain was a long time before he would consent to any terms of peace that did not concede it to her. It was not until the King had uttered threats against him that he would give way. As for Madame des Ursins, she had counted upon this sovereignty with as much certainty as though it were already between her fingers. She had counted too, with equal certainty upon exchanging it with our King, for the sovereignty of Touraine and the Amboise country; and had actually charged her faithful Aubigny to buy her some land near Amboise to build her there a vast palace, with courts and out-buildings; to furnish it with magnificence, to spare neither gilding nor paintings, and to surround the whole with the most beautiful gardens. She meant to live there as sovereign lady of the country. Aubigny had at once set about the work to the surprise of everybody: for no one could imagine for whom such a grand building could be designed. He kept the secret, pretended he was building a house for himself and pushed on the works so rapidly that just as peace was concluded without the stipulation respecting Madame des Ursins being inserted in the treaty, nearly all was finished. Her sovereignty scheme thoroughly failed; and to finish at once with that mad idea I may as well state, that ashamed of her failure, she gave this palace to Aubigny, who lived there all the rest of his life: Chanteloup, for so it is called, has since passed into the hands of Madame d'Armantières, his daughter. It is one of the most beautiful and most singular places in all France, and the most superbly furnished.

This sovereignty, coveted by Madame des Ursins, exceedingly offended Madame de Maintenon and wounded her pride. She felt, with jealousy, that the grand airs Madame des Ursins gave herself were solely the effect of the protection she had accorded her. She could not bear to be outstripped in importance by the woman she herself had elevated. The King, too, was much vexed with Madame des Ursins; vexed also to see peace delayed; and to be obliged to speak with authority and menace to the King of Spain, in order to compel him to give up the idea of this precious sovereignty. The King of Spain did not yield until he was threatened with abandonment by France. It may be imagined what was the rage of Madame des Ursins upon missing her mark after having, before the eyes of all Europe, fired at it with so much perseverance, nay with such unmeasured obstinacy. From this time there was no longer the same concert between Madame de Maintenon and Madame des Ursins that had formerly existed. But the latter had reached such a point in Spain, that she thought this was of no consequence.

It has been seen with what art Madame des Ursins had unceasingly isolated the King of Spain; in what manner she had shut him up with the Queen, and rendered him inaccessible, not only to his Court but to his grand officers, his ministers, even his valets, so that he was served by only three or four attendants, all French, and entirely under her thumb. At the death of the Queen this solitude continued. Under the pretext that his grief demanded privacy, she persuaded the King to leave his palace and to instal himself in a quiet retreat, the palace of Medina-Celi, near the Buen-Retiro, at the other end of the city. She preferred this because it was infinitely smaller than the Royal Palace, and because few people, in consequence, could approach the King. She herself took the Queen's place; and in order to have a sort of pretext for being near the King, in the same solitude, she caused herself to be named governess of his children. But in order to be always there, and so that nobody should know when they were together, she had a large wooden corridor made from the cabinet of the King to the apartment of his children, in which she lodged. By this means they could pass from one to the other without being perceived, and without traversing the long suite of rooms, filled with courtiers, that were between the two apartments. In this manner it was never known whether the King was alone or with Madame des Ursins; or which of the two was in the apartments of the other. When they were together or how long is equally unknown. This corridor, roofed and glazed, was proceeded with in so much haste, that the work went on, in spite of the King's devotion, on *fête* days and Sundays. The whole Court, which perfectly well knew for what use this corridor was intended, was much displeased. Those who directed the works were the same. Of this good proof was given. One day the Comptroller of the royal buildings, who had been ordered to keep the men hard at it, Sundays and *fête* days, asked the Père Robinet, the King's confessor, and the only good one he ever had; he asked, I say, in one of those rooms Madame des Ursins was so anxious to avoid, and in the presence of various courtiers, if the work was to be continued on the morrow, a Sunday, and the next day, the *fête* of the Virgin. Robinet replied, that the King had said nothing to the contrary; and met a second appeal with the same answer. At the third, he added, that before saying anything he would wait till the King spoke on the subject. At the fourth appeal he lost patience, and said that if for the purpose of destroying what had been commenced, be believed work might be done even on Easter day itself; but if for the purpose of continuing the corridor, he did not think a Sunday or a *fête* day was a fitting time. All the Court applauded; but Madame des Ursins, to whom this sally was soon carried, was much irritated.

It was suspected that she thought of becoming something more than the mere companion of the King. There were several princes. Reports were spread which appeared equivocal and which terrified. It was said that the King had no need of posterity, with all the children it had pleased God to bless him with; but now he only needed a wife who could take charge of those children. Not content with passing all her days with the King, and allowing him, like the deceased Queen, to work with his ministers only in her presence, the Princess des Ursins felt that to render this habit lasting she must assure herself of him at all moments. He was accustomed to take the air, and he was in want of it all the more now because he had been much shut up during the last days of the Queen's illness, and the first which followed her death. Madame des Ursins chose four or five gentlemen to accompany him, to the exclusion of all others, even his chief officers, and people still more necessary. These gentlemen charged with the amusement of the King, were called *recreadores*. With so much circumspection, importunity, preparation, and rumor carefully circulated, it was not doubted that Madame des Ursins intended to marry him; and the opinion, as well as the fear, became general. The King (Louis XIV.) was infinitely alarmed; and Madame de Maintenon, who had twice tried to be proclaimed Queen and twice failed, was distracted with jealousy. However, if Madame des Ursins flattered herself then, it was not for long.

The King of Spain, always curious to learn the news from France, often demanded them of his confessor, the only man to whom he could speak who was not under the thumb of Madame des Ursins. The clever and courageous Robinet, as disturbed as others at the progress of the design, which nobody in the two Courts of France and Spain doubted was in execution, allowed himself to be pressed by questions — in an embrasure where the King had drawn him — played the reserved and the mysterious in order to excite curiosity more. When he saw it was sufficiently excited, he said that since he was forced to speak, his news from France was the same as that at Madrid, where no one doubted that the King would do the Princess des Ursins the honor to espouse her. The King blushed and hastily replied, " Marry her! oh no! not that! » and quitted him.

Whether the Princess des Ursins was informed of this sharp repartee, or whether she despaired already of success, she changed about; and judging that this interregnum in the palace of Medina-Celi could not last forever, resolved to assure herself of the King by a Queen who should owe to her such a grand marriage, and who, having no other support, would throw herself into her arms by gratitude and necessity. With this view she explained herself to Alberoni, who, since the death of the Duc de Vendôme, had remained at Madrid charged with the affairs of Parma; and proposed to him the marriage of the Princess of Parma, daughter of the Duchess and of the late Duke of Parma, who had married the widow of his brother.

Alberoni could with difficulty believe his ears.   An alliance so disproportioned appeared to him so much the
more incredible, because he thought the Court of France
would never consent to it, and that without its consent
the marriage could not be concluded.   The Princess in
question was the issue of double illegitimacy; by her
father descended from a pope, by her mother from a natural daughter of Charles Quint.   She was daughter of a
petty Duke of Parma, and of a mother, entirely Austrian,
sister of the Dowager Empress and of the Dowager
Queen of Spain (whose acts had excited such disapproval
that she was sent from her exile at Toledo to Bayonne), sister
too of the Queen of Portugal, who had induced the King,
her husband, to receive the Archduke at Lisbon, and to
carry the war into Spain.   It did not seem reasonable,
therefore, that such a princess would be accepted as a
wife for the King of Spain.

Nothing of all this, however, stopped the Princess des
Ursins; her own interest was the most pressing consideration with her; the will of the King of Spain was entirely subject to her; she felt all the change toward her
of our King and of Madame de Maintenon; she no longer
hoped for a return of their favor; she believed that she
must look around for support against the very authority
which had established her so powerfully, and which could
destroy her; and occupied herself solely in pushing forward a marriage from which she expected everything by
making the same use of the new queen as she had made
of the one just dead.   The King of Spain was devout, he
absolutely wanted a wife, the Princess des Ursins was of
an age when her charms were but the charms of art; in
a word, she set Alberoni to work, and it may be believed
she was not scrupulous as to her means as soon as they
were persuaded at Parma that she was serious and not
joking.   Orry, always united with Madame des Ursins,
and all-powerful by her means, was her sole confidant in
this important affair.

At that time the Marquis de Brancas was French ambassador at Madrid.   He had flattered himself that Madame des Ursins would make him one of the grandees of
Spain.   Instead of doing so she simply bestowed upon

him the order of the Golden Fleece. He had never pardoned her for this. Entirely devoted to Madame de Maintenon, he became on that very account an object of suspicion to Madame des Ursins, who did not doubt that he cherished a grudge against her, on account of the favor he had missed. She allowed him no access to her, and had her eyes open upon all he did. Brancas in like manner watched all her doings. The confessor, Robinet, confided to him his fears respecting Madame des Ursins, and the chiefs of a court universally discontented, went and opened their hearts to him, thinking it was France alone which could set to rights the situation of Spain.

Brancas appreciated all the importance of what was told him, but warned by the fate of the Abbé d'Estrées, fearing even for his couriers, he took the precaution of sending word to the King that he had pressing business to acquaint him with, which he could not trust to paper, and that he wished to be allowed to come to Versailles for a fortnight. The reply was the permission asked for, accompanied, however, with an order to communicate *en route* with the Duc de Berwick, who was about to pass to Barcelona.

Madame des Ursins, who always found means to be informed of everything, immediately knew of Brancas's projected journey, and determined to get the start of him. At once she had sixteen relays of mules provided upon the Bayonne road, and suddenly sent off to France, on Holy Thursday, Cardinal del Giudice, grand inquisitor and minister of state, who had this mean complaisance for her. She thus struck two blows at once; she got rid, at least for a time, of a Cardinal minister who troubled her, and anticipated Brancas, which in our Court was no small point.

Brancas, who felt all the importance of arriving first, followed the Cardinal on Good Friday, and moved so well that he overtook him at Bayonne, at night while he was asleep; Brancas passed straight on, charging the commandant to amuse and to delay the Cardinal as long as possible on the morrow; gained ground, and arrived at Bordeaux with twenty-eight post horses that he had carried off with him from various stations to keep them from the Cardinal. He arrived at Paris in this manner two days before the other, and went straight to Marly where the King was, to explain the business that had led him there. He had a long audience with the King, and received a lodging for the rest of the visit.

The Cardinal del Giudice rested four or five days at Paris, and then came to Marly where he was introduced to the King. The Cardinal was somewhat embarrassed; he was charged with no business; all his' mission was to praise Madame des Ursins, and complain of the Marquis de Brancas. These praises of Madame des Ursins were but vague; she had not sufficient confidence in the Cardinal to admit to him her real position in our Court, and to give him instructions accordingly, so that what he had to say was soon all said; against the Marquis de Brancas he had really no fact to allege, his sole crime was that he was too sharp sighted and not sufficiently devoted to the Princess.

The Cardinal was a courtier, a man of talent, of business, of intrigue, who felt, with annoyance, that for a person of his condition and weight, such a commission as he bore was very empty. He appeared exceedingly agreeable in conversation, of pleasant manners, and was much liked in good society. He was assiduous in his attentions to the King, without importuning him for audiences that were unnecessary; and by all his conduct, he gave reason for believing that he suspected Madame des Ursins's decadence in our Court, and sought to gain esteem and confidence, so as to become by the support of the King, prime minister in Spain; but as we shall soon see, his ultramontane hobbies hindered the accomplishment of his measures. All the success of his journey consisted in hindering Brancas from returning to Spain. This was no great punishment, for Brancas had nothing more to hope for from Madame des Ursins, and was not a man to lose his time for nothing.

Up to this period not a word had been said to the King (Louis XIV.) by the King of Spain upon the subject of his marriage; not a hint had been given that he meant to remarry, much less with a Parma princess. This proceeding, grafted upon the sovereignty claimed by the Princess des Ursins, and all her conduct with the King of Spain since the death of the Queen, resolved our King to disgrace her without appeal.

A remark upon Madame des Ursins, accompanied by a smile, escaped from the King, generally so complete a master of himself, and appeared enigmatical to such an extent, although striking, that Torcy, to whom it was addressed, understood nothing. In his surprise, he related to Castries what the King had said; Castries told it to Madame la Duchess d'Orléans, who reported it to M. d'Orléans and to me. We racked our brains to comprehend it, but in vain; nevertheless, such an unintelligible remark upon a person like Madame des Ursins, who up to this time had been on such good terms with the King and Madame de Maintenon, did not appear to me to be favorable. I was confirmed in this view by what had just happened with regard to her sovereignty; but I was a thousand leagues from the thunderbolt which this lightning announced, and which only declared itself to us by its fall.

It was not until the 27th of June that the King was made acquainted by the King of Spain with his approaching marriage. Of course, through other channels, he had not failed to hear of it long before. He passed in the lightest and gentlest manner in the world over this project, and the mystery so long and so complete with which it had been kept from him, stranger, if possible, than the marriage itself. He could not hinder it; but from this moment he was sure of his vengence against her who had arranged and brought it about in this manner. The disgrace of Madame des Ursins was in fact determined on between the King and Madame de Maintenon, but in a manner so secret before and since, that I know nobody who has found out by whom or how it was carried out. It is good to admit our ignorance, and not to give fictions and inventions in place of what we are unacquainted with.

I know not why, but a short time after this, the Princess des Ursins conceived such strong suspicion of the lofty and enterprising spirit of the Princess of Parma that she repented having made this marriage, and wished to break it off. She brought forward, therefore, I know not what difficulties, and dispatched a courier to Rome to Cardinal Acquaviva, who did the King of Spain's business there, ordering him to delay his journey to Parma, where he had been commanded to ask the hand of the Princess, and to see her provisionally espoused. But Madame des Ursins had changed her mind too late. The courier did not find Acquaviva at Rome. That cardinal was already far away on the road to Parma, so that there were no means of retreat.

Acquaviva was received with great honor and much magnificence; he made his demand, but delayed the espousals as long as he could, and this caused much remark. The marriage, which was to have been celebrated on the 25th of August, did not take place until the 15th of September. Immediately after the ceremony the new Queen set out for Spain.

An envoy from Parma, with news of the marriage of the Princess, arrived at Fontainebleau on the 11th of October, and had an audience with the King. This was rather late in the day. For dowry she had one hundred thousand pistoles, and three hundred thousand livres' worth of jewels. She had embarked for Alicante at Sestri di Levante. A violent tempest sickened her of the sea. She landed, therefore, at Monaco, in order to traverse by land Provence, Languedoc, and Guienne, so as to reach Bayonne, and see there the Queen Dowager of Spain; sister of her mother, and widow of Charles II. Desgranges, master of the ceremonies, was to meet her in Provence, with orders to follow her, and to command the governors, lieutenants general, and intendants to follow her also, and serve her, though she traveled incognito.

The new Queen of Spain, on arriving at Pau, found the Queen Dowager, her aunt, had come expressly from Bayonne to meet her. As they approached each other, they both descended at the same time, and after saluting, mounted alone into a beautiful *calèche* that the Queen Dowager had brought with her, and that she presented to her niece. They supped together alone. The Queen Dowager conducted her to Saint Jean Pied-de-Port (for in that country, as in Spain, the entrances to mountain passes are called *ports*). They separated there, the Queen Dowager making the Queen many presents, among others a garniture of diamonds. The Duc de St. Aignan joined the Queen of Spain at Pau, and accompanied her by command of the King to Madrid. She sent Grillo, a Genoese noble, whom she has since made grandee of Spain, to thank the King for sending her the Duc de St. Aignan, and for the present he brought with him. The officers of her household had been named by Madame des Ursins.

The Queen of Spain advanced toward Madrid with the attendants sent to accompany her. She was to be met by the King of Spain at Guadalaxara, which is about the same distance from Madrid as Paris is from Fontaine-bleau. He arrived there, accompanied by the attendants that the Princess des Ursins had placed near him, to keep him company, and to allow no one else to approach him. She followed in her coach, so as to arrive at the same time, and immediately afterward he shut himself up alone with her, and saw nobody until he went to bed. This was on the 22d of September. The next day the Princess des Ursins set out with a small suite for a little place, seven leagues further, called Quadraqué, where the Queen was to sleep that night. Madame des Ursins counted upon enjoying all the gratitude that the Queen would feel for the unhoped-for grandeur she had obtained by her means: counted upon passing the evening with her, and upon accompanying her next day to Guadalaxara. She found, upon arriving at Quadraqué, that the Queen had already reached there. She at once entered into a lodging that had been prepared for her, opposite that of the Queen. She was in a full Court dress. After adjusting it in a hurried manner, she went to the Queen. The coldness and stiffness of her reception surprised her extremely. She attributed it in the first place to the embarrassment of the Queen, and tried to melt this ice. Everybody withdrew, in order to leave the two alone.

Then the conversation commenced. The Queen would not long allow Madame des Ursins to continue it; but burst out into reproaches against her for her manners, and for appearing there in a dress that showed want of respect for the company she was in. Madame des Ursins, whose dress was proper, and who, on account of her respectful manners and her discourse, calculated to win the Queen, believed herself to be far from meriting this treatment, was strangely surprised, and wished to excuse herself; but the Queen immediately began to utter offensive words, to cry out, to call aloud, to demand the officers of the guard, and sharply to command Madame des Ursins to leave her presence. The latter wished to speak and defend herself against the reproaches she heard; but the Queen, increasing her fury and her menaces, cried out to her people to drive this mad woman from her presence and from the house; and absolutely had her turned out by the shoulders. Immediately afterward she called Amenzago, lieutenant of the bodyguard, and at the same time the *écuyer* who had the control of her equipages. She ordered the first to arrest Madame des Ursins, and not quit her until he had placed her in a coach, with two sure officers of the guard and fifteen soldiers as sentinels over her; the second she commanded to provide instantly a coach and six, with two or three footmen, and send off in it the Princess des Ursins toward Burgos and Bayonne, without once stopping on the road. Amenzago tried to represent to the Queen that the King of Spain alone had the power to give such commands; but she haughtily asked him if he had not received an order from the King of Spain to obey her in everything, without reserve and without comment. It was true he had received such an order, though nobody knew a word about it.

Madame des Ursins was then immediately arrested, and put into a coach with one of her waiting women, without having had time to change her costume or her headdress, to take any precaution against the cold, to provide herself with any money or other things, and without any kind of refreshment in the coach, or a chemise; nothing, in fact, to change or to sleep in! She was shipped off thus (with two officers of the guard, who were ready as soon as the coach), in full Court dress, just as she left the Queen. In the very short and tumultuous interval which elapsed, she sent a message to the Queen, who flew into a fresh passion upon not being obeyed, and made her set out immediately.

It was then nearly seven o'clock in the evening, two days before Christmas, the ground all covered with snow and ice, and the cold extreme and very sharp and bitter, as it always is in Spain. As soon as the Queen learned that the Princess des Ursins was out of Quadraqué, she wrote to the King of Spain, by an officer of the guards whom she dispatched to Guadalaxara. The night was so dark that it was only by means of the snow that anything could be seen.

It is not easy to represent the state of Madame des Ursins in the coach. An excess of astonishment and bewilderment prevailed at first, and suspended all other sentiment; but grief, vexation, rage, and despair, soon followed. In their turn succeeded sad and profound reflections upon a step so violent, so unheard of, and so unjustifiable as she thought. Then she hoped everything from the friendship of the King of Spain and his confidence in her; pictured his anger and surprise, and those of the group of attached survitors, by whom she had surrounded him, and who would be so interested in exciting the King in her favor. The long winter's night passed thus; the cold was terrible, there was nothing to ward it off; the coachman actually lost the use of one hand. The morning advanced; a halt was necessary in order to bait the horses; as for the travelers there is nothing for them even in the Spanish inns. You are simply told where each thing you want is sold. The meat is ordinarily alive; the wine, thick, flat, and stong; the bread bad; the water is often worthless; as to beds, there are some, but only for the mule drivers, so that you must carry everything with you, and neither Madame des Ursins nor those with her had anything whatever. Eggs, when they could find any, were their sole resource; and these, fresh or not, simply boiled, supported them during all the journey.

Until this halt for the horses, silence had been profound and uninterrupted; now it was broken. During all this long night the Princess des Ursins had had leisure to think upon the course she should adopt, and to compose her face. She spoke of her extreme surprise, and of the little that had passed between her and the Queen. In like manner the two officers of the guard accustomed, as was all Spain, to fear and respect her more than their King, replied to her from the bottom of that abyss of astonishment from which they had not yet arisen. The horses being put to, the coach soon started again. Soon, too, the Princess des Ursins found that the assistance she expected from the King did not arrive. No rest, no provisions, nothing to put on, until St. Jean de Luz was reached. As she went further on, as time passed and no news came, she felt she had nothing more to hope for. It may be imagined what rage succeeded in a woman so ambitious, so accustomed to publicly reign, so rapidly and shamefully precipitated from the summit of power by the hand that she herself had chosen as the most solid support of her grandeur. The Queen had not replied to the last two letters Madame des Ursins had written to her. This studied negligence was of bad augury, but who would have imagined treatment so strange and so unheard of?

Her nephews, Lanti and Chalais, who had permission to join her, completed her dejection. Yet she was faithful to herself. Neither tears nor regrets, neither reproaches, nor the slightest weakness escaped her; not a complaint even of the excessive cold, of the deprivation of all things, or of the extreme fatigue of such a journey. The two officers who guarded her could not contain their admiration.

At St. Jean de Luz, where she arrived on the 14th of January, 1715, she found at last her corporeal ills at an end. She obtained a bed, change of dress, food, and her liberty. The guards, their officers, and the coach which had brought her, returned; she remained with her waiting maid and her nephews. She had leisure to think what she might expect from Versailles. In spite of her mad sovereignty scheme so long maintained, and her hardihood in arranging the King of Spain's marriage without consulting our King, she flattered herself she should find resources in a Court she had so long governed. It was from St. Jean de Luz that she dispatched a courier

charged with letters for the King, for Madame de Maintenon, and for her friends. She briefly gave us an account in those letters of the thunderbolt which had fallen
on her, and asked permission to come to the Court to
explain herself more in detail. She waited for the return of her courier in this her first place of liberty and
repose, which of itself is very agreeable. But this first
courier dispatched, she sent off Lanti with letters written
less hastily, and with instructions. Lanti saw the King
in his cabinet on the last of January, and remained there
some moments. From him it was known that as soon as
Madame des Ursins dispatched her first courier, she had
sent her compliments to the Queen Dowager of Spain at
Bayonne, who would not receive them. What cruel mor-
tifications attend a fall from a throne! Let us now return to Guadalaxara.

CHAPTER XXVII.

The King of Spain Acquiesces in the Disgrace of Madame des Ursins—
Its Origin—Who Struck the Blow—Her Journey to Versailles—
Treatment There—My Interview with Her—She Retires to Genoa
—Then to Rome—Dies.

THE officer of the guards, whom the Queen dispatched
with a letter for the King of Spain as soon as Madame des Ursins was out of Quadraqué, found the
King upon the point of going to bed. He appeared
moved, sent a short reply to the Queen, and gave no
orders. The officer returned immediately. What is singular is, that the secret was so well kept that it did not
transpire until the next morning at ten o'clock. It may be
imagined what emotion seized the whole Court, and what
divers movements there were among all at Guadalaxara.
However, nobody dared to speak to the King, and much
expectation was built upon the reply he had sent to the
Queen. The morning passed and nothing was said; the
fate of Madame des Ursins then became pretty evident.

Chalais and Lanti made bold to ask the King for permission to go and join the Princess in her isolation. Not
only he allowed them to do so, but charged them with a
letter of simple civility, in which he told her he was very
sorry for what had happened; that he had not been able
to oppose the Queen's will; that he should continue to her
her pensions, and see that they were punctually paid.
He was as good as his word: as long as she lived she
regularly received them.

The Queen arrived at Guadalaxara on the afternoon of
the day before Christmas day, at the hour fixed, and as
though nothing had occurred. The King received her in
the same manner on the staircase, gave her his hand,
and immediately led her to the chapel, where the marriage was at once celebrated; for in Spain the custom is
to marry after dinner. After that he led her to her

chamber, and straightway went to bed; it was before six
o'clock in the evening, and both got up again for the
midnight mass. What passed between them upon the
event of the previous evening was entirely unknown, and
has always remained so. The day after Christmas day
the King and Queen alone together in a coach, and followed by all the Court, took the road for Madrid, where
there was no more talk of Madame des Ursins than if
the King had never known her. Our King showed not
the least surprise at the news brought to him by a courier
dispatched from Guadalaxara by the Duke de Saint Aignan, though all the Court was filled with emotion and
affright after having seen Madame des Ursins so triumphant.

Let us now look about for some explanations that will
enable us to pierce this mystery — that remark to Torcy
which escaped the King, which Torcy could not comprehend, and which he related to Castries, who told it to
Madame la Duchess d'Orléans, from whom I learned it!
Can we imagine that a Parma princess brought up in a
garret by an imperious mother, would have dared to take
upon herself, while six leagues from the King of Spain
whom she had never seen, a step so bold and unheard
of, when we consider against whom directed, a person
possessing the entire confidence of that King and
reigning openly? The thing is explained by the order,
so unusual and so secret, that Amenzago had from
the King of Spain to obey the Queen in everything,
without reserve and without comment; an order that
became known only at the moment when she gave orders to arrest Madame des Ursins and take her away.

Let us remark, too, the tranquillity with which our King
and the King of Spain received the first intelligence of
this event; the inactivity of the latter, the coldness of
his letter to Madame des Ursins, and his perfect indifference what became of a person who was so cherished
the day before, and who yet was forced to travel, deprived of everything, by roads full of ice and snow. We
must recollect that when the King banished Madame des
Ursins before, for opening the letter of the Abbé d'Estrées, and for the note she sent upon it, he did not dare

to have his orders executed in the presence of the King of Spain. It was on the frontier of Portugal where our King wished him to go for the express purpose, that the King of Spain signed the order by which the Princess des Ursins was forced to withdraw from the country. Now we had a second edition of the same volume. Let me add what I learned from the Maréchal de Brancas, to whom Alberoni related, a long while after this disgrace, that one evening as the Queen was traveling from Parma to Spain, he found her pacing her chamber, with rapid step and in agitation muttering to herself, letting escape the name of the Princess des Ursins, and then saying with heat, " I will drive her away, the first thing." He cried out to the Queen and sought to represent to her the danger, the madness, the inutility of the enterprise which overwhelmed him. " Keep all this quiet," said the Queen, " and never let what you have heard escape you. Not a word! I know what I am about."

All these things together threw much light upon a catastrophe equally astonishing in itself and in its execution, and clearly show our King to have been the author of it; the King of Spain a consenting party and assisting by the extraordinary order given to Amenzago; and the Queen the actress, charged in some manner by the two Kings to bring it about. The sequel in France confirmed this opinion.

The fall of the Princess des Ursins caused great changes in Spain. The Comtesse d'Altamire was named Camarera Mayor, in her place. She was one of the greatest ladies in all Spain, and was hereditary Duchess of Cardonne. Cellamare, nephew of Cardinal del Giudice, was named her grand *écuyer;* and the Cardinal himself soon returned to Madrid and to consideration. As a natural consequence, Macanas was disgraced. He and Orry had orders to leave Spain, the latter without seeing the King. He carried with him the maledictions of the public. Pompadour, who had been named ambassador in Spain only to amuse Madame des Ursins, was dismissed, and the Duc de Saint-Aignan invested with that character, just as he was about to return after having conducted the Queen to Madrid.

In due time the Princess des Ursins arrived in Paris, and took up her quarters in the house of the Duc de Noirmoutiers, her brother, in the Rue St. Dominique, close to mine. This journey must have appeared to her very different from the last she had made in France, when she was Queen of the Court. Few people except her former friends and those of her former cabal, came to see her; yet, nevertheless, some curious folks appeared, so that for the first few days there was company enough; but after that, solitude followed when the ill success of her journey to Versailles became known. M. d'Orléans, reunited now with the King of Spain, felt that it was due to his interest even more than to his vengeance to show in a striking manner, that it was solely owing to the hatred and artifice of Madame des Ursins that he had fallen into such disfavor on account of Spain, and had been in danger of losing his head. Times had changed. Monseigneur was dead, the Meudon cabal annihilated; Madame de Maintenon had turned her back upon Madame des Ursins; thus M. d'Orléans was free to act as he pleased. Incited by Madame la Duchess d'Orléans, and more still by Madame, he begged the King to prohibit Madame des Ursins from appearing anywhere (Versailles not even excepted) where she might meet Madame la Duchess de Berry, Madame, Monsieur le Duc, and Madame la Duchess d'Orléans, who at the same time strictly forbade their households to see her, and asked the persons to whom they were particularly attached to hold no intercourse with her. This made a great stir, openly showed that Madame des Ursins had utterly lost the support of Madame de Maintenon and the King, and much embarrassed her.

I could not feel that M. d'Orléans was acting wrong, in thus paying off his wrongs for the injuries she had heaped upon him, but I represented to him, that as I had always been an intimate friend of Madame des Ursins, putting aside her conduct toward him and making no comparison between my attachment for him and my friendship for her, I could not forget the marks of consideration she had always given me, particularly in her last triumphant journey (as I have already explained), and that it would be hard if I could not see her. We capitulated then,

and M. le Duc and Madame la Duchess d'Orléans permitted me to see her twice — once immediately; once
when she left — giving my word that I would not see her
three times, and that Madame de Saint-Simon should not
see her at all; which latter clause we agreed to very unwillingly, but there was no remedy. As I wished at least
to profit by my chance, I sent word to Madame des Ursins,
explaining the fetters that bound me, and saying that as
I wished to see her at all events at my ease since I should
see her so little, I would let pass the first few days and
her first journey to Court, before asking her for an audience. My message was very well received; she had known
for many years the terms on which I was with M. d'Orléans; she was not surprised with these fetters, and was
grateful to me for what I had obtained. Some days after
she had been to Versailles, I went to her at two o'clock
in the day. She at once closed the door to all comers,
and I was *tête-à-tête* with her until ten o'clock at night.

It may be imagined what a number of things were
passed in review during this long discourse. Our eight
hours of conversation appeared to me like eight moments.
She related to me her catastrophe, without mixing up the
King or the King of Spain, of whom she spoke well;
but, without violently attacking the Queen, she predicted
what since has occurred. We separated at supper time,
with a thousand reciprocal protestations and regret that
Madame de Saint-Simon could not see her. She promised
to inform me of her departure early enough to allow us
to pass another day together.

Her journey to Versailles did not pass off very pleasantly. She dined with the Duchess de Luders, and then
visited Madame de Maintenon; waited with her for the
King, but when he came did not stop long, withdrawing
to Madame Adam's, where she passed the night. The
next day she dined with the Duchess de Ventadour, and
returned to Paris. She was allowed to give up the pension she received from the King, and in exchange to have
her Hôtel de Ville stock increased, so that it yielded
forty thousand livres a year. Her income, besides being
doubled, was thus much more sure than would have been
a pension from the King which she doubted not M. d'Or-

léans as soon as he became master, would take from her. She thought of retiring into Holland, but the States-General would have nothing to do with her, either at the Hague, or at Amsterdam. She had reckoned upon the Hague. She next thought of Utrecht, but was soon out of conceit with it, and turned her regards toward Italy.

The health of the King, meanwhile, visibly declining, Madame des Ursins feared lest she should entirely fall into the clutches of M. d'Orléans. She fully resolved, therefore, to make off, without knowing, however, where to fix herself; and asked permission of the King to come and take leave of him at Marly. She came there from Paris on Tuesday, the 6th of August, so as to arrive as he left dinner, that is, about ten o'clock. She was immediately admitted into the cabinet of the King, with whom she remained *tête-à-tête* full half an hour. She passed immediately to the apartments of Madame de Maintenon, with whom she remained an hour; and then got into her coach and returned to Paris. I only knew of this leave-taking by her arrival at Marly, where I had some trouble in meeting her. As chance would have it, I went in search of her coach to ask her people what had become of her, and was speaking to them when, lo and behold! she herself arrived. She seemed very glad to see me, and made me mount with her into her coach, where for little less than an hour we discoursed very freely. She did not dissimulate from me her fears; the coldness the King and Madame de Maintenon had testified for her through all their politeness; the isolation she found herself in at the Court, even in Paris; and the uncertainty in which she was as to the choice of a retreat; all this in detail, and nevertheless without complaint, without regret, without weakness; always reassured and superior to events, as though some one else were in question. She touched lightly upon Spain, upon the ascendency the Queen was acquiring already over the King, giving me to understand that it could not be otherwise; running lightly and modestly over the Queen, and always praising the goodness of the King of Spain. Fear, on account of the passers-by, put an end to our conversation. She was very gracious to me; expressed regret that we must part; proceeded to tell me when she should start in time for us to have another day together; sent many compliments to Madame de Saint-Simon; and declared herself sensible of the mark of friendship I had given her, in spite of my engagement with M. d'Orléans. As soon as I had seen her off, I went to M. d'Orléans, to whom I related what I had just done; said I had not paid a visit, but had had simply a meeting; that it was true I could not hinder myself from seeking it, without prejudice to the final visit he had allowed me. Neither he nor Madame la Duchess d'Orléans complained. They had fully triumphed over their enemy, and were on the point of seeing her leave France forever, without hope in Spain.

Until now, Madame des Ursins amused by a residue of friends, increased by those of M. de Noirmoutiers with whom she lodged and who had money, had gently occupied herself with the arrangement of her affairs, changed as they were, and in withdrawing her effects from Spain. The fear lest she should find herself in the power of a Prince whom she had so cruelly offended, and who showed, since her arrival in France, that he felt it, hurried all her measures. Her terror augmented by the change in the King that she found at this last audience had taken place since her first. She no longer doubted that his end was very near; and all her attention was directed to the means by which she might anticipate it, and be well informed of his health; this she believed her sole security in France. Terrified anew by the accounts she received of it, she no longer gave herself time for anything, but precipitately set out on the 14th of August, accompanied as far as Essonne by her two nephews. She had not time to inform me, so that I have never seen her since the day of our conversation at Marly in her coach. She did not breathe until she arrived at Lyons.

She had abandoned the project of retiring into Holland, where the States General would not have her. She herself, too, was disgusted with the equality of a republic, which counterbalanced in her mind the pleasure of the liberty enjoyed there. But she could not resolve to return to Rome, the theater of her former reign, and appear there proscribed and old, as in an asylum. She feared, too, a bad reception, remembering the quarrels that had taken place between the Courts of Rome and Spain. She had lost many friends and acquaintances; in fifteen years of absence all had passed away, and she felt the trouble she might be subjected to by the ministers of the Emperor, and by those of the two Crowns, with their partisans. Turin was not a Court worthy of her; the King of Sardinia had not always been pleased with her, and they knew too much for each other. At Venice she would have been out of her element.

While agitated in this manner, without being able to make up her mind, she learned that the King was in extreme danger, a danger exaggerated by rumor. Fear seized her lest he should die while she was in his realm. She set off immediately, therefore, without knowing where to go; and solely to leave France went to Chambéry, as the nearest place of safety, arriving there out of breath, so to say.

Every place being well examined, she preferred Genoa; its liberty pleased her; there was intercourse there with a rich and numerous nobility; the climate and the city were beautiful; the place was in some sort a center and halting point between Madrid, Paris, and Rome, with which places she was always in communication, and always hungered after all that passed there. Genoa determined on, she went there. She was well received, hoped to fix her tabernacle there, and indeed stayed some years. But at last *ennui* seized her; perhaps vexation at not being made enough of. She could not exist without meddling, and what is there for a superannuated woman to meddle with at Genoa? She turned her thoughts, therefore, toward Rome. Then, on sounding, found her course clear, quitted Genoa and returned to her nest.

She was not long there before she attached herself to the King and Queen of England (the Pretender and his wife), and soon governed them openly. What a poor resource! But it was courtly and had a flavor of occupation for a woman who could not exist without movement. She finished her life there remarkably healthy in mind and body, and in a prodigious opulence, which was not without its use in that deplorable Court. For the rest, Madame des Ursins was in mediocre estimation at Rome, was deserted by the Spanish, little visited by the French, but always faithfully paid by France and Spain, and unmolested by the Regent. She was always occupied with the world, and with what she had been, but was no longer; yet without meanness, nay, with courage and dignity.

The loss she experienced in January, 1720, of the Cardinal de la Trémoille, although there was no real friendship between them, did not fail to create a void in her. She survived him three years, preserved all her health, her strength, her mind until death, and was carried off, more than eighty years of age, at Rome, on the 5th of December, 1722, after a very short illness.

She had the pleasure of seeing Madame de Maintenon forgotten and annihilated in Saint Cyr, of surviving her, of seeing at Rome her two enemies, Giudice and Alberoni, as profoundly disgraced as she,—one falling from the same height,—and of relishing the forgetfulness, not to say contempt, into which they both sank. Her death, which, a few years before, would have resounded throughout all Europe, made not the least sensation. The little English Court regretted her, and some private friends also, of whom I was one. I did not hide this, although, on account of M. le Duc d'Orléans, I had kept up no intercourse with her; for the rest, nobody seemed to perceive she had disappeared. She was, nevertheless, so extraordinary a person, during all the course of her long life, everywhere, and had so grandly figured, although in various ways; had such rare intellect, courage, industry, and resources; reigned so publicly and so absolutely in Spain; and had a character so sustained and so unique, that her life deserves to be written, and would take a place among the most curious fragments of the history of the times in which she lived.

19

CHAPTER XXVIII.

Sudden Illness of the Duc de Berry — Suspicious Symptoms — The
Duchess Prevented from Seeing Him — His Death — Character —
Manners of the Duchess de Berry.

B UT I must return somewhat now, in order to make
way for a crowd of events which have been pressing forward all this time, but which I have passed
by, in going straightforward at once to the end of
Madame des Ursins's history.

On Monday, the 30th of April, 1714, the King took medicine, and worked after dinner with Pontchartrain. This
was at Marly. About six o'clock he went to M. le Duc de
Berry, who had had fever all night. M. le Duc de
Berry had risen without saying anything, had been with
the King at the medicine hour, and intended to go stag
hunting; but on leaving the King's chamber shivering
seized him, and forced him to go back again. He was
bled while the King was in his chamber, and the blood
was found very bad; when the King went to bed the
doctors told him the illness was of a nature to make
them hope that it might be a case of contagion. M. le
Duc de Berry had vomited a good deal — a black vomit.
Fagon said, confidently, that it was from the blood; the
other doctors fastened upon some chocolate he had taken
on the Sunday. From this day forward I knew what
was the matter. Boulduc, apothecary of the King, and
extremely attached to Madame de Saint-Simon and to me,
whispered in my ear that M. le Duc de Berry would not
recover, and that, with some little difference, his malady
was the same as that of which the Dauphin and Dauphine
died. He repeated this the next day, and never once
varied afterward; saying to me on the third day, that
none of the doctors who attended the Prince were of a
different opinion, or hid from him what they thought.

On Tuesday, the 1st of May, the Prince was bled in

the foot at seven o'clock in the morning, after a very
bad night; took emetics twice, which had a good effect;
then some manna; but still there were two accesses.
The King went to the sick room afterward, held a finance
council, would not go shooting, as he had arranged, but
walked in his gardens. The doctors, contrary to their
custom, never reassured him. The night was cruel. On
Wednesday, the 2d of May, the King went, after mass,
to M. le Duc de Berry, who had been again bled in the
foot. The King held the council of state, as usual,
dined in Madame de Maintenon's rooms, and afterward
reviewed his Guards. Coettenfao, *chevalier d'honneur* of
Madame la Duchess de Berry, came during the morning
to beg the King, in her name, that Chirac, a famous doctor of M. d'Orléans, should be allowed to see M. le Duc
de Berry. The King refused, on the ground that all the
other doctors were in accord, and that Chirac, who might
differ with them, would embarrass them. After dinner
Mesdames de Pompadour and la Vieuville arrived, on the
part of Madame la Duchess de Berry, to beg the King
that she might be allowed to come and see her husband,
saying that she would come on foot rather than stay
away. It would have been better, surely, for her to come
in a coach, if she so much wished, and, before alighting,
to send to the King for permission so to do. But the
fact is, she had no more desire to come than M. de Berry
had to see her. He never once mentioned her name, or
spoke of her, even indirectly. The King replied to those
ladies by saying that he would not close the door against
Madame la Duchess de Berry, but, considering the state
she was in, he thought it would be very imprudent on
her part to come. He afterward told M. le Duc and
Madame la Duchess d'Orléans to go to Versailles and
hinder her from coming. Upon returning from the review the King went again to see M. le Duc de Berry.
He had been once more bled in the arm, had vomited
all day — much blood too — and had taken some Robel
water three times, in order to stop his sickness. This
vomiting put off the communion. Père de la Rue had
been by his side ever since Tuesday morning, and found
him very patient and resigned.

On Thursday, the 3d, after a night worse than ever, the doctors said they did not doubt that a vein had been broken in the stomach. It was reported that this accident had happened by an effort M. de Berry made when out hunting on the previous Thursday, the day the Elector of Bavaria arrived. His horse slipped; in drawing the animal up, his body struck against the pommel of the saddle, so it was said, and ever since he had spit blood every day. The vomiting ceased at nine o'clock in the morning, but the patient was no better. The King, who was going stag hunting, put it off. At six o'clock at night M. de Berry was so choked that he could no longer remain in bed; about eight o'clock he found himself so relieved that he said to Madame, he hoped he should not die; but soon after, the malady increased so much that Père de la Rue said it was no longer time to think of anything but God, and of receiving the Sacrament. The poor Prince himself seemed to desire it.

A little after ten o'clock at night the King went to the chapel, where a consecrated host had been kept prepared ever since the commencement of the illness. M. le Duc de Berry received it, with extreme unction, in presence of the King, with much devotion and respect. The King remained nearly an hour in the chamber, supped alone in his own, did not receive the Princesses afterward, but went to bed. M. le Duc d'Orléans, at ten o'clock in the morning, went again to Versailles, as Madame la Duchess de Berry wished still to come to Marly. M. le Duc de Berry related to Père de la Rue, who at least said so, the accident just spoken of; but, it was added, "his head was then beginning to wander." After losing the power of speech, he took the crucifix Père de la Rue held, kissed it, and placed it upon his heart. He expired on Friday, the 4th of May, 1714, at four o'clock in the morning, in his twenty-eighth year, having been born at Versailles, the last day of August, 1686.

M. le Duc de Berry was of ordinary height, rather fat, of a beautiful blonde complexion, with a fresh, handsome face, indicating excellent health. He was made for society, and for pleasure, which he loved; the best, gentlest, most compassionate, and accessible of men, without pride, and without vanity, but not without dignity or self-appreciation. He was of medium intellect, without ambition or desire, but had very good sense, and was capable of listening, of understanding, and of always taking the right side in preference to the wrong, however speciously put. He loved truth, justice, and reason; all that was contrary to religion pained him to excess, although he was not of marked piety. He was not without firmness, and hated constraint. This caused it to be feared that he was not supple enough for a younger son, and, indeed, in his early youth he could not understand that there was any difference between him and his eldest brother, and his boyish quarrels often caused alarm.

He was the most gay, the most frank, and consequently the most loved of the three brothers; in his youth nothing was spoken of but his smart replies to Madame and M. de la Rochefoucauld. He laughed at preceptors and at masters — often at punishment. He scarcely knew anything except how to read and write; and learned nothing after being freed from the necessity of learning. This ignorance so intimidated him, that he could scarcely open his mouth before strangers, or perform the most ordinary duties of his rank; he had persuaded himself that he was an ass and a fool, fit for nothing. He was so afraid of the King that he dared not approach him, and was so confused if the King looked hard at him, or spoke of other things than hunting, or gaming, that he scarcely understood a word, or could collect his thoughts. As may be imagined, such fear does not go hand in hand with deep affection.

He commenced life with Madame la Duchess de Berry as do almost all those who marry very young and green. He became extremely amorous of her; this, joined to his gentleness and natural complaisance, had the usual effect, which was to thoroughly spoil her. He was not long in perceiving it; but love was too strong for him. He found a woman proud, haughty, passionate, incapable of forgiveness, who despised him, and who allowed him to see it, because he had infinitely less head than she; and because, moreover, she was supremely false and strongly determined. She piqued herself upon both these qualities,

and on her contempt for religion, ridiculing M. le Duc
de Berry for being devout; and all these things became
insupportable to him. Her gallantries were so prompt,
so rapid, so unmeasured, that he could not help seeing
them. Her endless private interviews with M. le Duc
d'Orléans, in which everything languished if he was
present, made him furious. Violent scenes frequently
took place between them; the last, which occurred at
Rambouillet, went so far that Madame la Duchess de
Berry received a kick . . . , and a menace that she
should be shut up in a convent for the rest of her life;
and when M. le Duc de Berry fell ill, he was thumbing
his hat, like a child, before the King, relating all his
grievances, and asking to be delivered from Madame la
Duchess de Berry. Hitherto I have only alluded to
Madame la Duchess de Berry, but, as will be seen, she
became so singular a person when her father was Regent,
that I will here make her known more completely than
I have yet done.

She was tall, handsome, well made, with, however, but
little grace, and had something in her eyes which made you
fear what she was. Like her father and mother she spoke
well and with facility. Timid in trifles, yet in other
things terrifyingly bold,—foolishly haughty sometimes,
and sometimes mean to the lowest degree,—it may be
said that she was a model of all the vices, avarice excepted, and was all the more dangerous because she had
art and talent. I am not accustomed to overcolor the
picture I am obliged to present to render things understood, and it will easily be perceived how strictly I am
reserved upon the ladies, and upon all gallantries, not
intimately associated with what may be called important
matters. I should be so here, more than in any other
case, from self-love, if not from respect for the sex and
dignity of the person. The considerable part I played
in bringing about Madame la Duchess de Berry's marriage, and the place that Madame de Saint-Simon, in
spite of herself and of me, occupied in connection with
her, would be for me reasons more than enough for
silence, if I did not feel that silence would throw obscurity over all the sequel of this history. It is then

to the truth that I sacrifice my self-love, and with the same truthfulness I will say that if I had known or merely suspected, that the Princess was so bad as she showed herself directly after her marriage, and always more and more since, she would never have become Duchess de Berry.

I have already told how she annoyed M. le Duc de Berry by ridiculing his devotion. In other ways she put his patience to severe trials, and more than once was in danger of public exposure. She partook of few meals in private, at which she did not get so drunk as to lose consciousness, and to bring up all she had taken on every side. The presence of M. le Duc de Berry, of M. le Duc and Madame la Duchess d'Orléans, of ladies with whom she was not on familiar terms, in no way restrained her. She complained even of M. le Duc de Berry for not doing as she did. She often treated her father with a haughtiness which was terrifying on all accounts.

In her gallantries she was as unrestrained as in other things. After having had several favorites, she fixed herself upon La Haye, who from King's page had become private *écuyer* of M. le Duc de Berry. The oglings in the *salon* of Marly were perceived by everybody; nothing restrained them. At last, it must be said, for this fact incloses all the rest, she wished La Haye to run away with her from Versailles to the Low Countries, while M. le Duc de Berry and the King were both living. La Haye almost died with fright at this proposition, which she herself made to him. His refusal made her furious. From the most pressing entreaties she came to all the invectives that rage could suggest, and that torrents of tears allowed her to pronounce. La Haye had to suffer her attacks — now tender, now furious; he was in the most mortal embarrassment. It was a long time before she could be cured of her mad idea, and in the meanwhile she subjected the poor fellow to the most frightful persecution. Her passion for La Haye continued until the death of M. le Duc de Berry, and some time after.

M. le Duc de Berry was buried at St. Denis on Wednesday, the 16th of May; M. le Duc d'Orléans was to

have headed the procession, but the same odious reports
against him that had circulated at the death of the
Dauphin had again appeared, and he begged to be let
off. M. le Duc filled his place. Madame la Duchess de
Berry, who was in the family way, kept her bed; and in
order that she should not be seen there when people
came to pay her the usual visits of condolence, the room
was kept quite dark. Many ridiculous scenes and much
indecent laughter, that could not be restrained, thus arose.
Persons accustomed to the room could see their way, but
those unaccustomed stumbled at every step, and had need
of guidance. For want of this, Père du Trevoux, and
Père Tellier after him, both addressed their compliments
to the wall; others to the foot of the bed. This became
a secret amusement, but happily did not last long.

As may be imagined, the death of M. le Duc de Berry
was a deliverance for Madame la Duchess de Berry. She
was, as I have said, in the family way; she hoped for a
boy, and counted upon enjoying as a widow more liberty
than she had been able to take as a wife. She had a
miscarriage, however, on Saturday, the 16th of June, and
was delivered of a daughter which lived only twelve
hours. The little corpse was buried at St. Denis, Madame de Saint-Simon at the head of the procession. Madame la Duchess de Berry, shortly before this event,
received two hundred thousand livres income of pension;
but the establishment she would have had if the child
had been a boy was not allowed her.

CHAPTER XXIX.

Maisons Seeks My Acquaintance — His Mysterious Manner — Increase of the Intimacy — Extraordinary News — The Bastards Declared Princes of the Blood — Rage of Maisons and Noailles — Opinion of the Court and Country.

IT is time now that I should say something about an event that caused an immense stir throughout the land, and was much talked of even in foreign parts. I must first introduce, however, a sort of a personage whose intimacy was forced upon me at this period; for the two incidents are in a certain degree associated together.

M. d'Orléans for some little time had continually represented to me, how desirous one of his acquaintances was to secure my friendship. This acquaintance was Maisons, president in the Parliament, grandson of that superintendent of the finances who built the superb *château* of Maisons, and son of the man who had presided so unworthily at the judgment of our trial with M. de Luxembourg, which I have related in its place. Maisons was a person of much ambition, exceedingly anxious to make a name, gracious and flattering in manners to gain his ends, and amazingly fond of grand society.

The position of Maisons, where he lived, close to Marly, afforded him many opportunities of drawing there the principal people of the Court. It became quite the fashion to go from Marly to his *château*. The King grew accustomed to hear the place spoken of, and was in no way displeased. Maisons had managed to become very intimate with M. le Duc and M. le Prince de Conti. These two princes being dead, he turned his thoughts toward M. d'Orléans. He addressed himself to Canillac who had always been an intimate friend of M. d'Orléans, and by him soon gained the intimacy of that prince.

But he was not yet satisfied. He wished to circumvent
M. d'Orléans more completely than he could by means
of Canillac. He cast his eye, therefore, upon me. I
think he was afraid of me on account of what I have related concerning his father. He had an only son about
the same age as my children. For a long time he had
made all kinds of advances, and visited them often. The
son's intimacy did not, however, assist the father; so that
at last Maisons made M. le Duc d'Orléans speak to me
himself.

I was cold; tried to get out of the matter with compliments and excuses. M. d'Orléans, who believed he
had found a treasure in his new acquaintance, returned
to the charge; but I was not more docile. A few days
after, I was surprised by an attack of the same kind
from M. de Beauvilliers. How or when he had
formed an intimacy with Maisons, I have never been
able to unravel; but formed it, he had; and he importuned me so much, nay exerted his authority over me,
that at last I found I must give way. Not to offend
M. d'Orléans by yielding to another after having refused
to yield to him, I waited until he should again speak to
me on the subject, so that he might give himself the
credit of vanquishing me. I did not wait long. The
Prince attacked me anew, maintained that nothing would
be more useful to him than an intimacy between myself
and Maisons, who scarcely dared to see him, except in
secret, and with whom he had not the same leisure or
liberty for discussing many things that might present
themselves. I had replied to all this before; but as I had
resolved to surrender to the Prince (after the authority
of the Duc de Beauvilliers had vanquished me), I complied with his wish.

Maisons was soon informed of it, and did not let my
resolution grow cold. M. le Duc d'Orléans urged me to
go and sleep a night in Paris. Upon arriving there, I
found a note from Maisons, who had already sent an
ocean of compliments to me by the Prince and the Duke.
This note, for reasons to be told me afterward, appointed
a meeting at eleven o'clock this night, in the plain behind
the Invalides, in a very mysterious manner. I went

there with an old coachman of my mother's and a lackey to put my people off the scent. There was a little moonlight. Maisons in a small carriage awaited me. We soon met. He mounted into my coach. I never could comprehend the mystery of this meeting. There was nothing on his part but advances, compliments, protestations, allusions to the former interview of our fathers; only such things, in fact, as a man of cleverness and breeding says when he wishes to form a close intimacy with anyone. Not a word that he said was of importance or of a private nature.

I replied in the most civil manner possible to the abundance he bestowed upon me. I expected afterward something that would justify the hour, the place, the mystery, in a word, of our interview. What was my surprise to hear no syllable upon these points. The only reason Maisons gave for our secret interview was that from that time he should be able to come and see me at Versailles with less inconvenience, and gradually increase the number and the length of his visits until people grew accustomed to see him there! He then begged me not to visit him in Paris, because his house was always too full of people. This interview lasted little less than half an hour. It was long indeed, considering what passed. We separated with much politeness, and the first time he went to Versailles he called upon me toward the middle of the day.

In a short time he visited me every Sunday. Our conversation by degrees became more serious. I did not fail to be on my guard, but drew him out upon various subjects; he being very willing.

We were on this footing when, returning to my room at Marly about midday on Sunday, the 29th of July, I found a lackey of Maisons with a note from him, in which he conjured me to quit all business and come immediately to his house at Paris, where he would wait for me alone, and where I should find that something was in question, that could not suffer the slightest delay, that could not even be named in writing, and which was of the most extreme importance. This lackey had long since arrived, and had sent my people everywhere in search of me. I was engaged that day to dine with M. and Madame de Lauzun. To have broken my engagement would have been to set the curiosity and the malignity of M. de Lauzun at work. I dared not disappear; therefore I gave orders to my coachman, and as soon as I had dined I vanished. Nobody saw me get into my chaise; and I quickly arrived at Paris, and immediately hastened to Maisons's with eagerness easy to imagine.

I found him alone with the Duc de Noailles. At the first glance I saw two dismayed men, who said to me in an exhausted manner, but after a heated though short preface, that the King had declared his two bastards, and their male posterity to all eternity, real princes of the blood, with full liberty to assume all their dignities, honors, and rank, and capacity to succeed to the throne in default of the others.

At this news, which I did not expect, and the secret of which had hitherto been preserved without a particle of it transpiring, my arms fell. I lowered my head and remained profoundly silent, absorbed in my reflections. They were soon disturbed by cries which aroused me. These two men commenced pacing the chamber; stamped with their feet; pushed and struck the furniture; raged as though each wished to be louder than the other, and made the house echo with their noise. I avow that so much hubbub seemed suspicious to me on the part of two men, one so sage and so measured, and to whom this rank was of no consequence; the other always so tranquil, so crafty, so master of himself. I knew not why this sudden fury succeeded to such dejected oppression, and I was not without suspicion that their passion was put on merely to excite mine. If this was their design, it succeeded ill. I remained in my chair, and coldly asked them what was the matter. My tranquillity sharpened their fury. Never in my life have I seen anything so surprising.

I asked them if they had gone mad, and if, instead of this tempest, it would not be better to reason, and see whether something could not be done. They declared it was precisely because nothing could be done against a thing not only resolved on, but executed, declared, and sent to the Parliament, that they were so furious; that M. le Duc d'Orléans, on the terms he was with the King, would not dare even to whisper objections; that the Princes of the blood, mere children as they were, could only tremble; that the Dukes had no means of opposition, and that the Parliament was reduced to silence and slavery. Thereupon they set to work to see who could cry the louder and reviled again, sparing neither things nor persons.

I, also, was in anger, but this racket kept me cool and made me smile. I argued with them and said, that after all I preferred to see the bastards Princes of the blood, capable of succeeding to the throne, than to see them in the intermediary rank they occupied. And it is true that as soon as I had cooled myself, I felt thus.

At last the storm grew calm, and they told me that the Chief President and the Attorney-General — who, I knew, had been at Marly very early in the morning at the Chancellor's — had seen the King in his cabinet soon after he rose, and had brought back the declaration, all prepared. Maisons must, however, have known this earlier; because when the lackey he sent to me set out from Paris, those gentlemen could not have returned there. Our talk led to nothing, and I regained Marly in all haste, in order that my absence might not be remarked.

Nevertheless it was toward the King's supper hour when I arrived. I went straight to the *salon*, and found it very dejected. People looked, but scarcely dared to approach each other; at the most, a sign or a whisper in the ear, as the courtiers brushed by one another, was ventured on. I saw the King sit down to table; he seemed to me more haughty than usual, and continually looked all around. The news had only been known one hour; everybody was still congealed and upon his guard.

As soon as the King was seated (he had looked very hard at me in passing) I went straight to M. du Maine's. Although the hour was unusual, the doors fell before me. I saw a man who received me with joyful surprise, and who, as it were, moved through

the air toward me, all lame that he was. I said that I
came to offer him a sincere compliment, that we (the
dukes) claimed no precedence over the Princes of the
blood; but what we claimed was, that there should be nobody between the Princes of the blood and us; that as
this intermediary rank no longer existed, we had nothing
more to say, but to rejoice that we had no longer to
support what was insupportable. The joy of M. du Maine
burst forth at my compliments, and he startled me with a
politeness inspired by the transport of triumph.

But if he was delighted at the declaration of the King,
it was far otherwise with the world. Foreign dukes and
princes fumed, but uselessly. The Court uttered dull
murmurs more than could have been expected. Paris and
the provinces broke out; the Parliament did not keep
silent. Madame de Maintenon, delighted with her work,
received the adoration of her familiars.

As for me, I will content myself with but few reflections upon this most monstrous, astounding, and frightful
determination of the King. I will simply say, that it is
impossible not to see in it an attack upon the Crown;
contempt for the entire nation, whose rights are trodden
under foot by it; insult to all the Princes of the blood; in
fact, the crime of high treason in its most rash and most
criminal extent. Yes! however venerable God may have
rendered in the eyes of men the majesty of kings and
their sacred persons, which are his anointed; however
execrable may be the crime known as high treason,— of
attempting their lives; however terrible and singular
may be the punishments justly invented to prevent that
crime, and to remove by their horror the most infamous
from the infernal resolution of committing it,— we cannot help finding in the crime in question a plenitude
not in the other, however abominable it may be. Yes!
to overthrow the most holy laws that have existed ever
since the establishment of monarchy; to extinguish a
right the most sacred — the most important — the most
inherent in the nation: to make succession to the throne,
purely, supremely, and despotically arbitrary; in a word,
to make of a bastard a crown prince,— is a crime more

black, more vast, more terrible, than that of high treason against the chief of the state.*

* I have endeavored to preserve the tone of majestic indignation which Saint-Simon indulges in on this inadequate occasion. After all, the King merely exercised the imperial right of adoption; and it is perfectly immaterial whether the persons chosen were his natural children or not. The Duc du Maine was not a very estimable person, though we must remember that Saint-Simon visits on him the sins of his father; but the Comte de Toulouse seems to have been more respectable than any member of the royal family then living, legitimate or not.

CHAPTER XXX.

The King Unhappy and Ill at Ease—Court Paid to Him—A New
Scheme to Rule Him—He Yields—New Annoyances—His Will
—Anecdotes Concerning It—Opinions of the Court—M. du Maine.

BUT let me now explain by what means the King was induced to arrive at, and publish this terrible determination.

He was growing old, and though no external change in him was visible, those near him had for some time begun to fear that he could not live long. This is not the place to descant upon a health hitherto so good and so even: suffice it to mention, that it silently began to give way. Overwhelmed by the most violent reverses of fortune after being so long accustomed to success, the King was even more overwhelmed by domestic misfortunes. All his children had disappeared before him, and left him abandoned to the most fatal reflections. At every moment he himself expected the same kind of death. Instead of finding relief from his anguish among those who surrounded him, and whom he saw most frequently, he met with nothing but fresh trouble there. Excepting Maréchal, his chief surgeon, who labored unceasingly to cure him of his suspicions, Madame de Maintenon, M. du Maine, Fagon, Bloin, the other principal valets sold to the bastard and his former governors,—all sought to augment these suspicions; and in truth it was not difficult to do so. Nobody doubted that poison had been used, nobody could seriously doubt it; and Maréchal, who was as persuaded as the rest, held a different opinion before the King only to deliver him from a useless torment which could not but do him injury. But M. du Maine, and Madame de Maintenon also, had too much interest to maintain him in this fear, and by their art filled him with horror against M. d'Orléans, whom they named as the author of these crimes, so that the King

with this Prince before his eyes every day, was in a per-
petual state of alarm.

With his children the King had lost, and by the same
way, a princess, who in addition to being the soul and
ornament of his Court, was, moreover, all his amusement, all his joy, all his affection, in the hours when he
was not in public. Never, since he entered the world,
had he become really familiar with anyone but her; it
has been seen elsewhere to what extent. Nothing could
fill up this great void: the bitterness of being deprived
of her augmented, because he could find no diversion.
This unfortunate state made him seek relief everywhere
in abandoning himself more and more to Madame de
Maintenon and M. du Maine.

They soon managed to obtain possession of him, as it
were, entirely; leaving no art unexhausted in order to
flatter, to amuse, to please, and to interest him. He was
made to believe that M. du Maine was utterly without
ambition; like a good father of a family, solely occupied
with his children, touched with the grandeur of his near-
ness to the King, simple, frank, upright, and one who,
after working at his duties all day, and after giving himself time for prayer and piety, amused himself in hunting, and drew upon his natural gayety and cheerfulness,
without knowing anything of the Court, or of what was
passing! Compare this portrait with his real character,
and we shall feel with terror what a rattlesnake was introduced into the King's privacy.

Established thus in the mind and heart of the King,
the opportunity seemed ripe for profiting by precious
time that could not last long. Everybody smiled upon
the project of M. du Maine and Madame de Maintenon.
They had rendered M. d'Orléans odious in the eyes of
the King and of the whole country, by the most execrable
calumnies. How could he defend himself? shut up as
the King was, how oppose them? how interfere with their
dark designs? M. du Maine wished not only to be made
Prince of the blood, but to be made guardian of the heir
to the throne, so as to dwarf the power of the Regent
as much as possible. He flattered himself that the feeling he had excited against M. d'Orléans in the Court in

20

Paris, and in the provinces would be powerfully strengthened by dispositions so dishonorable; that he should find himself received as the guardian and protector of the life of the royal infant, to whom was attached the salvation of France, of which he would then become the idol; that the independent possession of the young King, and of his military and civil households, would strengthen with the public applause the power with which he would be invested in the state by this testament; that the Regent, reviled and stripped in this manner, not only would be in no condition to dispute anything, but would be unable to defend himself from any attempts the bastard might afterward make against him. M. du Maine wished in fact to take from M. d'Orléans everything, except the name of Regent, and to divide all the power between himself and his brother. Such was his scheme, that the King by incredible art was induced to sanction and approve.

But the schemers had tough work before they obtained this success. They found that the King would not consent to their wishes without much opposition. They hit upon a devilish plan to overpower his resistance. Hitherto, they had only been occupied in pleasing him, in amusing him, in anticipating his wishes, in praising him — let me say the word — in adoring him. They had redoubled their attention, since, by the Dauphine's death, they had become his sole resource. Not being able now to lead him as they wished, but determined to do so at all cost, they adopted another system, certain as they were that they could do so with impunity. Both became serious, oftentimes dejected, silent, furnishing nothing to the conversation, letting pass what the King forced himself to say, sometimes not even replying, if it was not a direct interrogation. In this manner all the leisure hours of the King were rendered dull and empty; his amusements and diversions were made fatiguing and sad and a weight was cast upon him, which he was the more unable to bear because it was quite new to him, and he was utterly without means to remove it. The few ladies who were admitted to the intimacy of the King knew not what to make of the change they saw in Madame de

Maintenon. They were duped at first by the plea of illness; but seeing at last that its duration passed all bounds, that it had no intermission, that her face announced no malady, that her daily life was in no way deranged, that the King became as serious and as sad as she, they sounded each other to find out the cause. Fear, lest it should be something in which they, unknowingly, were concerned, troubled them; so that they became even worse company to the King than Madame de Maintenon.

There was no relief for the King. All his resource was in the common-place talk of the Count de Toulouse, who was not amusing, although ignorant of the plot, and the stories of the valets, who lost their tongue as soon as they perceived that they were not seconded by the Duc du Maine in his usual manner. Maréchal and all the rest, astonished at the mysterious dejection of the Duc du Maine, looked at each other without being able to divine the cause. They saw that the King was sad and bored; they trembled for his health, but not one of them dared to do anything. Time ran on, and the dejection of M. du Maine and Madame de Maintenon, increased. This is as far as the most instructed have ever been able to penetrate. To describe the interior scenes that doubtless passed during the long time this state of things lasted, would be to write romance. Truth demands that we should relate what we know, and admit what we are ignorant of. I cannot go further, therefore, or pierce deeper into the density of these dark mysteries.

What is certain is, that cheerfulness came back all at once, with the same surprise to the witnesses of it, as the long-continued dejection had caused them, simply because they understood no more of the end than of the commencement. The double knowledge did not come to them until they heard the frightful crash of the thunderbolt which fell upon France and astonished all Europe.

To give some idea of the opposition from the King, M. du Maine and Madame de Maintenon had to overcome, and to show how reluctantly he consented to their wishes, more than one incident may be brought forward. Some days before the news transpired, the King, full of the enormity of what he had just done for his bastards, looked at them in his cabinet, in presence of the valets, and of D'Antin and D'O, and in a sharp manner, that told of vexation, and with a severe glance, suddenly thus addressed himself to M. du Maine: "You have wished it; but know that however great I may make you, and you may be in my lifetime, you are nothing after me; and it will be for you then to avail yourself of what I have done for you, if you can."

Everybody present trembled at a thunderclap so sudden, so little expected, so entirely removed from the character and custom of the King, and which showed so clearly the extreme ambition of the Duc du Maine, and the violence he had done to the weakness of the King, who seemed to reproach himself for it, and to reproach the bastard for his ambition and tyranny. The consternation of M. du Maine seemed extreme at this rough sally, which no previous remark had led to. The King had made a clean breast of it. Everybody fixed his eyes upon the floor and held his breath. The silence was profound for a considerable time: it finished only when the King passed into his wardrobe. In his absence everybody breathed again. The King's heart was full to bursting with what he had just been made to do; but like a woman who gives birth to two children, he had at present brought but one into the world, and bore a second of which he must be delivered, and of which he felt all the pangs without any relief from the suffering the first had caused him.

Again, on Sunday, the 27th of August, the Chief President and the Attorney General were sent for by the King. He was at Versailles. As soon as they were alone with him, he took from a drawer, which he unlocked, a large and thick packet, sealed with seven seals (I know not if by this M. du Maine wished to imitate the mysterious book with Seven Seals, of the Apocalypse, and so sanctify the packet). In handing it to them, the King said: "Gentlemen, this is my will. No one but myself knows its contents. I commit it to you to keep in the Parliament, to which I cannot give a greater testimony of my esteem and confidence than by rendering it the depository of it. The example of the Kings, my predecessors, and that of the will of the King, my father, do not allow me to be ignorant of what may become of this; but they would have it; they have tormented me; they have left me no repose, whatever I might say. Very well! I have bought my repose. Here is the will; take it away: come what may of it, at least, I shall have rest, and shall hear no more about it."

At this last word, that he finished with a dry nod, he turned his back upon them, passed into another cabinet, and left them both nearly turned into statues. They looked at each other frozen by what they had just heard, and still more by what they had just seen in the eyes and the countenance of the King; and as soon as they had collected their senses, they retired, and went to Paris. It was not known until after dinner that the King had made a will and given it to them. In proportion as the news spread, consternation filled the Court, while the flatterers, at bottom as much alarmed as the rest, and as Paris was afterward, exhausted themselves in praises and eulogies.

The next day, Monday, the 28th, the Queen of England came from Chaillot, where she almost always was, to Madame de Maintenon's. As soon as the King perceived her, "Madame," said he to her, like a man full of something and angry, "I have made my will; I have been tormented to do it;" then casting his eyes upon Madame de Maintenon, "I have bought repose; I know the powerlessness and inutility of it. We can do all we wish while we live; afterward we are less than the meanest. You have only to see what became of my father's will immediately after his death, and the wills of so many other kings. I know it well; but nevertheless they have wished it; they gave me no rest nor repose, no calm until it was done; ah, well! then, Madame, it is done; come what may of it, I shall be no longer tormented."

Words such as these so expressive of the extreme violence suffered by the King, of his long and obstinate battle before surrendering, of his vexation, and uneasiness, demand the clearest proofs. I had them from people who heard them, and would not advance them unless I were perfectly persuaded of their exactness.

As soon as the Chief President and the Attorney General returned to Paris, they sent for some workmen, whom they led into a tower of the Palace of Justice, behind the Buvette, or drinking place of the grand chamber and the cabinet of the Chief President. They had a big hole made in the wall of this tower, which is very thick, deposited the testament there, closed up the opening with an iron door, put an iron grating by way of second door, and then walled all up together. The door and the grating each had three locks, the same for both; and a different key for each of the three, which consequently opened each of the two locks, the one in the door and the one in the grating. The Chief President kept one key, the Attorney General another, and the Chief Greffier of the Parliament the third. The Parliament was assembled and the Chief President flattered the members as best he might upon the confidence shown them in intrusting them with this deposit.

At the same time was presented to the Parliament an edict that the Chief President and the Attorney General had received from the hand of the Chancellor at Versailles the same morning the King had given them his will, and the edict was registered. It was very short. It declared that the packet committed to the Chief President and to the Attorney General contained the will of the King, by which he had provided for the protection and guardianship of the young King, and had chosen a Regency Council, the dispositions of which for good reasons he had not wished to publish; that he wished this deposit should be preserved during his life in the registry of the Parliament, and that at the moment when it should please God to call him from the world, all the chambers of the Parliament, all the Princes of the royal house, and all the peers who might be there, should assemble and open the will; and that after it was read, all its dispositions should be made public and executed, nobody to be permitted to oppose them in any way.

Notwithstanding all this secrecy, the terms of the will were pretty generally guessed, and as I have said, the consternation was general. It was the fate of M. du Maine to obtain what he wished; but always with the

maledictions of the public. This fate did not abandon
him now, and as soon as he felt it, he was overwhelmed,
and Madame de Maintenon exasperated, and their attentions and their care redoubled, to shut up the King, so
that the murmurs of the world should not reach him.
They occupied themselves more than ever to amuse and
to please him, and to fill the air around him with praises,
joy, and public adoring at an act so generous and so
grand, and at the same time so wise and so necessary
to the maintenance of good order and tranquillity, which
would cause him to reign so gloriously even after his reign.

This consternation was very natural, and is precisely
why the Duc du Maine found himself deceived and
troubled by it. He believed he had prepared everything,
smoothed everything, in rendering M. d'Orléans so suspected and so odious; he had succeeded, but not so much
as he imagined. His desires and his emissaries had exaggerated everything; and he found himself overwhelmed
with astonishment, when instead of the public acclamations with which he had flattered himself the will would
be accompanied, it was precisely the opposite.

It was seen very clearly that the will assuredly could
not have been made in favor of M. d'Orléans, and although public feeling against him had in no way changed,
no one was so blind as not to see that he must be Regent by the incontestable right of his birth; that the
dispositions of the testament could not weaken that
right, except by establishing a power that should bal-
ance his; and that thus two parties would be formed in
the State, the chief of each of which would be interested
in vanquishing the other, everybody being necessitated
to join one side or other, thereby running a thousand risks without any advantage. The rights of the two
disputants were compared. In the one they were found
sacred, in other they could not be found at all. The
two persons were compared. Both were found odious,
but M. d'Orléans was deemed superior to M. du Maine.
I speak only of the mass of uninstructed people, and of
what presented itself naturally and of itself. The better
informed had even more cause to arrive at the same decision.

M. d'Orléans was stunned by the blow; he felt that it fell directly upon him, but during the lifetime of the King he saw no remedy for it. Silence respectful and profound appeared to him the sole course open; any other would only have led to an increase of precautions. The King avoided all discourse with him upon this matter; M. Du Maine the same. M. d'Orléans was contented with a simple approving monosyllable to both, like a courtier who ought not to meddle with anything; and he avoided conversation upon this subject, even with Madame la Duchess d'Orléans, and with anybody else. I was the sole person to whom he dared to unbosom himself; with the rest of the world he had an open, an ordinary manner, was on his guard against any discontented sign, and against the curiosity of all eyes. The inexpressible abandonment in which he was, in the midst of the Court, guaranteed him at least from all remarks upon the will. It was not until the health of the King grew more menacing that he began to speak and be spoken to thereon.

As for M. du Maine, despite his good fortune, he was not to be envied. At Sceaux, where he lived, the Duchess du Maine, his wife, ruined him by her extravagance. Sceaux was more than ever the theater of her follies, and of the shame and embarrassment of her husband, by the crowd from the Court and the town, which abounded there and laughed at them. She herself played there Athalie (assisted by actors and actresses) and other pieces several times a week. Whole nights were passed in coteries, games, *fêtes*, illuminations, fireworks,—in a word, fancies and fripperies of every kind and every day. She reveled in the joy of her new greatness — redoubled her follies; and the Duc du Maine, who always trembled before her, and who, moreover, feared that the slightest contradiction would entirely turn her brain, suffered all this, even piteously doing the honors as often as he could without ceasing in his conduct to the King.

However great might be his joy, whatever the unimaginable greatness to which he had arrived, he was not tranquil. Like those tyrants who have usurped by their crimes the sovereign power and who fear as so many con-

spiring enemies all their fallen citizens they have en-
slaved — he felt as though seated under that sword that
Dionysius, tyrant of Syracuse, suspended by a hair over
his table, above the head of a man whom he placed
there because he believed him happy, and in this manner wished to make him feel what passed unceasingly in
himself. M. du Maine, who willingly expressed in pleasantry the most serious things, frankly said to his familiars, that he was " like a louse between two finger nails "
(the princes of the blood and the peers), by which he
could not fail to be cracked if he did not take care! This
reflection troubled the excess of his pleasure, and that
of the greatness and the power to which so many artifices had elevated him. He feared the Princes of the
blood as soon as they should be of age to feel the in-
famy and the danger of the wound he had given them;
he feared the parliament, which even under his eyes had
not been able to dissimulate its indignation at the violence he had committed against the most holy and the
most inviolable laws; he even feared the Dukes, so timid
are injustice and tyranny!

CHAPTER XXXI.

A New Visit from Maisons — His Violent Project — My Objections — He Persists — His Death and That of His Wife — Death of the Duc de Beauvilliers — His Character — Of the Cardinal d'Estrées — Anecdotes — Death of Fénelon.

L ET me return now to Maisons. Five days after the King's will had been walled up, in the manner I have described, he came to me and made a pathetic discourse upon the injustice done to M. le Duc d'Orléans by this testament, and did all he could to excite me by railing in good set terms against dispositions intended to add to the power and grandeur of the bastards.

When he had well harangued, I said he had told me nothing new; that I saw the same truths as he with the same evidence; that the worst thing I found was that there was no remedy.

"No remedy!" he exclaimed, interrupting me, with his sly and cunning laugh; "courage and ability can always find one for everything, and I am astonished that you, who have both, should have nothing to suggest while everything is going to confusion."

I asked him how it was possible to suppress a will registered by edict; a document solemn and public deposited with ceremony in the very depths of the palace, with precautions known to everybody — nature and art combining to keep it in safety?

"You are at a loss to know!" replied Maisons to me. "Have ready at the instant of the King's death sure troops and sensible officers, all ready and well instructed; and with them, masons and locksmiths — march to the palace, break open the doors and the wall, carry off the will, and let it never be seen."

In my extreme surprise I asked him, what he expected would be the fruit of such violence? I pointed out that to seize by force of arms a public and solemn document, in the midst of the capital, in despite of all law and

order, would be to put weapons into the hands of the enemies of M. le Duc d'Orléans, who assuredly would be
justified in crying out against this outrage, and who would
find the whole country disposed to echo their cries. I
said too, that if in the execution of such an odious scheme
a sedition occurred, and blood were shed, universal hatred and opprobrium would fall upon the head of M. le
Duc d'Orléans, and deservedly so.

We carried on our discussion a long time, but Maisons
would in no way give up his scheme. After leaving me
he went to M. le Duc d'Orléans and communicated it to
him. Happily it met with no success with the Duke.
Indeed, he was extremely astonished at it; but what astonished us more was, that Maisons persisted in it up to
his death, which preceded by some few days that of the
King, and pressed it upon M. le Duc d'Orléans and myself till his importunity became persecution.

It was certainly not his fault that I over and over
again refused to go to the Grand Chamber of the Parliament to examine the place, as Maisons wished me to
do,—I who never went to the Parliament except for the
reception of the peers or when the King was there. Not
being able to vanquish what he called my obstinacy,
Maisons begged me at the least to go and fix myself
upon the Quai de la Megisserie, where so much old iron
is sold, and examine from that spot the tower where the
will was; he pointed it out to me; it looked out upon the
Quai des Morfondus, but was behind the buildings on
the quai. What information could be obtained from such
a point of view may be imagined. I promised to go
there, not to stop, and thus awake the attention of the
passers-by, but to pass along and see what was to be
seen; adding, that it was simply out of complaisance to
him, and not because I meant to agree in any way to
his enterprise.

What is incomprehensible is, that for a whole year
Maisons pressed his charming project upon us. The
worst enemy of M. le Duc d'Orléans could not have
devised a more rash and ridiculous undertaking. I doubt
whether many people would have been found in all Paris
sufficiently deprived of sense to fall in with it. What

are we to think then of a Parliamentary President of
such consideration as Maisons had acquired at the Palace
of Justice, at the Court, in the town, where he had always
passed for a man of intellect, prudent, circumspect, intel-
ligent, capable, measured? Was he vile enough, in concert
with M. du Maine, to open this gulf beneath our feet, to
push us to our ruin, and by the fall of M. le Duc d'Orléans
—the sole Prince of the blood old enough to be Regent
—to put M. le Duc du Maine in his place, from which
to the crown there was only one step, as none are ignorant, left to be taken? It seems by no means impossible;
M. du Maine, that son of darkness, was, judging him by
what he had already done, quite capable of adding this
new crime to his long list.

The mystery was, however, never explained. Maisons
died before its darkness could be penetrated. His end
was terrible. He had no religion; his father had had
none. He married a sister of the Maréchal de Villars,
who was in the same case. Their only son they specially
educated in unbelief. Nevertheless, everything seemed
to smile upon them. They had wealth, consideration,
distinguished friends. But mark the end.

Maisons is slightly unwell. He takes rhubarb twice
or thrice, unseasonably; more unseasonably comes Cardinal de Bissy to him, to talk upon the constitution, and
thus hinder the operation of the rhubarb; his inside
seems on fire, but he will not believe himself ill; the
progress of his disease is great in a few hours; the doctors, though soon at their wits' ends, dare not say so;
the malady visibly increases; his whole household is in
confusion; he dies, forty-eight years of age, in the midst
of a crowd of friends, of clients, without power or leisure to think for a moment what is going to happen to
his soul!

His wife survives him ten or twelve years, opulent,
and in consideration, when suddenly she has an attack
of apoplexy in her garden. Instead of thinking of her
state, and profiting by leisure, she makes light of her
illness, has another attack a few days after, and is carried
off on the 5th of May, 1727, in her forty-sixth year, without having had a moment free.

Her son, for a long time much afflicted, seeks to distinguish himself and acquire friends. Taking no warning from what has occurred, he thinks only of running after the fortune of this world, and is surprised at Paris by the smallpox. He believes himself dead, thinks of what he has neglected all his life, but fear suddenly seizes him, and he dies in the midst of it, on the 13th of September, 1731, leaving an only son, who dies a year after him, eighteen months old, all the great wealth of the family going to collateral relatives.

These "Memoirs" are not essays on morality, therefore I have contented myself with the most simple and the most naked recital of facts; but I may, perhaps, be permitted to apply here those two verses of the 37th Psalm, which appear so expressly made for the purpose: "I have seen the impious exalted like the cedars of Lebanon. Yet he passed away, and, lo, he was not: yea, I sought him, but he could not be found."

But let me leave this subject now, to treat of other matters. On Friday, the last day of August, I lost one of the best and most revered of friends, the Duc de Beauvilliers. He died at Vaucresson after an illness of about two months, his intellect clear to the last, aged sixty-six years, having been born on the 24th of October, 1648.

He was the son of M. de Saint Aignan, who with honor and valor was truly romantic in gallantry, in *belles-lettres*, and in arms. He was Captain of the Guards of Gaston, and at the end of 1649 bought of the Duc de Liancourt the post of first gentleman of the King's chamber. He commanded afterward in Berry against the party of M. le Prince, and served elsewhere subsequently. In 1661 he was made Chevalier of the Order, and in 1661 Duke and Peer. His first wife he lost in 1679. At the end of a year he married one of her chambermaids, who had been first of all engaged to take care of her dogs. She was so modest, and he so shamefaced, that in despite of repeated pressing on the part of the King, she could not be induced to take her taboret. She lived in much retirement, and had so many virtues that she made herself respected all her life, which was long. M. de

Beauvilliers was one of the children of the first marriage.

I know not what care M. and Madame de Saint Aignan
took of the others, but they left him, until he was six
or seven years of age, to the mercy of their lodge keeper.
Then he was confided to the care of a canon of Notre
Dame de Clery. The household of the canon consisted
of one maidservant, with whom the little boy slept; and
they continued to sleep together until he was fourteen or
fifteen years old, without either of them thinking of evil,
or the canon remarking that the lad was growing into a
man. The death of his eldest brother called M. de
Beauvilliers home. He entered the army, served with
distinction at the head of his regiment of cavalry, and
was brigadier.

He was tall, thin, had a long and ruddy face, a large
aquiline nose, a sunken mouth, expressive, piercing eyes,
an agreeable smile, a very gentle manner, but ordinarily
retiring, serious, and concentrated. By disposition he was
hasty, hot, passionate, fond of pleasure. Ever since God
had touched him, which happened early in his life, he
had become gentle, modest, humble, kind, enlightened,
charitable, and always full of real piety and goodness.
In private, where he was free, he was gay, joked, and
bantered pleasantly, and laughed with good heart. He
liked to be made fun of: there was only the story of his
sleeping with the canon's servant that wounded his modesty, and I have seen him embarrassed when Madame de
Beauvilliers has related it,— smiling, however, but praying her sometimes not to tell it. His piety, which, as I
have said, commenced early in life, separated him from
companions of his own age. At the army one day, during a promenade of the King, he walked alone, a little
in front. Some one remarked it, and observed, sneeringly,
that " he was meditating." The King, who heard this,
turned toward the speaker, and, looking at him, said:
" Yes, 'tis M. de Beauvilliers, one of the best men of the
Court, and of my realm." This sudden and short apology
caused silence, and food for reflection, so that the fault-
finders remained in respect before his merit.

The King must have entertained a high regard for him,

to give him, in 1670, the very delicate commission he intrusted to him. Madame had just been so openly poisoned, the conviction was so complete and so general that it was very difficult to palliate it. Our King and the King of England between whom she had just become a stronger bond, by the journey she had made into England, were penetrated by grief and indignation, and the English could not contain themselves. The King chose the Duc de Beauvilliers to carry his compliments of condolence to the King of England, and under this pretext to try to prevent this misfortune interfering with their friendship and their union, and to calm the fury of London and the nation. The King was not deceived; the prudent dexterity of the Duc de Beauvilliers brought round the King of England, and even appeased London and the nation.

M. de Beauvilliers had expressed a wish to be buried at Montargis, in the Benedictine monastery, where eight of his daughters had become nuns. Madame de Beauvilliers went there, and by an act of religion, terrible to think of, insisted upon being present at the interment. She retired to her house at Paris, where during the rest of her life she lived in complete solitude, without company or amusement of any kind. For nearly twenty years she remained there, and died in 1733, seventy-five years of age, infinitely rich in alms and all sorts of good works.

The King taxed the infantry regiments, which had risen to an excessive price. This venality of the only path by which the superior grades can be reached is a great blot upon the military system, and stops the career of many a man who would become an excellent soldier. It is a gangrene which for a long time has eaten into all the orders and all the parties of the state, and under which it will be odd if all do not succumb. Happily it is unknown, or little known, in all the other countries of Europe!

Toward the end of this year Cardinal d'Estrées died in Paris at his abbey of Saint Germain des Prés, nearly eighty-seven years of age, having always enjoyed perfect health of body and mind until this illness, which was very short, and which left his intellect clear to the last. It is proper and curious to pause for a moment upon a personage, all his life of importance, and who at his death was Cardinal, Bishop of Albano, Abbé of Longpont, of Mont Saint Eloi, of Saint Nicholas-aux-Bois, of La Staffarde in Piedmont (where Catinat gained a celebrated battle before being Maréchal of France), of Saint Claude in Franche-Comté, of Anchin in Flanders, and of Saint Germain des Prés in Paris. He was also Commander of the Order of the promotion of 1688.

Merit, aided by the chances of fortune, made out of an obscure family of the Boulonais country, a singularly illustrious race in the fourth generation, of which Mademoiselle de Tourbes alone remains. The cardinal, brother of the last Maréchal d'Estrées, their uncle, used to say, that he knew his fathers as far as the one who had been page of Queen Anne, Duchess of Brittany; but beyond that he knew nothing, and it was not worth while searching. Gabrielle d'Estrées, mistress of Henry IV., whose beauty made her father's fortune, and whose history is too well known to be here alluded to, was sister of the cardinal's father, but died thirty years before he was born. It was through her that the family became elevated. The father of Cardinal d'Estrées was distinguished all his life by his merit, his capacity, and the authority and elevated posts he held. He was made Marshal of France in 1626, and it is a thing unique that he, his son, and his grandson were not only Marshals of France, but all three were in succession seniors of that corps for a long time.

The Cardinal d'Estrées was born in 1627, and for forty years lived with his father, profiting by his lessons and his consideration. He was of the most agreeable manners, handsome, well made, full of honor, wit, and ability; in society the pleasantest person in the world, and yet well instructed; indeed, of rare erudition, generous, obliging, dignified, incapable of meanness, he was with so much talent and so many great and amiable qualities generally loved and respected, and deserved to be. He was made Cardinal in 1671, but was not declared until after many delays had occurred. These delays much disturbed him. It was customary, then, to pay many visits. One evening the Abbé de la Victoire, one of his friends, and very witty, arrived very late at a supper, in a house where he was expected. The company importunely asked him where he had been, and what had delayed him.

"Alas!" replied the Abbé, in a tone of sadness, "where have I been? I have been all day accompanying the body of poor M. de Laon." [The Cardinal d'Estrées was then Bishop and Duke of Laon.]

"M. de Laon!" cried everybody, "M. de Laon dead! Why, he was quite well yesterday. 'Tis dreadful. Tell us what has happened."

"What has happened?" replied the Abbé, still with the same tone. "Why, he took me with him when he paid his visits, and though his body was with me, his spirit was at Rome, so that I quitted him very wearied." At this recital grief changed into merriment.

That grand dinner at Fontainebleau for the Prince of Tuscany, at which the Prince was to be the only guest, and yet never received his invitation from the Cardinal, I have already mentioned. He was oftentimes thus absent, but never when business or serious matters were concerned, so that his forgetfulness was amusing. He never could bear to hear of his domestic affairs. Pressed and tormented by his steward and his *maître d'hôtel* to overlook their accounts, that he had not seen for many years, he appointed a day to be devoted to them. The two financiers demanded that he should close his door so as not to be interrupted; he consented with difficulty, then changed his mind, and said that if Cardinal Bonzi came he must be admitted, but that it was not likely he would come on that particular day. Directly afterward he sent a trusty servant to Cardinal Bonzi, entreating him to come on such and such a day, between three and four o'clock, conjuring him not to fail, and begging him above all to come as of his own accord, the reason to be explained afterward. On the appointed day Cardinal d'Estrées told his porter to let no one enter in the afternoon except Cardinal Bonzi, who assuredly was not likely to come, but who was not to be sent away if he did. His people delighted at having their master to themselves all day without interruption, arrived about three o'clock; the Cardinal quitted his family and the few friends who had that day dined with him, and passed into a cabinet where his business people laid out their papers. He said a thousand absurdities to them upon his expenditure, of which he understood nothing, and unceasingly looked toward the window, without appearing to do so, secretly sighing for a prompt deliverance. A little before four o'clock, a coach arrived in the courtyard; his business people, enraged with the porter, exclaimed that there will then be no more opportunity for working. The Cardinal in delight referred to the orders he had given. "You will see," he added, "that it is Cardinal Bonzi, the only man I expected, and who, of all days in the world, comes to-day."

Immediately afterward, the Cardinal was announced, and the intendant and *maître d'hôtel* were forced to make off with their papers and their table. As soon as he was alone with Bonzi, he explained why he had requested this visit, and both laughed heartily. Since then his business people have never caught him again, never during the rest of his life would he hear speak of them.

He must have had honest people about him; for every day his table was magnificent, and filled at Paris and at the Court with the best company. His equipages were so, also; he had numberless domestics, many gentlemen, chaplains, and secretaries. He gave freely to the poor, and to his brother the Maréchal and his children (who were not well off), and yet died without owing a crown to a living soul.

His death, for which he had been long prepared, was fine — edifying and very christianlike. He was universally regretted. A joke of his with the King is still remembered. One day, at dinner, where he always paid much attention to the Cardinal, the King complained of the inconvenience he felt in no longer having teeth.

"Teeth, Sire!" replied the Cardinal; "why, who HAS any teeth?"

The joke is that the Cardinal, though old, still had very white and very beautiful teeth, and that his mouth, large, but agreeable, was so shaped that it showed them plainly in speaking. Therefore the King burst out laughing at this reply, and all present also, including the Cardinal, who was not in the slightest degree embarrassed. I might go on forever telling about him, but enough, perhaps, has been already said.

The commencement of the new year, 1715, was marked by the death of Fénelon, at Cambrai, where he had lived in disgrace so many years. I have already said something about him, so that I have now but little to add. His life at Cambrai was remarkable for the assiduity with which he attended to the spiritual and temporal wants of his flock. He was indefatigable in the discharge of his functions, and in endeavoring to gain all hearts. Cambrai is a place much frequented; through which many people pass. During the war the number of wounded soldiers he had received into his house or attended to in the hospitals passes all belief. He spared nothing for them, neither physical comforts nor spiritual consolations. Thus it is incredible to what an extent he became the idol of the whole army. His manners, to high and low, were most affable, yet everywhere he was the prelate, the gentleman, the author of "Telemachus." He ruled his diocese with a gentle hand, in no way meddled with the Jansenists; he left all untouched. Take him for all in all, he had a bright genius and was a great man. His admiration true or feigned for Madame Guyon remained to the last, yet always without suspicion of impropriety. He had so exactly arranged his affairs that he died without money, and yet without owing a sou to anybody.

CHAPTER XXXII.

THE reign of Louis XIV. was approaching its conclusion, so that there is now nothing more to relate but what passed during the last month of his life, and scarcely so much. These events, indeed, so curious and so important, are so mixed up with those that immediately followed the King's death, that they cannot be separated from them. It will be interesting and is necessary to describe the projects, the thoughts, the difficulties, the different resolutions, which occupied the brain of the Prince, who, despite the efforts of Madame de Maintenon and M. du Maine, was of necessity about to be called to the head of affairs during the minority of the young King. This is the place, therefore, to explain all these things, after which we will resume the narrative of the last month of the King's life, and go on to the events which followed his death.

But, as I have seen, before entering upon this thorny path, it will be as well to make known, if possible, the chief personage of the story, the impediments interior and exterior in his path, and all that personally belonged to him.

M. le Duc d'Orléans was, at the most, of mediocre stature, full-bodied without being fat; his manner and his deportment were easy and very noble; his face was broad and very agreeable, high in color; his hair black, and wig the same. Although he danced very badly, and had but ill succeeded at the riding school, he had in his face, in his gestures, in all his movements, infinite grace, and so natural that it adorned even his most ordinary commonplace actions. With much ease when nothing constrained him, he was gentle, affable, open, of facile and charming access; the tone of his voice was agreeable, and he had a surprisingly easy flow of words upon all subjects which nothing ever disturbed, and which never failed to surprise; his eloquence was natural and extended even to his most familiar discourse, while it equally entered into his observations upon the most abstract sciences, on which he talked most perspicuously; the affairs of government, politics, finance, justice, war, the Court, ordinary conversation, the arts, and mechanics. He could speak as well too upon history and memoirs, and was well acquainted with pedigrees. The personages of former days were familiar to him; and the intrigues of the ancient Courts were to him as those of his own time. To hear him, you would have thought him a great reader. Not so. He skimmed; but his memory was so singular that he never forgot things, names, or dates, cherishing remembrance of things with precision; and his apprehension was so good, that in skimming thus it was, with him, precisely as though he had read very laboriously. He excelled in unpremeditated discourse, which, whether in the shape of repartee or jest, was always appropriate and vivacious. He often reproached me, and others more than he, with "not spoiling him"; but I often gave him praise merited by few, and which belonged to nobody so justly as to him; it was, that besides having infinite ability and of various kinds, the singular perspicuity of his mind was joined to so much exactness, that he would never have made a mistake in anything if he had followed the first suggestions of his judgment. He oftentimes took this my eulogy as a reproach, and he was not always wrong, but it was not the less true. With all this he had no presumption, no trace of superiority natural or acquired; he reasoned with you as with his equal, and struck the most able with surprise. Although he never forgot his own position, nor allowed others to forget it, he carried no constraint with him but put everybody at his ease, and placed himself upon the level of all others.

He had the weakness to believe that he resembled Henry IV. in everything, and strove to affect the manners, the gestures, the bearing, of that monarch. Like Henry IV. he was naturally good, humane, compassionate; and, indeed, this man, who has been so cruelly accused of the blackest and most inhuman crimes, was more opposed to the destruction of others than anyone I have ever known, and had such a singular dislike to causing anybody pain that it may be said, his gentleness, his humanity, his easiness, had become faults; and I do not hesitate to affirm, that that supreme virtue which teaches us to pardon our enemies he turned into vice, by the indiscriminate prodigality with which he applied it; thereby causing himself many sad embarrassments and misfortunes, examples and proofs of which will be seen in the sequel.

I remember that about a year, perhaps, before the death of the King, having gone up early after dinner into the apartments of Madame la Duchess d'Orléans at Marly, I found her in bed with the meagrims, and M. d'Orléans alone in the room, seated in an armchair at her pillow. Scarcely had I sat down than Madame la Duchess began to talk of some of those execrable imputations concerning M. d'Orleans unceasingly circulated by Madame de Maintenon and M. du Maine: and of an incident arising therefrom, in which the Prince and the Cardinal de Rohan had played a part against M. d'Orléans. I sympathized with her all the more because the Duke, I know not why, had always distinguished and courted those two brothers, and thought he could count upon them. "And what will you say of M. d'Orleans," added the Duchess, "when I tell you that since he has known this, known it beyond doubt, he treats them exactly the same as before?"

I looked at M. d'Orléans, who had uttered only a few words to confirm the story, as it was being told, and who was negligently lolling in his chair, and I said to him with warmth:

"Oh, as to that, Monsieur, the truth must be told;

since Louis the Débonnaire, never has there been such a Débonnaire as you.»

At these words he rose in his chair, red with anger to the very whites of his eyes, and blurted out his vexation against me for abusing him, as he pretended, and against Madame la Duchess d'Orléans for encouraging me and laughing at him.

« Go on,» said I, «treat your enemies well, and rail at your friends. I am delighted to see you angry. It is a sign that I have touched the sore point, when you press the finger on it the patient cries. I should like to squeeze out all the matter, and after that you would be quite another man, and differently esteemed.»

He grumbled a little more, and then calmed down. This was one of two occasions only, on which he was ever really angry with me.

Two or three years after the death of the King, I was chatting in one of the grand rooms of the Tuileries, where the Council of the Regency was, according to custom soon to be held, and M. d'Orléans at the other end was talking to some one in a window recess. I heard myself called from mouth to mouth, and was told that M. d'Orléans wished to speak to me. This often happened before the Council. I went therefore to the window where he was standing. I found a serious bearing, a concentrated manner, an angry face, and was much surprised.

« Monsieur,» said he to me at once, « I have a serious complaint against you; you, whom I have always regarded as my best of friends.»

« Against me! Monsieur!» said I, still more surprised. « What is the matter, then, may I ask?»

« The matter!» he replied with a mien still more angry; « something you cannot deny; — verses you have made against me.»

« I — verses!» was my reply. « Why, who the devil has been telling you such nonsense? You have been acquainted with me nearly forty years, and do you not know, that never in my life have I been able to make a single verse — much less verses.»

« No, no, by Heaven,» replied he, « you cannot deny

these;" and forthwith he began to sing to me a street song in his praise, the chorus of which was: OUR REGENT IS DÉBONNAIRE, LA, LA, HE IS DÉBONNAIRE, with a burst of laughter.

"What!" said I, "you remember it still!" and smiling, I added also, "since you are revenged for it, remember it in good earnest." He kept on laughing a long time before going to the Council, and could not hinder himself. I have not been afraid to write this trifle, because it seems to me that it paints the man.

M. d'Orléans loved liberty, and as much for others as for himself. He extolled England to me one day on this account, as a country where there are no banishments, no *lettres de cachet*, and where the King may close the door of his palace to anybody, but can keep no one in prison; and thereupon related to me with enjoyment, that besides the Duchess of Portsmouth, Charles II. had many subordinate mistresses; that the Grand Prieur, young and amiable in those days, driven out of France for some folly, had gone to England to pass his exile and been well received by the King. By way of thanks he seduced one of those mistresses, by whom the King was then so smitten, that he sued for mercy, offered money to the Grand Prieur, and undertook to obtain his reconciliation in France. The Grand Prieur held firm. Charles prohibited him the palace. He laughed at this, and went every day to the theater with his conquest, and placed himself opposite the King. At last, Charles not knowing what to do to deliver himself from his tormentor, begged our King to recall him, and this was done. But the Grand Prieur said he was very comfortable in England and continued his game. Charles outraged, confided to the King (Louis XIV.) the state he was thrown into by the Grand Prieur, and obtained a command so absolute and so prompt, that his tormentor was afterward obliged to go back into France.

M. d'Orléans admired this; and I know not if he would not have wished to be the Grand Prieur. He always related this story with delight. Thus, of ambition for reigning or governing, he had none. If he made a false move in Spain it was because he had been misdirected.

What he would have liked best would have been to command armies while war lasted, and divert himself the rest of the time without constraint to himself or to others. He was, in fact, very fit for this. With much valor, he had also much foresight, judgment, coolness, and vast capacity. It may be said that he was captain, engineer, and army purveyor; that he knew the strength of his troops, the names and the company of the officers, and the most distinguished of each corps; that he knew how to make himself adored, at the same time keeping up discipline, and could execute the most difficult things, while unprovided with everything. Unfortunately there is another side of this picture, which it will be as well now to describe.

M. d'Orléans, by disposition so adapted to become the honor and the masterpiece of an education, was not fortunate in his teachers. Saint Laurent, to whom he was first confided, was, it is true, the man in all Europe best fitted to act as the instructor of Kings, but he died before his pupil was beyond the birch, and the young Prince, as I have related, fell entirely into the hands of the Abbé Dubois. This person has played such an important part in the State since the death of the King, that it is fit that he should be made known. The Abbé Dubois was a little, pitiful, wizened, herring-gutted man, in a flaxen wig, with a weazel's face, brightened by some intellect. In familiar terms, he was a regular scamp. All the vices unceasingly fought within him for supremacy, so that a continual uproar filled his mind. Avarice, debauchery, ambition, were his gods; perfidy, flattery, footlicking his means of action; complete impiety was his repose; and he held the opinion as a great principle, that probity and honesty are chimeras, with which people deck themselves, but which have no existence. In consequence, all means were good to him. He excelled in low intrigues; he lived in them, and could not do without them; but they always had an aim, and he followed them with a patience terminated only by success, or by firm conviction that he could not reach what he aimed at, or unless, as he wandered thus in deep darkness, a glimmer of light came to him from some other cranny. He passed thus his days in sapping and counter-sapping. The most impudent deceit had become natural to him, and was concealed under an air that was simple, upright, sincere, often bashful. He would have spoken with grace and forcibly, if, fearful of saying more than he wished, he had not accustomed himself to a fictitious hesitation, a stuttering which disfigured his speech, and which, redoubled when important things were in question, became insupportable and sometimes unintelligible. He had wit, learning, knowledge of the world, much desire to please and insinuate himself, but all was spoiled by an odor of falsehood which escaped in spite of him through every pore of his body — even in the midst of his gayety, which made whoever beheld it sad. Wicked besides, with reflection, both by nature and by argument, treacherous and ungrateful, expert in the blackest villanies, terribly brazen when detected; he desired everything, envied everything, and wished to seize everything. It was known afterward, when he no longer could restrain himself, to what an extent he was selfish, debauched, inconsistent, ignorant of everything, passionate, headstrong, blasphemous and mad, and to what an extent he publicly despised his master, the State, and all the world, never hesitating to sacrifice everybody and everything to his credit, his power, his absolute authority, his greatness, his avarice, his fears and his vengeance.

Such was the sage to whom M. le Duc d'Orléans was confided in early youth!

Such a good master did not lose his pains with his new disciple, in whom the excellent principles of Saint Laurent had not had time to take deep root, whatever esteem and affection he may have preserved through life for that worthy man. I will admit here, with bitterness, for everything should be sacrificed to the truth, that M. le Duc d'Orléans brought into the world a failing — let us call things by their names — a weakness, which unceasingly spoiled all his talents, and which were of marvelous use to his preceptor all his life. Dubois led him into debauchery, made him despise all duty and all decency, and persuaded him that he had too much mind to be the dupe of religion, which he said was a

politic invention to frighten ordinary intellects, and keep
the people in subjection. He filled him too with his
favorite principle, that probity in man and virtue in
woman, are mere chimeras, without existence in anybody
except a few poor slaves of early training. This was
the basis of the good ecclesiastic's doctrines, whence
arose the licence of falsehood, deceit, artifice, infidelity,
perfidy; in a word, every villainy, every crime, was
turned into policy, capacity, greatness, liberty and depth
of intellect, enlightenment, good conduct, if it could be
hidden, and if suspicions and common prejudices could
be avoided.

Unfortunately all conspired in M. d'Orléans to open his
heart and his mind to this execrable poison; a fresh and
and early youth, much strength and health, joy at escaping from the yoke as well as vexation at his marriage,
the wearisomeness produced by idleness, the impulse of
his passions, the example of other young men, whose
vanity and whose interest it was to make him live like
them. Thus he grew accustomed to debauchery, above
all to the uproar of it, so that he could not do without
it, and could only divert himself by dint of noise, tumult,
and excess. It is this which led him often into such
strange and such scandalous debauches, and as he wished
to surpass all his companions, to mix up with his parties
of pleasure the most impious discourses, and as a precious
refinement, to hold the most outrageous orgies on the
most holy days,—as he did several times during his Regency on Good Friday, by choice, and on other similar
days. The more debauched a man was, the more he
esteemed him; and I have unceasingly seen him in admiration, that reached almost to veneration for the Grand
Prieur,—because for forty years he had always gone to
bed drunk, and had never ceased to keep mistresses in
the most public manner, and to hold the most impious
and irreligious discourses. With these principles, and the
conduct that resulted from them, it is not surprising that
M. le Duc d'Orléans was false to such an extent that he
boasted of his falsehood, and plumed himself upon being
the most skillful deceiver in the world. He and Madame
la Duchess de Berry sometimes disputed which was the

cleverer of the two; and this in public before M. le Duc
de Berry, Madame de Saint-Simon, and others!*

M. le Duc d'Orléans, following out the traditions of the
Palais Royal, had acquired the detestable taste and habit
of embroiling people one with the other, so as to profit
by their divisions. This was one of his principal occupations during all the time he was at the head of affairs,
and one that he liked the best; but which, as soon as
discovered, rendered him odious, and caused him a thousand annoyances. He was not wicked, far from it; but
he could not quit the habits of impiety, debauchery, and
deceit into which Dubois had led him. A remarkable
feature in his character is, that he was suspicious and
full of confidence at the same time with reference to the
very same people.

It is surprising that with all his talents he was totally
without honest resources for amusing himself. He was
born bored; and he was so accustomed to live out of himself, that it was insufferable to him to return, incapable
as he was of trying even to occupy himself. He could
only live in the midst of the movement and torrent of
business; at the head of an army for instance, or in the
cares that arose out of the execution of campaign projects, or in the excitement and uproar of debauchery.
He began to languish as soon as he was without noise,
excess, and tumult, the time painfully hanging upon his
hands. He cast himself upon painting, when his great
fancy for chemistry had passed or grown deadened, in
consequence of what had been said upon it. He painted
nearly all the afternoon at Versailles and at Marly. He
was a good judge of pictures, liked them, and made a
collection, which in number and excellence was not surpassed by those of the Crown. He amused himself afterward in making composition stones and seals over charcoal,
the fumes of which often drove me away; and the strongest perfumes, which he was fond of all of his life, but
from which I turned him because the King was very
much afraid of them and soon sniffed them. In fact,

---

* These curious admissions of Saint-Simon as to the execrable hypocrisy of his favorite prince, singularly diminish our faith in his innocence of the many horrible crimes laid to his charge.

never was man born with so many talents of all kinds, so much readiness and facility in making use of them, and yet never was man so idle, so given up to vacuity and weariness. Thus Madame painted him very happily by an illustration from fairy tales, of which she was full.

She said, that all the fairies had been invited to his birth; that all came, and that each gave him some talent, so that he had them all. But, unfortunately, an old fairy, who had disappeared so many years that she was no longer remembered, had been omitted from the invitation lists. Piqued at this neglect, she came supported upon her little wand, just at the moment when all the rest had endowed the child with their gifts. More and more vexed, she revenged herself by rendering useless all the talents he had received from the other fairies, not one of which, though possessing them all, in consequence of her malediction, was he able to make use of. It must be admitted, that on the whole this is a speaking portrait.

One of the misfortunes of this prince was being incapable of following up anything, and an inability to comprehend, even, how anyone else could do so. Another, was a sort of insensibility which rendered him indifferent to the most mortal and the most dangerous offenses; and as the nerve and principle of hatred and friendship, of gratitude and vengence, are the same, and as they were wanting in him, the consequences were infinite and pernicious. He was timid to excess, knew it, and was so ashamed that he affected to be exactly the reverse, and plumed himself upon his daring. But the truth is, as was afterward seen, nothing could be obtained from him, neither grace, nor justice, except by working upon his fears, to which he was very susceptible; or by extreme importunity. He tried to put people off by words, then by promises, of which he was monstrously prodigal, but which he only kept when made to people who had good firm claws. In this manner he broke so many engagements that the most positive became counted as nothing; and he promised, moreover, to so many different people what could only be given to one, that he thus opened out a copious source of discredit to himself and caused

much discontent. Nothing deceived or injured him more
than the opinion he had formed, that he could deceive
all the world. He was no longer believed, even when he
spoke with the best faith, and his facility much diminished the value of everything he did. To conclude, the
obscure, and for the most part blackguard, company
which he ordinarily frequented in his debauches, and
which he did not scruple publicly to call his *roués*, drove
away all decent people, and did him infinite harm.

His constant mistrust of everything and everybody was
disgusting, above all, when he was at the head of affairs.
The fault sprang from his timidity, which made him fear
his most certain enemies, and treat them with more distinction than his friends,—from his natural easiness, from
a false imitation of Henry IV., in whom this quality was
by no means the finest, and from that unfortunate opinion which he held, that probity was a sham. He was,
nevertheless, persuaded of my probity; and would often
reproach me with it as a fault and prejudice of education which had cramped my mind and obscured my understanding, and he said as much of Madame de Saint-
Simon, because he believed her virtuous. I had given
him so many proofs of my attachment that he could not
very well suspect me; and yet, this is what happened
two or three years after the establishment of the Regency.
I give it as one of the most striking of the touches that
paint his portrait.

It was autumn. M. d'Orléans had dismissed the Councils for a fortnight. I profited by this to go and spend
the time at La Ferté. I had just passed an hour alone
with the Duke, and had taken my leave of him and gone
home, where, in order to be in repose, I had closed my
door to everybody. In about an hour at most, I was
told that Biron, with a message from M. le Duc d'Orléans was at the door, with orders to see me, and that
he would not go away without. I allowed Biron to enter,
all the more surprised because I had just quitted M. le
Duc d'Orléans, and eagerly asked him his news. Biron was
embarrassed, and in his turn asked where was the Marquis
de Ruffec (my son). At this my surprise increased, and
I demanded what he meant. Biron, more and more con-

fused, admitted that M. le Duc d'Orléans wanted information on this point, and had sent him for it. I replied,
that my son was with his regiment at Besançon, lodging
with M. de Levi, who commanded in Franche Comté.

"Oh," said Biron, "I know that very well; but have
you any letter from him?"

"What for?" I asked.

"Because, frankly, since I must tell you all," said he,
"M. le Duc d'Orléans wishes to see his handwriting."

He added, that soon after I had quitted M. le Duc
d'Orléans, while he was walking at Montmartre in a
garden with his *roués* and his harlots, some letters had
been brought to him by a post-office clerk, to whom he
had spoken in private; that afterward he, Biron, had
been called by the Duke, who showed him a letter from
the Marquis de Ruffec to his master, dated "Madrid,"
and charged him, thereupon, with this present commission.

At this recital I felt a mixture of anger and compassion, and I did not constrain myself with Biron. I
had no letters from my son, because I used to burn them,
as I did all useless papers. I charged Biron to say to
M. le Duc d'Orléans a part of what I felt; that I had
not the slightest acquaintance with anybody in Spain;
that I begged him at once to dispatch a courier there
in order to satisfy himself that my son was at Besançon.

Biron, shrugging his shoulders, said all that was very
good but that if I could find a letter from the Marquis
de Ruffec it would be much better; adding, that if one
turned up and I sent it to him, he would take care that
it reached M. le Duc d'Orléans at table, in spite of the
privacy of his suppers. I did not wish to return to the
Palais Royal to make a scene there, and dismissed Biron.
Fortunately, Madame de Saint-Simon came in some time
after. I related to her this adventure. She found the
last letter of the Marquis de Ruffec, and we sent it to
Biron. It reached the table as he had promised. M. le
Duc d'Orléans seized it with eagerness. The joke is that
he did not know the handwriting. Not only did he look
at the letter, but he read it; and as he found it diverting,
regaled his company with it; it became the topic of their

discourse, and entirely removed his suspicions. Upon my return from La Ferté, I found him ashamed of himself, and I rendered him still more so by what I said to him on the subject.

I learned afterward that this Madrid letter, and others that followed, came from a sham Marquis de Ruffec, that is to say, from the son of one of Madame's porters, who passed himself off as my son. He pretended that he had quarreled with me, and wrote to Madame de Saint-Simon, begging her to intercede for him; and all this that his letters might be seen, and that he might reap substantial benefits from his imposture in the shape of money and consideration. He was a well-made fellow, had much address and effrontery, knew the Court very well, and had taken care to learn all about our family, so as to speak within limits. He was arrested at Bayonne, at the table of Dadoncourt, who commanded there, and who suddenly formed the resolution, suspecting him not to be a gentleman, upon seeing him eat olives with a fork! When in gaol he confessed who he was. He was not new at the trade and was confined some little time.

CHAPTER XXXIII.

Bᴜᴛ to return to M. le Duc d'Orléans. His curiosity, joined to a false idea of firmness and courage, had early led him to try and raise the devil and make him speak. He left nothing untried, even the wildest reading, to persuade himself there was no God; and yet believed meanwhile in the devil, and hoped to see him and converse with him! This inconsistency is hard to understand, and yet is extremely common. He worked with all sorts of obscure people, and above all with Mirepoix, sublieutenant of the Black Musketeers, to find out Satan. They passed whole nights in the quarries of Vanvres and of Vaugirard uttering invocations. M. le Duc d'Orléans, however, admitted to me that he had never succeeded in hearing or seeing anything, and at last had given up this folly.

At first it was only to please Madame d'Argenton, but afterward from curiosity, that he tried to see the present and the future in a glass of water; so he said, and he was no liar. To be false and to be a liar are not one and the same thing, though they closely resemble each other, and if he told a lie it was only when hard pressed upon some promise or some business, and in spite of himself, so as to escape from a dilemma.

Although we often spoke upon religion, to which I tried to lead him so long as I had hope of success, I never could unravel the system he had formed for himself, and I ended by becoming persuaded that he wavered unceas-

22

ingly without forming any religion at all. His passionate
desire, like that of his companions in morals, was this,
that it would turn out that there is no God; but he had
too much enlightenment to be an atheist,—who is a particular kind of fool much more rare than is thought.
This enlightenment importuned him; he tried to extinguish it and could not. A mortal soul would have been
to him a resource; but he could not convince himself of
its existence. A God and an immortal soul threw him
into sad straits, and yet he could not blind himself to the
truth of both the one and the other. I can say, then, this,
I know of what religion he was not; nothing more. I am
sure, however, that he was very ill at ease upon this point,
and that if a dangerous illness had overtaken him, and he
had had the time, he would have thrown himself into the
hands of all the priests and all the Capuchins of the town.
His great foible was to pride himself upon his impiety and
to wish to surpass in that everybody else.

I recollect that one Christmas time, at Versailles,
when he accompanied the King to morning prayers and
to the three midnight masses, he surprised the Court by
his continued application in reading a volume he had
brought with him, and which appeared to be a prayer
book. The chief *femme de chambre* of Madame la
Duchess d'Orléans, much attached to the family, and
very free, as all good old domestics are, transfixed with
joy at M. le Duc d'Orléans's application to his book,
complimented him upon it the next day, in the presence
of others. M. le Duc d'Orléans allowed her to go on
some time, and then said, " You are very silly, Madame
Imbert. Do you know what I was reading? It was
' Rabelais, ' that I brought with me for fear of being
bored. "

The effect of this reply may be imagined. The thing
was too true, and was pure braggadocio; for, without
comparison of the places, or of the things, the music of
the chapel was much superior to that of the opera, and
to all the music of Europe; and at Christmas it surpassed itself. There was nothing so magnificent as the
decoration of the chapel, or the manner in which it was
lighted. It was full of people; the arches of the tribune

were crowded with the Court ladies, in undress, but ready for conquest. There was nothing so surprising as the beauty of the spectacle. The ears were charmed also. M. le Duc d'Orléans loved music extremely; he could compose, and had amused himself by composing a kind of little opera, La Fare writing the words, which was performed before the King. This music of the chapel, therefore, might well have occupied him in the most agreeable manner, to say nothing of the brilliant scene, without his having recourse to "Rabelais." But he must needs play the impious, and the wag.

Madame la Duchess d'Orléans was another kind of person. She was tall, and in every way majestic; her complexion, her throat, her arms, were admirable; she had a tolerable mouth, with beautiful teeth, somewhat long; and cheeks too broad, and too hanging, which interfered with, but did not spoil, her beauty. What disfigured her most was her eyebrows, which were, as it were, peeled and red, with very little hair; she had, however, fine eyelashes, and well-set, chestnut colored hair. Without being humpbacked or deformed, she had one side larger than the other, and walked awry. This defect in her figure indicated another, which was more troublesome in society, and which inconvenienced herself. She had a good deal of intellect, and spoke with much ability. She said all she wished, and often conveyed her meaning to you without directly expressing it; saying, as it were, what she did not say. Her utterance was, however, slow and embarrassed, so that unaccustomed ears with difficulty followed her.

Every kind of decency and decorum centered themselves in her, and the most exquisite pride was there upon its throne. Astonishment will be felt at what I am going to say, and yet, however, nothing is more strictly true: it is, that at the bottom of her soul she believed that she, bastard of the King, had much honored M. d'Orléans in marrying him! M. le Duc d'Orléans often laughed at her pride, calling her Madame Lucifer, in speaking to her, and she admitted that the name did not displease her. She always received his advances with coldness, and a sort of superiority of greatness. She was a princess to the backbone, at all hours, and in all places. Yet, at the same time, her timidity was extreme. The King could have made her feel ill with a single severe look; and Madame de Maintenon could have done likewise, perhaps. At all events, Madame la Duchess d'Orléans trembled before her; and upon the most commonplace matters never replied to either him or her without hesitation, fear printed on her face.

M. le Duc and Madame la Duchess d'Orléans lived an idle, languishing, shameful, indecent, and despised life, abandoned by all the Court. This, I felt, was one of the first things that must be remedied. Accordingly, I induced Madame la Duchess d'Orléans to make an effort to attract people to her table. She did so, persevering against the coldness and aversion she met with, and in time succeeded in drawing a tolerably numerous company to her dinners. They were of exquisite quality, and people soon got over their first hesitation, when they found everything orderly, free, and unobjectionable. At these dinners, M. d'Orléans kept within bounds, not only in his discourse, but in his behavior. But oftentimes his *ennui* led him to Paris, to join in supper parties and debauchery. Madame la Duchess d'Orléans tried to draw him from these pleasures by arranging small parties at her pretty little villa, l'Etoile (in the park of Versailles), which the King had given to her, and which she had furnished in the most delightful manner. She loved good cheer, the guests loved it also, and at table she was altogether another person — free, gay, exciting, charming. M. le Duc d'Orléans cared for nothing but noise, and as he threw off all restraint at these parties, there was much difficulty in selecting guests, for the ears of many people would have been much confused at his loose talk, and their eyes much astonished to see him get drunk at the very commencement of the repast, in the midst of those who thought only of amusing and recreating themselves in a decent manner, and who never approached intoxication.

As the King became weaker in health, and evidently drew near his end, I had continued interviews with Madame d'Orléans upon the subject of the regency, the plan of government to be adopted, and the policy he should follow. Hundreds of times before we had reasoned together upon the faults of the Government, and the misfortunes that resulted from them. What we had to do was to avoid those faults, educate the young King in good and national maxims, so that when he succeeded to power he might continue what the Regency had not had time to finish. This, at least, was my idea, and I labored hard to make it the idea of M. le Duc d'Orléans. As the health of the King diminished I entered more into details; as I will explain.

What I considered the most important thing to be done, was to overthrow entirely the system of government in which Cardinal Mazarin had imprisoned the King and the realm. A foreigner, risen from the dregs of the people, who thinks of nothing but his own power and his own greatness, cares nothing for the State, except in its relation to himself. He despises its laws, its genius, its advantages: he is ignorant of its rules and its forms; he thinks only of subjugating all, of confounding all, of bringing all down to one level. Richelieu and his successor, Mazarin, succeeded so well in this policy that the nobility, by degrees, became annihilated, as we now see them. The pen and the robe people, on the other hand, were exalted; so that now things have reached such a pretty pass that the greatest lord is without power, and in a thousand different manners is dependent upon the meanest plebeian. It is in this manner that things hasten from one extreme to the other.

My design was to commence by introducing the nobility into the ministry, with the dignity and authority due to them, and by degrees to dismiss the pen and robe people from all employ not purely judicial. In this manner the administration of public affairs would be entirely in the hands of the aristocracy. I proposed to abolish the two offices of secretary of state for the war department, and for foreign affairs, and to supply their places by councils; also, that the offices of the navy should be managed by a council. I insisted upon the distinct and perfect separation of these councils, so that their authority should never be confounded, and the public should never have

the slightest trouble in finding out where to address itself
for any kind of business.

M. le Duc d'Orléans exceedingly relished my project,
which we much discussed. This point arrived at, it became necessary to debate upon the persons who were to
form these councils. I suggested names, which were accepted or set aside, according as they met his approval
or disapprobation. "But," said M. le Duc d'Orléans, after
we had been a long time at this work, "you propose
everybody and never say a word of yourself. What do
you wish to be?"

I replied, that it was not for me to propose, still less
to choose any office, but for him to see if he wished to
employ me, believing me capable, and in that case to
determine the place he wished me to occupy. This
was at Marly, in his chamber, and I shall never forget it.

After some little debate, that between equals would
have been called complimentary, he proposed to me the
presidency of the council of finance. But I had good
reasons for shrinking from this office. I saw that dis-
ordered as the finances had become there was only one
remedy by which improvement could be effected; and
this was National Bankruptcy. Had I occupied the
office, I should have been too strongly tempted to
urge this view, and carry it out, but it was a responsi-
bility I did not wish to take upon myself before God
and man. Yet, I felt as I said, that to declare the State
bankrupt would be the wisest course, and I am bold
enough to think, that there is not a man, having no personal interest in the continuance of imposts, who of two
evils, viz, vastly increased taxation, and national failure,
would not prefer the latter. We were in the condition
of a man who unfortunately must choose between passing
twelve or fifteen years in his bed, in continual pain, or
having his leg cut off. Who can doubt this? He would
prefer the loss of his leg by a painful operation, in order to find himself two months after quite well, free
from suffering and in the enjoyment of all his faculties.

I shrank accordingly from the finances for the reason
I have above given and made M. le Duc d'Orléans so

angry by my refusal to accept the office he had proposed to me, that for three weeks he sulked and would not speak to me, except upon unimportant matters.

At the end of that time, in the midst of a languishing conversation, he exclaimed, "Very well, then. You stick to your text, you won't have the finances?"

I respectfully lowered my eyes and replied, in a gentle tone, that I thought that question was settled. He could not restrain some complaints, but they were not bitter, nor was he angry, and then rising and taking a few turns in the room, without saying a word, and his head bent, as was his custom when embarrassed, he suddenly spun round upon me, and exclaimed, "But whom shall we put there?"

I suggested the Duc de Noailles, and although the suggestion at first met with much warm opposition from M. le Duc d'Orléans, it was ultimately accepted by him.

The moment after we had settled this point he said to me, "And you! what will you be?" and he pressed me so much to explain myself that I said at last if he would put me in the council of affairs of the interior, I thought I should do better there than elsewhere.

"Chief, then," replied he with vivacity.

"No, no! not that," said I; "simply a place in the council."

We both insisted, he for, I against. "A place in that council," he said, "would be ridiculous, and cannot be thought of. Since you will not be chief, there is only one post which suits you, and which suits me also. You must be in the council I shall be in,— the Supreme Council."

I accepted the post, and thanked him. From that moment this distinction remained fixed.

I will not enter into all the suggestions I offered to M. le Duc d'Orléans respecting the Regency, or give the details of all the projects I submitted to him. Many of those projects and suggestions were either acted upon only partially, or not acted upon at all, although nearly every one met with his approval. But he was variable as the winds, and as difficult to hold. In my dealings with him I had to do with a person very different from that estimable Dauphin who was so rudely taken away from us.

But let me, before going further, describe the last days of the King, his illness, and death, adding to the narrative a review of his life and character.

CHAPTER XXXIV.

Louis XIV. began, as I have before remarked, sensibly
to decline, and his appetite, which had always been
good and uniform, very considerably diminished.
Even foreign countries became aware of this. Bets were
laid in London that his life would not last beyond the
first of September, that is to say, about three months,
and although the King wished to know everything, it
may be imagined that nobody was very eager to make
him acquainted with the news. He used to have the
Dutch papers read to him in private, by Torcy, often
after the Council of State. One day as Torcy was reading, coming unexpectedly — for he had not examined
the paper — upon the account of these bets, he stopped,
stammered, and skipped it. The King, who easily perceived this, asked him the cause of his embarrassment,
what he was passing over, and why? Torcy blushed to the
very whites of his eyes, and said that it was a piece of
impertinence unworthy of being read. The King insisted; Torcy also: but at last thoroughly confused, he
could not resist the reiterated command he received,
and read the whole account of the bets. The King
pretended not to be touched by it, but he was, and profoundly, so that sitting down to table immediately afterward, he could not keep himself from speaking of it,
though without mentioning the gazette.

This was at Marly, and by chance I was there that day. The King looked at me as at the others, but as though asking for a reply. I took good care not to open my mouth, and lowered my eyes. Cheverny (a discreet man), too, was not so prudent, but made a long and ill-timed rhapsody upon similar reports that had come to Copenhagen from Vienna while he was ambassador at the former place seventeen or eighteen years before. The King allowed him to say on, but did not take the bait. He appeared touched, but like a man who does not wish to seem so. It could be seen that he did all he could to eat, and to show that he ate with appetite. But it was also seen that the mouthfuls loitered on their way. This trifle did not fail to augment the circumspection of the Court, above all of those who by their position had reason to be more attentive than the rest. It was reported that an aide-de-camp of Lord Stair, who was then English ambassador of our Court, and very much disliked for his insolent bearing and his troublesome ways, had caused these bets by what he had said in England respecting the health of the King. Stair, when told this, was much grieved, and said 'twas a scoundrel he had dismissed.

As the King sensibly declined I noticed that although terror of him kept people as much away from M. d'Orléans as ever, I was approached even by the most considerable. I had often amused myself at the expense of these prompt friends; I did so now and diverted M. d'Orléans by warning him beforehand what he had to expect.

On Friday, the 9th of August, 1713, the King hunted the stag after dinner in his *calèche*, that he drove himself as usual. 'Twas for the last time. Upon his return he appeared much knocked up. There was a grand concert in the evening in Madame de Maintenon's apartment.

On Saturday, the 10th of August, he walked before dinner in his gardens at Marley; he returned to Versailles about six o'clock in the evening, and never again saw that strange work of his hands. In the evening he worked with the Chancellor in Madame de Maintenon's rooms, and appeared to everybody very ill. On Sunday, the eleventh of August, he held the Council of State, walked after dinner to Trianon, never more to go out again during life.

On the morrow, the 12th of August, he took medicine as usual, and lived as usual the following days. It was known that he complained of sciatica in the leg and thigh. He had never before had sciatica, or rheumatism, or a cold; and for a long time no touch of gout. In the evening there was a little concert in Madame de Maintenon's rooms. This was the last time in his life that he walked alone.

On Tuesday, the 13th of August, he made a violent effort, and gave a farewell audience to a sham Persian ambassador, whom Pontchartrain had imposed upon him; this was the last public action of his life. The audience, which was long, fatigued the King. He resisted the desire for sleep which came over him, held the finance council, dined, had himself carried to Madame de Maintenon's, where a little concert was given, and on leaving his cabinet stopped for the Duchess de la Rochefoucauld, who presented to him the Duchess de la Rocheguyon, her daughter-in-law, who was the last lady presented to him. She took her taboret that evening at the King's grand supper, which was the last he ever gave. On the morrow he sent some precious stones to the Persian ambassador just alluded to. It was on this day that the Princess des Ursins set off for Lyons, terrified at the state of the King as I have already related.

For more than a year the health of the King had diminished. His valets noticed this first, and followed the progress of the malady, without one of them daring to open his mouth. The bastards, or to speak exactly, M. du Maine, saw it; Madame de Maintenon also; but they did nothing. Fagon, the chief physician, much fallen off in mind and body, was the only one of the King's intimates who saw nothing. Maréchal, also chief physician, spoke to him (Fagon) several times, but was always harshly repulsed. Pressed at last by his duty and his attachment, he made bold one morning toward Whitsuntide to go to Madame de Maintenon. He told her what he saw and how grossly Fagon was mistaken. He assured her that the King, whose pulse he had often felt, had had for some time a slow internal fever; that his constitution was so good that with remedies and attention all would go well, but that if the malady were allowed to grow there would no longer be any resource. Madame de Maintenon grew angry, and all he obtained for his zeal was her anger. She said that only the personal enemies of Fagon could find fault with his opinion upon the King's health, concerning which the capacity, the application, the experience of the chief physician could not be deceived. The best of it is that Maréchal, who had formerly operated upon Fagon for stone, had been appointed chief surgeon by him, and they had always lived on the best of terms. Maréchal, annoyed as he related to me, could do nothing more, and began from that time to lament the death of his master. Fagon was in fact the first physician in Europe, but for a long time his health had not permitted him to maintain his experience; and the high point of authority to which his capacity and his favor had carried him, had at last spoiled him. He would not hear reason, or submit to reply, and continued to treat the King as he had treated him in early years; and killed him by his obstinacy.

The gout of which the King had had long attacks, induced Fagon to swaddle him, so to say, every evening in a heap of feather pillows, which made him sweat all night to such an extent that it was necessary in the morning to rub him down and change his linen before the grand chamberlain and the first gentleman of the chamber could enter. For many years he had drunk nothing but Burgundy wine, half mixed with water, and so old that it was used up instead of the best champagne which he had used all his life. He would pleasantly say sometimes that foreign lords who were anxious to taste the wine he used, were often mightily deceived. At no time had he ever drank pure wine, or made use in any way of spirits, or even tea, coffee, or chocolate. Upon rising, instead of a little bread and wine and water, he had taken for a long time two glasses of sage and veronica; often between his meals, and always on going to bed, glasses of water with a little orange-flower water in them, and always iced.

Even on the days when he had medicine he drank this, and always also at his meals, between which he never ate anything except some cinnamon lozenges that he put into his pocket at his dessert, with a good many cracknels for the bitches he kept in his cabinet.

As during the last year of his life the King became more and more costive, Fagon made him eat at the commencement of his repasts many iced fruits, that is to say, mulberries, melons, and figs rotten from ripeness; and at his dessert many other fruits, finishing with a surprising quantity of sweetmeats. All the year round he ate at supper a prodigious quantity of salad. His soups, several of which he partook of morning and evening, were full of gravy, and were of exceeding strength, and everything that was served to him was full of spice, to double the usual extent, and very strong also. This regimen and the sweetmeats together Fagon did not like, and sometimes while seeing the King eat, he would make most amusing grimaces, without daring however to say anything except now and then to Livry and Benoist, who replied that it was their business to feed the King, and his to doctor him. The King never ate any kind of venison or waterfowl, but otherwise partook of everything, *fête* days and fast days alike, except that during the last twenty years of his life he observed some few days of Lent.

This summer he redoubled his *régime* of fruits and drinks. At last the former clogged his stomach, taken after soup, weakened the digestive organs and took away his appetite, which until then had never failed him all his life, though however late dinner might be delayed he never was hungry or wanted to eat. But after the first spoonful of soup, his appetite came, as I have several times heard him say, and he ate so prodigiously and so solidly morning and evening that no one could get accustomed to see it. So much water and so much fruit unconnected by anything spirituous, turned his blood into gangrene; while those forced night sweats diminished its strength and impoverished it; and thus his death was caused, as was seen by the opening of his body. The organs were found in such good and healthy condition that there is reason to believe he would have lived beyond his hundredth year. His stomach above all astonished, and also his bowels by their volume and extent, double that of the ordinary, whence it came that he was such a great yet uniform eater. Remedies were not thought of until it was no longer time, because Fagon would never believe him ill, or Madame de Maintenon either; though at the same time she had taken good care to provide for her own retreat in the case of his death. Amid all this, the King felt his state before they felt it, and said so sometimes to his valets: Fagon always reassured him, but did nothing. The King was contented with what was said to him without being persuaded, but his friendship for Fagon restrained him, and Madame de Maintenon still more.

On Wednesday, the 14th of August, the King was carried to hear mass for the last time; held the Council of State, ate a meat dinner, and had music in Madame de Maintenon's rooms. He supped in his chamber, where the court saw him as at his dinner; was with his family a short time in his cabinet, and went to bed a little after ten.

On Thursday, the Festival of the Assumption, he heard mass in his bed. The night had been disturbed and bad. He dined in his bed, the courtiers being present, rose at five and was carried to Madame de Maintenon's, where music was played. He supped and went to bed as on the previous evening. As long as he could sit up he did the same.

On Friday, the 16th of August, the night had been no better; much thirst and drink. The King ordered no one to enter until ten. Mass and dinner in his bed as before; then he was carried to Madame de Maintenon's; he played with the ladies there, and afterward there was a grand concert.

On Saturday, the 17th of August, the night as the preceding. He held the finance council, he being in bed; saw people at his dinner, rose immediately after; gave audience in his cabinet to the General of the order of Sainte-Croix de la Bretonnerie; passed to Madame de Maintenon's, where he worked with the Chancellor. At night, Fagon slept for the first time in his chamber.

Sunday, the 18th of August, passed like the preceding days. Fagon pretended there had been no fever. The King held a Council of State before and after his dinner; worked afterward upon the fortifications with Pelletier; then passed to Madame de Maintenon's, where there was music.

Monday, the 19th, and Tuesday, the 20th of August, passed much as the previous days, excepting that on the latter the King supped in his dressing gown, seated in an armchair; and that after this evening he never left his room or dressed himself again. That same day Madame de Saint-Simon, whom I had pressed to return, came back from the waters of Forges. The King, entering after supper into his cabinet, perceived her. He ordered his chair to be stopped; spoke to her very kindly upon her journey and her return; then had himself wheeled on by Bloin into the other cabinet. She was the last Court lady to whom he spoke. I don't count those who were always near him, and who came to him when he could no longer leave his room. Madame de Saint-Simon said to me in the evening that she should not have recognized the King if she had met him anywhere else. Yet she had left Marly for Forges only on the 6th of July.

On Wednesday, the 21st of August, four physicians saw the King, but took care to do nothing except praise Fagon, who gave him cassia. For some days it had been perceived that he ate meat and even bread with difficulty (though all his life he had eaten but little of the latter, and for some time only the crumb, because he had no teeth). Soup in larger quantity, hash very light, and eggs compensated him; but he ate very sparingly.

On Thursday, the 22d of August, the King was still worse. He saw four other physicians, who, like the first four, did nothing but admire the learned and admirable treatment of Fagon, who made him take toward evening some Jesuit bark and water and intended to give him at night ass's milk. This same day, the King ordered the Duc de la Rochefoucauld to bring him his clothes on the morrow, in order that he might choose which he would wear upon leaving off the mourning he wore for a son of Madame la Duchess de Lorraine. He had not been able to quit his chamber for some days; he could scarcely eat anything solid; his physician slept in his chamber, and yet he reckoned upon being cured, upon dressing himself again, and wished to choose his dress! In like manner there was the same round of councils, of work, of amusements. So true it is, that men do not wish to die, and dissimulate from themselves the approach of death as long as possible. Meanwhile, let me say, that the state of the King, which nobody was ignorant of, had already changed M. d'Orléans's desert into a crowded city.

Friday, the 23d of August, the night was as usual, the morning also. The King worked with Père Tellier, who tried, but in vain, to make him fill up several benefices that were vacant; that is to say, Père Tellier wished to dispose of them himself, instead of leaving them to M. le Duc d'Orléans. Let me state at once, that the feebler the King grew, the more Père Tellier worried him; so as not to lose such a rich prey, or miss the opportunity of securing fresh creatures for his service. But he could not succeed. The King declared to him that he had enough to render account of to God, without charging himself with this nomination, and forbade him to speak again upon the subject.

On Saturday evening, the 24th of August, he supped in his dressing gown, in presence of the courtiers, for the last time. I noticed that he could only swallow liquids, and that he was troubled if looked at. He could not finish his supper, and begged the courtiers to pass on, that is to say, go away. He went to bed, where his leg, on which were several black marks, was examined. It had grown worse lately and had given him much pain. He sent for Père Tellier and made confession. Confusion spread among the doctors at this. Milk, and Jesuit bark and water had been tried and abandoned in turns; now, nobody knew what to try. The doctors admitted that they believed he had had a slow fever ever since Whitsuntide; and excused themselves for doing nothing on the ground that he did not wish for remedies.

On Sunday, the 25th of August, no more mystery was made of the King's danger. Nevertheless, he expressly

commanded that nothing should be changed in the usual
order of this day (the *fête* of St. Louis), that is to say,
that the drums and the hautboys, assembled beneath his
windows, should play their accustomed music as soon as
he awoke, and that the twenty-four violins should play
in the antechamber during his dinner. He worked afterward with the Chancellor, who wrote under his dictation,
a codicil to his will, Madame de Maintenon being present.
She and M. du Maine, who thought incessantly of themselves, did not consider the King had done enough for
them by his will; they wished to remedy this by a codicil,
which equally showed how enormously they abused the
King's weakness in this extremity, and to what an excess
ambition may carry us. By this codicil the King submitted all the civil and military household of the young
King to the Duc du Maine, and under his orders to
Maréchal de Villeroy, who, by this disposition, became
the sole masters of the person and the dwelling place of
the King, and of Paris, by the troops placed in their
hands; so that the Regent had not the slightest shadow
of authority and was at their mercy; certainly liable to
be arrested or worse, any time it should please M. du
Maine.

Soon after the Chancellor left the King, Madame de
Maintenon who remained, sent for the ladies; and the
musicians came at seven o'clock in the evening. But
the King fell asleep during the conversation of the ladies.
He awoke; his brain confused, which frightened them
and made them call the doctors. They found his pulse
so bad that they did not hesitate to propose to him, his
senses having returned, to take the Sacrament without delay. Père Tellier was sent for; the musicians who had
just prepared their books and their instruments, were
dismissed, the ladies also; and in a quarter of an hour
from that time, the King made confession to Père Tellier,
the Cardinal de Rohan, meanwhile, bringing the Holy
Sacrament from the Chapel, and sending for the *curé*
and holy oils. Two of the King's chaplains, summoned
by the Cardinal, came, and seven or eight candlesticks
were carried by valets. The Cardinal said a word or two
to the King upon this great and last action, during which

23

the King appeared very firm, but very penetrated with what he was doing. As soon as he had received Our Savior and the holy oils, everybody left the chamber except Madame de Maintenon and the Chancellor. Immediately afterward, and this was rather strange, a kind of book or little tablet was placed upon the bed, the codicil was presented to the King, and at the bottom of it he wrote four or five lines, and restored the document to the Chancellor.

After this, the King sent for M. le Duc d'Orléans, showed him much esteem, friendship, and confidence; but what is terrible, with Jesus Christ still upon his lips — the Sacrament he had just received — he assured him, he would find nothing in his will with which he would not feel pleased. Then he recommended to him the state and the person of the future King.

On Monday, the 26th of August, the King called to him the Cardinals de Rohan and de Bissy, protested that he died in the faith, and in submission to the Church, then added, looking at them, that he was sorry to leave the affairs of the Church as they were; that they knew he had done nothing except what they wished; that it was therefore for them to answer before God for what he had done; that his own conscience was clear, and that he was an ignorant man who had abandoned himself entirely to them. What a frightful thunderbolt was this to the two cardinals; for this was an illusion to the terrible constitution they had assisted Père Tellier in forcing upon him. But their calm was superior to all trial. They praised him and said he had done well, and that he might be at ease as to the result.

This same Monday, 26th of August, after the two Cardinals had left the room, the King dined in his bed in the presence of those who were privileged to enter. As the things were being cleared away, he made them approach and addressed to them these words, which were stored up in their memory: "Gentlemen, I ask your pardon for the bad example I have given you. I have much to thank you for the manner in which you have served me, and for the attachment and fidelity you have always shown for me. I am very sorry I have not done for you all I should have wished to do; bad times have been the cause. I ask for my grandson the same application and the same fidelity you have had for me. He is a child who may experience many reverses. Let your example be one for all my other subjects. Follow the orders my nephew will give you; he is to govern the realm; I hope he will govern it well; I hope also that you will all contribute to keep up union, and that if anyone falls away you will aid in bringing him back. I feel that I am moved, and that I move you also. I ask your pardon. Adieu, gentlemen, I hope you will sometimes remember me.»

A short time after he called the Maréchal de Villeroy to him, and said he had made him governor of the Dauphin. He then called to him M. le Duc and M. le Prince de Conti, and recommended to them the advantages of union among princes. Then, hearing women in the cabinet, questioned who were there, and immediately sent word they might enter. Madame la Duchess de Berry, Madame la Duchess d'Orléans, and the Princesses of the blood forthwith appeared, crying. The King told them they must not cry thus, and said a few friendly words to them, and dismissed them. They retired by the cabinet, weeping and crying very loudly, which caused people to believe outside that the King was dead, and, indeed, the rumor spread to Paris, and even to the provinces.

Some time after the King requested the Duchess de Ventadour to bring the little Dauphin to him. He made the child approach, and then said to him, before Madame de Maintenon and the few privileged people present, "My child, you are going to be a great king; do not imitate me in the taste I have had for building, or in that I have had for war; try, on the contrary, to be at peace with your neighbors. Render to God what you owe him; recognize the obligations you are under to him; make him honored by your subjects. Always follow good counsels; try to comfort your people, which I unhappily have not done. Never forget the obligation you owe to Madame de Ventadour. Madame (addressing her), let me embrace him (and while embracing him), my dear child, I give you my benediction with my whole heart."

As the little Prince was about to be taken off the bed, the King redemanded him, embraced him again, and raising hands and eyes to heaven, blessed him once more. This spectacle was extremely touching.

On Tuesday, the 27th of August, the King said to Madame de Maintenon, that he had always heard, it was hard to resolve to die; but that as for him, seeing himself upon the point of death, he did not find this resolution so difficult to form. She replied that it was very hard when we had attachments to creatures, hatred in our hearts, or restitutions to make. "Ah," rejoined the King, "as for restitutions, to nobody in particular do I owe any; but as for those I owe to the realm, I hope in the mercy of God."

The night which followed was very agitated. The King was seen at all moments joining his hands, striking his breast, and was heard repeating the prayers he ordinarily employed.

On Wednesday morning, the 28th of August he paid a compliment to Madame de Maintenon, which pleased her but little, and to which she replied not one word. He said that what consoled him in quitting her was that, considering the age she had reached, they must soon meet again!

About seven o'clock in the morning, he saw in the mirror two of his valets at the foot of the bed weeping, and said to them, "Why do you weep? Is it because you thought me immortal? As for me, I have not thought myself so, and you ought, considering my age, to have been prepared to lose me."

A very clownish Provençal rustic heard of the extremity of the King, while on his way from Marseilles to Paris, and came this morning to Versailles with a remedy, which he said would cure the gangrene. The King was so ill, and the doctors so at their wits' ends, that they consented to receive him. Fagon tried to say something, but this rustic, who was named Le Brun, abused him very coarsely, and Fagon accustomed to abuse others was confounded. Ten drops of Le Brun's mixture in Alicante wine were therefore given to the King about eleven o'clock in the morning. Some time after he became stronger, but the pulse falling again and becoming bad, another dose was given to him about four o'clock, to recall him to life, they told him. He replied, taking the mixture, "To life or to death as it shall please God."

Le Brun's remedy was continued. Some one proposed that the King should take some broth. The King replied that it was not broth he wanted, but a confessor, and he sent for him. One day, recovering from loss of consciousness, he asked Père Tellier to give him absolution for all his sins. Père Tellier asked him if he suffered much? "No," replied the King, "that's what troubles me: I should like to suffer more for the expiation of my sins."

On Thursday, the 29th of August, he grew a little better; he even ate two little biscuits steeped in wine, with a certain appetite. The news immediately spread abroad that the King was recovering. I went that day to the apartments, of M. le Duc d'Orléans, where, during the previous eight days, there had been such a crowd that, speaking exactly, a pin would not have fallen to the ground. Not a soul was there! As soon as the Duke saw me he burst out laughing, and said, I was the first person who had been to see him all the day! And until the evening he was entirely deserted. Such is the world!

In the evening it was known that the King had only recovered for the moment. In giving orders during the day, he called the young Dauphin "the young King." He saw a movement among those around him. "Why not?" said he, "that does not trouble me." Toward eight o'clock he took the elixir of the rustic. His brain appeared confused; he himself said he felt very ill. Toward eleven o'clock his leg was examined. The gangrene was found to be in the foot and the knee; the thigh much inflamed. He swooned during this examination. He had perceived with much pain that Madame de Maintenon was no longer near him. She had in fact gone off on the previous day with very dry eyes to St. Cyr, not intending to return.* He asked for her several times during the day. Her departure could not be hidden. He sent for her to St. Cyr, and she came back in the evening.

Friday, August the 30th, was a bad day preceded by a bad night. The King continually lost his reason. About five o'clock in the evening Madame de Maintenon left him, gave away her furniture to the domestics, and went to St. Cyr never to leave it.

On Saturday, the 31st of August, everything went from bad to worse. The gangrene had reached the knee and all the thigh. Toward eleven o'clock at night the King was found to be so ill that the prayers for the dying were said. This restored him to himself. He repeated the prayers in a voice so strong that it rose above all the other voices. At the end he recognized Cardinal de Rohan, and said to him, "These are the last favors of the Church." This was the last man to whom he spoke. He repeated several times, "*Nunc et in horâ mortis,*" then said, "Oh, my God, come to my aid; hasten to succor me."

These were his last words. All the night he was without consciousness and in a long agony, which finished on Sunday, the 1st of September, 1715, at a quarter past eight in the morning, three days before he had accomplished his seventy-seventh year, and in the seventy-second of his reign. He had survived all his sons and grandsons, except the King of Spain. Europe never saw so long a reign or France a King so old.

*If anything could make Madame de Maintenon more odious, it is this heartless desertion of the old King in his last moments of agony and penitence.

CHAPTER XXXV.

Early Life of Louis XIV. — His Education — His Enormous Vanity — His Ignorance — Cause of the War with Holland — His Mistakes and Weakness in War — The Ruin of France — Origin of Versailles — The King's Love of Adulation and Jealousy of People Who Came not to Court — His Spies — His Vindictiveness — Opening of Letters — Confidence Sometimes Placed in Him — A Lady in a Predicament.

I SHALL pass over the stormy period of Louis XIV.'s minority. At twenty-three years of age he entered the great world as King, under the most favorable auspices. His ministers were the most skillful in all Europe; his generals the best; his Court was filled with illustrious and clever men, formed during the troubles which had followed the death of Louis XIII.

Louis XIV. was made for a brilliant Court. In the midst of other men, his figure, his courage, his grace, his beauty, his grand mien, even the tone of his voice and the majestic and natural charm of all his person, distinguished him till his death as the King Bee, and showed that if he had only been born a simple private gentleman, he would equally have excelled in *fêtes*, pleasures, and gallantry, and would have had the greatest success in love. The intrigues and adventures which early in life he had been engaged in — when the Comtesse de Soissons lodged at the Tuileries, as superintendent of the Queen's household, and was the center figure of the Court group — had exercised an unfortunate influence upon him: he received those impressions with which he could never after successfully struggle. From this time, intellect, education, nobility of sentiment, and high principle, in others, became objects of suspicion to him, and soon of hatred. The more he advanced in years, the more this sentiment was confirmed in him. He wished to reign by himself. His jealousy on this point unceasingly became weakness. He reigned, indeed, in little things; the great he could never reach: even in the former, too, he was often governed. The superior ability of his early ministers and his early generals soon wearied him. He liked nobody to be in any way superior to him. Thus he chose his ministers, not for their knowledge, but for their ignorance; not for their capacity, but for their want of it. He liked to form them, as he said; liked to teach them even the most trifling things. It was the same with his generals. He took credit to himself for instructing them; wished it to be thought that from his cabinet he commanded and directed all his armies. Naturally fond of trifles, he unceasingly occupied himself with the most petty details of his troops, his household, his mansions; would even instruct his cooks, who received, like novices, lessons they had known by heart for years. This vanity, this unmeasured and unreasonable love of admiration, was his ruin. His ministers, his generals, his mistresses, his courtiers, soon perceived his weakness. They praised him with emulation and spoiled him. Praises, or to say truth, flattery, pleased him to such an extent, that the coarsest was well received, the vilest even better relished. It was the sole means by which you could approach him. Those whom he liked owed his affection for them, to their untiring flatteries. This is what gave his ministers so much authority, and the opportunities they had for adulating him, of attributing everything to him, and of pretending to learn everything from him. Suppleness, meanness, an admiring, dependent, cringing manner — above all, an air of nothingness — were the sole means of pleasing him.

This poison spread. It spread, too, to an incredible extent, in a prince who, although of intellect beneath mediocrity, was not utterly without sense, and who had had some experience. Without voice or musical knowledge, he used to sing, in private, the passages of the opera prologues that were fullest of his praises. He was drowned in vanity; and so deeply, that at his public suppers — all the Court present, musicians also — he would hum these self-same praises between his teeth, when the music they were set to was played.

And yet, it must be admitted, he might have done better. Though his intellect, as I have said, was beneath mediocrity, it was capable of being formed. He loved glory, was fond of order and regularity; was by disposition prudent, moderate, discreet, master of his movements and his tongue. Will it be believed? He was also by disposition good and just. God had sufficiently gifted him to enable him to be a good King; perhaps even A TOLERABLY GREAT KING! All the evil came to him from elsewhere. His early education was so neglected that nobody dared approach his apartment. He has often been heard to speak of those times with bitterness, and even to relate that, one evening he was found in the basin of the Palais Royal garden fountain, into which he had fallen. He was scarcely taught how to read or write, and remained so ignorant, that the most familiar historical and other facts were utterly unknown to him. He fell, accordingly, and sometimes even in public, into the grossest absurdities.

It was his vanity, his desire for glory, that led him soon after the death of the King of Spain, to make that event the pretext for war; in spite of the renunciations so recently made, so carefully stipulated in the marriage contract. He marched into Flanders; his conquests there were rapid; the passage of the Rhine was admirable; the triple alliance of England, Sweden, and Holland only animated him. In the midst of winter he took Franche-Comté, by restoring which at the peace of Aix-la-Chapelle, he preserved his conquests in Flanders. All was flourishing then in the State. Riches everywhere. Colbert had placed the finances, the navy, commerce, manufactures, letters even, upon the highest point; and this age, like that of Augustus, produced in abundance illustrious men of all kinds,— even those illustrious only in pleasures.

Le Tellier and Louvois, his son, who had the war department, trembled at the success and at the credit of Colbert, and had no difficulty in putting into the head of the King a new war, the success of which caused such fear to all Europe that France never recovered from it, and after having been upon the point of succumbing to this war, for a long time felt the weight and misfortune of it. Such was the real cause of that famous Dutch war, to which the King allowed himself to be pushed, and which his love for Madame de Montespan rendered so unfortunate for his glory and for his kingdom. Everything being conquered, everything taken, and Amsterdam ready to give up her keys, the King yields to his impatience, quits the army, flies to Versailles, and destroys in an instant all the success of his arms! He repaired this disgrace by a second conquest, in person, of Franche-Comté, which this time was preserved by France.

In 1676, the King having returned into Flanders, took Condé, while Monsieur took Bouchain. The armies of the King and of the Prince of Orange approached each other so suddenly and so closely, that they found themselves front to front near Heurtebise. According even to the admission of the enemy, our forces were so superior to those of the Prince of Orange, that we must have gained the victory if we had attacked. But the King, after listening to the opinions of his generals, some for, and some against giving battle, decided for the latter, turned tail, and the engagement was talked of no more. The army was much discontented. Everybody wished for battle. The fault therefore of the King made much impression upon the troops, and excited cruel railleries against us at home and in the foreign courts. The King stopped but little longer afterward in the army, although we were only in the month of May. He returned to his mistress.

The following year he returned to Flanders, and took Cambrai; and Monsieur besieged Saint Omer. Monsieur got the start of the Prince of Orange, who was about to assist the place, gave him battle near Corsel, obtained a complete victory, immediately took Saint Omer, and then joined the King. This contrast so affected the monarch that never afterward did he give Monsieur command of an army! External appearances were perfectly kept up, but from that moment the resolution was taken and always well sustained.

The year afterward the King led in person the siege of Ghent. The peace of Nimeguen ended this year the war with Holland, Spain, etc.; and on the commencement of the following year, that with the Emperor and the empire. America, Africa, the Archipelago, Sicily, acutely felt the power of France, and in 1684 Luxembourg was the price of the delay of the Spaniards in fulfilling all the conditions of the peace. Genoa, bombarded, was forced to come in the persons of its doge and four of its senators, to sue for peace at the commencement of the following year. From this date, until 1688, the time passed in the cabinet less in *fêtes* than in devotion and constraint. Here finishes the apogeum of this reign, and the fullness of glory and prosperity. The great captains, the great ministers, were no more, but their pupils remained. The second epoch of the reign was very different from the first; but the third was even more sadly dissimilar.

I have related the adventure which led to the wars of this period; how an ill-made window-frame was noticed at the Trianon, then building; how Louvois was blamed for it; his alarm lest his disgrace should follow; his determination to engage the King in a war which should turn him from his building fancies. He carried out his resolve: with what result I have already shown. France was ruined at home; and abroad, despite the success of her arms, gained nothing. On the contrary, the withdrawal of the King from Gembloux, when he might have utterly defeated the Prince of Orange, did us infinite harm, as I have shown in its place. The peace which followed this war was disgraceful. The King was obliged to acknowledge the Prince of Orange as King of England, after having so long shown hatred and contempt for him. Our precipitation, too, cost us Luxembourg; and the ignorance of our plenipotentiaries gave our enemies great advantages in forming their frontier. Such was the peace of Ryswick, concluded in September, 1697.

This peace seemed as though it would allow France some breathing time. The King was sixty years of age, and had, in his own opinion, acquired all sorts of glory. But scarcely were we at peace, without having had time to taste it, than the pride of the King made him wish to astonish all Europe by the display of a power that it believed prostrated. And truly he did astonish Europe. But at what a cost! The famous camp of Compiègne—

for 'tis to that I allude — was one of the most magnificent spectacles ever seen; but its immense and misplaced prodigality was soon regretted. Twenty years afterward, some of the regiments who took part in it were still in difficulties from this cause.

Shortly afterward, by one of the most surprising and unheard-of pieces of good fortune, the crown of Spain fell into the hands of the Duc d'Anjou, grandson of the King. It seemed as though golden days had come back again to France. Only for a little time, however, did it seem so. Nearly all Europe, as it has been seen, banded against France, to dispute the Spanish crown. The King had lost all his good ministers, all his able generals, and had taken good pains they should leave no successors. When war came, then, we were utterly unable to prosecute it with success or honor. We were driven out of Germany, of Italy, of the Low Countries. We could not sustain the war, or resolve to make peace. Every day led us nearer and nearer the brink of the precipice, the terrible depths of which were forever staring us in the face. A misunderstanding among our enemies, whereby England became detached from the grand alliance; the undue contempt of Prince Eugène for our generals, out of which arose the battle of Denain; saved us from the gulf. Peace came, and a peace, too, infinitely better than that we should have ardently embraced if our enemies had agreed among themselves beforehand. Nevertheless, this peace cost dear to France, and cost Spain half its territory — Spain, of which the King had said not even a windmill would he yield! But this was another piece of folly he soon repented of.

Thus we see this monarch grand, rich, conquering, the arbiter of Europe; feared and admired as long as the ministers and captains existed who really deserved the name. When they were no more, the machine kept moving some time by impulsion, and from their influence. But soon afterward we saw beneath the surface; faults and errors were multiplied, and decay came on with giant strides; without, however, opening the eyes of that despotic master, so anxious to do everything and direct everything himself, and who seemed to indemnify himself for disdain abroad by increasing fear and trembling at home.

So much for the reign of this vainglorious monarch.

Let me touch now upon some other incidents in his career, and upon some points in his character.

He early showed a disinclination for Paris. The troubles that had taken place there during the minority made him regard the place as dangerous; he wished, too, to render himself venerable by hiding himself from the eyes of the multitude; all these considerations fixed him at St. Germains soon after the death of the Queen, his mother. It was to that place he began to attract the world by *fêtes* and gallantries, and by making it felt that he wished to be often seen.

His love for Madame de la Vallière, which was at first kept secret, occasioned frequent excursions to Versailles, then a little card castle, which had been built by Louis XIII.— annoyed, and to his suite still more so, at being frequently obliged to sleep in a wretched inn there, after he had been out hunting in the forest of Saint Leger. That monarch rarely slept at Versailles more than one night, and then from necessity; the King, his son, slept there, so that he might be more in private with his mistress, pleasures unknown to the hero and just man, worthy son of Saint Louis, who built the little *château*.

These excursions of Louis XIV. by degrees gave birth to those immense buildings he erected at Versailles; and their convenience for a numerous court, so different from the apartments at St. Germains, led him to take up his abode there entirely shortly after the death of the Queen. He built an infinite number of apartments, which were asked for by those who wished to pay their court to him; whereas at St. Germains nearly everybody was obliged to lodge in the town, and the few who found accommodation at the *château* were strangely inconvenienced.

The frequent *fêtes*, the private promenades at Versailles, the journeys, were means on which the King seized in order to distinguish or mortify the courtiers, and thus render them more assiduous in pleasing him. He felt that of real favors he had not enough to bestow; in order to keep up the spirit of devotion, he therefore unceas-

ingly invented all sorts of ideal ones, little preferences
and petty distinctions, which answered his purpose as
well.

He was exceedingly jealous of the attention paid him.
Not only did he notice the presence of the most distinguished courtiers, but those of inferior degree also.   He
looked to the right and to the left, not only upon rising
but upon going to bed, at his meals, in passing through
his apartments, or his gardens of Versailles, where alone
the courtiers were allowed to follow him; he saw and
noticed everybody; not one escaped him, not even those
who hoped to remain unnoticed.   He marked well all
absentees from the Court, found out the reason of their
absence, and never lost an opportunity of acting toward
them as the occasion might seem to justify.   With some
of the courtiers (the most distinguished), it was a de-
merit not to make the Court their ordinary abode; with
others it was a fault to come but rarely; for those who
never or scarcely ever came it was certain disgrace.
When their names were in any way mentioned, " I do
not know them," the King would reply haughtily.   Those
who presented themselves but seldom were thus char-
acterized: " They are people I never see "; these decrees
were irrevocable.   He could not bear people who liked
Paris.

Louis XIV. took great pains to be well informed of
all that passed everywhere; in the public places, in the
private houses, in society, and familiar intercourse.   His
spies and tell-tales were infinite.   He had them of all
species; many who were ignorant that their information
reached him; others who knew it; others who wrote to
him direct, sending their letters through channels he indicated; and all these letters were seen by him alone,
and always before everything else; others who sometimes
spoke to him secretly in his cabinet, entering by the
back stairs.   These unknown means ruined an infinite
number of people of all classes, who never could discover the cause; often ruined them very unjustly; for
the King, once prejudiced, never altered his opinion, or
so rarely, that nothing was more rare.   He had, too,
another fault, very dangerous for others and often for

himself, since it deprived him of good subjects. He had
an excellent memory; in this way, that if he saw a man
who, twenty years before, perhaps, had in some manner
offended him, he did not forget the man, though he
might forget the offense. This was enough, however, to
exclude the person from all favor. The representations
of a minister, of a general, of his confessor even, could
not move the King. He would not yield.

The most cruel means by which the King was informed of what was passing — for many years before
anybody knew it — was that of opening letters. The
promptitude and dexterity with which they were opened
passes understanding. He saw extracts from all the letters in which there were passages that the chiefs of the
post-office, and then the minister who governed it,
thought ought to go before him; entire letters, too, were
sent to him, when their contents seemed to justify the
sending. Thus the chiefs of the post, nay, the principal clerks, were in a position to suppose what they
pleased and against whom they pleased. A word of contempt against the King or the Government, a joke, a
detached phrase, was enough. It is incredible how many
people, justly or unjustly, were more or less ruined,
always without resource, without trial, and without
knowing why. The secret was impenetrable; for nothing ever cost the king less than profound silence and
dissimulation.

This last talent he pushed almost to falsehood, but
never to deceit, pluming himself upon keeping his word,
— therefore he scarcely ever gave it. The secrets of others
he kept as religiously as his own. He was even flattered
by certain confessions and certain confidences; and there
was no mistress, minister, or favorite, who could have
wormed them out, even though the secret regarded
themselves.

We know, among many others, the famous story of a
woman of quality, who, after having been separated a
year from her husband, found herself in the family way
just as he was on the point of returning from the army,
and who, not knowing what else to do, in the most
urgent manner begged a private interview of the King.

She obtained it, and confided to him her position, as to the worthiest man in the realm, as she said. The King counseled her to profit by her distress, and live more wisely for the future, and immediately promised to retain her husband on the frontier as long as was necessary, and to forbid his return under any pretext, and in fact he gave orders the same day to Louvois, and prohibited the husband not only all leave of absence, but forbade him to quit for a single day the post he was to command all the winter. The officer who was distinguished, and who had neither wished nor asked to be employed all the winter upon the frontier, and Louvois, who had in no way thought of it, were equally surprised and vexed. They were obliged, however, to obey to the letter, and without asking why; and the King never mentioned the circumstance until many years afterward, when he was quite sure nobody could find out either husband or wife, as in fact they never could, or even obtain the most vague or the most uncertain suspicion.

CHAPTER XXXVI.

Excessive Politeness — Influence of the Valets — How the King Drove Out — Love of Magnificence — His Buildings—Versailles — The Supply of Water — The King Seeks for Quiet — Creation of Marly — Tremendous Extravagance.

NEVER did man give with better grace than Louis XIV., or augmented so much, in this way, the price of his benefits. Never did man sell to better profit his words, even his smiles, — nay, his looks. Never did disobliging words escape him; and if he had to blame, to reprimand, or correct, which was very rare, it was nearly always with goodness, never except on one occasion (the admonition of Courtenvaux, related in its place), with anger or severity. Never was man so naturally polite, or of a politeness so measured, so graduated, so adapted to person, time, and place. Toward women his politeness was without parallel. Never did he pass the humblest petticoat without raising his hat; even to chambermaids, that he knew to be such, as often happened at Marly. For ladies he took his hat off completely, but to a greater or less extent; for titled people half off, holding it in his hand or against his ear for some instants, more or less marked. For the nobility he contented himself by putting his hand to his hat. He took it off for the princes of the blood as for the ladies. If he accosted ladies he did not cover himself until he had quitted them. All this was out of doors, for in the house he was never covered. His reverences, more or less marked, but always light, were incomparable for their grace and manner; even his mode of half raising himself at supper for each lady who arrived at table. Though at last this fatigued him, yet he never ceased it; the ladies who were to sit down, however, took care not to enter after supper had commenced.

If he was made to wait for anything while dressing, it was always with patience. He was exact to the hours that he gave for all his day, with a precision clear and brief in his orders. If in the bad weather of winter, when he could not go out, he went to Madame de Maintenon's a quarter of an hour earlier than he had arranged (which seldom happened), and the captain of the guards was not on duty, he did not fail afterward to say that it was his own fault for anticipating the hour, not that of the captain of the guards for being absent. Thus, with this regularity which he never deviated from, he was served with the utmost exactitude.

He treated his valets well, above all those of the household. It was among them that he felt most at ease, and that he unbosomed himself the most familiarly, especially to the chiefs. Their friendship and their aversion have often had grand results. They were unceasingly in a position to render good and bad offices: thus they recalled those powerful enfranchised slaves of the Roman emperors, to whom the senate and the great people paid court and basely truckled. These valets during Louis XIV.'s reign were not less courted. The ministers, even the most powerful, openly studied their caprices; and the princes of the blood,— nay, the bastards,— not to mention people of lower grade, did the same. The majority were accordingly insolent enough; and if you could not avoid their insolence, you were forced to put up with it.

The King loved air and exercise very much, as long as he could make use of them. He had excelled in dancing, and at tennis and mall. On horseback he was admirable, even at a late age. He liked to see everything done with grace and address. To acquit yourself well or ill before him was a merit or a fault. He said that with things not necessary it was best not to meddle, unless they were done well. He was very fond of shooting, and there was not a better or more graceful shot than he. He had always in his cabinet seven or eight pointer bitches, and was fond of feeding them, to make himself known to them. He was very fond, too, of stag hunting; but in a *calèche*, since he broke his arm, while hunting at Fontainebleau, immediately after the death of the Queen. He rode alone in a species of "box," drawn by four little horses — with five or six relays, and

drove himself with an address and accuracy unknown
to the best coachmen. His postilions were children from
ten to fifteen years of age, and he directed them.

He liked splendor, magnificence, and profusion in everything: you pleased him if you shone through the brilliancy of your houses, your clothes, your table, your
equipages. Thus a taste for extravagance and luxury
was disseminated through all classes of society; causing
infinite harm, and leading to general confusion of rank
and to ruin.

As for the King himself, nobody ever approached his
magnificence. His buildings, who could number them?
At the same time who was there who did not deplore
the pride, the caprice, the bad taste seen in them? He
built nothing useful or ornamental in Paris, except the
Pont Royal, and that simply by necessity; so that despite its incomparable extent, Paris is inferior to many
cities of Europe. St. Germains, a lovely spot, with a
marvelous view, rich forest, terraces, gardens, and water
he abandoned for Versailles; the dullest and most ungrateful of all places, without prospect, without wood,
without water, without soil; for the ground is all shifting
sand or swamp, the air accordingly bad.

But he liked to subjugate nature by art and treasure.
He built at Versailles, on, on, without any general design, the beautiful and the ugly, the vast and the mean,
all jumbled together. His own apartments and those of
the Queen, are inconvenient to the last degree, dull, close,
stinking. The gardens astonish by their magnificence,
but cause regret by their bad taste. You are introduced
to the freshness of the shade only by a vast torrid zone,
at the end of which there is nothing for you but to
mount or descend; and with the hill, which is very short,
terminate the gardens. The violence everywhere done
to nature repels and wearies us despite ourselves. The
abundance of water, forced up and gathered together
from all parts, is rendered green, thick, muddy; it dis-
seminates humidity, unhealthy and evident; and an odor
still more so. I might never finish upon the monstrous
defects of a palace so immense and so immensely dear,
with its accompaniments, which are still more so.

But the supply of water for the fountains was all de-
fective at all moments, in spite of those seas of reser-
voirs which had cost so many millions to establish and
to form upon the shifting sand and marsh. Who could
have believed it? This defect became the ruin of the
infantry which was turned out to do the work. Madame
de Maintenon reigned. M. de Louvois was well with
her, then. We were at peace. He conceived the idea
of turning the river Eure between Chartres and Maintenon, and of making it come to Versailles. Who can say
what gold and men this obstinate attempt cost during
several years, until it was prohibited by the heaviest
penalties, in the camp established there, and for a long
time kept up; not to speak of the sick,—above all, of
the dead,—that the hard labor and still more the much
disturbed earth, caused? How many men were years in
recovering from the effects of the contagion! How many
never regained their health at all! And not only the
subofficers, but the colonels, the brigadiers and general
officers, were compelled to be upon the spot, and were
not at liberty to absent themselves a quarter of an hour
from the works. The war at last interrupted them in
1688, and they have never since been undertaken; only
unfinished portions of them exist which will immortalize
this cruel folly.

At last, the King, tired of the cost and bustle, persuaded himself that he should like something little and
solitary. He searched all around Versailles for some
place to satisfy this new taste. He examined several
neighborhoods, he traversed the hills near St. Germains,
and the vast plain which is at the bottom, where the
Seine winds and bathes the feet of so many towns, and
so many treasures in quitting Paris. He was pressed to
fix himself at Lucienne, where Cavoye afterward had a
house, the view from which is enchanting; but he replied
that, that fine situation would ruin him, and that as he
wished to go to no expense, so he also wished a situation which would not urge him into any. He found behind Lucienne a deep narrow valley, completely shut in,
inaccessible from its swamps, and with a wretched village
called Marly upon the slope of one of its hills. This

closeness, without drain or the means of having any, was
the sole merit of the valley. The King was overjoyed
at his discovery. It was a great work, that of draining
this sewer of all the environs, which threw there their
garbage, and of bringing soil thither! The hermitage
was made. At first, it was only for sleeping in three
nights, from Wednesday to Saturday, two or three times
a year, with a dozen at the outside of courtiers, to fill
the most indispensable posts.

By degrees, the hermitage was augmented, the hills
were pared and cut down, to give at least the semblance
of a prospect; in fine, what with buildings, gardens,
waters, aqueducts, the curious and well-known machine,
statues, precious furniture, the park, the ornamental
inclosed forest,—Marly has become what it is to-day,
though it has been stripped since the death of the King.
Great trees were unceasingly brought from Compiègne
or farther, three-fourths of which died and were immediately after replaced; vast spaces covered with thick
wood, or obscure alleys, were suddenly changed into immense pieces of water, on which people were rowed in gon-
dolas; then they were changed again into forest (I speak
of what I have seen in six weeks); basins were changed
a hundred times; cascades the same; carp ponds adorned
with the most exquisite painting, scarcely finished, were
changed and differently arranged by the same hands;
and this an infinite number of times; then there was
that prodigious machine just alluded to, with its immense
aqueducts, the conduit, its monstrous resources solely
devoted to Marly, and no longer to Versailles; so that I
am under the mark in saying that Versailles, even, did
not cost so much as Marly.

Such was the fate of a place the abode of serpents,
and of carrion, of toads and frogs, solely chosen to avoid
expense. Such was the bad taste of the King in all
things, and his proud, haughty pleasure in forcing nature;
which neither the most mighty war, nor devotion could
subdue!

CHAPTER XXXVII.

LET me now speak of the amours of the King which
were even more fatal to the State than his building
mania. Their scandal filled all Europe, stupefied
France, shook the State, and without doubt drew upon
the King those maledictions under the weight of which
he was pushed so near the very edge of the precipice,
and had the misfortune of seeing his legitimate posterity within an ace of extinction in France. These are
evils which became veritable catastrophes and which
will be long felt.

Louis XIV. in his youth more made for love than any
of his subjects — being tired of gathering passing sweets,
fixed himself at last upon La Vallière. The progress and
the result of his love are well known.

Madame de Montespan was she whose rare beauty
touched him next, even during the reign of Madame de
La Vallière. She soon perceived it, and vainly pressed
her husband to carry her away into Guienne. With
foolish confidence he refused to listen to her. She spoke
to him more in earnest. In vain. At last the King was
listened to, and carried her off from her husband, with
that frightful hubbub which resounded with horror among
all nations, and which gave to the world the new spectacle of two mistresses at once! The King took them to
the frontiers, to the camps, to the armies, both of them

in the Queen's coach. The people ran from all parts to look at the three queens; and asked each other in their simplicity if they had seen them. In the end, Madame de Montespan triumphed, and disposed of the master and his Court with an *éclat* that knew no veil; and in order that nothing should be wanting to complete the license of this life, M. de Montespan was sent to the Bastile; then banished to Guienne, and his wife was appointed superintendent of the Queen's household.

The accouchements of Madame de Montespan were public. Her circle became the center of the Court, of the amusements, of the hopes and of the fears of ministers and the generals, and the humiliation of all France. It was also the center of wit, and of a kind so peculiar, so delicate, and so subtle, but always so natural and so agreeable, that it made itself distinguished by its special character.

Madame de Montespan was cross, capricious, ill-tempered, and of a haughtiness in everything which reached to the clouds, and from the effects of which nobody, not even the King was exempt. The courtiers avoided passing under her windows, above all when the King was with her. They used to say it was equivalent to being put to the sword, and this phrase became proverbial at the Court. It is true that she spared nobody, often without other design than to divert the King; and as she had infinite wit and sharp pleasantry, nothing was more dangerous than the ridicule she, better than anybody, could cast on all. With that she loved her family and her relatives, and did not fail to serve people for whom she conceived friendship. The Queen endured with difficulty her haughtiness — very different from the respect and measure with which she had been treated by the Duchess de La Vallière, whom she always loved; whereas of Madame de Montespan she would say, " That strumpet will cause my death." The retirement, the austere penitence, and the pious end of Madame de Montespan have been already described.

During her reign she did not fail to have causes for jealousy. There was Mademoiselle de Fontange, who pleased the King sufficiently to become his mistress.

But she had no intellect, and without that it was impossible to maintain supremacy over the King. Her early death quickly put an end to this amour. Then there was Madame de Soubise, who, by the infamous connivance of her husband, prostituted herself to the King, and thus secured all sorts of advantages for that husband, for herself, and for her children. The love of the King for her continued until her death, although for many years before that he had ceased to see her in private. Then there was the beautiful Ludre, demoiselle of Lorraine, and maid of honor to Madame, who was openly loved for a moment. But this amour was a flash of lightning, and Madame de Montespan remained triumphant.

Let us now pass to another kind of amour which astonished all the world as much as the other had scandalized it, and which the King carried with him to the tomb. Who does not already recognize the celebrated Françoise d'Aubigné, Marquise de Maintenon, whose permanent reign did not last less than thirty-two years?

Born in the American islands, where her father, perhaps a gentleman, had gone to seek his bread, and where he was satisfied by obscurity, she returned alone and at haphazard into France. She landed at La Rochelle, and was received in pity by Madame de Neuillant, mother of the Maréchale Duchess de Navailles, and was reduced by that avaricious old woman to keep the keys of her granary, and to see the hay measured out to her horses, as I have already related elsewhere. She came afterward to Paris, young, clever, witty, and beautiful, without friends and without money; and by lucky chance made acquaintance with the famous Scarron. He found her amiable; his friends perhaps still more so. Marriage with this joyous and learned cripple appeared to her the greatest and most unlooked-for good fortune; and folks who were, perhaps, more in want of a wife than he, persuaded him to marry her, and thus raise this charming unfortunate from her misery.

The marriage being brought about the new spouse pleased the company which went to Scarron's house. It was the fashion to go there: people of wit, people of the Court and of the city, the best and most distinguished

went. Scarron was not in a state to leave his house,
but the charm of his genius, of his knowledge, of his
imagination, of that incomparable and ever fresh gayety
which he showed in the midst of his afflictions, that rare
fecundity, and that humor, tempered by so much good taste
that is still admired in his writings, drew everybody there.

Madame Scarron made at home all sorts of acquaintances, which, however, at the death of her husband,
did not keep her from being reduced to the charity of
the parish of St. Eustace. She took a chamber for herself and for a servant, where she lived in a very pinched
manner. Her personal charms by degrees improved her
condition. Villars, father of the Maréchal; Beuvron,
father of D'Harcourt; the three Villarceaux, and many
others kept her.

This set her afloat again, and, step by step, introduced
her to the Hotel d'Albret, and thence to the Hotel de
Richelieu, and elsewhere; so she passed from one house
to the other. In these houses Madame Scarron was far from
being on the footing of the rest of the company. She
was more like a servant than a guest. She was completely at the beck and call of her hosts; now to ask for
firewood; now if a meal was nearly ready; another time
if the coach of so-and-so or such a one had returned;
and so on, with a thousand little commissions which the
use of bells, introduced a long time after, differently dis-
poses of.

It was in these houses, principally in the Hotel de
Richelieu, much more still in the Hotel d'Albret, where
the Maréchal d'Albret lived in great state, that Madame
Scarron made the majority of her acquaintances. The
Maréchal was cousin-german of M. de Montespan, very
intimate with him, and with Madame de Montespan. When
she became the King's mistress he became her counselor,
and abandoned her husband.

To the intimacy between the Maréchal d'Albret and
Madame de Montespan Madame de Maintenon owed the
good fortune she met with fourteen or fifteen years later.
Madame de Montespan continually visited the Hotel
d'Albret, and was much impressed with Madame Scarron.
She conceived a friendship for the obliging widow, and

when she had her first children by the King,— M. du
Maine and Madame la Duchess, whom the King wished
to conceal,— she proposed that they should be confided
to Madame Scarron. A house in the Marais was accordingly given to her to lodge in with them, and the means
to bring them up, but in the utmost secrecy. Afterward,
these children were taken to Madame de Montespan, then
shown to the King, and then by degrees drawn from
secrecy and avowed. Their governess, being established
with them at the Court, more and more pleased Madame
de Montespan, who several times made the King give
presents to her. He, on the other hand, could not endure
her; what he gave to her, always little, was by excess
of complaisance and with a regret that he did not hide.

The estate of Maintenon being for sale, Madame de
Montespan did not let the King rest until she had drawn
from him enough to buy it for Madame Scarron, who
thenceforth assumed its name. She obtained enough also
for the repair of the *château*, and then attacked the King
for means to arrange the garden, which the former owners
had allowed to go to ruin.

It was at the toilet of Madame de Montespan that
these demands were made. The captain of the guards
alone followed the King there. M. le Maréchal de Lorges,
the truest man that ever lived, held that post then,
and he has often related to me the scene he witnessed.
The King at first turned a deaf ear to the request of
Madame de Montespan, and then refused. Annoyed
that she still insisted, he said he had already done more
than enough for this creature; that he could not understand the fancy of Madame de Montespan for her, and
her obstinacy in keeping her after he had begged her
so many times to dismiss her; that he admitted Madame
Scarron was insupportable to him, and provided he
never saw her more and never heard speak of her, he
would open his purse again, though, to say truth, he had
already given too much to a creature of this kind!
Never did M. le Maréchal de Lorges forget these words;
and he has always repeated them to me and others precisely as they are given here, so struck was he with
them, and much more after all that he saw since, so

astonishing and so contradictory. Madame de Montespan stopped short, very much troubled by having too far pressed the King.

M. du Maine was extremely lame; this was caused, it was said, by a fall he had had from his nurse's arms. Nothing done for him succeeded; the resolution was then taken to send him to various practicians in Flanders, and elsewhere in the realm, then to the waters, among others to Barèges. The letters that the governess wrote to Madame de Montespan, giving an account of these journeys, were shown to the King. He thought them well written, relished them, and the last ones made his aversion for the writer diminish.

The ill humor of Madame de Montespan finished the work. She had a good deal of that quality, and had become accustomed to give it full swing. The King was the object of it more frequently than anybody; he was still amorous; but her ill humor pained him. Madame de Maintenon reproached Madame de Montespan for this, and thus advanced herself in the King's favor. The King, by degrees, grew accustomed to speak sometimes to Madame de Maintenon; to unbosom to her what he wished her to say to Madame de Montespan; at last to relate to her the chagrins this latter caused him, and to consult her thereupon.

Admitted thus into the intimate confidence of the lover and the mistress, and this by the King's own doing, the adroit waiting woman knew how to cultivate it, and profited so well by her industry that by degrees she supplanted Madame de Montespan, who perceived, too late, that her friend had become necessary to the King. Arrived at this point, Madame de Maintenon made, in her turn, complaints to the King of all she had to suffer from a mistress who spared even him so little; and by dint of these mutual complaints about Madame de Montespan, Madame de Maintenon at last took her place, and knew well how to keep it.

Fortune, I dare not say Providence, which was preparing for the haughtiest of kings humiliation the most profound, the most public, the most durable, the most unheard-of, strengthened more and more his taste for this woman, so adroit and expert at her trade; while the continued ill humor and jealousy of Madame de Montespan rendered the new union still more solid. It was this that Madame de Sévigné so prettily paints, enigmatically, in her letters to Madame de Grignan, in which she sometimes talks of these Court movements; for Madame de Maintenon had been in Paris in the society of Madame de Sévigné, of Madame de Coulange, of Madame de La Fayette, and had begun to make them feel her importance. Charming touches are to be seen in the same style upon the favor, veiled but brilliant, enjoyed by Madame de Soubise.

It was while the King was in the midst of his partiality for Madame de Maintenon that the Queen died. It was at the same time, too, that the ill humor of Madame de Montespan became more and more insupportable. This imperious beauty, accustomed to domineer and to be adored, could not struggle against the despair which the prospect of her fall caused her. What carried her beyond all bounds, was that she could no longer disguise from herself, that she had an abject rival whom she had supported, who owed everything to her; whom she had so much liked that she had several times refused to dismiss her when pressed to do so by the King; a rival, too, so beneath her in beauty, and older by several years; to feel that it was this lady's maid, not to say this servant, that the King most frequently went to see; that he sought only her; that he could not dissimulate his uneasiness if he did not find her; that he quitted all for her; in fine, that at all moments she (Madame de Montespan) needed the intervention of Madame de Maintenon, in order to attract the King to reconcile her with him, or to obtain the favors she asked for. It was then, in times so propitious to the enchantress, that the King became free by the death of the Queen.

He passed the first few days at Saint Cloud, at Monsieur's, whence he went to Fontainebleau, where he spent all the autumn. It was there that his liking, stimulated by absence, made him find that absence insupportable. Upon his return it is pretended—for we must distinguish the certain from that which is not so—it is pretended,

I say, that the King spoke more freely to Madame de Maintenon, and that she, venturing to put forth her strength, retrenched herself behind devotion and prudery; that the King did not cease, that she preached to him and made him afraid of the devil, and that she balanced his love against his conscience with so much art, that she succeeded in becoming what our eyes have seen her, but what posterity will never believe she was.

But what is very certain and very true, is, that some time after the return of the King from Fontainebleau, and in the midst of the winter that followed the death of the Queen (posterity will with difficulty believe it, although perfectly true and proved), Père de la Chaise, confessor of the King, said mass at the dead of night in one of the King's cabinets at Versailles, Bontems, governor of Versailles, chief valet on duty, and the most confidential of the four, was present at this mass, at which the Monarch and La Maintenon were married in presence of Harlay, archbishop of Paris, as diocesan, of Louvois (both of whom drew from the King a promise that he would never declare this marriage), and of Montchevreuil. This last was relative and friend of Villarceaux, to whom during the summer he lent his house at Montchevreuil, remaining there himself, however, with his wife; and in that house Villarceaux kept Madame Scarron, paying all the expenses because his relative was poor, and because he (Villarceaux) was ashamed to take her to his own home, to live in concubinage with her in the presence of his wife whose patience and virtue he respected.

The satiety of the honeymoon, usually so fatal, and especially the honeymoon of such marriages, only consolidated the favor of Madame de Maintenon. Soon after, she astonished everybody by the apartments given to her at Versailles, at the top of the grand staircase facing those of the King and on the same floor. From that moment the King always passed some hours with her every day of his life; wherever she might be she was always lodged near him, and on the same floor if possible.

What manner of person she was,—this incredible enchantress,—and how she governed all-powerfully for more than thirty years, it behooves me now to explain!